Green Line 3

Lehrerband mit Kopiervorlagen

von
Vera Brunkau
Anette Christiani
Paul Dennis
Hartmut Klose
Antje Körber
Margitta Kuty
Axel Plitsch
Mario Rinvolucri
Stefanie Schneider
Harald Weisshaar

herausgegeben von
Harald Weisshaar

Ernst Klett Verlag
Stuttgart · Leipzig

Green Line 3   Lehrerband mit Kopiervorlagen

Herausgeber: Harald Weisshaar, Bisingen

Autoren: Vera Brunkau, Bergisch Gladbach; Anette Christiani, Dortmund; Paul Dennis, Lahnstein; Hartmut Klose, Seevetal; Antje Körber, Merseburg; Dr. Margitta Kuty, Greifswald; Axel Plitsch, Wülfrath; Mario Rinvolucri/Pilgrims, Canterbury/Kent; Dr. Stefanie Schneider, Recklinghausen; Harald Weisshaar, Bisingen

Abkürzungen und Symbole im Lehrerband:

G	Grammatikparagraf	S.	Seite
HA	Hausaufgabe	TA	Tafelanschrieb/-bild
HV	Hörverstehen	PA	Partnerarbeit
KV	Kopiervorlage	GA	Gruppenarbeit
L	Lehrerin/nen und Lehrer	SB	Schülerbuch
S	Schülerinnen und Schüler	WB	Workbook
pl.	Plural		Differenzierung nach oben
S.	Seite		Differenzierung nach unten
			Schreibübungen

Bildquellen:
UM1/UM4: Corbis/Skelley; **S. 68:** The Cartoon Bank, THE NEW YORKER Magazine (Peter Steiner), Yonkers, NY; **S. 165–167:** Klett-Archiv/Hill; **S. 184:** shutterstock (Pablo Eder), New York, NY; **S. 190:** (1) StockFood GmbH (Eising), München; (2–3) Getty Images RF (PhotoDisc), München; (4) StockFood GmbH (Eising), München; (5) iStockphoto (JKM191), Calgary, Alberta; **S. 226:** (1) Corbis (Ric Ergenbright), Düsseldorf; (3) Alamy Images RF (RF), Abingdon, Oxon; (4) Alamy Images RM (qaphotos), Abingdon, Oxon; (5) iStockphoto (RF/René Mansi), Calgary, Alberta; (6) shutterstock (Rachelle Burnside), New York, NY; (7) Getty Images RF (Photodisc), München; (8) Picture-Alliance (PA Steve Parsons), Frankfurt; (9) Alamy Images RM (eye35.com), Abingdon, Oxon; (10) Corbis (Reuters/Hodgson), Düsseldorf; (11) Corbis (Ward), Düsseldorf; (12) Alamy Images RM (Photolibrary, Wales), Abingdon, Oxon; **S. 286:** Alamy Images RM (Allstar), Abingdon, Oxon; **S. 288:** Avenue Images GmbH (Image Source), Hamburg; **S. 289:** Fotolia LLC (RF/Jason Stitt), New York; **S. 292–293:** MEW Verlag GmbH, Augsburg; **S. 338:** (1) Mauritius (age), Mittenwald; (2) Marco Polo Agence Photographique, Paris; (3) Corbis (Peter Fisher), Düsseldorf; (4) JupiterImages photos.com (RF/photos.com), Tucson, AZ; (5) Alamy Images RM (Janine Wiedel), Abingdon, Oxon; (6) Marco Polo Agence Photographique (F. Bouillot), Paris; (7) Image 100 (RF), Berlin; **S. 339:** (1) Image 100 RF, Berlin; **S. 341:** (1) Alamy Images Limited RF (BananaStock), Abingdon, Oxon; **S. 342:** (1) Alamy Images Limited RF (ImageFonds), Abingdon, Oxon

1. Auflage   1 9 8 7 6 5 | 2020 19 18 17 16

Alle Drucke dieser Auflage sind unverändert und können im Unterricht nebeneinander verwendet werden. Die letzte Zahl bezeichnet das Jahr des Druckes.

Das Werk und seine Teile sind urheberrechtlich geschützt. Jede Nutzung in anderen als den gesetzlich zugelassenen Fällen bedarf der vorherigen schriftlichen Einwilligung des Verlages.
Hinweis § 52 a UrhG: Weder das Werk noch seine Teile dürfen ohne eine solche Einwilligung eingescannt und in ein Netzwerk eingestellt werden. Dies gilt auch für Intranets von Schulen und sonstigen Bildungseinrichtungen. Fotomechanische oder andere Wiedergabeverfahren nur mit Genehmigung des Verlages.

© Ernst Klett Verlag GmbH, Stuttgart 2008.
Alle Rechte vorbehalten.
Internetadresse: www.klett.de

Redaktion: Anette Dangelmaier M.A., Martina Reckart

Gestaltung: Anita Bauch
Illustrationen: Lars Benecke, Hannover; Dorothee Wolters, Köln sowie Thomas Binder, Magdeburg; Andrea Büdinger, München; Christian Dekelver, Weinstadt; Naomi Fearn, Berlin; Martin Hoffmann, Stuttgart; Gerlinde Keller, München; Helga Merkle, Albershausen; David Norman, Meerbusch; Jürgen Wirth, Offenthal; Guy Delcourt Production, Paris
Umschlaggestaltung: Koma Amok, Stuttgart
Umschlagfoto: Ariel Skelley/Corbis
Reproduktion: Meyle + Müller, Medien-Management, Pforzheim
Satz: Satzkiste GmbH, Stuttgart
Druck: AZ Druck und Datentechnik GmbH, Kempten (Allgäu)

Printed in Germany
ISBN 978-3-12-547143-6

Inhaltsverzeichnis

Vorwort 4

A Allgemeiner Teil

I Das Lehrwerkskonzept
  1 Ziele und Aufgaben 5
  2 Die didaktischen Schwerpunkte 6
    2.1 Neuerungen in *Green Line* 3 6
    2.2 Solides Basiswissen 7
    2.3 Differenzierung und Individualisierung 8
    2.4 Textarbeit 8
    2.5 Übung, Transfer und Wiederholung 9
    2.6 Lernfortschrittsdokumentation und Selbstbewertungskompetenz 10
    2.7 Interkulturelle Kompetenz 10
    2.8 Anmerkungen zum Unterricht in 3-, 4- oder 5-stündigen Kursen ... 11

II Der Medienverbund
  1 Der Lehrerband 13
  2 Das Schülerbuch 13
  3 Das *Workbook* 14
  4 Weitere Werkteile für den Unterricht 15

B Unterrichtskommentare

Unit 1 16
⟨Project⟩ English and Computing 70
Unit 2 77
⟨Revision A⟩ 126
Unit 3 130
⟨Project⟩ English and Biology 186
Unit 4 192
⟨Revision B⟩ 244
Unit 5 248
⟨Project⟩ English and Geography 301
Unit 6 307
⟨Revision C⟩ 352
Mediation 358
⟨Free section⟩ 367
  ⟨The Spaniards are coming⟩ 367
  ⟨Authentic Britain⟩ 369
  ⟨Poems⟩ 370
  ⟨Working with films⟩ 373

Liebe Kolleginnen und Kollegen,

der Lehrerband von *Green Line* 3 führt die Konzeption der Lehrerbände von *Green Line* 1 und 2 fort:

1. Es gibt wieder vielfältige Hinweise zum methodischen Verfahren, zum Einsatz des *Workbooks*, der Folien, der CDs mit Trackangabe und der DVD. Außerdem finden Sie nützliche Hinweise zur Erweiterung des Pensums bis hin zum Einsatz der Kopiervorlagen. Tafelanschriebe, Tipps und Lösungen/Erwartungshorizonte zu den Aufgaben runden das Bild ab.

2. Darüber hinaus bietet auch dieser Lehrerband, wie die Lehrerbände von *Green Line* 1 und 2, etliche Neuerungen:

   - Der Lehrerband liegt als **Ordner** vor und ist somit leicht zu handhaben. Ihre eigenen Materialien können Sie gleich an Ort und Stelle einfügen.
   - Jeder Unit ist eine **Planungsübersicht** vorangestellt. So erhalten Sie einen Überblick über die jeweilige Unit mit Hinweisen zum Einsatz der relevanten Medien.
   - Mit der Seitenaufteilung in **drei Kolumnen** ist jede Seite übersichtlich: die linke Randspalte ist die Navigationsleiste, die breite Mittelspalte vermittelt die Inhalte, die rechte Randspalte koordiniert den Medienverbund und gibt die genauen Mediendaten an.
   - Bei der Mehrheit der Aufgaben und Texte folgt am Ende der methodischen Kommentare eine Rubrik **„Tipps für junge Lehrer"** mit Informationen und Anregungen für Kolleginnen und Kollegen, die zum ersten Mal in dieser Klassenstufe unterrichten.
   - An vielen Stellen in diesem Lehrerband finden sich Alternativvorschläge des bedeutenden britischen Didaktikers Mario Rinvolucri. Sie wurden von ihm eigens für diesen Lehrerband konzipiert und heißen **„Tipps von Mario Rinvolucri – The alternative way"**.
   - Begleitend zu jeder Unit gibt es ca. **10 Kopiervorlagen**, die zum Teil als Differenzierung nach unten und nach oben ausgewiesen sind. Auch zu den fakultativen Zusatztexten wurden Kopiervorlagen für diesen Lehrerband konzipiert.
   - Nach jeder Unit gibt es ein kleines **Diktat**.

Der vor Ihnen liegende Lehrerband verfolgt also nur ein Ziel: Er soll Ihnen die Arbeit erleichtern! Er steht im Zentrum des perfekt aufeinander abgestimmten Medienverbundes von *Green Line*, ist zentrales Steuerungselement und Ideengeber zugleich. Mit ihm können Sie Ihren Unterricht flexibel sowohl lang- als auch kurzfristig planen und die Vielfalt der Lehrwerksteile koordinieren.

Viel Freude und Erfolg beim Unterrichten mit *Green Line* wünscht Ihnen

Ihr Harald Weisshaar

A Allgemeiner Teil

I Das Lehrwerkskonzept

1. Ziele und Aufgaben

Ziele in Green Line

Die Zielsetzung in *Green Line* ist:
- Ausbildung einer allgemeinen Kommunikationsfähigkeit im Englischen.
- (Weiter-)Entwicklung der Fertigkeiten des Hör-/Hör-Sehverstehens, des Sprechens, des Leseverstehens und des Schreibens.
- Freude und Motivation beim Englischlernen – Englisch soll Spaß machen!
- Befähigung der Schülerinnen und Schüler (in der Folge: S) zur Sprachmittlung in zunehmend komplexen Alltagssituationen.
- Unterstützung der Persönlichkeitsbildung in intellektueller, sozialer, emotionaler und motorischer Hinsicht, u. a. durch die Beschäftigung mit einer Vielzahl fiktionaler und nichtfiktionaler Texte und durch die kreative Auseinandersetzung mit deren Inhalten.
- Weiterentwicklung eines interkulturellen Bewusstseins durch den Erwerb von Kenntnissen über englischsprachige Länder und durch die Auseinandersetzung mit deren Kulturen.
- Ausbau von Lerner- und Medienkompetenzen beim Erwerb und Gebrauch von (Fremd-)Sprachen.
- Aufbau einer Kultur der Selbsteinschätzung.
- Pflege und Erhaltung der Freude am Erlernen einer Fremdsprache in Hinblick auf lebenslanges Lernen und als Grundlage für den Aufbau von Mehrsprachigkeit.
- Anwendung des bereits Erlernten in fächerverbindenden Projekten, die sich an Standardsituationen unterschiedlicher Sachfächer orientieren.
- Ausbau der Methodenkompetenz durch vertiefte Beschäftigung mit zentralen *skills*.
- Erweiterung der kommunikativen Kompetenz durch Vermittlung und Betonung der Sprechfähigkeit in Alltagssituationen.

Gegenwärtige Situation

Der Englischunterricht in der Sekundarstufe I hat sich heute grundlegend geändert:
- Die S besitzen heute auch am Gymnasium sehr unterschiedliche Lernvoraussetzungen – eine Tatsache, die hohe Anforderungen an Differenzierung und Individualisierung stellt.
- Die Erkenntnisse aus der Neurolinguistik über die sehr unterschiedlichen Lernweisen von Kindern müssen ihre Auswirkungen auf das Aufgabenangebot haben.
- Kenntnisse über unterschiedliche Lernertypen sollten beachtet werden, um den Lernprozess bei allen Kindern optimal zu gestalten.
- Anspruchsvolle Forderungen aus Berufsleben und Wirtschaft tragen bei den S sehr früh zu dem Bedürfnis bei, etwas zu lernen, das sich im Berufsleben als nützlich erweist.
- Die veränderten Anforderungen an den Englischunterricht, basierend auf den Lehrgängen in der Primarstufe einerseits und den völlig veränderten Rahmenbedingungen durch den europäischen Referenzrahmen, durch einheitliche Prüfungsanforderungen und neue Bildungspläne und Standards andererseits, machen einen neuen Ansatz im Fremdsprachenunterricht unabdingbar.
- Die Betonung der Kommunikationsfähigkeit ist weiter ins Zentrum des Englischunterrichts gerückt. Hierzu gehört auch ein Ausbau der Methodenkompetenz.
- Motiviertes Lernen kann nur über lebendiges Englisch entwickelt werden – dazu gehören die situationsbezogene Vermittlung von Wortschatz und Grammatik ebenso wie ein Angebot altersgemäßer, vielfältiger Texte und Materialien.
- Für die S bedeutet autonomes Lernen: die eigenständige Überprüfung von Lernfortschritten, ein selbstständiger Umgang mit Audio-CDs und die Heranführung an den Umgang mit dem Wörterbuch – allesamt Grundbausteine für ein wirkliches *life-long learning*.

Zentrales Steuerungselement

Green Line 3 koordiniert eine Vielfalt an Aufgaben, Bedingungen und Angeboten im *Green Line*-Medienverbund. Das zentrale Steuerungselement dieses Verbundes ist der Lehrerband, der wie bereits in den Bänden 1 und 2
- nicht nur die Inhalte des Schülerbuches interpretiert, sondern den gesamten Unterrichtsprozess steuert.

A

- mit seinen Angeboten einen reibungslosen Unterricht vorbereitet, der auch die notwendigen Differenzierungsmaßnahmen enthält.
- auch die lehrwerksfreien Unterrichtsphasen mit einbezieht.
- die Möglichkeit bietet, die langfristige Planung der konkreten Klassensituation direkt anzupassen.
- weiterführende Anregungen für alternative Zugänge zum Lehrwerk enthält, die von dem bekannten Didaktiker **Mario Rinvolucri** speziell für *Green Line* entwickelt wurden.
- besondere Tipps für Lehrerinnen und Lehrer (in der Folge: L) bietet, die zum ersten Mal in dieser Klassenstufe unterrichten („Tipps für junge Lehrer").
- als Ordner vorliegt, um den Umgang damit zu erleichtern.
- mindestens 10 Kopiervorlagen pro Unit zu allen Bereichen des Schülerbuches enthält – auch zu den fakultativen Zusatztexten in *Green Line* 3.
- Und jetzt neu zusätzliche Angebote zum Lernen an Stationen und für die Freiarbeit bietet.

Darüber hinaus finden sich in diesem Lehrerband alle Elemente, die von einem solchen Instrument zu erwarten sind und die L bei seiner Arbeit entlastet – z. B. Angaben zur *storyline*, weiterführende Informationen zu geografischen/landeskundlichen Aspekten, zur Lexik, zur Grammatik, Vorschläge für Tafelbilder, Lösungen u.v.a.m.

2. Die didaktischen Schwerpunkte

2.1 Neuerungen in *Green Line* 3

Das Schülerbuch *Green Line* 3 setzt die Konzeption von *Green Line* 1 und 2 fort, hebt sich jedoch durch eine Vielzahl von neuen Elementen von den beiden Vorgängerbänden ab. War innerhalb der Jahrgangsstufen 5 und 6 die konzeptionelle Kontinuität gewährleistet, so entfielen im zweiten Lernjahr bereits die für den Übergang von der Grundschule ins Gymnasium notwendigen Aufgaben und Besonderheiten. In Band 3 wurde es nun notwendig, die den S bereits vertraute Unit-Struktur erneut leicht zu modifizieren bzw. neue Elemente einzuflechten, um schrittweise eine Heranführung an die Mittelstufe zu erreichen, gleichzeitig aber auch die Motivation und die Altersgemäßheit zu erhalten.

In *Green Line* 3 ergeben sich gegenüber *Green Line* 1 und 2 folgende konzeptionelle Neuerungen:
- In Band 3 gibt es erstmals nur sechs Units.
- Der zentrale Handlungsort Greenwich und die Lehrwerkscharaktere aus Band 1 und 2 werden von einer altersgemäßeren dezentralen Struktur abgelöst, mit unterschiedlichen Schauplätzen und einer Vielzahl von einprägsamen Charakteren.
- Das Maskottchen Tom wird in *Green Line* 3 durch das Mädchen Kelsey ersetzt, das sich auf S. 3 im Schülerbuch vorstellt.
- Die meisten Units haben nur noch zwei *Language*-Teile, mit Ausnahme von Unit 3 (drei *Language*-Teile).
- In jeder Unit erfahren die S durch eine *Did you know?*-Box außergewöhnliche Fakten zum zentralen Thema der Unit.
- Als weiteres neues Element findet sich in jeder Unit eine Aufgabe zu *Writing texts*. Diese bietet den S eine Hilfestellung beim Verfassen und kreativen Ausgestalten eigener Texte.
- Im Grammatikanhang wird jedes Pensum durch ein *English summary* ergänzt, das den S helfen soll, sich auch in der Zielsprache über grammatische Fragestellungen auszutauschen.
- In jeder Unit bietet *Green Line* 3 als neues Element zwischen den beiden *Language*-Teilen eine so genannte *Talkwise*-Seite an. Hier werden die S anhand gängiger Alltagssituationen über das Hörverstehen zum freien Sprechen geführt, z. B. zu den Themenbereichen „Vorschläge machen", „einen Kompromiss schließen", „Hilfe anbieten" bzw. „sich entschuldigen".
- Die aus den Vorgängerbänden bekannte Vermittlung von *skills* wird in Band 3 vertieft, indem zentralen Aspekten nun eine ganze *Skills*-Seite gewidmet ist, z. B. Unit 1: *Using a dictionary*, Unit 3: *Listening skills: Telephone messages*, Unit 6: *Small talk* etc. Dies ist eine Erweiterung der den S bereits aus *Green Line* 1 und 2 bekannten *Skills*-Box.
- In den Units 2, 4 und 6 gibt es nach dem *Check-out* je eine fakultative Doppelseite mit Textauszügen aus aktuellen Jugendromanen (Unit 2: *The ruby in the smoke*, Unit 4: *Benny and Omar*) und aus einer bekannten klassischen Erzählung (Unit 6: *Treasure Island*). Die hohe Textqualität der ersten beiden Bände wird somit fortgeführt, und dem Leseverstehen, vor allem auch durch die längeren Unit-Texte, zusätzliches Gewicht gegeben.

- Band 3 enthält drei fächerverbindende Projekte in Anlehnung an den bilingualen Unterricht in den Sachfächern, hier anhand der Themen *English and Computing, English and Biology* sowie *English and Geography*.
- Am Ende des Buches findet sich eine *time line of British history* mit interessanten Fakten aus der britischen Geschichte

2.2 Solides Basiswissen

Green Line 3, wie seine Vorgängerbände ein ausgesprochen systematisches, klar aufgebautes Lehrwerk, verhilft den S zu einem soliden Basiswissen. Siehe dazu auch unten, II. 2.

Wortschatz Die Wortschatzarbeit ist neben der Arbeit an der Grammatik eine der beiden Säulen des Fremdsprachenlernens. Die Wortschatzeinführung erfolgt schwerpunktmäßig in den Bereichen *Check-in*, *Language* und *Text*. Soweit wie möglich verfolgt *Green Line* die Trennung von Wortschatz- und Grammatikeinführung. *Vocabulary skills*-Aufgaben auf den *Wordwise*-Seiten, Wortfeldarbeit, Kollokationen, *Word pairs*, *Opposites*-Aufgaben, Wortbildungen durch Komposita und *Working with a dictionary* sind ständiges Angebot in der Aufgabentypologie. Auch spielerische Formen der Wortschatzarbeit, der Umgang mit unbekanntem Vokabular sowie *Mixed-bag*-Aufgaben zur integrativen Wortschatzwiederholung sichern den systematischen Aufbau des Wortschatzes auf Seite der Lernenden.

Wortschatzvernetzung und -festigung Hauptort der Umwälzung und Vernetzung ist die *Wordwise*-Seite (z. B. S. 36), auf der gezielt neuer Wortschatz vernetzt und so das Behalten und sofortige Abrufen ermöglicht werden soll.
In das Vokabular eingeschlossen sind auch eine Reihe von Redewendungen, die eine altersgemäße, umgangssprachliche Kommunikation ermöglichen. Diese Redewendungen befähigen die S dazu, auch Jugendsprache zu verstehen und stilistisch richtig einzuordnen.

Unitbegleitendes Vokabular Das unitbegleitende Vokabular befindet sich im Anhang (S. 154–182). Es ist eine dreispaltige Auflistung des neuen Wortschatzes in chronologischer Reihenfolge mit Angabe des Erstvorkommens.
Zusätzlich finden sich hier wertvolle Lerntipps:
- Gelb hinterlegte Boxen mit *Vocabulary skills* (z. B. S. 159) sollen den S Verfahren zum Erlernen und Einprägen von Wortschatz nahe bringen und ihnen so die Möglichkeit geben, die für sie am besten geeignete Methode zu finden. Auf diese Weise wird das bereits angebahnte individuelle Lernen im 3. Lernjahr fortgeführt.
- Die rechte Spalte gibt Erläuterungen zu Besonderheiten in Verwendung, Schreibung und Aussprache des neuen Wortschatzes.
- Boxen mit *Useful phrases* (z. B. S. 167) sichern vor allem leistungsschwächeren S einen kommunikativen Erfolg.
- Weitere, umrandete Boxen fassen vor allem Phänomene oder typische Fehlerquellen (z. B. S. 175 unten) übersichtlich zusammen.

Alphabetische Wortliste Die alphabetische Wortschatzliste mit dem Erstvorkommen in *Green Line* 1, 2 und 3 (Englisch-Deutsch sowie Deutsch-Englisch) im Anhang bereitet die S auf die Benutzung des Wörterbuches vor.

Grammatik *Green Line* 3 zeichnet sich durch eine klare Progression der Grammatik aus. Der Stellenwert der Grammatik als sprachliches Gerüst ist hoch. Anhand funktionalisierter Texte werden Pensen *en bloc* eingeführt und anschließend sukzessive ausgewertet. Dabei gilt das Prinzip von geschlossenen hin zu offenen Aufgaben. Die Grammatik wird nur themenorientiert angeboten, d. h. eingebunden in das Thema der jeweiligen Unit. Auch die Einschleifaufgaben sind weitgehend kontextualisiert. Sie führen jedoch so bald wie möglich in eine sinnvolle Kommunikation über. Die Arbeitsanweisungen sind stets einfach gehalten; ein Beispiel gibt den S Hilfestellung. Neben vermehrt induktiven werden gelegentlich auch deduktive Verfahren angewandt.

Die Aufgaben unterliegen den folgenden Grundsätzen:
- vom Einfachen zum Schweren
- von geschlossenen zu offenen Aufgaben
- von der Reproduktion zum Transfer
- von Drillaufgaben und Automatismen über variierende Aufgaben zur freien Äußerung
- von kommunikationsvorbereitenden zu kommunikativen Aufgaben
- vom Isolierten zum Komplexen

Umfangreicher Grammatikstoff

Umfangreicher Grammatikstoff bedarf einer besonderen Betrachtung, Bewusstmachung und Übung. In den Units gibt es dazu eine knappe Darstellung der Formen in einer gelb unterlegten *Tip*-Box mit einem entsprechenden Verweis auf den Paragrafen im Grammatikanhang (z. B. S. 61 oben). Wo eine *Tip*-Box nicht genügt, finden sich systematische *Grammar*-Boxen in den Units eingestreut, die das neue Phänomen ausführlich und übersichtlich erläutern (z. B. S. 83 oben).

Grammatikanhang

Der Grammatikanhang (S. 124–153) ist eine vereinfachte Regelgrammatik mit weiteren Aussagen zu Struktur, Funktion, Form und Bedeutung eines grammatischen Phänomens. Neben seiner Funktion als Nachschlagewerk (Wiederholung und Hausaufgaben) dient dieser Anhang verstärkt als Lern- und Arbeitshilfe bei der Erarbeitung von Grammatik im Unterricht. Der Grammatikanhang soll den S bewusst machen, wie die Sprache funktioniert.

2.3 Differenzierung und Individualisierung

Binnendifferenzierende Maßnahmen

Die im Schülerbuch und in den Materialien des Medienverbundes angebotenen Texte und Aufgaben gehen von einem mittleren Lernerniveau aus. An geeigneten Stellen werden speziell gekennzeichnete Aufgaben angeboten und Hinweise für eine Differenzierung nach oben bzw. nach unten gegeben. Das Symbol für Differenzierung nach oben ist ⌐⌐. Das Symbol für Differenzierung nach unten – nur hier im Lehrerband und bei den Kopiervorlagen sowie im *Workbook* – ist ⌐⌐.

Die binnendifferenzierenden Maßnahmen beinhalten im Wesentlichen:
- ein im Anspruchsniveau variierendes, umfangreiches Aufgabenangebot.
- vielfältige Aufgaben für unterschiedliche Lernertypen.
- ausgewiesene Differenzierungsaufgaben auf unterschiedlichen Niveaustufen.
- offene Aufgaben, die individuell auf unterschiedlichen Niveaus erfüllt werden können.

Differenzierung ist möglich:
- durch Aufgaben im Schülerbuch für alle Lernziele zur Differenzierung nach oben ⌐⌐, z. B. Unit 4 *Wordwise*, S. 70, *ex.* 4.
- durch Teilaufgaben im Schülerbuch für alle Lernziele zur Differenzierung nach oben ⌐⌐, z. B. Unit 3 *Wordwise*, S. 54, *ex.* 1c).
- durch zusätzliche Tafelanschriebe, Kopiervorlagen, Wortgerüste, deutsche/englische Aufgabenstellungen etc. mit Hinweisen zur Umsetzung der Differenzierung nach oben und unten im Lehrerband (Teil B Unterrichtskommentare, z. B. Lehrerband S. 21).
- durch differenzierendes Arbeiten mit dem *Workbook* und dem Medienverbund (z. B. *Workbook* S. 45).
- durch gezielten Einsatz der *Mediation* (S. 110–115) und der *Free section* (S. 116–123) sowie der fakultativen Zusatztexte in Schülerbuch und *Workbook*.
- durch Einsatz der Wiederholungsaufgaben *Revision* A, B und C sowie generell der *Check-out*-Seiten.

2.4 Textarbeit

Textqualität

Auch in *Green Line* 3 wird wieder gezielt auf eine gymnasialgerechte und hohe Textqualität geachtet. Sehr kurze, unnatürliche und nur zur Einführung eines einzelnen Grammatik-Teilpensums dienende Texte werden vermieden. Gleichzeitig werden längere Lesetexte und eine vertiefte Textauswertung angeboten. Dem 7. Schuljahr entsprechend werden die Kinder behutsam an literarische Erzählqualitäten herangeführt. *Pre-, while-* und *post-reading activities* sind nun in allen Units angelegt.
Die besondere Bedeutung der Textarbeit, die der Lese- und Verständnisschwäche vieler S entgegenwirkt, wird nochmals durch den zweiseitigen, im Ansatz literarischen fakultativen Zusatztext am Ende von drei der sechs Units unterstrichen. Drei weitere Texte werden als fakultative Lesetexte im *Workbook* angeboten, Unterrichtsideen hierzu finden sich ebenfalls in diesem Lehrerband.
Der Authentizität der Texte wurde besondere Beachtung geschenkt; auch Sachtexte kommen wieder zum Einsatz. Beim Verfassen der Texte wird u. a. den Aspekten der Altersgemäßheit, dem Rollenverständnis von Jungen und Mädchen und der Motivation und Anregung zum weiteren selbständigen Lesen in der Fremdsprache besondere Beachtung beigemessen. Gefördert wird insbesondere das *Free voluntary reading*, das seinen Höhepunkt im Verlauf des 5. Lernjahres finden wird, jedoch in *Green Line* bereits von Anfang an angelegt ist.
Wie in der realen Kommunikation sind Texte Grundlage der Entwicklung rezeptiver Fertigkeiten (Lesen, Hören, Hör-Sehen) und Ausgangspunkt für sprachproduktive Tätigkeiten (Sprechen und Schreiben).

Ebenso dienen sie als situative Grundlage dem Erwerb sprachlicher Mittel (Wortschatz, Grammatik, Phonetik).

Textsortenvielfalt Neben der gegenüber früheren Lehrwerken erhöhten Textmenge spielt in *Green Line* die Textsortenvielfalt eine besondere Rolle. Beispiele hierfür sind Sachtexte, E-Mails, Briefe, Telefongespräche, Bildergeschichten etc. Die Textsortenvielfalt führt zu einem deutlich erweiterten Aufgabenspektrum.

Erweiterter Textbegriff Texte haben zentrale Bedeutung: sie sind ein wichtiger Motivationsfaktor und der Ausgangspunkt für jegliche Kommunikation. Zu ihnen gehören deshalb nicht nur die Grundlagentexte in *Check-in* und den *Language*-Seiten, der Hauptlesetext einer jeden Unit *(Text)* sowie die fakultativen Zusatztexte, sondern auch die Hörverstehenstexte und Bildergeschichten (z. B. S. 37), die als Ausgangspunkt für Sprachhandlungen dienen.

Basis der Kommunikation Neu an diesem Textbegriff ist, dass Unterricht ungeachtet seiner speziellen Zielstellung immer vom Text (Hörtext, Hör-Sehtext, Lesetext oder Bild) ausgeht. Wie in der realen Kommunikation sind Texte Grundlage der Entwicklung rezeptiver Fertigkeiten (Lesen, Hören, Hör-Sehen) und Ausgangspunkt für sprachproduktive Tätigkeiten (Sprechen und Schreiben). Die in den Bildungs- und Rahmenplänen geforderte stärkere Verzahnung der Fertigkeiten im Unterricht wird hierdurch ermöglicht.

Vom Buchtext zum Schülertext An die Bearbeitung des jeweiligen Textes schließt sich eine auf das spezielle Unterrichtsziel zugeschnittene Aufgabenkette an, die zum Abschluss in das kommunikative Ziel, den Schülertext, mündet. Diese Vorgehensweise vom Buchtext zum Schülertext überbrückt die häufig bestehende Kluft zwischen der Vermittlung von Wortschatz und Grammatik auf der einen und der Entwicklung der Fertigkeiten auf der anderen Seite. Um diesem Ansatz gerecht zu werden, findet sich in allen Teilen der Units eine Vielzahl kommunikativer Aufgaben (*Your turn: …*, z. B. S. 10, *ex.* 3; *Listening: …*, z. B. S. 15, *ex.* 8; *A game: …*, z. B. S. 64, *ex.* 4 etc.).

Der Hauptlesetext Der Hauptlesetext jeder Unit ist mit entsprechenden Anregungen und Aufgaben zur Auswertung *(pre-, while-* und *post-reading)* versehen. Er dient vor allem der Auswertung von Texten und führt die S früh an Lesetechniken in der Fremdsprache heran. Dem produktiven Schreiben wird besonderes Gewicht beigemessen. Anhand von *How to*-Aufgaben zur Erarbeitung der notwendigen sprachlichen Inventare (Strukturen, Wortschatz, Redemittel), möglicher Inhalte und der jeweiligen Textmerkmale werden die S sukzessive an ein systematisches, reflektierendes Verfahren herangeführt, das sie in Zukunft selbständig anwenden sollen. Textrezeption und Textproduktion bilden so zunehmend eine Einheit.
Beispielhaft sei auf die Aufbereitung des Hauptlesetextes der Unit 1 verwiesen: Hier finden sich auf einer ganzen Seite (S. 18) Anregungen zur Auswertung und Weiterführung, die selbstverständlich nicht alle im Unterricht behandelt werden können. Je nach Leistungsstand der Klasse kann hier eine Differenzierung erfolgen. Denkbar ist auch eine gruppenteilige Auswertung, z. B. durch die Bearbeitung des Rollenspiels (*ex.* 4) von der einen Hälfte der Klasse und der Textproduktion (*ex.* 5) von der anderen Hälfte. Die Auswahl kann mit der Klasse getroffen werden, um bereits hier ein Verfahren anzubahnen, welches in *Green Line* 4 und 5 weitere Bedeutung erlangen wird. In jeder zweiten Unit findet sich außerdem, wie bereits erwähnt, ein zweiseitiger fakultativer Lesetext.

2.5 Übung, Transfer und Wiederholung

Aufgabenformen In der Erarbeitungs- und Transferphase bietet *Green Line* neben der deutlich erhöhten Aufgabenzahl eine im Vergleich zu früheren Lehrwerksgenerationen ebenso deutlich erhöhte Vielfalt an Aufgaben an, die von den einfachsten Drillaufgaben bis hin zu spielerischen und im Sinne eines motorischen Lernanreizes auch sensorischen Aufgabenformen reichen. Die Aufgaben decken die Bereiche der sprachlichen und grammatikalischen Fähigkeiten sowie die der vier *skills* umfangreich ab. Dabei wird eine Gleichgewichtung der *skills* angestrebt. Die Festigung der Strukturen wird in sinnvollen Sprachkontexten geübt. Da der Auftakt zu den einzelnen Doppelseiten jeweils mehrere Phänomene zusammenfasst, wird ein höheres Maß an authentischer Sprache als bisher erreicht; der Anteil des „Schulbuchenglisch" konnte zurückgedrängt werden. Die Grammatik wird systematisch anhand gestaffelter Aufgaben vertieft. Eine unnötige Zerstückelung in sehr kleine Pensen gibt es dabei nicht. Darüber hinaus wurde neben der Verwendung von den S bereits bekannten Aufgabenformen auf eine große Menge leicht erfassbarer Aufgaben geachtet. Sie bilden die Grundlage für spätere gemischte Aufgabenformen, aber auch für die eigenständige Produktion im Sinne eines *creative writing*.

Das Spektrum der Aufgaben reicht somit von eher formbezogenen Aufgaben mit kommunikationsvorbereitender Funktion („geschlossene Aufgaben") bis hin zu komplexen Simulationen und realitätsnaher Kommunikation („offene Aufgaben").

Folgende Aufgabentypen erscheinen regelmäßig in den Units und sind besonders gekennzeichnet:

Listening:	bezeichnet jede Form von Höraufgaben (auch zu *Sounds*).
Sounds:	heißen die Aufgaben, die Aussprache und die Intonation schulen.
Role play:	übt Dialoge und Situationen im Spiel ein.
How to:	sind Aufgaben zur Vermittlung von bestimmten Methoden.
Your turn:	fordert die S zu mündlichen Stellungnahmen und/oder zum kreativen Schreiben auf.
Revision:	wiederholt bereits bekannte Strukturen.
A song:	kennzeichnet die Lieder.
A game:	gibt der Handlungsorientierung breiten Raum.
Writing texts:	schult das Schreiben und kreative Ausgestalten eigener Texte, in der Regel auf Grundlage eines Ausgangstextes sowie nach gezielten Vorgaben und Hinweisen.

Verzahnung von Schülerbuch und Workbook

Erhalten bleibt die sehr enge Verzahnung mit dem *Workbook*, das Aufgaben jeweils im gleichen Bereich, zum gleichen Schwerpunkt und in analoger Form wie das Schülerbuch anbietet. Damit wird zum einen die Aufgabenmenge drastisch erhöht, zum anderen durch die schriftliche Übung auch den stärker schreibgesteuerten Lernertypen eine zusätzliche Übungsmöglichkeit angeboten.

Wiederholung

Wortschatz, Grammatik, Sprechintentionen und Fertigkeiten werden spiralcurricular innerhalb des Lehrwerks wiederholt. Auch *Green Line* 3 arbeitet mit einem **dreifachen Wiederholungsnetz** – Wiederholung innerhalb der Unit, Wiederholung am Ende einer jeden Unit und Wiederholungsdoppelseiten, die jeweils mehrere Units zusammenfassen und standardgemäße Aufgabenformen anbieten.

1. Im *Language*-Teil finden sich mit *Revision* gekennzeichnete Aufgaben (z. B. S. 48, *ex.* 7), die zielgerichtet bestimmte sprachliche Phänomene aufgreifen.
2. Auf der *Check-out*-Seite wird der in der Unit behandelte Stoff wiederholt und zusammengefasst, wobei ein selbstständiger Umgang mit den Aufgaben durch die Lösungen am Ende des Schülerbuches (S. 214–216) gefördert wird (siehe auch unten, 2.6).
3. Die grün hinterlegten Doppelseiten *Revision* A, B und C sind ein fakultatives Aufgabenangebot.

2.6 Lernfortschrittsdokumentation und Selbstbewertungskompetenz

Lernfortschritte

Durch die wachsende Bedeutung autonomer und individualisierter Lernprozesse müssen die S heute zunehmend selbstständig über erreichte Lernfortschritte nachdenken und diese dokumentieren.
Auf der *Check-out*-Seite jeder Unit können die S ihre Lernleistung in der jeweiligen Unit einschätzen. Anhand unterschiedlicher Aufgabentypen überprüfen sie, ob sie die Pensen der Unit anwenden können.

Portfolio

So wird eine ständige Ergebnissicherung gewährleistet. Erarbeitete Produkte werden im *English folder* (z. B. S. 18, *ex.* 5) gesammelt. Selbstbewertungskompetenz wird auch im *Workbook* mit dem Portfolio (Lernstandsüberprüfung in der Heftmitte, zum Heraustrennen) entwickelt.
Diese didaktischen Schwerpunkte gelangen in ihrem Zusammenwirken in den einzelnen Teilen des Medienverbundes erst richtig zur Entfaltung und werden durch den Lehrerband optimal koordiniert.

2.7 Interkulturelle Kompetenz

Die Begegnung mit der Zielkultur geschieht nicht nur durch die *constellation of characters*. Auf den landeskundlichen Einführungsseiten jeder Unit, der *Check-in*-Doppelseite, erhalten die S sprachliche, soziale, kulturelle und geografische Informationen über das Zielland. Diese Informationen werden so weit wie möglich mit der eigenen Erfahrungswelt unserer S in Bezug gesetzt. Das Ziel der einführenden Doppelseite und aller anderen Seiten, die landeskundliche Informationen direkt und indirekt vermitteln, liegt nicht darin, abstrakte, scheinbar objektive Landeskunde vorzuführen. Wo immer möglich sollen Vergleiche zur eigenen Lebenswelt stattfinden können, auch im sprachlichen Bereich. Die Präsentation eines vielfältigen Bildes des Ziellandes wird konsequent verfolgt. Bei den neu hinzugekommenen Elementen *Talkwise* und den ausgeweiteten *Skills*-Seiten ist es außerdem möglich, einen vertieften Zugang zum interkulturellen Lernen zu schaffen.

2.8 Anmerkungen zum Unterricht in 3-, 4- oder 5-stündigen Kursen

Green Line 3 hat insgesamt nur 77 Seiten Obligatorik von Unit 1 bis Unit 6. Der Anteil der einzelnen Buchteile am Gesamtumfang ist wie folgt:

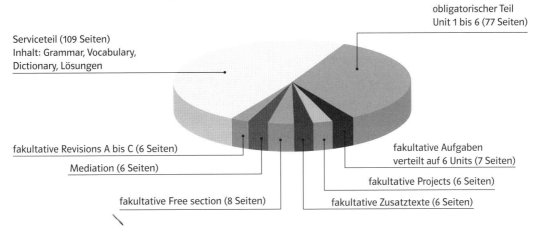

Empfehlungen für 3-, 4- und 5-stündige Kurse in Klasse 7:

	Klasse 7: 3-stündig	Klasse 7: 4-stündig	Klasse 7: 5-stündig
⟨Fakultatives Aufgaben-angebot⟩	weitestgehend weglassen	gelegentlich Aufgaben (je nach Leistungsstand) auswählen	zahlreiche Aufgaben auswählen
Aufgaben zur Differenzierung nach oben	weitestgehend weglassen	gelegentlich Aufgaben (je nach Leistungsstand) auswählen	zahlreiche Aufgaben auswählen
English folder	u. a. zu Hause	zu Hause/in der Schule	u. a. im Unterricht
Aufgaben mit Schreibsymbol	u. a. als Hausaufgabe	in der Schule/als Hausaufgabe	u. a. im Verlauf des Unterrichts
Listening	Kürzungsmöglichkeit!	Aufgaben dazu u. a. mündlich	Aufgaben auch schriftlich
Aufgaben	Aufgaben im Unterricht einführen, zu Hause schriftlich fixieren lassen; zeitintensive Aufgabenformen (Schreiben, Abschreiben, Zeichnen, Gestalten, *classroom posters* etc.) kürzen; wenig Gruppenarbeit einsetzen	Aufgaben im Wechsel schriftlich/mündlich; gelegentlich zeitintensivere Arbeitsformen oder Sozialformen einstreuen. Aufgaben mit Gestaltungselementen zu Hause anfertigen lassen	Aufgaben im Wechsel schriftlich/mündlich; gelegentlich zeitintensivere Arbeitsformen oder Sozialformen einstreuen. Aufgaben mit Gestaltungselementen gelegentlich im Unterricht anfertigen lassen
Aufgaben mit zeichnerischen Elementen	weglassen bzw. zu Hause anfertigen	zu Hause anfertigen, gelegentlich im Unterricht	sowohl im Unterricht als auch zu Hause vertiefen lassen
Revisions	u. a. zu Hause; Lösungsblatt anbieten/Selbstkontrolle	einige Aufgaben im Unterricht, andere zu Hause oder als Freiarbeitsmaterialien	Aufgaben im Plenum als Freiarbeitsmaterialien
Wordwise	zügig bearbeiten; Kürzungsmöglichkeiten bei zeichnerischer Umsetzung und zeitintensiven Aufgabenformen	im Unterricht, aber auch zu Hause erledigen	im Unterricht, aber auch zu Hause erledigen

A

	Klasse 7: 3-stündig	Klasse 7: 4-stündig	Klasse 7: 5-stündig
Check-out	zu Hause und Selbstkontrolle	im Unterricht anüben, zu Hause mit Selbstkontrolle	im Wechsel: im Unterricht, z. B. für Lernzirkel, aber auch zu Hause
Lautes Lesen in der Klasse	Texte von CD, S lesen mit; S lesen Texte 1–2 Mal	Texte von CD, L liest Texte, S lesen mit; S lesen Texte 1–2 Mal bzw. spielen Dialoge/Rollenspiele vor	Texte von CD, L liest Texte, S lesen mit; S lesen Texte 2–3 Mal, auch in Partnerarbeit, bzw. spielen Dialoge/Rollenspiele vor
Einsatz des *Workbook*	Aufgaben immer wieder mündlich durchgehen; L liest den Textteil, S dürfen die einzusetzenden Wörter laut rufen; u. a. Tandem-Aufgaben und Aufgaben mit Partner im Unterricht; Hörverstehen mit CD zu Hause!	Aufgaben schriftlich/mündlich gemischt; als Methodenwechsel auch ruhigere schriftliche Phasen im Unterricht zur Vertiefung einplanen	Aufgaben schriftlich/mündlich gemischt; als Methodenwechsel immer wieder ruhigere schriftliche Phasen im Unterricht zur Vertiefung einplanen
Einsatz der DVD	gelegentlich	regelmäßig	konsequent
⟨Fakultative Zusatztexte⟩	*free voluntary reading*	anfänglich im Unterricht gemeinsam, gestützt durch Kopiervorlagen, zunehmend autonom	autonom, aber durch Kopiervorlagen gestützt, im Unterricht aufgreifen und vertiefen
⟨*Free section*⟩	selektiv, zur Anbahnung des Hör-Sehverstehens aber v. a. *Working with films*; einige wenige *poems*	selektiv und zur Auflockerung	durchgängig, v. a. auch die eigene Textproduktion von *poems*
Mediation	sehr selektiv	gelegentlich	regelmäßig
Skills/How to …	unverzichtbar	unverzichtbar	unverzichtbar

II Der Medienverbund

1. Der Lehrerband

Zentrales Steuerungselement
Der Lehrerband ist das zentrale Steuerungselement für den Unterricht.

Unitteil Kommentare
Er besteht aus zwei Hauptteilen:
- Teil A – Allgemeiner Teil
- Teil B – Unterrichtskommentare

Teil B
Der Teil B des Lehrerbands folgt dem Aufbau des Schülerbuches.

Materialübersicht
Jeder Unit ist eine Planungsübersicht vorangestellt. Darin wird ein Überblick gegeben über die einzelnen Abschnitte der Unit: Wortschatz- und Grammatikpensen, die Fundstelle im Grammatikanhang, *Workbook*-Aufgaben, CD-Tracks, Kopiervorlagen, Folien und DVD-Einsatz.

Hinweise
Nach den landeskundlichen Informationen zum jeweiligen Schauplatz und einer kurzen Inhaltsangabe zur Unit *(Storyline)* folgt der eigentliche methodische Kommentar zur Unterrichtsgestaltung.

Komplexe Unterrichtsabläufe
Die linke Randspalte führt mit ihren Rubriken durch die Unterrichtsabläufe. Die breite Mittelspalte beschreibt die methodischen Abläufe, erteilt Ratschläge oder erläutert Möglichkeiten zur Differenzierung etc. Hier erscheinen ebenfalls die Tafelbilder, Erweiterungen im Unterricht und Lösungen. Die Koordinierung mit den anderen Teilen des Medienverbundes ist in der rechten Randspalte anschaulich dargestellt.
Es wird immer Unterricht in seiner Gesamtheit beschrieben, d. h. über die Erläuterungen zum Funktionieren der Lehrwerksteile hinausgehend, werden komplexe Unterrichtsabläufe beschrieben, wie sie die L täglich bewältigen müssen.
Eine Besonderheit stellen die **„Tipps für junge Lehrer"** dar, die Informationen für Kolleginnen und Kollegen enthalten, die zum ersten Mal in dieser Klassenstufe unterrichten.
Darüber hinaus finden sich an unterschiedlichen Stellen Tipps des bedeutenden englischen Didaktikers Mario Rinvolucri, die alternative Zugänge zu einzelnen Texten/ Aufgaben eröffnen: **„Tipps von Mario Rinvolucri – The alternative way"**.

2. Das Schülerbuch

Charaktere und Situationen
Es wurde große Sorgfalt darauf verwendet, Charaktere und Situationen authentisch zu gestalten. Topografische Gegebenheiten der einzelnen Schauplätze sind auch in den Details authentisch. Es treten nun auch vermehrt authentische Personen auf, z. B. „Eddie the Eagle" etc. In Band 3 gibt es keinen zentralen Handlungsort mehr. Die Lehrwerkscharaktere sind durch eine Vielzahl von Personen abgelöst. Zentral ist dabei der Ansatz, unterschiedliche Regionen Großbritanniens kennen zu lernen. Das den S aus Band 1 und 2 bekannte begleitende Filmmaterial *Action UK!* führt diesen Ansatz in Band 3 konsequent weiter. Die drei Charaktere des Films bleiben im Sinne einer einfacheren Identifikation auch in Band 3 erhalten.

Aufbau des Schülerbuches
Der Aufbau des Schülerbuches im Überblick:
- 6 Units mit den fakultativen *Revisions* A, B und C nach den Units 2, 4 und 6
- fakultative zweiseitige Lektüre in jeder zweiten Unit (ergänzt durch fakultative Texte im *Workbook*)
- Sprachmittlung *(Mediation)*
- fakultative *Free section* mit einem historischen Augenzeugenbericht, der authentischen Problemseite eines Jugendmagazins, Anregungen zum Umgang mit Gedichten sowie einer ersten Filmanalyse
- drei *Project*-Doppelseiten nach den Units 1, 3 und 5: *English and Computing, English and Biology, English and Geography*
- Grammatikanhang
- Unitvokabular
- Alphabetische Wortliste Englisch-Deutsch und Deutsch-Englisch von *Green Line* 1, 2 und 3
- Liste der unregelmäßigen Verben
- *Classroom phrases*
- Lösungen zu den *Check-out*-Seiten
- Zeitstrahl zur britischen Geschichte

Zu den Neuerungen in Band 3 siehe oben, 2.1.

Alle Units des Schülerbuches sind einheitlich gegliedert. Jede der sechs Units des Schülerbuches besteht aus den unten aufgelisteten Teilen. Diese führen über einen Text oder Dialog, über Bilder etc. in ein bzw. mehrere Phänomen(e) gleichzeitig ein, die dann sukzessive behandelt werden. Am Ende steht jeweils eine Aufgabe, mit der die gesamten Pensen des Unitteils nochmals zusammengebracht und wiederholt werden.

Check-in:	Einstimmen auf das Thema, neuer Themenwortschatz, Erwerb landeskundlichen Orientierungswissens
Language:	Vermittlung der vier *skills*, von Wortschatz und Grammatik
Talkwise:	Hinführung zum Sprechen über unterschiedliche Themenbereiche
Skills:	Erweitertes Methodentraining zu den vier *skills*
Text:	Hauptlesetext mit Auswertung
Wordwise:	Wiederholung und Vernetzung insbesondere des neuen Unit-Wortschatzes
Check-out:	Selbstevaluation mit Lösungen hinten im Schülerbuch (S. 213–216).

In den Units 2, 4 und 6 zusätzlich:
⟨Text⟩: Zweiter, fakultativer Lesetext mit Auswertung nur im Lehrerband, um das unmittelbare Leseerlebnis der S nicht zu beeinträchtigen

Nach den Units 1, 3 und 5 zusätzlich:
⟨Project⟩: drei fächerverbindende fakultative Projekte zu verschiedenen Themen

Nach den Units 2, 4 und 6 zusätzlich:
⟨Revision⟩: Wiederholung von Wortschatz und Grammatik zur Vorbereitung auf Standardprüfungen

3. Das *Workbook*

Für den Unterricht und zu Hause
Alle Aufgaben der sechs *Workbook*-Units sind für ihren optimalen Einsatzort im Schülerbuch selbst und hier im Lehrerband gekennzeichnet. Das *Workbook* kann sowohl für die Arbeit zu Hause als auch im Unterricht eingesetzt werden.

Einige Elemente sind: große Aufgabenvielfalt, viele Aufgaben, vertiefende Textarbeit zu den Schülerbuch-Texten, Tandem-Aufgaben, eine Liste der (bis dahin bekannten) unregelmäßigen Verben u.v.m. Authentische Materialien werden so früh wie möglich angeboten. Zum Portfolio siehe oben, 2.6!
Dem *Workbook* ist eine vierseitige Grammatikübersicht der wichtigsten Pensen von *Green Line* 3 (in der Heftmitte) zum Heraustrennen beigeheftet.

***Workbook* mit Audio-CD (für Schüler)**
Das *Workbook* (Klett-Nr. 547145) enthält zahlreiche Aufgaben zum Hörverstehen. Zum einen beziehen sich diese auf Hörverstehenstexte und -aufgaben des Schülerbuches. Zum anderen enthält jede Unit einen zusätzlichen Hörverstehenstext mit dazugehöriger Aufgabe. Alle Hörverstehenstexte und -aufgaben des *Workbooks* befinden sich auf zwei Audio-CDs, die – wie beim *Workbook* von *Green Line* 1 und 2 – hinten in das Heft eingelegt sind. Darüber hinaus umfassen diese Audio-CDs den Hauptlesetext jeder Schülerbuch-Unit.

***Workbook* mit Audio-CD und Lernsoftware (für Schüler)**
Das *Workbook* mit zusätzlicher Lernsoftware enthält neben den Audio-CDs den auf *Green Line* zugeschnittenen Sprachtrainer für Grammatik, Vokabeln und Kommunikation, der zum Üben zu Hause und für den Unterricht die richtige Ergänzung zu den Schülermaterialien anbietet (Klett-Nr. 547148).

Netzwerkversion (für Lehrer)
Auch als Netzwerkversion für die Schule erhältlich: Klett-Nr. 990683.

***Workbook* mit Lösungen (für Lehrer)**
Das *Workbook* mit Lösungen ist für die Arbeit der Lehrer/innen gedacht und enthält die Lösungen und Texte zu allen Aufgaben des *Workbooks* (Klett-Nr. 547146).

4. Weitere Werkteile für den Unterricht

- **Bildfolien** (Klett-Nr. 547142): Der Folienordner enthält 15 farbige Folien mit Angeboten zur Semantisierung, zusätzlichen Aufgaben zu Wortschatz und Grammatik sowie Transferaufgaben.

- **Standardaufgaben mit Audio-CD und Lehrersoftware** (Klett-Nr. 547144): Aufgaben zum Hör- und Leseverstehen, zu Grammatik, Wortschatz und Mediation zu jeder Unit, v. a. als Material zur Leistungsmessung.

- **Tonträger** (Klett-Nr. 547149): 4 Audio-CDs für den Unterricht, für die Arbeit des Lehrers/der Lehrerin mit **allen** Tonaufnahmen von Schülerbuch und *Workbook* rund um *Green Line*.

- **„Action UK!" 3 (DVD, Klett-Nr. 585213):** Diese DVD bietet ansprechende und motivierende Filmsequenzen in unterschiedlichen Regionen Großbritanniens, ausgehend von einer Rahmenhandlung, bei der die drei Filmemacher aus Greenwich an einem Wettbewerb teilnehmen. *Action UK!* trainiert das Hör- und Sehverstehen und ist auf das Schülerbuch abgestimmt. Somit können im Unterricht auch visuell viele Alltagsszenen in Großbritannien vorgeführt werden, wodurch der Sprachlehrgang durch die Gestik und Mimik von Muttersprachlern authentischer wird.
  Den meisten Schülerinnen und Schülern ist das Medium inzwischen geläufig. Eine Reihe von Einsatzmöglichkeiten bieten sich an, so z. B. die gezielte Schulung des Hör-Sehverstehens und das anschließende Nachspielen. Die Charaktere aus *Green Line* 3 kommen im Film nicht vor. Er kann deshalb unabhängig von der unmittelbaren Progression eingesetzt werden. Das Begleitheft liefert klare Hinweise für den Unterrichtseinsatz.

- **Begleitheft zur DVD** (Klett-Nr. 585223): Das Lehrerbegleitheft zu *Action UK!* enthält detaillierte Hinweise zum Einsatz der DVD im Unterricht.

- **Lehrersoftware** (**nur mit Standardaufgaben** Klett-Nr. 547144 erhältlich): Die CD-ROM bietet eine Sammlung von bearbeitbaren Standardaufgaben, Texten, Aufgaben und Bildern zur Gestaltung des Unterrichts. Zusätzlich ist ein Lexikon mit dem gesamten Wortschatz des Schülerbuches enthalten sowie ein Aufgabengenerator, der eigene Texte nach vorhandenen Wortschatzkenntnissen überprüft und daraus Aufgaben erstellt. Ebenfalls integriert sind Filmausschnitte aus *Action UK!* (siehe oben, **Standardaufgaben**).

- **PONS Green Line** Wörterbuch (Klett-Nr. 517679, für Schüler): Das PONS-Wörterbuch zu *Green Line* ist Englisch-Deutsch und Deutsch-Englisch gestaltet. Es enthält 77 000 Stichworte und Wendungen sowie den Wortschatz des Schülerbuches. Die wichtigsten Wörter werden gekennzeichnet. Das Wörterbuch enthält außerdem zahlreiche farbige Informationskästen.

B Unterrichtskommentare
Planung Unit 1
Übersicht
Bearbeitungszeitraum: 22 Unterrichtsstunden

Abschnitt	SB-Seiten	Ziele	Wortschatz/Grammatik & skills	WB-Übungen	CD-Tracks Kopiervorlagen Folien DVD	Gramm. Anhang (SB)
Check-in *The world of sport*	8–9	Beliebte Sportarten und ihre Regeln kennen lernen. Über die eigene sportliche Betätigung sprechen. Sportreportagen im Radio verstehen	Wortfeld „Sport" Ein persönliches Vokabular zusammenstellen	S. 4/ex. 1–3	Schüler-CD 1/1–4 Lehrer-CD 1/1–4, 5–8 KV 1, 2 Folie 1, 2 DVD: A Sport, Part A	
Language 1 *A new trick*	10–11	Über Termine und Vereinbarungen in der Zukunft sprechen. Um Hilfe bitten und Hilfe anbieten	Das *simple present* und das *present progressive* zur Wiedergabe der Zukunft	S. 5/ex. 4–6 S. 6/ex. 7–9	Lehrer-CD 1/9 KV 3, 4	G2–4
Talkwise *Is it important to win?*	12	Die *Talkwise*-Seiten im SB und ihre Funktion kennen lernen. Ein Streitgespräch verstehen und führen Zustimmung und Ablehnung ausdrücken	*Useful phrases: Agreeing and disagreeing*	S. 7/ex. 10–12	Lehrer-CD 1/10 Folie 3	
Language 2 *Did you know?*	13–15	Einige kuriose Sportfakten kennen lernen. Personen und Dinge näher bestimmen	Das Wortfeld „Sport" vertiefen *Defining relative clauses/contact clauses* How to: Wortschatzlücken durch Paraphrasieren umgehen R: *Simple present vs. present progressive*	S. 8/ex. 13–15 S. 9/ex. 16–18	Schüler-CD 1/5 Lehrer-CD 1/11, 12, 13 KV 5, 6	G5–7
Text *Eddie the Eagle*	16–18	Eine Sportlerbiografie lesen. Über Personen und deren Gefühle sprechen	Wortfelder „Charakterisierung" und „Gefühle" *Writing texts*: Kuriose Sportfakten zusammenstellen	S. 10/ex. 19, 20	Schüler-CD 1/6–10 Lehrer-CD 1/14–18, 19 KV 7, 8 DVD: A Sport, Part B	
Skills *Using a German-English dictionary*	19	Das Arbeiten mit dem zweisprachigen Wörterbuch schulen	*Vocabulary Skills*: Das deutsch-englische Wörterbuch Das Wortfeld „Sport" vertiefen Die Bedeutung des Sinnzusammenhangs für die Wortwahl erkennen	S. 11/ex. 21, 22	KV 9	

Abschnitt	SB-Seiten	Ziele	Wortschatz/Grammatik & skills	WB-Übungen	CD-Tracks Kopiervorlagen Folien DVD	Gramm. Anhang (SB)
Wordwise	20	Den Wortschatz der Unit umwälzen und vernetzen	Den Wortschatz zum Thema „Sport" sammeln und systematisieren Präpositionen wiederholen Verb-Nomen-Paare kennen lernen *Sounds*: Die Aussprache im Satzzusammenhang üben	S. 12/ *ex.* 24–26	Lehrer-CD 1/20 KV 10	
Check-out	21	Selbstkontrolle Die Lernziele der Unit 1 überprüfen	Wortschatz- und Grammatikschwerpunkte der Unit: „Sport", *present progressive to express the future, defining relative clauses/ contact clauses* Ein *word web* anlegen	S. 13/ *ex.* 28–30	KV 11	
⟨Text⟩ *Point Blank*		Einen Auszug aus einem Jugendroman eigenständig erschließen		S. 14	Schüler-CD 1/11 Lehrer-CD 1/21	

Unit 1 The world of sport

Hinweise

LANDESKUNDE

Danny Way (born April 15, 1974 in Portland, Oregon) is a professional skateboarder. He started skating at the age of four and won his first competition when he was eleven. In 1989 he turned pro and since then he has won lots of competitions and awards. He is still continually pushing himself and his skateboarding to the next limit, knowing that there will always be another injury and another rehabilitation to work through (→ Between 1999 and 2002 he had to undergo seven operations, five on his knees and two on his shoulder!). In 2005 (July 9) he became the first person to jump the Great Wall of China on a skateboard.

The 1988 Winter Olympics, Calgary/Canada: For the first time, Canada hosted the Winter Olympic Games (officially known as the XV Olympic Winter Games) which were extended from 12 to 16 days (February 13–28), including three weekends. 57 nations with 1,423 athletes (301 women, 1,122 men) took part in 46 events; 9,498 volunteers helped and 6,838 media people were present (2,477 written press, 4,361 broadcasters). The USSR was the most successful nation (11 gold medals), followed by the German Democratic Republic (9 gold medals) and Switzerland (5 gold medals); the Federal Republic of Germany sent two winners to Calgary. These were the first smoke-free Olympic Games. Two competitors, Eddie Edwards in ski jumping and the bobsleighing team from Jamaica, entered their competitions with little experience and no chance of winning any medals:

Michael Edwards (born December 5, 1963 in Cheltenham, England), better known as **Eddie 'the Eagle' Edwards**, was the first athlete to represent the British team in an Olympic ski jumping competition. Edwards was ranked 55th in the world when he qualified, as the only British applicant, for the Calgary games. He was handicapped by his weight – at about 82 kg, more than 9 kg heavier than the next heaviest competitor – and by his lack of financial support for training – he was totally self-funded, – and so he finished last in both the 70 m and 90 m events. Another problem was that he was very farsighted, so that he had to wear his glasses at all times. When he was skiing they fogged so much that he could hardly see anything. His determination, however, to compete in spite of being outmatched by the other ski jumpers won the affection of the spectators which even overshadowed the actual medal winners. People loved him because he demonstrated the true Olympic spirit.

The Jamaican Bobsleigh Team: The first Jamaican four-man bobsleigh team made history in the Calgary Olympic Winter Games. In their first games ever the team from a country which had never seen snowfall was regarded as a novelty. They had many technical difficulties, injuries and crashes, but nevertheless became crowd favourites and a media sensation. In 1993 their story was made into a Walt Disney film called *Cool Runnings*: http://www.answers.com/topic/cool-runnings.

STORYLINE

Im Mittelpunkt der Unit steht die Begegnung mit der Welt des Sports, wobei es weniger um Bestleistungen und Rekorde als vielmehr um die manchmal eher skurrilen und weniger im Blickpunkt der Öffentlichkeit stehenden Seiten des Sports geht. Ausgehend von der zu diskutierenden Frage, wie wichtig es im Einzelfall ist, einen Wettkampf zu gewinnen, beschäftigen sich die S eingehend mit Eddie Edwards, einem überhaupt nicht ins Bild des typischen Sportlers passenden britischen Skispringer.

Check-in

Seite 8–9

Ziele
- Beliebte Sportarten und ihre Regeln kennen lernen
- Über die eigene sportliche Betätigung sprechen
- Den individuellen Wortschatz erweitern
- Sportreportagen im Radio verstehen

Fotos	**The world of sport**	Seite 8–9

Ziel
- Die Bildbeschreibung üben

Wortschatz *oval, pitch, referee, to control, baseball, ice, stick, base, field, bat, cricket, to go on, athletics, rugby, track, skateboarding, American, helmet, racket, umpire, court, ice hockey, race, brake*

Methodisches Vorgehen
- Zur Einstimmung auf den inhaltlichen Rahmen der Unit berichtet L in einem kurzen Vortrag über die eigenen sportlichen Aktivitäten in den Sommerferien, z. B. *In the summer holidays I went to Garmisch-Partenkirchen in Bavaria. There I did a lot of hiking/mountain climbing and I often went swimming in one of the wonderful lakes. Back at home I often played tennis with a friend.*
- L startet als *warming-up exercise* eine S-S-Kette, indem ein symbolischer „Staffelstab" (z. B. ein Tennisball) weitergereicht wird: *What sports did you do in the summer holidays? Think about what you did and finish the sentence: In the summer holidays I …* Benötigte Redemittel können an die Tafel geschrieben werden; so empfiehlt sich etwa eine begleitende Phase der Wortschatzarbeit (siehe TA), in der Sportarten den Verben *to play, to do* und *to go* zugeordnet werden.
- L leitet zum SB über: *Now open your books and look at the pictures on pages 8–9. Describe them in a few words to a partner/the class. Don't read the texts, please.*
- Die S stellen anschließend Vermutungen über den Inhalt der Unit an: *What will you talk about in Unit 1?*

TA

```
                        | often played …
In the summer holidays I| did a lot of …
                        | sometimes went …

to play:  football, basketball, volleyball, cricket, rugby, …
to do:    athletics, …
to go:    swimming, jogging, surfing, abseiling, …
```

Erweiterung
- Leistungsstärkere S können Kurzreferate vorbereiten, in denen sie ihren Mitschüler/innen die hier vorgestellten Sportarten und die wichtigsten Regeln vorstellen. Zur Unterstützung erhalten die S **KV 1: Preparing a talk to the class**, die auch in der weiteren Arbeit mit dem SB bei anderen Themen genutzt werden kann.

Material
Kopiervorlage 1

Text/Fotos	**1 Work with the photos**	Seite 8

Ziel
- Das Textverständnis durch Zuordnen von Fotos nachweisen
- Wörter aus dem Textzusammenhang erschließen

Methodisches Vorgehen
- a) PA: Die S lesen die Notizen zu den einzelnen Sportarten, ordnen sie den Fotos zu und erschließen den neuen Wortschatz aus dem Kontext.
- Vergleich der Ergebnisse mit einem anderen Schülerpaar, anschließend Besprechung im Plenum.
- b) Spontane Schüleräußerungen. Teilaufgabe b) kann auch direkt im Zusammenhang mit der Auswertung von Teilaufgabe a) bearbeitet werden.

1 Check-in

- c) wird schriftlich als Hausaufgabe bearbeitet.
- Anschließend kann **KV 2: Our sports** eingesetzt werden; ggf. auch als Hausaufgabe zur Vorbereitung der folgenden Unterrichtsstunden.

HA Auch als HA geeignet

Erweiterung
- Die in der *Tip*-Box vorgeschlagene Zusammenstellung von *personal vocabulary* kann im Verlauf des Schuljahres sukzessive erweitert werden.
- Folie 1: **What's their sport?** übt das Erkennen von Sportarten und das Zuordnen von *equipment* anhand von Bildern.

Lösung

> baseball: B/3 – cricket: A/4 – athletics: F/5 – rugby: D/1 – skateboarding: E/6 – tennis: C/7 – ice hockey: G/2

Tipps für junge Lehrer

Quiz game: Die S schreiben die Fragen und Antworten (*ex.* 1c) auf Karteikarten, die eingesammelt werden. L übernimmt die Rolle des Spielleiters (bzw. bestimmt hierfür eine/n S) und liest eine beliebige Frage vor. Das Quiz wird als Gruppenwettkampf durchgeführt. Für jede richtige Antwort erhält die jeweilige Gruppe einen Punkt. Das Quiz kann auch in Kleingruppen gespielt werden. Hierzu erhält jede Gruppe einen Teil der Fragekarten; ein mehrmaliger Austausch der Karten zwischen den Gruppen ist möglich.

Material
Workbook S. 4/1, 3
Kopiervorlage 2
Folie 1

Üben 2 Listening: Sports news

Seite 9

HV-Text

One *(slight British accent)*
And it's a good start by Dabrovski. But Auermann gets away fastest. And Rossi is also running well. Now it's Martinez and Stavros. Oh, but here comes Miller between them. Stavros tries to fight back, but – no – Miller wins! He holds his arms in the air. World champion over a hundred metres. At last all his dreams …

Two *(slight Australian accent)*
… and Chang turns and comes back down the pool for the last time. Only fifty more metres. Nobody can catch her now. She's so far in front. She's still moving beautifully through the water. This girl isn't only strong – she also has great style. The clock shows that she is going to be well inside her personal best time of one …

Three *(light American accent)*
Murray serves. Another ace. *(umpire heard giving score: Thirty-fifteen)* Murray is playing brilliantly today – gets ready for his next serve – this time Petrovic gets to the ball with his racket – hits it low and hard into the opposite corner of the court *(linesperson heard shouting: Out!)* – Oh! Petrovic doesn't like that call. He thinks the ball landed on the line. Now he's looking angrily at the umpire, but the umpire doesn't want to know. *(umpire heard giving score: Forty-fifteen)* Petrovic still isn't happy. He throws his racket down. Wow! He's very angry. Let's wait and see what the umpire is going to do …

Four *(light Scottish accent)*
… and Jones brings the ball down with her left foot – passes to Thompson – a great ball almost to the other side of the pitch. Thompson collects and takes the ball down the line. Now Singh has the ball – runs almost to the goal line and – Oh, that was a bad foul by Dixon! Yes, that's no surprise. The referee shows her the yellow card. But Singh is OK. She gets up again and takes the free kick quickly. Thompson is waiting for the ball and – Goal! Thompson has scored again! This time with her head. A brilliant header right into the top corner! Well, this really is turning into a great game …

Ziel
- Kurze Ausschnitte aus Radio-Sportreportagen mit unterschiedlichen regionalen Akzenten verstehen

| | | Check-in | 1 |

Methodisches Vorgehen

Pre-listening:
- a) L bereitet die S kurz auf die HV-Texte vor: *You are going to listen to four short reports from different sports events. Be careful: The reporters come from different parts of the English-speaking world – so they have different accents. Can you guess where they come from?*
- Die S lesen den Arbeitsauftrag im SB und fertigen ein einfaches Lösungsraster für ihre Notizen an.

While-listening:
- L präsentiert die vier Live-Mitschnitte von Sportreportagen nacheinander von CD und macht jeweils eine kurze Pause, damit die S Stichworte notieren können.
- In einem zweiten Durchgang werden alle vier Mitschnitte unmittelbar hintereinander vorgespielt; die S vervollständigen ihre Notizen.

Post-listening:
- Vergleich und Diskussion der Notizen in PA. Anschließend stellen mehrere Schülerpaare ihre Ergebnisse im Plenum vor.
- b) L startet die Diskussion. Mögliche Leitfragen können zur Orientierung für die ganze Klasse an die Tafel/auf Folie geschrieben werden, da b) Differenzierung nach oben ist.

TA

> Have you ever listened to a sports programme on the radio?
> What sports do you listen to on the radio?
> How often do you listen to sports on the radio?
> When/Where do you listen to sports programmes?

- Anschließend Beantwortung der Frage aus dem SB, wobei es sicherlich keine für alle S zutreffende „richtige" Antwort gibt. Aufgrund des Schwierigkeitsgrads der Fragestellung leitet L die Diskussion und hilft bei Wortschatzproblemen.

Lösung

	Sport	Sounds	Words
1	athletics (reporter: English)	shot to start the race	good start running well a hundred metres
2	swimming (reporter: Australian)	water	pool moving through the water
3	tennis (reporter: American)	whacks of tennis ball voices of umpire/linesperson	30-15/40-15/Out! next serve racket, court on the line
4	football (reporter: Scottish)	background noise of typical football crowd	ball → left foot passes to … (goal) line, bad foul referee → yellow card free kick, score/goal header

Material
- s 1/1–4
- L 1/1–4, 5–8
- Workbook S. 4/2
- Ggf. Leerfolie

Üben **3 Your turn: You and sports** Seite 9

Ziel
- Über in Deutschland beliebte bzw. weniger beliebte Sportarten sprechen
- Die eigene(n) Sportart(en) vorstellen

Methodisches Vorgehen
- a) Zuerst notieren die S in Einzelarbeit, welche Sportarten sie für beliebt bzw. weniger beliebt halten und führen mögliche Gründe an. Anschließend

1 Check-in

Gruppenbildung (3–4 S); die S tauschen sich aus und besprechen ihre individuellen Einschätzungen. Ein Gruppenmitglied trägt das Ergebnis der Diskussion im Plenum vor.

- b) Zur Vorbereitung dieser Aufgabe fordert L die S auf, ein Foto mitzubringen, das sie bei der Ausübung „ihrer" Sportart zeigt, im Verein oder unorganisiert in der Freizeit. Alternativ wählen sie ein Foto aus Zeitung, Zeitschrift o. Ä., in dem diese Sportart dargestellt ist. Außerdem bereiten die S einen Kurzvortrag zur Vorstellung der jeweiligen Sportart vor (*show and tell*: nicht länger als zwei Minuten!). Hierzu ist ggf. eigenständiges Arbeiten mit dem Wörterbuch erforderlich. Zur Unterstützung der S in der Vorbereitung des Vortrags kann auch **KV 1: Preparing a talk to the class** eingesetzt werden, falls sie noch nicht bearbeitet wurde.

Erweiterung

- L stellt das Ergebnis einer Untersuchung für das Jahr 2006 bezogen auf die Mitgliederzahlen in Sportvereinen in Deutschland vor: 1. Fußball (6,4 Millionen); 2. Turnen (5,1 Millionen); 3. Fitnesscenter (4,2 Millionen); 4. Tennis (1,7 Millionen); 5. Schützen (1,5 Millionen); 6. Leichtathletik (900 000).
- Die S vergleichen die Statistik mit ihrer eigenen Einschätzung und diskutieren die Frage, ob es in der Beliebtheitsskala Unterschiede gibt, wenn es nicht um aktiv im Verein betriebene Sportarten geht, sondern um Sportarten, die man gerne im Fernsehen oder live sieht (= *spectator sports*).
- **Folie 2: A class survey: Popular sports** übt die Durchführung einer Klassenumfrage zum Thema „Sport" mit anschließender Auswertung.

Tipps für junge Lehrer

Zur Vorbereitung der GA kann (statt Folie 2) auch kurz ein *class survey* an der Tafel durchgeführt werden: L schreibt die Überschrift *Our favourite sports* mittig auf die Tafel. Links werden auf Zuruf der S acht bis zehn Sportarten aufgeführt, die die S aktiv, d. h. im Verein, betreiben (z. B.: *volleyball, basketball, football, swimming, jogging, karate, gymnastics, handball, tennis, hockey*). Die S kommen abwechselnd an die Tafel und tragen sich mit Strichen ein; ggf. trägt ein/e S seine/ihre Sportart nach, wenn sie in der Liste fehlt bzw. legt eine weitere Zeile an für solche S, die nicht in einem Verein aktiv sind. Die Ergebnisse werden im Plenum versprachlicht: *Five people in our class play basketball./Most people in our class play football./Only two people go jogging./Ten people are not in a sports club./…* Auch eine geschlechterspezifische Aussage ist denkbar, z. B.: *Girls do …/Boys play …/Many girls like … better than …/… is more popular with boys./…*

> **TIP**
> Aus Zeitgründen empfiehlt es sich, die Zahl der Sportarten einzugrenzen (z. B.: "Top/Flop 3") Sammeln von *personal vocabulary* für den *folder*

Material
Kopiervorlage 1
Folie 2
Im Anschluss an *ex.* 3: *Action UK!* 3, A Sport, Part A: *Greg, the 'Super Surfer'* sowie *Action UK!* 3, Begleitheft zu den Filmsequenzen, Unit 1 A

Language 1 — Seite 10–11

Ziele
- Über Termine und Vereinbarungen in der Zukunft sprechen
- Um Hilfe bitten und Hilfe anbieten

Text: A new trick — Seite 10

Ziel
- Das Hör-/Leseverstehen üben
- Bekannte Futurformen wiederholen

Wortschatz event, chance, arrangement, feeling, not until

Strukturen
- Verschiedene Formen des *future tense*

Methodisches Vorgehen
- SB geschlossen. L präsentiert den Dialog von CD und stellt Fragen zum Globalverständnis (z. B.: *What are the speakers' names? What is their sport? What big event are they training for? What does Harry want Laura to do? Why doesn't she want to teach him her trick?*). In diesem Kontext semantisiert L den neuen Wortschatz und schreibt die neuen Wörter an die Tafel.
- SB geöffnet. L präsentiert die Tonaufnahme ein zweites Mal; die S lesen leise mit. Anschließend Lesen mit verteilten Rollen.
- Ausgehend von der Zeitbestimmung *next weekend* nennen die S die beiden bereits bekannten Futurformen, erläutern ihre Anwendung, suchen die entsprechenden Belegsätze aus dem Text heraus und notieren sie im Heft.

Tipps für junge Lehrer
Der Text eignet sich gut für eine szenische Umsetzung und bietet so die Möglichkeit, nach der langen Sommerpause möglichst alle S zum Sprechen zu bringen. Hierzu lernen alle Mädchen die Rolle Lauras und alle Jungen die Rolle Harrys als Hausaufgabe auswendig. Durch Losverfahren werden dann Spielpaare gebildet, die den Dialog entweder anderen Paaren oder der Klasse vorspielen. Anschließend findet eine *feedback*-Runde statt, in der Stärken und Schwächen der einzelnen Darbietungen angesprochen werden.

Material
 1/9

TIPPS VON MARIO RINVOLUCRI – THE ALTERNATIVE WAY

Dear colleague,

I am told that some teachers using Green Line 1 and Green Line 2 have found the „Tipps" I wrote for these two volumes useful with their pupils. Perhaps this is what has prompted the people at Klett to ask me to provide a new set of teaching suggestions for Green Line 3.

I am aware that I am a 'guest methodologist' and that in this role my task is to look at some of the texts in the book with a fresh eye and see what new possibilities they offer. My role is **not** to upset the tripartite balance between you, the coursebook authors and your pupils.

Some of the ideas I suggest will make sense to you and some will not appeal. Some of the suggestions that you like will go down well with your classes and some things that you like and want to use will bomb. Exercises, as we all know, can go pear-shaped because of the time of day, because of the mood the group brought with them from the last lesson or because certain leading pupils take against the particular task.

My hope is that some of the activities will go so well in your classes that they are admitted to your personal repertoire of staple procedures. This has to be the hope in the heart of any methodologist, and there is plenty of evidence that such miracles do, from time to time, happen!

The set of teaching techniques presented here are* different to the ideas proposed in my „Tipps" in the two previous books, so if you find good things in

Language 1

this book, then have a look back over the exercise proposals in the earlier books, as many of the ideas are generic and so applicable to different texts. You will possibly find yourself looking at an exercise suggestion and realizing that there is a much better way of doing it. If you find that your pupils' reaction confirms your insight you may decide to share the new exercise you have thus created with fellow language teachers. If you want more people than your immediate colleagues to have the chance of reading and using your new exercise then why not send it for publication to HUMANISING LANGUAGE TEACHING which you will find at www.hltmag.co.uk. The editor is Hanna Kryszewska (hania.kryszewska@pilgrims.co.uk).

If you want to learn more in depth about humanistic teaching ideas you might apply for an EU funded grant and come and do an in-service TT course with us in Canterbury, UK. To find out more, go to the teacher training part of this website: www.pilgrims.co.uk.

Yours, Mario Rinvolucri

*Grammar note:
You will have noticed the use of 'are' with a singular subject, 'the set of …'. I guess I would have marked this wrong in a pupil's work back in the sixties or seventies of last century. This kind of loosening of strict grammatical concordance is now common in the private and public speech of university-educated middle class Brits. By my criteria and those of *The Cambridge Grammar of English* (Carter and McCarthy) this makes it inevitably linguistically acceptable. (Please don't throw a wobbly!)

With neither head nor tail
A new trick (p. 10)

a) In your preparation photocopy **KV 3: With neither head nor tail** so that every three pupils can be given a copy.

b) In class tell the pupils to shut their books and form groups of three. Give each group a copy of the head- and tailless text.

c) Tell the class that the title of the passage is *A new Trick*. Ask the pupils to listen as you read the full text to them and to follow the truncated text with their eyes. Read fairly fast. Now ask them to add the missing letters, working in their teams of three.

d) Tell them to open the book and check their texts against the book version.

Pluses: In this activity pupils with good aural memories help the pupils who naturally tend to accomplish the task in visual puzzle-solving mode. Both approaches are useful. Done more than once this exercise helps improve pupils' spelling.

Minuses: Some pupils are put off by the Russian salad look of the page.

Material
Kopiervorlage 3

Enroling as a character
A new trick (p. 10)

a) Once the pupils have done normal language work on the conversation between Laura and Harry, ask them to write adjectives on the board, in mother tongue or English, that describe Laura.

b) Ask the pupils as a group to turn all the mother tongue adjectives on the board into English. You help when they get stuck. All the German words should vanish into English!

c) Ask each pupil to draw a picture of the way they imagine Laura's face. Ask them to draw their picture using the whole of an A4 page.

d) Tell the class that they are going to interview Laura about her life and about her childhood. Ask each pupil to write seven questions directly addressed to Laura in the second person. Move round the room helping the pupils with grammar and giving them new words they need.

e) Stick six of the Laura portraits on the board above an empty chair. Ask for a volunteer to come and sit in the empty chair and become Laura. The volunteer can be a girl or a boy.

f) Your role now is a back seat one as the pupils ask 'Laura' the questions they have written down and more that occur to them during the interview.

g) Round off the exercise by asking 'Laura' how he or she felt and by asking some of the interviewers how they felt. Make sure the 'Laura' impersonator is properly out of role.

Variations:

a) Bring in a poster or big photo of a person well known to your pupils. Your pupils interview the picture following steps d) to g) above. (You tell them that the person in the picture has lost his or her voice and that you need a 'volunteer voice'.) If you use the picture of a well-known contemporary person the pupils are working with information they have previously heard or read.

b) You may choose to bring in a more ambiguous and distant picture, e.g. the picture of an Ancient Egyptian courtier or the head of a person so old that no one is sure of their gender. This provokes more imaginative and projective interviewing.

c) You group the pupils in fours or fives. You ask one person in each group to bring to mind an old person they know and whom they are willing to talk about in their group. You ask them how the old person is dressed, how he/she typically sits and what sort of voice he/she has. You ask the volunteer pupil to imitate the seated posture of the old person and to speak in a voice similar to his/hers, i.e. to step into role. The other pupils in the fivesome then interview the old person. In a warmed-up group of pupils this exercise can become so fascinating they nearly forget they are speaking and usefully fumble and stumble in a foreign tongue.

Pluses: For some, even many, pupils speaking English is easier when they are playing a role. A second plus is that Laura, on p. 10, is a 'third person' character. She connects with Harry but not directly with us. In the role play Laura goes into 'I-you mode' with the interviewing pupils. The 'I-you mode' is more gripping than 'third person' work when you are learning a foreign language.

Minuses: If the pupils are not warmed up and are not used to this kind of activity, you can expect that the first run-through of an activity like this will be angular, stilted and lacking in flow and rhythm. Things usually get better second time round.
When you first meet this set of role-playing ideas you may dismiss them as being contrivances from the dark side of the moon.

Acknowledgement: These ideas are inspired by John Morgan's section of *The Standby Book: Activities for the Language Classroom*, ed. Seth Lindstromberg, Cambridge University Press, 1997.

1 Language 1

Üben	**1 Put the right parts together**	Seite 10

Ziel
- Das Textverständnis durch Zusammenfügen von Satzelementen nachweisen

Strukturen
- Verschiedene Formen des *future tense*

Methodisches Vorgehen
- Die S lösen die Aufgabe in Einzelarbeit schriftlich.
- SB geschlossen. In der gemeinsamen Besprechung im Plenum sortieren die S vorbereitete Folienstreifen mit den Satzelementen auf dem OHP. Danach weist L die S darauf hin, dass die Lösungssätze zwei weitere Futurformen beinhalten. Die S benennen das *simple present* und das *present progressive* und formulieren einfache Aussagen zum Gebrauch der beiden Zeitformen.
Alternative in leistungsstärkeren Klassen: SB geöffnet. Nach der Besprechung gemeinsames Lesen der beiden *Grammar*-Boxen auf S. 10/11 und Anwenden der Regeln auf die Lösungssätze.

Auch als HA geeignet

Lösung
1. *Harry is sure Laura will win the competition next weekend.*
2. *Laura's dad is picking her up soon.*
3. *The football match doesn't go on the whole day tomorrow.*
4. *The boys' competition starts at 10 o'clock next Saturday.*
5. *Laura will teach Harry her trick next Sunday.*

Material
Ggf. Leerfolie

Üben	**2 What do you think?**	Seite 10

Ziel
- Eine eigene Stellungnahme formulieren

Wortschatz *to offer*

Methodisches Vorgehen
- Die S erhalten einige Minuten Zeit, sich Gedanken zu Lauras Verhalten zu machen. Beim anschließenden Unterrichtsgespräch achtet L darauf, dass die S ihre Meinung angemessen begründen.

TIP
Ggf. Vorgriff auf die *Useful phrases*, S. 12

Üben	**3 Your turn: What, where and when?**	Seite 10

Ziel
- Das *simple present* für feste Termine in der Zukunft anwenden

Strukturen
- *Simple present for 'timetable' information about events in the future*

Methodisches Vorgehen
- a) Zur Einstimmung auf die Aufgabe erkundigt sich L nach aktuellen Sportveranstaltungen an der Schule/am Wohnort/in der Region. Die S äußern sich spontan. L erläutert die Aufgabe im SB, die als Hausaufgabe zu bearbeiten ist, und legt fest, bis wann die Informationen zusammengetragen werden müssen.
- b) Auswertung in PA wie im SB dargestellt.

TIP
G 2

HA

Erweiterung
- Die S können die Termine (z. B. der nächsten vier Wochen) in einer Übersicht als Veranstaltungskalender zusammenstellen und im Klassenraum aushängen. Die dort eingetragenen Termine dienen dann als Redeanlässe, indem sich L z. B. erkundigt, wer eine bestimmte Sportveranstaltung besucht hat, wie ein Spiel ausgegangen ist, wann ein bestimmtes Turnier stattfindet etc.

Material
Workbook S. 5/4

Üben	**4 What is happening next week?**	Seite 11

Ziel
- Das *present progressive* für Vereinbarungen in der Zukunft anwenden

Wortschatz *to open*

Strukturen
- *Present progressive to express arrangements for the future*

26

Language 1

Methodisches Vorgehen	• a) L erläutert die Aufgabenstellung; ein/e S liest das Beispiel laut vor. • Die S bearbeiten die Aufgabe mündlich mit einem/r Partner/in, indem sie abwechselnd einen Tag bearbeiten. Anschließend Wechsel der Tage, so dass am Ende jede/r S die ganze Aufgabe bearbeitet hat. • b) Die S notieren unter Verwendung des *present progressive* ihre festen Pläne für die kommende Woche im Heft/auf einem Zettel. Anschließend tauschen sie sich mit einem/r Partner/in über ihre Pläne aus.
Erweiterung	• Textproduktion (Differenzierung nach oben, ggf. auch als Hausaufgabe): Die S machen sich bei der gegenseitigen Befragung Notizen und schreiben anschließend einen kurzen Text über die geplanten Aktivitäten der/des Partners/in. • Ergänzend kann **KV 4: What are they doing this afternoon?** eingesetzt werden.

TIP

G 3
Aktuelle Infos, Fotos und Videos zu Danny Way finden sich auf seiner Homepage: www.dannyway.com

Auch als HA geeignet

Lösung	– On Monday he's arriving in the UK. – On Tuesday morning he's doing an interview with 'Sidewalk' magazine. In the afternoon he's talking on the radio. – On Wednesday he's making a skateboard video at Playstation Skatepark in London. – On Thursday morning he's opening a sports shop in Swansea. In the afternoon he's meeting fans at Swansea Skatepark. – On Friday he's teaching tricks to kids in Leicester. – On Saturday he's giving prizes at a skateboard competition in Birmingham.
Tipps für junge Lehrer	Spielidee: L stellt eine Frage, z. B.: *What are you doing this Saturday afternoon?* Die S schreiben die geplante Tätigkeit und ihren Namen auf Zettel/Karteikärtchen, die L einsammelt. Ein/e S übernimmt die Spielleitung, zieht einen Zettel, nennt die geplante Tätigkeit, z. B.: *Somebody is playing football with his team*, und startet eine Musik-CD. Die übrigen S bewegen sich im Klassenraum. Wenn der/die Spielleiter/in die Musik stoppt, befragen sich gegenüberstehende S gegenseitig. Diejenigen S, die von ihrem Gegenüber auf die Frage *What are you doing this afternoon?* die richtige Antwort erhalten, dürfen weiterhin im Spiel bleiben. Die übrigen S müssen sich setzen.

Material
Workbook S. 5/5, 6
Kopiervorlage 4
Ggf. Karteikarten

Üben	**5 Events and arrangements**
Ziel	• Das *simple present* und das *present progressive* zur Wiedergabe der Zukunft anwenden und festigen
Strukturen	• *Simple present and present progressive to express the future*
Methodisches Vorgehen	• L erläutert die Aufgabenstellung. Ein/e S liest das Beispiel (Satz 1) laut vor. Die S erklären, warum im ersten Satz das *simple present* (→ fester Termin) und im zweiten Satz das *present progressive* (→ Vereinbarung) verwendet wird. L verweist auf G 2 und G 3 (S. 127) im Grammatikanhang. • Die S bearbeiten die Sätze 2–6 in Einzelarbeit. • Als Hausaufgabe können die S analog eigene Sätze bilden (z. B. 10 Sätze, davon fünf Sätze mit *simple present* und fünf Sätze mit *present progressive*, nach Möglichkeit als sinngemäß zusammengehörige Satzpaare).

Seite 11

TIP
G 2, G 3

Lösung	2 *is taking – starts* 3 *is sending – arrives* 4 *finishes – are starting* 5 *are going – leaves* 6 *opens – is opening*
Tipps für junge Lehrer	Mit Blick auf den Bereich *language awareness* empfiehlt es sich, anhand des Hinweises in G 2 die Unterschiede im Zeitgebrauch im Vergleich zur deutschen Sprache bewusst zu machen.

Material
Workbook S. 6/7

1 Language 1 — Talkwise

Üben	**6 Asking for help and giving help**		Seite 11

Ziel
- Das *will future* zur Wiedergabe spontaner Entscheidungen verwenden

Wortschatz *situation*

Strukturen
- *Will future to express spontaneous decisions*

Methodisches Vorgehen
- a) SB geöffnet. Die S betrachten die beiden Bilder und beschreiben die dargestellten Situationen, z. B. *In the first picture a small man is carrying two heavy bags. A big, strong man sees that and asks if he can help. – In the second picture …*
- Die S fassen zusammen (*someone is giving help/asking for help*) und leiten eine einfache Regel ab. Anschließend gemeinsames Lesen von G 4 (S. 127).
- b) wird im Unterricht vorbereitet und schriftlich als Hausaufgabe bearbeitet.

TIP G 4

Auch als HA geeignet

Erweiterung
- Leistungsstärkere S notieren auf einer Folie 8–10 ähnliche Situationen, zu denen dann die Mitschülern/innen analog zur Lehrbuchaufgabe Sätze mit *will future* formulieren.

Lösung
1 Will you play tennis with me, please? 2 I'll get it (the golf ball) for you.
3 Will you explain the rules (for baseball) to me, please? 4 Will you help me (to mend my skateboard), please? 5 I'll tell you the way (to the skatepark).
6 I'll be your referee. 7 Will you lend me your cricket bat, please?
8 I'll put it (the sports equipment) away.

Material
Workbook S. 6/8, 9
Ggf. Leerfolie

Talkwise
Seite 12

Ziele
- Die neuen *Talkwise*-Seiten im SB und ihre Funktion kennen lernen
- Ein Streitgespräch verstehen
- Zustimmung und Ablehnung ausdrücken
- Ein Streitgespräch führen

Text	**Is it important to win?**	Seite 12

Ziel
- Die neuen *Talkwise*-Seiten kennen lernen

Wortschatz *talkwise, agreeing, disagreeing*

Methodisches Vorgehen
- SB geöffnet. L oder ein/e S liest den Text in der Sprechblase vor.
- L erläutert die Funktion der neuen *Talkwise*-Seiten und bespricht mit den S, wie sie das neue Sprachmaterial sinnvoll sammeln (z. B. durch Anlegen einer neuen Rubrik in ihrem *folder*), sukzessive erweitern und lernen können.

TIP
Sammeln der *Useful phrases* für den *folder*

Text/Bild	**1 A cartoon**	Seite 12

Ziel
- Die Aussage einer Karikatur verstehen und versprachlichen

Wortschatz *wheelchair*

Methodisches Vorgehen
- Nachdem die S die Karikatur maximal eine Minute betrachtet haben, stellt L einige Fragen dazu, z. B. *What are the people in the cartoon going to do? Where are they? Who are these people? Who is the man in the black and white shirt? What is he doing?*

	• L lenkt die Aufmerksamkeit auf den einzelnen Spieler im Zentrum der Karikatur und führt hierbei das neue Wort *wheelchair* ein, ggf. wird in diesem Zusammenhang auch schon das Adjektiv *disabled* (siehe Text, S. 13) eingeführt. Anschließend beantworten die S die Frage im SB.	**TIP** Karikatur auf Folie kopieren, um die Aufmerksamkeit der S auf die Bildaussage zu lenken
Erweiterung	• **Folie 3: That's not fair!** übt das Erzählen einer Bildergeschichte zum Thema „Fair Play im Sport".	
Lösung	*Erwartungshorizont: sitting in very big wheelchair – easy to score points – can drop ball into basket – unfair player – other team can't stop him*	**Material** Folie 3 Ggf. Leerfolie

Üben **2 Listening: A sports discussion** Seite 12

HV-Text
Julie: Look, you two. There's Adam.
Tracy: Oh yes. Let's go and talk to him.
Marcus: Hi, Adam!
Adam: Oh, it's you lot. Hello.
Julie: Hey, you sound fed up!
Adam: I *am* fed up. I lost my tennis match this afternoon.
Marcus: Oh, bad luck. But it isn't so important to win all the time, is it?
Adam: Yes, it is! *Of course* it's important when you want to be the best.
Julie: I agree, Adam. I don't play tennis, but I do athletics. It's important to me to win, too, because my dream is to become a champion.
Tracy: But the fact is, not everybody *can* win. So why get fed up when you don't? It's silly.
Marcus: You're right, Tracy. Sports is for fun. Even when you lose, you can enjoy it.
Adam: Don't be silly! You look like an idiot when you lose.
Marcus: No, you don't.
Julie: But it's much cooler to win!
Adam: That's what I think, too, Julie. Everybody loves a winner.
Marcus: Well, I don't agree. I don't like people just because they're good at sport. There are much more important things than sports.
Tracy: Exactly, Marcus! Actually, my father says it's *good* to lose sometimes.
Julie: What?! Good to *lose*?!
Tracy: Yes. He says it's an important lesson in life to learn how to lose.
Adam: I don't think that's true. It's better to learn how to win.
Julie: Adam is right. When you win it makes you happy. Doesn't everybody want to be happy?
Tracy: But my father says –
Marcus: Oh, forget your father, Tracy! I can see we aren't going to agree about this. Come on, let's all go to my house and watch …

Ziel • Einem Streitgespräch zielgerichtet Informationen entnehmen

Wortschatz *once, to agree, exactly, rubbish*

Methodisches Vorgehen
Pre-listening:
• a) L leitet von der Aussage des *cartoons* zur Thematik des HV-Textes über. Der konkrete Einstieg erfolgt dann über ein kurzes *brainstorming*, ggf. auch in PA. Die S legen zwei Listen an; anschließend werden die S-Antworten unkommentiert an der Tafel gesammelt.
While-listening:
• b) L präsentiert den Dialog von CD, die S ergänzen ihre Listen. Vergleich der Ergebnisse im Plenum.
• Ein/e S fasst das Gespräch kurz zusammen. Im folgenden Unterrichtsgespräch sollte deutlich werden, dass die Personen einen Sachverhalt diskutieren und hierbei Zustimmung bzw. Ablehnung zum Ausdruck bringen.

1 Talkwise

- c) Die S lesen die *Useful phrases*, hören das Gespräch ein weiteres Mal an und notieren dabei die *phrases*, die nicht im Text vorkommen. Vergleich in PA.
  Post-listening:
- Siehe *ex.* 4.

Lösung

b)
It **is** important to win …	It **is not** important to win …
– when you want to be the best. – when you want to become a champion. – because you look like an idiot when you lose. – because it's much cooler to win. – because everybody loves a winner. – because it's better to learn how to win. – because it makes you happy when you win.	– because not everybody can win. – because sports is for fun. You can enjoy it even when you lose. – because you don't look like an idiot when you lose. – because there are much more important things than sports. – because not everybody loves winners. – because it's a good lesson to learn how to lose.

c) *Sorry, but you're wrong./Rubbish!*

Tipps für junge Lehrer
In leistungsschwächeren bzw. zurückhaltenderen Lerngruppen sollten, u. a. mit Blick auf die abschließende GA (*ex.* 4), die Argumente auf jeden Fall auf Folie (und nicht an der Tafel!) gesammelt werden. Diese Folie kann dann in den folgenden Unterrichtsphasen zur Unterstützung der Schüleraktivitäten wieder in die Arbeit einbezogen werden.

Material
◎L 1/10
Workbook S. 7/10, 11
Ggf. Leerfolie

Üben   **3 Short answers**   Seite 12

Ziel
- Ablehnung mit Hilfe von *short answers* zum Ausdruck bringen

Wortschatz   *luck*

Methodisches Vorgehen
- Die S lesen die Beispielsätze im SB und formulieren schriftlich eine einfache Regel zum Gebrauch der *short answers*. Vergleich in PA oder im Plenum.
- Die S bilden nach dem Muster der Beispielsätze je einen Satz mit einem Vollverb, einem Hilfsverb und einer Form von *to be*. L schreibt einige der Sätze an die Tafel, die S stimmen zu oder lehnen ab.

TIP
In diesem Kontext lassen sich auch gut die *question tags* wiederholen

TA
> Many athletes want to make a lot of money. — Yes, they do./No, they don't.
> Girls can't play American football. — Yes, they can./No, they can't.
> Winners are lucky sometimes. — Yes, they are./No, they aren't.

Lösung
a) *Individuelle S-Antworten*
b) 1 *Yes, they do.*   2 *No, it isn't.*   3 *No, there aren't.*   4 *Yes, you can.*
    5 *No, you don't.*

Material
Workbook S. 7/12

Üben   **4 Your turn: Is it important to win?**   Seite 12

Ziel
- Ein Streitgespräch führen

Methodisches Vorgehen
- Da es sich hier um eine sehr komplexe Aufgabenstellung handelt, empfiehlt es sich vor der eigentlichen GA, eine Phase des kooperativen Lernens nach der *Think-Pair-Share*-Methode vorzuschalten:

Schritt 1: *Think*
L schreibt die Leitfrage *Is it important to win?* an die Tafel und fordert die S auf: *Think carefully about this question and write down your ideas.*
Schritt 2: *Pair*
Nach der Einzelarbeit finden sich die S in Paaren zusammen.
Schritt 3: *Share*
L führt die S in die nächste Aufgabe ein: *Share your answers with a partner and prepare to share them with a larger group of your classmates.*
Im Gespräch mit dem/r Partner/in tauschen die S ihre Ideen aus aus, kontrollieren ihr eigenes Verständnis der Fragestellung und organisieren ihre Antworten in Stichpunkten.
- Erst im nächsten Schritt findet der Austausch in Vierer-Gruppen statt, indem sich je zwei Schülerpaare gegenseitig ihre Ergebnisse vorstellen.
- Abschließend präsentieren einzelne S die Ergebnisse der Gruppen im Plenum.

Tipps für junge Lehrer Anregungen und Hilfen zu den Strategien des kooperativen Lernens finden sich in zahlreichen empfehlenswerten Internetangeboten, z. B.
http://www.learn-line.nrw.de/angebote/greenline
http://www.kooperatives-lernen.de

Language 2

Seite 13–15

Ziele
- Einige kuriose Sportfakten kennen lernen
- Personen und Dinge mit Hilfe von *relative clauses* näher bestimmen
- Wortschatzlücken durch Paraphrasieren umgehen

 L Text **Did you know?** Seite 13

Ziel
- Einfache Informationstexte lesen und verstehen

Wortschatz *relative clause, which, American football, half* pl. *halves, channel, that, commercial break, commercial, who, also, unusual, bobsleigh, snow, whose, rowing, the lungs* (pl.), *swimming, scientist, disabled, athlete, gold medal, record, marathon, love*

Methodisches Vorgehen
- Die sechs Kurztexte eignen sich besonders zum Üben des schnellen Erfassens wichtiger Textinformationen *(scanning)*, da aufgrund der Erschließbarkeit der Kurztexte hier auf eine Vorentlastung des neuen Vokabulars verzichtet werden kann. L gibt je nach Leistungsstärke der Klasse den Zeitrahmen vor (3–5 Minuten) und überprüft, wie weit die einzelnen S in dieser Zeit gekommen sind.
- Anschließend lautes Lesen und Klären des neuen Wortschatzes, den die S nicht aus dem Kontext heraus erschließen konnten.
- Alternative: *pair reading:* Jedes Schülerpaar entscheidet sich für zwei der Kurztexte und teilt diese untereinander auf. Nach dem Lesen beantwortet S1 Fragen des/der Partners/in zum ersten Text. S2 macht sich Notizen und fasst den Text noch einmal kurz zusammen. Anschließend Rollentausch. Wenn alle S die Aufgabe bearbeitet haben, fordert L nach dem Zufallsprinzip einzelne Schülerpaare auf, die Texte im Plenum vorzustellen. Diejenigen Paare, die die gleichen Texte bearbeitet haben, korrigieren bzw. ergänzen ggf. die Informationen.

TA

American football (l. 2)	gold medal (l. 32)	record (l. 33)
bobsleigh (l. 13)	Great Wall (l. 42)	scientist (l. 24)
commercial break (l. 7)	love (ll. 35, 36)	skateboard (l. 41)
Cool Runnings (l. 12)	marathon (l. 34)	Winter Olympic Games (l. 18)

1 Language 2

Erweiterung
- *Translation exercise:* Die S bilden Dreier-Gruppen. S 1 übersetzt die braun unterlegten, S 2 die grün unterlegten und S 3 die gelb unterlegten Texte. Nach einer vorher vereinbarten Zeit (7–10 Minuten, je nach Leistungsstärke der S) wird das Blatt an den/die nächste/n S gegeben, der/die Korrektur liest. Nach weiteren fünf Minuten bekommt der/die dritte S die Übersetzung. Abschließend wird eine der Übersetzungen im Plenum vorgelesen und mit dem englischen Originaltext verglichen.

Tipps für junge Lehrer
Das *scanning* lässt sich auch spielerisch trainieren, indem man gelegentlich kleine Wettbewerbe durchführt:
- Die Klasse wird in zwei oder drei Gruppen eingeteilt, die jeweils eine unterschiedliche „Lesezeit" zur Verfügung haben (z. B. 2, 3, 4 Minuten); anschließend Vergleich, wie weit die einzelnen Gruppen gekommen sind.
- L schreibt *keywords* in alphabetischer Reihenfolge an die Tafel (siehe TA), die von den S möglichst rasch in den Texten gefunden werden müssen. Die S notieren die Zeilenangabe. Hier kann auch neuer Wortschatz aufgeführt werden, der dann direkt aus dem Kontext heraus erläutert wird.

Material
L 1/11

TIPPS VON MARIO RINVOLUCRI – THE ALTERNATIVE WAY

Speaking clearly and listening well
Did you know? (p. 13)

a) In preparation, add two more surprising paragraphs to the six given on p. 13. Choose things that are topical at this time in your part of the world. Make sure you use relative clauses in your new paragraphs!
You now have eight paragraphs. Photocopy them so that you can give one paragraph to each person in the class. Do the necessary scissors work.

b) Ask the pupils to make groups of eight, or thereabouts. Within each eight-some give each pupil a different paragraph. Give the longer paragraphs to the stronger pupils. Tell them to read their text over and over until they have it firmly memorized.

c) The pupils put their texts down on their chairs, stand up and find a partner within their own group. Each pupil tells the other their own memorized text. The listening pupil needs to pay a lot of attention as he/she needs to remember the new text.
The pupils change partners within their group of eight. They tell their new partner the paragraph they have just heard.
Second change of partner. They tell their partner the last paragraph they have heard.
Third change of partner. They tell their partner the last paragraph they have heard.

d) Bring the whole class back together and ask three or four people to recite the last paragraph they have heard. After each recitation allow the 'experts' on this paragraph to add things that have been missed out and correct things that have been said wrong.

Pluses: This activity entails accurate and clear speaking and attentive, receptive listening. It puts social pressure on the lazier pupils to perform.

Minuses: Pupils who live very visually or very kinaesthetically are at a disadvantage compared to auditorily acute pupils. But then, language is primarily a reality in the world of sound.

Language 2 | 1

Üben	**1 Play a game with the texts**		Seite 13
Ziel	• Das Textverständnis spielerisch überprüfen		
Methodisches Vorgehen	• Es empfiehlt sich, zunächst den Arbeitsauftrag gemeinsam mit den S zu lesen, um sicherzustellen, dass die anschließende PA problemlos durchgeführt werden kann. L schreibt ggf. Beispielsätze an die Tafel, z. B.		
TA	Michael Phelps has very large <u>hands</u>. → feet Tanni Grey-Thompson from <u>Scotland</u> is a disabled athlete. → Wales		

Üben	**2 Find the rule**		Seite 13
Ziel	• Eine Regel zur Verwendung der Relativpronomen aufstellen		
Wortschatz	*relative pronoun*		**TIP**
Strukturen	• *Defining relative clauses*		G 5a, 6 Die Regel sollte um den Bereich „Tiere" erweitert werden: *A cat is an animal which/that catches mice.*
Methodisches Vorgehen	• a) Schriftliche Bearbeitung in PA. Die S übertragen die Tabelle ins Heft, lesen die Texte noch einmal durch und tragen die gesuchten Relativpronomen ein. • Ein leistungsstärkeres Schülerpaar erhält eine vorbereitete Folie und trägt hier die Lösungen in die Tabelle ein. Anschließend Ergebnissicherung mit Hilfe der Folie. • b) Die S formulieren eine einfache Regel zum Gebrauch der Relativpronomen; danach Vergleich mit den Erläuterungen in G 5a, G 6 (S. 128/129).		
Lösung	*who:* referee, people *which:* event, film *that:* TV channel, country, tennis players *whose:* people, athlete		**Material** Ggf. Leerfolie

Üben	**3 What relative pronouns can you use?**		Seite 14
Ziel	• Den Gebrauch der Relativpronomen anwenden und festigen		
Wortschatz	*sweat, oddity*		Auch als HA geeignet
Strukturen	• *Defining relative clauses*		
Methodisches Vorgehen	• a) Im ersten Teil der Aufgabe ergänzen die S die unvollständigen Sätze mündlich in PA. Anschließend Kontrolle im Plenum, z. B. als Kettenübung, damit möglichst viele Schülerpaare an die Reihe kommen. Schriftliche Bearbeitung als Hausaufgabe möglich. • b) SB geschlossen. L schreibt *No sweat!* an die Tafel und erläutert die Wortbedeutung von *sweat* anhand eines Beispiels (*Phew! The sun is shining today. It's really hot in the classroom. ...*) und/oder pantomimisch. Die S stellen Vermutungen an, was die Aussage *No sweat!* in Bezug auf Sport bedeuten könnte. Anschließend beschreiben die S das abgebildete Buchcover.		**TIP** Falls ein Farbkopierer zur Verfügung steht, kann das Cover auf Folie kopiert werden
Erweiterung	• **KV 5: Sports dominoes:** Die Wortkärtchen werden mit der Schrift nach unten auf den Tisch gelegt. Jede/r S zieht sieben Kärtchen. Ein/e Spieler/in mit einem Satzanfang (*) beginnt. Die Mitspieler/innen müssen nun im Uhrzeigersinn ihre Karten so anlegen, dass ein inhaltlich und grammatisch korrekter Satz entsteht. Satzanfänge können jederzeit gelegt werden. Wer nicht anlegen kann, zieht ein weiteres Kärtchen; wer einen Fehler macht, setzt einmal aus. Sieger ist, wer zuerst alle Kärtchen angelegt hat.		
Lösung	a) 1 *that/which* 2 *that/who* 3 *that/which* 4 *whose* 5 *that/which* 6 *that/who* 7 *whose* 8 *that/which* b) *football, tennis, cricket, ice hockey, American football, rugby*		**Material** *Workbook* S. 8/13 Kopiervorlage 5

1 Language 2

Üben	**4 A game: Sports words**	Seite 14

Ziel
- Personen und Dinge aus dem Wortfeld „Sport" näher bestimmen

Wortschatz *definition*

Strukturen
- *Definining relative clauses*

Methodisches Vorgehen
- *Warm-up:* L beginnt etwa so: *It's a person who wants to buy something in a shop.* Die S antworten entsprechend: *It's a customer.* / L: *It's something which many people in Britain drink in their tea.* S: *Milk.*
- SB geöffnet. L erläutert die Aufgabenstellung und macht deutlich, dass für die PA das Thema „Sport" verbindlich vorgegeben ist.
- Anschließend kann das Spiel auch als Wettbewerb durchgeführt werden: Die Klasse wird in zwei Gruppen aufgeteilt. Je zwei S befragen sich gegenseitig; dann kommt das nächste Schülerpaar an die Reihe. Für eine grammatisch richtige Definition und die zutreffende Antwort gibt es je einen Punkt.

Erweiterung
- Eine thematische Ausweitung auf andere Wortfelder (*school/home town/hobbies/…*) erhöht die Übungsmöglichkeiten. Hierzu können in GA zu unterschiedlichen Themenbereichen Definitionen erstellt werden (5–8 je Gruppe und Thema).

> **TIP**
> In leistungsschwächeren Klassen sollte auf die thematische Eingrenzung verzichtet werden

Material
Workbook S. 8/14

> **!**
>
> **TIPPS VON MARIO RINVOLUCRI – THE ALTERNATIVE WAY**
>
> **Grammar practice – relative pronouns**
>
> a) Get a volunteer pupil to sit with you in front of the class. The pupil is to ask you one simple question, but to put it to you over and over again. He/she should question you in a friendly way. The question is:
>
> **Who are you?**
> Your demonstration could go something like this:
>
> Pupil: Who are you?
> Teacher: I'm a teacher.
> Pupil: Who are you?
> Teacher: Well, I'm your teacher.
> Pupil: Who are you?
> Teacher: I'm a teacher who is strict about homework.
> Pupil: Who are you?
> Teacher: I'm a person that gets angry quite easily.
> Pupil: Who are you?
> Teacher: I'm a person whose children come to this school.
> etc.
>
> b) Group the pupils in threes. Person A is the questioner, Person B is to give the answers and Person C writes all the answers down. They use the insistence question *Who are you?*. Tell them to do two minutes of this. You time it.
>
> c) Person C then reads B's answers to the others and the groups can check with you for language accuracy.
>
> d) They swap roles twice and repeat steps b) and c).
>
> *Variation:* If you want the pupils to work on spatial prepositions then have them use the repeated question: *Where do you live?*.
>
> *Pluses:* This activity has pupils speaking about themselves in a meaningful way while virtually locked into a drill pattern. Naturally they are thinking about themselves much more than about language.

> *Minuses:* Some introverted pupils may sometimes blurt out things they later regret having said. This is a disadvantage with this sort of exercise in any of the rather reticent Northern European cultures. You wouldn't need to worry about this if you were working in Brazil!

Üben	**5 What can sports fans buy on the Internet?**	Seite 14

Ziel • Die Stellung von Präpositionen im notwendigen Relativsatz einüben

Strukturen • *Prepositions in defining relative clauses*

Methodisches Vorgehen
- L erläutert die Stellung der Präpositionen bei geöffnetem SB. Für leistungsschwächere S kann L das Beispiel auch an die Tafel schreiben und die Bildung des Relativsatzes schrittweise erarbeiten und veranschaulichen.
- Die S bearbeiten die Aufgabe in Einzelarbeit; anschließend Partnerkontrolle und Vergleich der Ergebnisse im Plenum.
- Als Hausaufgabe formulieren die S weitere Sätze nach den Beispielen im SB.

Lösung
1 *There's a pair of shoes which/that Kelly Holmes won a gold medal in.*
2 *There's a cricket bat which/that the English team wrote their names on.*
3 *There's a tennis racket which/that Roger Federer played at Wimbledon with.*
4 *There's a bottle which/that Lance Armstrong drank water from.*
5 *There's a skateboard which/that Danny Way broke a record on.*
6 *There's a ball which/that David Beckham scored a goal with.*

Material
Workbook S. 8/15
Ggf. bunte Kreide

Üben	**6 Contact clauses**	Seite 14

Ziel • Die *contact clauses* kennen lernen und anwenden

Wortschatz *contact clause*

Strukturen • *Contact clauses*

Methodisches Vorgehen
- a) Die S erarbeiten das Grammatikkapitel anhand der Hilfen im SB und der Erläuterungen in G 5b (S. 129) selbstständig in Einzelarbeit oder PA.
- b) Die S überprüfen ihr Regelverständnis durch Bearbeitung der Aufgabe in Einzelarbeit. Anschließend Partnerkontrolle und Vergleich der Ergebnisse im Plenum.

TIP
G 5b

Erweiterung • Die S lesen den Text in *ex.* 3 noch einmal durch und nennen die Sätze, in denen das Relativpronomen weggelassen werden kann.

Lösung b) 1 – 2 *They test athletes trainers send to them.* 3 *The information they collect is useful.* 4 – 5 *They know about the food athletes should eat.* 6 *They also help athletes with the computer technology they use.*

Tipps für junge Lehrer In leistungsschwächeren Lerngruppen empfiehlt sich einleitend unbedingt eine kurze Grammatikwiederholung (Satzteile), um sicher zu stellen, dass die Regeln verstanden werden.

Üben	**7 Make one sentence from two**	Seite 15

Ziel • Zwei Hauptsätze durch Bildung von *contact clauses* verknüpfen

Strukturen • *Contact clauses*

1 Language 2

Methodisches Vorgehen
- SB geöffnet. Der erste *contact clause* wird von den S anhand des Beispiels mündlich gebildet. Ein/e S beschreibt die Vorgehensweise, z. B. *In the second sentence I left out the personal pronoun.*
- Die S bearbeiten die Aufgabe schriftlich in Einzelarbeit oder PA; anschließend Kontrolle im Plenum.

Erweiterung
- Zur weiteren Festigung und Übung der Relativsätze kann **KV 6: The relative clause race** eingesetzt werden.

Lösung
1. *Last year I went to London with a friend I know from school.*
2. *We waited in a good place we found near the Cutty Sark.*
3. *Then we saw the car the athletes were running behind.*
4. *This was the big moment everyone was waiting for.*
5. *It was so exciting to be near famous athletes you usually only see on TV.*
6. *Lots of people were also running for charities they wanted to make money for.*
7. *A man shouted 'thank you' for the money we threw in his box.*

Material
Workbook S. 9/16
Kopiervorlage 6

Üben

8 Listening: A cricket bat   Seite 15

HV-Text

Methodisches Vorgehen	*Pre-listening:*
	• a) L führt kurz in die Situation des HV-Textes ein: *Well, we're going to a sports shop now. We'll meet three people there: Tim and his father and a shop assistant.*
	• Die S lesen die Arbeitsanweisung durch und äußern spontan ihre Vermutungen. Ein/e S notiert diese in Stichworten an der Tafel.
	While-listening:
	• b) L präsentiert den HV-Text mindestens zweimal. Die S machen sich während des Hörens Notizen und formulieren in Einzelarbeit ihre Antworten zu den im SB gestellten Aufgaben.
	Post-listening:
	• Die S vergleichen ihre Ergebnisse mit einem/r Partner/in oder in Kleingruppen.
	• Abschließend stellen die Schülerpaare/Kleingruppen ihr gemeinsames Ergebnis im Plenum vor. Die S diskutieren, welchem Lösungsvorschlag sie am ehesten zustimmen würden.
Lösung	b) *Erwartungshorizont: The cricket bat (which/that) Tim wants is very expensive. Because Tim hasn't played much cricket yet, nobody knows how good he is going to be. So his father doesn't know if he should buy one of the expensive bats or a cheaper one. I think Tim's father will buy the cheaper bat because he doesn't want to spend a lot of money.*

Material
L 1/12

Üben

Listening: A ball kid at Wimbledon

Workbook Seite 9

HV-Text
Workbook

Girl:
Guess what I'm doing this week and next week – I'm one of the ball kids at Wimbledon! You know – we're the girls and boys that help in the matches. We collect the tennis balls and give them to the players and all that. It's quite hard work, but it's great fun, too. I really enjoy it. Every match is different. And all kinds of funny things can happen.

Yesterday was a really special day. I mean, three funny things happened in the same match!

First, just when the players were ready to start the match, a silly bird flew down and landed on the court. It didn't do anything. It just stood there and looked around and didn't want to leave. We waited for a time because we wanted to be kind to it. But we couldn't wait for too long. So in the end I chased it away. It flew up into the air again and everybody clapped. I'm not sure if they were clapping for me or for the bird. But anyway, at last the match could begin!

Then, after a few games, the next thing happened. One of the players ran to the ball when it came to him, and he just got to it, but he couldn't control it like he wanted. And so it went the wrong way and – smack! – the ball hit the umpire on the head! It was so hard – you could really hear it! The poor man almost fell out of his chair. Anyway, I was down on my knees in my place next to his chair, and I was scared that he could fall out of the chair on top of me. So I jumped up and ran away. Of course everybody laughed. Well, almost everybody. The umpire didn't think it was so funny. I expect he had a headache!

That wasn't the only mistake that player made in the match. He wasn't a very good player – and it was even worse for him because the other player was so much better. So he lost game after game after game and he didn't know what to do to change the match. I mean, he didn't give up, but he knew he didn't really have any hope. And finally, in one game, when he made a really bad mistake, he called me to him and gave me his racket. So I took his place as a player and he took my place as a ball kid! It was only a joke, of course, and it was only for a moment. Then he took his racket back and the game went on.

Like I said, you never know what's going to happen. Sorry, but I've got to go now. My next match starts soon and I have to …

Material
S 1/5
L 1/13
Workbook S. 9/17

1 Language 2

Üben	**9 How to: Explain words you don't know**	Seite 15

Ziel
- Wortschatzlücken durch Paraphrasieren umgehen

Wortschatz *exact*

Methodisches Vorgehen
- Gemeinsames Lesen des Arbeitsauftrags; anschließend Umschreibung der vorgegebenen Begriffe in PA.
- Die S schreiben ihre Lösungen in veränderter Reihenfolge auf einen Zettel; Austausch der Zettel mit einem anderen Schülerpaar, das versucht, die deutsche Bedeutung zu erschließen.
- Die Schülerpaare besprechen die Qualität der vorliegenden Umschreibungen (*peer editing*); anschließend werden gelungene Umschreibungen im Plenum vorgestellt.

Erweiterung
- In leistungsstärkeren Lerngruppen kann folgendes Rollenspiel durchgeführt werden: Ein/e S aus Deutschland fährt zu einem Sportvergleichswettkampf in die britische Partnerstadt. L bereitet Karteikärtchen mit deutschen Wörtern vor, die dem/der S zur Verständigung fehlen könnten. Ein/e S übernimmt die Rolle des deutschen Gastes, zwei oder drei S die Rolle der britischen Gastgeber, die anhand der Umschreibungen herausfinden müssen, welches deutsche Wort paraphrasiert wird: z. B. *Oh, you're looking for the English word for the German „Freistoß"*. Bei richtiger Lösung nennt L das gesuchte englische Wort. Eine andere Schülergruppe macht weiter.

Lösung *Individuelle S-Antworten*

Material *Workbook* S. 9/18

Üben	**10 Revision: Simple present or present progressive?**	Seite 15

Ziel
- Die Unterscheidung von *simple present* und *present progressive* wiederholen und festigen

Strukturen
- *Simple present vs. present progressive*

Methodisches Vorgehen
- a) L schreibt an die Tafel: *Danny Way/to train hard/ + signal word* und fordert die S auf, je einen Satz im *simple present* und im *present progressive* zu bilden (siehe TA).
- Die S nennen die entsprechenden Regeln und lösen anschließend die Aufgabe schriftlich in Einzelarbeit.
- Alternativ kann die Aufgabe nach einer Wiederholung der Grammatikregeln im Unterricht auch als Hausaufgabe bearbeitet werden.
- b) Die S formulieren als Hausaufgabe Fragen für ein mögliches Interview.

Auch als HA geeignet
HA

TA

```
                         Danny Way/to train hard/+ signal word
    simple present:      Danny Way trains hard every day.
    present progressive: Danny Way is training hard right now.
```

Lösung
a) 1 *I'm training for the Olympic Games at the moment.* (Alternative: *At the moment I'm training…*) 2 *I come to this track every day.* 3 *I usually meet my group at 2 o'clock.* 4 *Our trainer always gives us lots of help.* 5 *Today he is checking our fitness over 400 metres.* 6 *I'm starting to feel really strong now.* 7 *The others are waiting for me right now.* 8 *Champions never stop and talk.*
b) *Individuelle S-Antworten*

| | | Text | 1 |

Text
Seite 16–18

| **Ziele** | • Eine Sportlerbiografie lesen
• Ein Interview mit einem Sportler führen
• Einen Text zu kuriosen Sportfakten schreiben |

| Fotos/Üben | **1 Before you read** | Seite 16 |

| Ziel | • Das persönliche Vorwissen aktivieren
• Über bekannte Sportler/innen sprechen |

| Methodisches Vorgehen | • Der Arbeitsauftrag im SB dient als *pre-reading activity*. Die S äußern sich spontan im Unterrichtsgespräch. L oder die S notieren die Namen der genannten Sportler und die Kurzbeschreibungen in Stichworten an der Tafel. L gibt ggf. Hilfestellung bei Wortschatzproblemen.
• Anschließend betrachten die S die Fotos im SB und stellen Vermutungen zum Inhalt des Textes an. |

| TA | Michael Ballack: very good player, good-looking, a lot of money …
Anni Friesinger: world champion, very fast, friendly smile, …
Dirk Nowitzki: great basketball player, very tall, … |

| Erweiterung | • **KV 7: My favourite sports star**: Als Hausaufgabe bereiten die S anhand der Kopiervorlage ein Poster zu ihrem Lieblingssportler vor. Die fertigen Poster können nach der Präsentation im Klassenraum aufgehängt werden. | HA |

| Tipps für junge Lehrer | Diese Aufgabe kann zur Einstimmung auf den Text als Hausaufgabe bearbeitet werden. Die S erhalten den Auftrag, zu fünf Sportlern beschreibendes Wortmaterial zu sammeln, ggf. mit Hilfe des Wörterbuchs. Bei der Besprechung im Unterricht werden die Stichpunkte an der Tafel/auf Folie gesammelt und können später zum Vergleich mit der Hauptfigur des Textes, Eddie the Eagle, genutzt werden. | Auch als HA geeignet

Material
Kopiervorlage 7 |

| Text | **Eddie the Eagle** | Seite 16–17 |

| Ziel | • Das Textverständnis spielerisch überprüfen |

| Wortschatz | *eagle, glasses* (pl.), *ski jump, ski, jump, at last, press conference, to mist up, goggles* (pl.), *ski jumper, van, tradition, far, might, to slide, to flap, place, to wave* |

| Methodisches Vorgehen | • SB geöffnet. L präsentiert den ersten Teil des Textes (bis Z. 25) von CD, die S lesen leise mit. Jede/r S erhält zwei laminierte Karten (siehe **KV 8: YES or NO?**). L trifft Aussagen zur Überprüfung des Textverständnisses, etwa:

– *This story happened in Canada in 1988.*
– *It was the time of the Summer Olympic Games.*
– *Eddie Edwards arrived in Calgary early in the morning.*
– *He didn't look like a sports star.*
– *Edwards wanted to win the ski jump competitions.*
– *He was happy to be in Canada.*
– *His Canadian fans were already waiting for him at the airport.*
– *First he had problems with his bags, then he couldn't find the doors.*
– *Eddie didn't know the way to the Olympic village, but a fan helped him.*
– *He reached the village at two o'clock in the night.*

Die S entscheiden, ob die Aussagen richtig oder falsch sind und halten die entsprechende Karte hoch. Nicht zutreffende Aussagen werden von den S mündlich korrigiert.
• L spielt den restlichen Text von CD vor; die S lesen leise mit. | **TIP**
Karten laminieren und für spätere Textauswertungen wieder einsammeln |

39

1 Text

- Anschließend Weiterarbeit in möglichst heterogen zusammengesetzten Gruppen (3–4 S pro Gruppe). Jede Gruppe erstellt zu einem Textabschnitt 6–8 Aussagesätze, die teils richtig und teils falsch sind.
- Die Gruppen tragen nacheinander ihre Sätze vor, wobei jedes Gruppenmitglied mindestens zwei Sätze übernimmt, ansonsten analoges Vorgehen wie oben (Aufzeigen der Karten und Korrektur).

Material
◎s 1/6–10
◎L 1/14–18
Kopiervorlage 8
Ggf. laminierte Karten

!

TIPPS VON MARIO RINVOLUCRI – THE ALTERNATIVE WAY

Cooperative Dictation
Eddie the Eagle (p. 16–18)

a) In preparation, choose a slice of the text near the middle and make six photocopies of it. I would suggest lines 26 to 51.

b) Have the pupils group themselves in fours at one end of the classroom. Stick your six copies to the wall at the other end of the room. Tell the pupils to shut their coursebooks.

c) Ask the pupils to decide who is A, B, C and D in their four. Tell the A and the B people from each four to go to the opposite wall, read a few words of the text, run back across the room and dictate the words to C and D. A and B then dash back to bring more text back and dictate it to C and D. Make it clear to the pupils that A and B should collaborate closely and make sure that C and D both take down the dictation separately but suggest they help each other with words that are hard to spell.

d) Half way through the exercise ask the 'dictators' to reverse roles with the writers. A and B continue the texts started by C and D.

e) When the running is done ask the pupils to open their books at p. 16 and check their texts.

Note: This exercise is a significant variation of my „Tipp" Running Dictation in Green Line 1 Teacher's Book, p. 42. The main difference between the two processes is that in Cooperative Dictation each task is performed by **two** pupils who help each other out. The proverb that two heads are better than one can sometimes be true!

Pluses: When you present the pupils with a fairly long text like that on pp. 16–17 it makes sense to get them working on parts of it actively. Movement dictation is rapidly becoming a 'classic' exercise across World EFL.

Minuses: This is a boisterous exercise which is appropriate for a teenage group but which can get noisy. It is worth maybe warning colleagues working in adjacent rooms. A silent music lesson is hard to imagine … Ditto a silent language lesson.

Acknowledgement: On January 3, 2008 I presented Running Dictation to a group of London Further Education teachers. One of them offered the group the variation I am presenting to you here. I am simply acting as a transmitter wire. It is this sort of 'exercise dialogue' that allows EFL techniques to creatively multiply.

		Text	1

Üben	**2 Talk about Eddie Edwards**		Seite 18
Ziel	• Die Personenbeschreibung üben		**TIP**
Methodisches Vorgehen	• a) Die S vergleichen im Unterrichtsgespräch ihre Ergebnisse aus *ex.* 1 mit der Hauptfigur des Textes. • b) + c) Die S bereiten die Aufgaben schriftlich vor; anschließend Diskussion im Plenum.		Ein interessantes Video-Interview des kanadischen Fernsehens gibt es im Internet: http://archives.cbc.ca/IDC-1-41-1322-8081/sports/calgary_olympic_games/clip8
Erweiterung	• *Think in pairs* (hier: Differenzierung nach oben): *Talk to a partner about what Eddie Edwards did. Would you start in an important sports competition although you know that you have no chance to win? Each of you reports your partner's answer back to the class.*		

Fotos/Üben	**3 ⟨Feelings in sport⟩**		Seite 18
Ziel	• Anhand von Fotos die Gefühle anderer beschreiben		
Methodisches Vorgehen	• Zur Vorbereitung der Aufgabe sammeln die S Adjektive, mit denen man positive bzw. negative Gefühle zum Ausdruck bringen kann. Zwei S schreiben die Adjektive auf Zuruf an die Tafel:		
TA	positive feelings: ☺ happy excited glad fantastic fine ...	negative feelings: ☹ angry nervous aggressive scared sad ...	
	• a) Die S beschreiben die Gefühle des Skispringers vor, während und nach dem Wettkampf. Leistungsstärkere S begründen zusätzlich die Wahl geeigneter Adjektive aus der jeweiligen Situation heraus. • *Show and tell:* Jede/r S bringt ein geeignetes (Sport)Foto mit und stellt die dort abgebildete Situation (Ort, Anlass, Person(en), Gefühle) in einem *one-minute talk* vor. Hierzu notieren sich die S Stichwörter auf Karteikarten, die sie während des Vortrags benutzen dürfen.		
Erweiterung	• L bringt mehrere Sportfotos mit und legt sie im Klassenraum aus. Jede/r S wählt das Foto aus, das sie/ihn am meisten anspricht. Die S beschreiben reihum, welches Foto sie ausgewählt haben und begründen kurz ihre Wahl (Differenzierung nach oben). Auch die *Frozen-picture*-Methode kann zur Bildauswertung genutzt werden.		**TIP** Die Fotos auf Karton aufkleben, um sie mehrfach einsetzen zu können
Tipps für junge Lehrer	Zeitungsfotos zu den unterschiedlichsten Themen bieten eine Vielzahl von Möglichkeiten zum kreativen Umgang mit der Sprache. Hier z. B. könnte der Arbeitsauftrag lauten: *Make up a story about what happened before, during, or after the photo was taken.*		**Material** Sportfotos

Üben	**4 Role play: Eddie's press conference**		Seite 18
Ziel	• Ein Rollenspiel schreiben und vorspielen		
Methodisches Vorgehen	• Bearbeitung in PA; anschließend üben die S das Interview ein und spielen es anderen Gruppen/im Plenum vor.		
Erweiterung	• *In the spot:* Ein/e S schlüpft in die Rolle von Eddie Edwards und nimmt auf dem „Heißen Stuhl" Platz. Er/Sie beantwortet eine von L vorgegebene Anzahl an Fragen der Mitschüler/innen aus der Sicht des Sportlers im Jahr 1988.		

	• Für leistungsstärkere S kann die Situation so abgeändert werden, dass die Befragung des Ex-Sportlers zum augenblicklichen Zeitpunkt stattfindet und er die Fragen in der Rückschau beantwortet und kommentiert. So können in die Antworten auch spätere Erfahrungen und Reflexionen mit einfließen.	**Material** *Workbook* S. 10/19
Üben	**5 Writing texts: Write your own *Did you know?* sports text**	Seite 18
Ziel	• Einen Text zu kuriosen Sportfakten schreiben • Ein Gruppenposter erstellen	
Methodisches Vorgehen	• a) Da der Ablauf des Schreibprozesses *(Plan your text. → Write a first draft. → Correct your text. → Share your text.)* den S bekannt ist, kann die Bearbeitung vollständig als Hausaufgabe erfolgen. • Alternativ kann die Planung und Korrektur der Texte auch in PA erfolgen. • b) Die Schülertexte können auf einem „Gruppenposter" zusammengefasst werden. Je 3–5 S übertragen ihre Texte auf ein gemeinsames Poster und illustrieren es mit Fotos und/oder Zeichnungen. Die fertigen Poster werden im Klassenraum oder an geeigneter Stelle im Schulgebäude präsentiert.	
Tipps für junge Lehrer	Je nach Schreiberfahrung der Klasse kann es sich anbieten, die Korrekturphase *(peer editing)* nicht in Paaren, sondern in Kleingruppen durchführen zu lassen. L gibt folgende Anweisung, ggf. schriftlich (Tafel, Folie, Arbeitsblatt): *It can be lots of fun to improve your writing skills with your classmates. So get together in small groups to check your first drafts. Remember to follow these steps:* *– First tell the classmate what you think he or she did well.* *– Then give the classmate some ideas about how to improve his or her text. (Did he/she choose the best words? Did he/she use enough/too few/too many details? Is the structure OK?).* *– Finally check your classmate's text for spelling, grammar mistakes and missing punctuation.* *But remember: Always try to stay positive!*	**Material** *Workbook* S. 10/20
⊚L **Song**	**6 ⟨A song: You'll never walk alone⟩**	Seite 18
HV-Text	Identisch mit SB-Text	
Ziel	• Die Wirkung eines typischen „Fußballsongs" diskutieren	
Wortschatz	*to be afraid (of), the dark, golden, silver, lark, to walk on, though your dreams be tossed and blown*	**Material** ⊚L 1/19 Im Anschluss an *ex. 6: Action UK! 3, A Sport, Part B: Surfing in Cornwall* sowie *Action UK! 3*, Begleitheft zu den Filmsequenzen, Unit 1 B
Methodisches Vorgehen	• Gemeinsames Lesen des Texts im SB und Klären des unbekannten Wortschatzes. • L spielt den Song von CD vor. Die S diskutieren unter Rückbezug auf die *Talkwise*-Seite die Frage der Wirkung des Liedes auf die Zuhörenden.	
Erweiterung	• Interessierte S stellen andere populäre Fußball-/Sportsongs bzw. häufig bei sportlichen Anlässen gespielte Lieder vor, z. B. *We are the champions* von Queen (in *Green Line* 2, S. 69).	

Skills

Seite 19

Ziele
- Das Arbeiten mit dem zweisprachigen Wörterbuch schulen
- Die Bedeutung des Sinnzusammenhangs für die Wortwahl erkennen

Using a German-English dictionary

Seite 19

Wortschatz *context*

Methodisches Vorgehen Es empfiehlt sich, wenn möglich, im Klassenschrank eine ausreichende Anzahl zweisprachiger Wörterbücher bereit zu halten, so dass bei Bedarf für jeweils zwei S ein Wörterbuch vorhanden ist.

Material Wörterbücher

Üben **1 What's 'null' in English?**

Seite 19

Ziel
- Die Bedeutung des Sinnzusammenhangs für die Wortwahl erkennen

Methodisches Vorgehen
- Die S bereiten die Lösungen in Einzelarbeit vor; anschließend Besprechung im Plenum.
- Die S wenden jede Übersetzungsmöglichkeit in einem situativen Kontext an (3–5 Sätze). Bearbeitung mündlich in PA, dann schriftlich als Hausaufgabe.

HA

Lösung
1 *tennis: love* 2 *telephone number: oh* 3 *temperature: zero* 4 *soccer: nil*

Material *Workbook* S. 11/21

Üben **2 Not word for word**

Seite 19

Ziel
- Grenzen der Wort-für-Wort-Übersetzung erkennen

Methodisches Vorgehen
- Bearbeitung in Einzelarbeit; anschließend Partnerkontrolle.
- In PA erstellen die S zu 1. und 2. kurze Texte oder Dialoge; anschließend Vergleich im Plenum. Bearbeitung von 3. und 4. als Hausaufgabe.

Erweiterung
- Jede/r S sucht im Wörterbuch ein weiteres Wortbeispiel heraus und schreibt analog zum SB Sätze zu verschiedenen Situationen auf einen Zettel. Ein/e Partner/in löst die Aufgabe.

HA

Lösung
1 *What a stroke of luck!* 2 *Good luck!* 3 *You were lucky there.*
4 *You were out of luck/unlucky!*

Üben **3 Put it into English**

Seite 19

Ziel
- Die Bedeutung des Sinnzusammenhangs für die Wortwahl erkennen

Methodisches Vorgehen
- Die S suchen die passende Übersetzung der deutschen Wörter heraus; Vergleich mit einem/r Partner/in oder im Plenum.

Erweiterung
- KV 9: What a match! kann als Hausaufgabe bearbeitet werden.

Lösung
1 *count* 2 *offside* 3 *half* 4 *penalty* 5 *half-time* 6 *in a draw*

Material *Workbook* S. 11/22
Kopiervorlage 9

Üben **4 ⟨A joke⟩**

Seite 19

Ziel
- Ein Wortspiel verstehen

1 Skills — Wordwise

Methodisches Vorgehen
- Diese fakultative Aufgabe dient zur Auflockerung des Unterrichts. Die S suchen die zweite Bedeutung des Wortes *racket* heraus und erläutern das Wortspiel in eigenen Worten.

Erweiterung
- L schreibt weitere *jokes* an die Tafel; die S erläutern die Wortspiele anhand des Wörterbuchs. Einige Beispiele (weitere finden sich auf zahlreichen EFL-Seiten im Internet):
    - Q: What did the ocean say to the beach?
      A: Nothing, it just waved!
    - I hear this new cemetery is very popular. People are just dying to get in.
    - I was arrested at the airport. Just because I was saying 'hello' to my cousin Jack! All that I shouted was, "Hi, Jack!"

Wordwise

Seite 20

Ziele
- Den Wortschatz der Unit umwälzen und vernetzen
- Den persönlichen Wortschatz durch Verb-Nomen-Paare erweitern

Stationenlernen
Vor der Arbeit an *Wordwise* kann das Stationenlernen zur Wiederholung des bisher Gelernten durchgeführt werden (**Kopiervorlagen 12–16**). Dabei ist Folgendes zu beachten:

TIP
Stationenlernen vor *Wordwise* einsetzen

- Vorbereitung:
    - Kopieren Sie **KV 17: Arbeitsbericht** in Klassenstärke und geben Sie diese zu Beginn des Stationenlernens an die S aus.
    - Kopieren Sie die Arbeitsaufträge für die einzelnen Stationen mehrfach in Klassenstärke.
    - Nummerieren Sie kleine Aufstellkarten zum Aufbau der Stationen und zur schnellen Orientierung für die S.
- Durchführung:
    - Die einzelnen Stationen werden (unter Nutzung aller verfügbaren Abstellflächen) gleichmäßig im Klassenraum verteilt (Vermeidung von „Stau") und mit den entsprechend nummerierten Aufstellkärtchen versehen.
    - Die S entscheiden sich für die Bearbeitung einer Station und absolvieren diese entsprechend ihrem individuellen Lerntempo.
    - Sie übernehmen die Rolle des/der Beraters/in und Beobachters/in. Vereinbaren Sie mit den S, ab wann Sie konsultiert werden dürfen und ermutigen Sie die S zur gegenseitigen Hilfe und Unterstützung.
    - Nachdem die S eine Station bearbeitet haben, tragen sie die benötigte Zeit ein, kontrollieren die Aufgabe selbstständig, vermerken dies auf ihrem Arbeitsbericht (gegebenenfalls mit einem Vermerk bezüglich der Fehleranzahl) und lassen sich anschließend von einem/r Partner/in kontrollieren (wird ebenfalls im Arbeitsbericht vermerkt).
    - Wenn Sie Zeit haben, können auch Sie die Fremdkontrolle übernehmen. Dabei ist es nicht notwendig, dass Sie alles kontrollieren – eine Konzentration auf schwächere S ist sinnvoll.
- Auswertung:
    - Die Lösungen zu den Stationen finden sich jeweils nach der letzten Station als Kopiervorlage.

Üben	**1 Make a grid for sports words**		Seite 20
Ziel	• Den Wortschatz zum Thema „Sport" systematisch zusammenstellen		Auch als HA geeignet
Methodisches Vorgehen	• Bearbeitung in Einzelarbeit oder PA; auch als Hausaufgabe geeignet.		
Erweiterung	• Zur spielerischen Festigung und Übung des themenspezifischen Wortschatzes kann **KV 10: A letter grid** eingesetzt werden. Die S spielen in Gruppen (3–4 S). Aufgabe ist es, ausschließlich mit den vorgegebenen 16 Buchstaben Wörter aus dem Wortfeld „Sport" zu bilden. Anrechenbare Wörter müssen mindestens drei Buchstaben haben, zusammengesetzte Substantive sind erlaubt. Für jedes gefundene Wort und für jeden eingesetzten Buchstaben erhält die Gruppe einen Punkt.		**Material** *Workbook* S. 12/24, 25 Kopiervorlage 10

Üben	**2 Put in the correct prepositions**		Seite 20
Ziel	• Den Gebrauch von Präpositionen wiederholen		Auch als HA geeignet
Methodisches Vorgehen	• Die S bearbeiten die Aufgabe schriftlich in Einzelarbeit oder als Hausaufgabe und überprüfen ihre Lösungen eigenständig anhand des Lesetextes (S. 16/17).		
Lösung	1 *like* 2 *to* 3 *for* 4 *in* 5 *at* 6 *of* 7 *on* 8 *at* 9 *to* 10 *than*		
Tipps für junge Lehrer	Die Aufgabe kann auch als Tandemaufgabe in PA gelöst werden: Partner A löst die Sätze 1–5 schriftlich, Partner B die Sätze 6–10. Partner B schließt dann das Buch und Partner A liest den ersten Satz ohne Präposition vor. Partner B macht einen Lösungsvorschlag, der von A akzeptiert oder als falsch zurückgewiesen wird. Nach Satz 5 werden die Rollen getauscht.		**Material** *Workbook* S. 12/26

Üben	**3 Words as verbs and nouns**		Seite 20
Ziel	• Verb-Nomen-Paare zur Erweiterung des individuellen Wortschatzes kennen lernen		Auch als HA geeignet
Methodisches Vorgehen	• a) + b) werden schriftlich in der Stunde oder als Hausaufgabe bearbeitet; Vergleich der Ergebnisse im Plenum.		
Erweiterung	• Gruppenwettkampf: *Write down all the words which you already know that can be a verb <u>and</u> a noun. You've got five minutes from now. Ready, steady, go!* L legt vorab fest, ob das *Dictionary* im SB benutzt werden darf oder nicht. • Auswertung und Siegerehrung im Plenum.		
Lösung	a) 1 *A fan in the crowd shouted.* 2 *He jumped over 100 metres.* 3 *He kicked the ball.* 4 *Two bikes in the race crashed.* 5 *Athletes should sleep a lot.* b) 1 *It was a surprise for everyone when I won.* 2 *I think there will be snow before the game ends.* 3 *The Olympics are her dream.* 4 *There was an interview with the winner.* 5 *Look, there's a queue for tickets.*		
Tipps für junge Lehrer	Zur Kontrolle der S-Antworten lässt sich hier gut das *peer correcting* einsetzen, d. h. die S bilden „Korrekturpaare", die ihre Ergebnisse vergleichen. Die hierzu benötigten Redemittel müssen den S bekannt sein (z. B. *Come on, let's start./Yes, I've got that, too. – No, I've got a different answer here./Yes, that's right. – No, I think your answer is wrong./What have you got as first sentence?/I'm not sure. Let's ask someone else./Can you explain that to me?/…*).		

1 Wordwise — Check-out

| ⊙L Üben | **4 Sounds: Words that you link** | Seite 20 |

HV-Text Identisch mit SB-Text

Ziel
- Die Aussprache im Satzzusammenhang üben

Methodisches Vorgehen
- SB geöffnet. Die S lesen die Aufgabenstellung.
- a) L spielt die sechs Sätze von CD vor. Die S lesen leise mit.
- Beim zweiten Vorspielen macht L nach jedem Satz eine Pause; die S sprechen im Chor, in Gruppen und einzeln nach.
- Die S formulieren anhand der Beispiele eine einfache Regel (*consonant followed by vowel/same consonant*).
- b) Die S wählen in Einzelarbeit drei Sätze aus und üben leise die Aussprache.
- Alle S schlagen S. 16/17 auf. Ein/e S gibt die Zeile(n) des ausgewählten Satzes an und liest vor. Kontrolle durch die Mitschüler/innen.

Material
⊙L 1/20

Check-out   Seite 21

Ziele
- Die Lernziele der Unit in Selbstkontrolle überprüfen

| Üben | **1 A game** | Seite 21 |

Ziel
- Ein *word web* zu einer Sportart erstellen
- Die Sportart in einem Kurzvortrag vorstellen

Methodisches Vorgehen
- Die S erstellen in Einzelarbeit bzw. als Hausaufgabe ein *word web* zu einer von ihnen selbst gewählten Sportart.
- In GA stellen die S abwechselnd den Mitschülern/innen ihre Sportart vor.

Auch als HA geeignet

Erweiterung
- Zur weiteren spielerischen Festigung und Übung des themenspezifischen Wortschatzes kann **KV 11: A crossword race** eingesetzt werden. Die S spielen in Gruppen (3–5 S). Aufgabe ist es, vom Startbereich links oben in den Zielbereich rechts unten zu gelangen. Die S tragen reihum im Kreuzwortsystem ein Wort aus dem Wortfeld „Sport" ein. Wer passen muss oder einen Rechtschreibfehler macht, scheidet aus. Sieger ist der/die S, der/die mit seinem/ihrem Wort in den Zielbereich gelangt. Das Spiel kann auch mit Hilfe einer vorbereiteten Folie im Plenum gespielt werden.

Material
Kopiervorlage 11
Ggf. Leerfolie

Lösung *Siehe SB S. 214*

| Üben | **2 What are they doing at the weekend?** | Seite 21 |

Ziel
- Das *present progressive* für Vereinbarungen in der Zukunft wiederholen und anwenden

Strukturen
- *Present progressive to express arrangements for the future*

Methodisches Vorgehen
- L weist eingangs auf G 3 hin.
- Die S bearbeiten die Aufgabe in Einzelarbeit; anschließend Selbstkontrolle anhand der Lösungen auf S. 214.

TIP
G 3

Material
Workbook S. 13/28

Lösung *Siehe SB S. 214*

46

| | | Check-out | ⟨Text⟩ | 1 |

| Üben | **3 Make sentences with relative clauses** | Seite 21 |

| Ziel | • Die Bildung von notwendigen Relativsätze und *contact clauses* wiederholen und anwenden |

TIP
G 5
Die S können die Aufgabe durch eigene Relativsätze erweitern

| Strukturen | • *Defining relative clauses, contact clauses* |

| Methodisches Vorgehen | • a)+b) L weist eingangs auf G 5 hin; die S bearbeiten die Aufgaben schriftlich in Einzelarbeit. Anschließend Selbstkontrolle anhand der Lösungen auf S. 214. |

| Lösung | Siehe SB S. 214 |

Material
Workbook S. 13/29

| Üben | **4 Your turn: Do you agree?** | Seite 21 |

| Ziel | • Zustimmung bzw. Ablehnung ausdrücken |

| Methodisches Vorgehen | • Nach einer kurzen Vorbereitung in Einzelarbeit nehmen die S in PA Stellung zu den Aussagen im SB. |

| Lösung | Siehe SB S. 214 |

Material
Workbook S. 13/30

Dictation

Soccer is very popular all over the world because it is so simple. All that you need to play soccer is a ball and two goals. You can even play the game without special shoes and you can play it almost everywhere, in the park, in the street or on the beach. The big football teams play on a grass field, or pitch. A game has two halves and each team has eleven players. A team scores a point when one of the players kicks the ball into the goal. The team that scores the most goals wins, but sometimes a match ends in a draw.

⟨Text⟩

Workbook Seite 14

| Ziele | • Einen adaptierten Auszug aus einem Roman eigenständig erschließen
• Das ganzheitliche Leseerlebnis kennen lernen
• Das *creative writing* üben |

◎S ◎L Text **⟨Point Blank⟩** Workbook Seite 14

| Ziel | • Einen Auszug aus einem Jugendroman eigenständig erschließen
• Vermutungen zum weiteren Verlauf der Handlung anstellen |

| Wortschatz | Annotationen *Workbook* S. 14 |

| Methodisches Vorgehen | *Pre-reading:*
• Die S lesen den kursiv gedruckten Einführungstext. Unbekanntes Vokabular wird durch die Annotationen oder ein Wörterbuch erschlossen. |

- L stellt Fragen in Bezug auf James Bond: *Think about a James Bond movie. Who follows whom? How can the person in front get away from his followers? What sounds would you hear?*

While-reading:
- L leitet zur Lektüre des Textes über. Präsentation von CD, die S lesen leise mit.
- Beim erneuten Lesen des Textes machen sich die S Notizen zu folgender Aufgabe: *Now listen to the story of how Alex Rider gets away from the school. You don't have to understand every single word. Just imagine what Alex can see, hear, smell and feel while snowboarding down the hill.*

TA

see	hear	smell	feel

- Die S vergleichen und ergänzen ihre Ergebnisse in PA; anschließend Besprechung im Plenum.

Post-reading:
- L stellt Fragen zum Textverständnis: *What do you find out about Dr Grief and Mrs Stellenbosch from this passage?*
- *What do you think happens next? Would you like to read more? Say why/why not.*

Erweiterung
- *Link this passage to the text about 'Eddie the Eagle' in your book. Find at least three similarities and three differences.*
- *Find out more about a) Anthony Horowitz, b) The Alex Rider novels (Stormbreaker, Point Blanc, Skeleton Key, Eagle Strike, Scorpia, Ark Angel and Snakehead – out October 2007). Ein hilfreicher Link: http://www.alexrider.com/*

Lösung

Erwartungshorizont:
While-reading: see: slope, trees, snow, train; **hear:** wind, snowboard on snow, snowmobiles, machine guns, train; **smell:** cold air, snow; **feel:** cold air, snow, pain

Post-reading: Dr Grief: his name = Kummer, Sorge; wears a silver dressing gown, that means he is rich and he is the boss; realizes that Alex is very clever; acts with certainty; sends men with snowmobiles and machine guns; wants to kill Alex; very cruel
Mrs Stellenbosch: purrs like a cat; admires Dr Grief; cruel like her boss

Erweiterung: similarities: winter sports, down the hill, not scared
differences: ski-jumping – snowboarding, during the day – at night, Eddie is doing sports – Alex has to run away

⟨Freiarbeit⟩ **1**

⟨Freiarbeit⟩

Ziele • Den Wortschatz der Unit 1 und des *Project: English and Computing* anwenden und festigen

Methodisches Vorgehen
- Die Aufgaben wälzen sowohl das Vokabular des in Unit 1 erarbeiteten Wortfeldes „Sport" als auch dasjenige des *Project: English and Computing* um. Daher sollten **KV 18: English and Computing** und **KV 19: The world of sports** erst nach Bearbeitung des *Project* eingesetzt werden.
- Der Rätselcharakter der Materialien spricht die S an und ermöglicht Selbstkontrolle bzw. *peer evaluation*.

TIP
Freiarbeit nach Project *English and Computing* einsetzen

Lösung

KV 18:
1
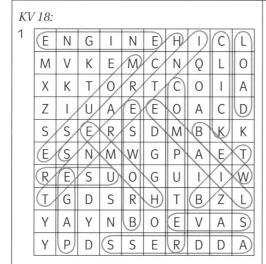

2 *On the Internet, nobody knows you're a dog.*
3 *41 % had their own computer. / 59 % could use a computer at home. / 96 % (only) played games on the computer. / 22 % had their own email address. / 55 % used the Internet. / 84 % liked listening to music. / 65 % liked adventure games or other games. / 72 % never read texts on the Internet.*

KV 19:
Individuelle S-Antworten

Material
Kopiervorlage 18, 19

49

KV 1: Preparing a talk to the class

When you are preparing a talk to your classmates, you need to collect information first. Then you must organise it to make your talk interesting. Here is some help for planning and preparing a talk in class. Follow these steps and make your notes.

My talk is about:

Introduction: *How will I make the talk interesting for my classmates?*

Important information:

-
-
-
-
-
-
-

Conclusion: *How will I finish my talk?*

Things I will show to my classmates:

KV 2: Our sports

a) *Read the questions and answer them for yourself.*
b) *Choose two classmates and ask them the questions. Fill in your classmates' lists.*
c) *Tell the class about your sports and your classmates' sports.*

Questions	YOU	Your classmate 1	Your classmate 2
1 What is your favourite sport?			
2 What is your favourite team?			
3 Who is your favourite player/sports(wo)man?			
4 Are you in a club? What's the name of the club?			
5 Can you do your sport near your home/in your town/in your village?			
6 How often do you practise every week?			
7 Can you do your sport at school?			
8 What is your favourite school sport?			
9 What kind of sports do you watch on TV?			
10 …			

KV 3: With neither head nor tail

A new ric

aur is ractisin at pi katepar in irmingha for a big ven ex ee .

Harry: Wow, aur ! I've eve ee ha ric efor ! It's rillian . Who augh you?

Laura: obod . It's my own pecia ric . I'm oin to do it in the ompetitio ex ee .

Harry: it a rea new ric ik ha I'm ur you'll win. il you eac me, leas ? he I'll av a ette han in the oy ' ompetitio .

Laura: Oh, I – aven' got im now. My ad' ickin me up oo .

Harry: el , et' ee gai er omorro . I'll pay for ou icke , no roble .

Laura: Hm. I'm atchin the big ootbal atc on TV omorro .

Harry: Me, too. But the atc oesn' go on the hol day, oe it?

KV 4: What are they doing this afternoon?

a) *It is Saturday afternoon and the sun is shining. Look at the picture and talk about the people's arrangements with a partner.*

b) *And what about your arrangements for this weekend? They can be fantasy arrangements, too. Fill in the table. Talk about your weekend with a partner.*

	FRIDAY	SATURDAY	SUNDAY
morning	school		
afternoon			
evening			

Lösung: a) The man is playing tennis. The girl is riding her bike, and the two other girls are playing basketball. The three boys are playing football. The woman is walking the dog.

GREEN LINE 3

1 Kopiervorlagen

KV 5: Sports dominoes

Cut out the cards. Play the game in groups of three or four.

*Tennis	is	a	sport
which	you	play	with
a racket.	*Fans	are	people
who	follow	their teams.	*Cricket
is	a	game	that
can go on	for days.	*Ice-hockey	is
a	sport	which	comes
from Canada.	*A	referee	is
someone	who	controls	a
football	match.	*Sometimes	champions
are	people	whose	bodies
are	different.	*Baseball	is
a	sport	that	is
very	popular	in	America.

KV 6: The relative clause race

a) *First make a grid. You and your partner have 15 minutes to describe the people and things in the pictures. Use relative clauses. You can write your sentences in any order. The winner is the person who has the most points after 15 minutes. You get two points for a correct relative clause/contact clause.*

b) *Give your list to your partner and read your partner's sentences. Can you match each sentence to a picture? Write the correct number next to the sentence.*

Example:

relative clause	contact clause
A policeman is a person who catches thieves.	A policeman is a person you can ask for help when you are in trouble.

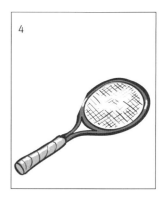

Lösungsvorschlag: 1. A cricket bat is something (which/that) a cricket player needs. 2. A hotel is a house which/that has got many rooms for tourists. 3. A fan is a person who/that loves his or her club. 4. A tennis racket is the thing (which/that) a tennis player hits the ball with. 5. An umpire is a person who/that controls a tennis match. 6. Soap is something (which/that) you can wash your hands with. 7. A medal is a prize (which/that) you can win in a competition. 8. A helmet is something (which/that) you wear when you ride your bike. 9. A horse is an animal which/that can jump and which/that can run in a (horse) race. 10. A radio reporter is a person who/that talks on the radio. 11. Tea is something (which/that) you can drink. 12. A doctor is a person who/that helps you when you are ill.

KV 7: My favourite sports star

Who is your favourite sports star? Find a nice photo and collect words and phrases that describe him/her best.

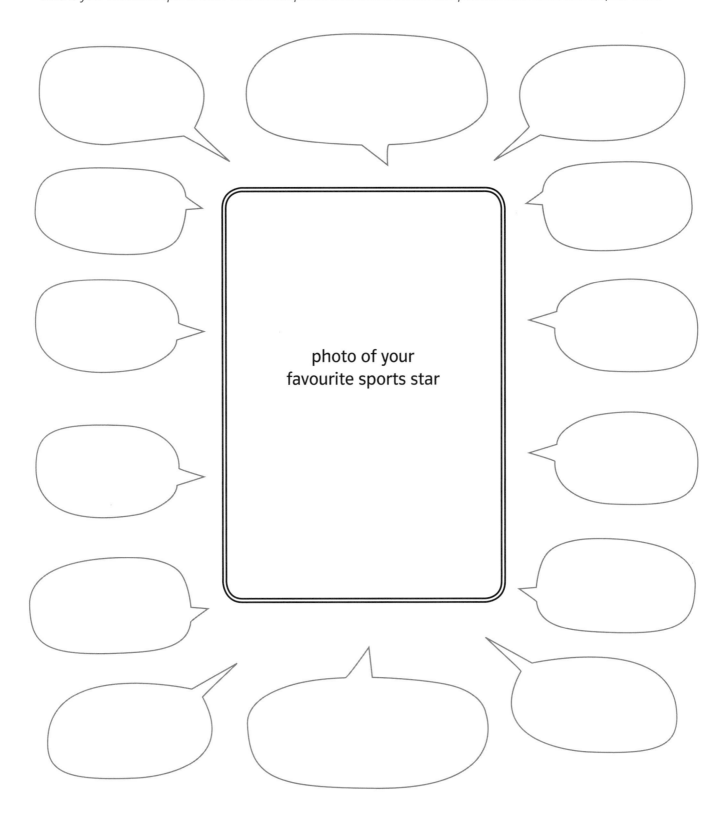

KV 8: YES or NO?

KV 10: A letter grid

Work in groups of three or four. How many sports words can you make with these letters?
Note: You can make one word with all 16 letters!

A	B	B	P
K	Y	A	A
L	E	E	S
L	L	T	R

1 _____
2 _____
3 _____
4 _____
5 _____
6 _____
7 _____
8 _____
9 _____
10 _____
11 _____
12 _____
13 _____
14 _____
15 _____
16 _____
17 _____
18 _____
19 _____
20 _____
21 _____
22 _____
23 _____
24 _____
25 _____
26 _____
27 _____
28 _____
29 _____
30 _____

Lösung: Das Ausgangswort lautet basketball player.

KV 11: A crossword race

	P					
C	R	I	C	K	E	T
	T					
	C					
	H					

KV 12: Stationenlernen Unit 1 (Wordwise)

Station 1: What a sportsman!

Fill in the missing words. What is wrong in the picture?

Station 2: Rubbish!

Work in groups. Cut out the cards and mix them. Put them face down on the table.
Decide who starts. Choose a card, read the sentence and agree or disagree. Don't forget to give reasons for your (dis)agreement. Use the phrases on page 12 in your book. Take turns.

You always need luck.	Never play in a team.
It's more important to play fairly.	Not everybody can win.
	Sport should be fun.
The best player always wins.	It's important to lose sometimes.
When you lose, you smile!	When you lose, you can't smile.
Football is the best sport in the world.	When you lose, people laugh.

KV 13: Stationenlernen Unit 1 (Wordwise)

Station 3: Guess the word

Work in groups. Cut out the cards and put them on the table so that everyone can see the words. Decide who starts.
Choose one word and give a definition – if possible, use a relative clause. Don't say the word, let the others guess. If someone knows the word, he/she says STOP and says the word. If it is right, he/she gets the card. If nobody gets it right, the next player goes on. Take turns.
The winner is the one who gets the most cards.

pitch	place	athlete
umpire	press conference	referee
brakes	ice	disabled
arrangement	commercial	track

―――――✂―――――――――――――――――――――――

Station 4: Sports words

a) *Choose a colour for each of these categories:*

kinds of sports   **place/equipment**   **activities**

Now look at the words in the box and sort them into the three categories (mark them with the right colour). Be careful: You don't need all the words!

b) *Make a grid in your folder and fill in the words. Be careful: Some of the words fit into more than one category!*

c) *Compare your grid with a partner's.*

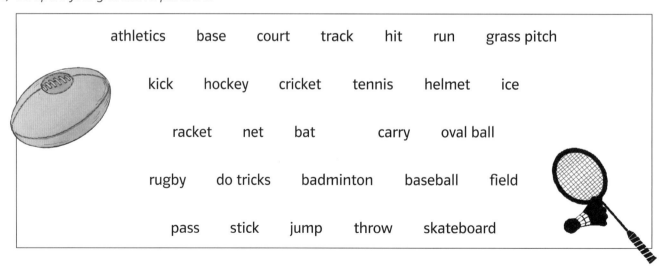

athletics   base   court   track   hit   run   grass pitch

kick   hockey   cricket   tennis   helmet   ice

racket   net   bat   carry   oval ball

rugby   do tricks   badminton   baseball   field

pass   stick   jump   throw   skateboard

KV 14: Stationenlernen Unit 1 (Wordwise)

Station 5: Find someone who ...

a) *Read the sentences to your partner. Take turns.*
b) *Walk around the class and find a classmate for each sentence. Who finishes first?*
c) *Compare the sentences with your partner.*

Find someone who ...

1. likes your favourite sport.
2. knows the name of a famous tennis player.
3. can explain the rules for football.
4. is good at athletics.
5. knows the equipment for cricket.
6. goes jogging at the weekend.
7. doesn't find it important to win every time.
8. knows the name of a famous American skateboard champion.
9. can tell you what the Superbowl is.
10. can give you five verbs for what you can do with a ball.
11. can explain what a referee is.
12. likes to watch ski jumping on TV.

Station 6: A game

Decide who starts. Throw the dice¹ and answer the question or do the activity. If your answer is correct or you do the activity well, you may continue and throw the dice again. If not, you'll have to wait for the next round. The person who gets to "Finish" first is the winner. Good luck!

🍀 You're lucky! Throw the dice again.

☹ Bad luck! Go back three squares².

START →	☹	Say three sentences about your favourite sportsman/ sportswoman.	Baseball is a famous sport in ...	Name ten kinds of sport.	🍀
Jump like a kangaroo.	What kind of equipment do you need for rugby?	Ask one of the other players two questions about tennis.	☹	Jump ten times on your left foot.	What is the word for the person who helps athletes?
Name five ball games.	How many players are there in an ice-hockey team?	🍀	Describe your favourite sport and let the others guess.	Explain the word "marathon".	Name two skateboard tricks.
FINISH ←	☹	What is the German word for "brake"?	Bend your knees ten times.	🍀	Spell the English word for "Werbespot".

¹**dice** [daɪs] = Würfel • ²**square** [skweə] = Spielfeld

KV 15: Stationenlernen Unit 1 (Wordwise)

Station 7: Plans for the weekend

a) *With a partner, decide who is A and who is B. Cut the card in half. Don't show your card to your partner.*

b) *Look at the pictures. Decide what you are doing and what you aren't doing at the weekend.*

c) *Think of one more activity for the weekend and draw a picture in the box next to the four pictures.*

d) *Now work with your partner. Find out what he/she is doing at the weekend.*
   Take turns to ask and answer questions:

   A: Are you playing tennis at the weekend? – B: Yes, I am./No, I'm not.

   When you get an activity right, draw it in one of the empty boxes.

e) *Compare your cards.*

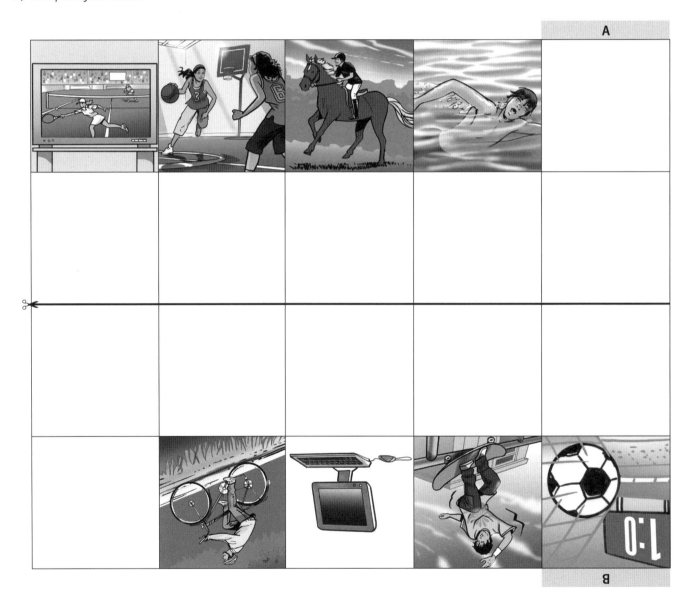

KV 16: Stationenlernen Unit 1 (Wordwise)

Station 8: Verbs and nouns

a) *Find 12 words in the grid that can be verb **and** noun.*

b) *Choose five of them and form two sentences with each: one with the verb and one with the noun. Be careful with the meaning of the words!*

E	K	Z	Z	M	A	T	C	H	B	B	R	E	A	K	S	K
G	S	K	F	I	D	P	G	N	W	M	Y	J	S	C	U	S
H	R	A	I	N	R	L	J	S	J	Z	J	N	E	O	W	U
J	J	V	E	C	R	A	S	H	A	H	U	R	U	O	T	R
O	R	K	L	W	K	C	T	P	V	J	M	V	C	K	S	F
G	A	F	D	N	W	T	S	H	B	S	P	O	R	T	J	P
W	A	T	C	H	F	O	E	O	U	T	W	R	A	T	K	H
V	L	J	A	N	Y	R	G	P	U	N	D	W	S	X	S	G
Y	D	U	E	H	B	I	X	E	I	P	B	A	N	G	J	W
G	U	W	H	N	Z	O	K	O	D	S	U	R	W	Q	X	G
L	M	H	A	H	D	X	O	K	W	O	R	K	Y	E	U	A

Station 9: All about football

a) *Work in groups of three or four. Draw a picture to explain the following football words. You can use your dictionary.*

b) *Can you find more football words? Make a mind map in your folder.*

| corner | throw in | foul | linesman | goalpost | touchline | penalty area |
| penalty | goal | goal line | goal area | free kick | header | offside |

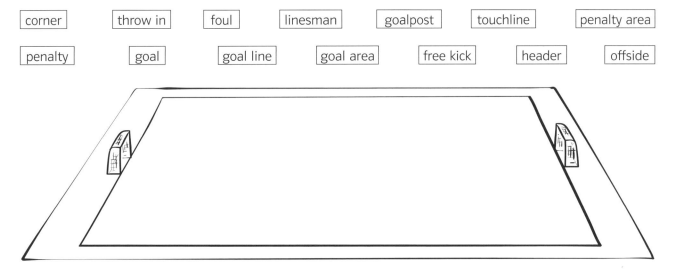

KV 17: Arbeitsbericht

Dieses Formular ist ein Arbeitsbericht. Trage nach Abschluss einer Aufgabe das Datum, die Uhrzeit und die Station ein. Kontrolliere dann deine Aufgabe und unterschreibe im Feld „Selbstkontrolle".
Lass deine Ergebnisse anschließend von einem Klassenkamerad oder einer Klassenkameradin kontrollieren und lass ihn/sie unter „Fremdkontrolle" unterschreiben. Bei Partneraufgaben kann hier dein Partner/deine Partnerin unterschreiben.

Station	Datum/Uhrzeit	Selbstkontrolle	Fremdkontrolle

Lösungen zu den Stationen

Station 1:
1 *helmet* 2 *suit* 3 *oval ball* 4 *boots* 5 *racket* 6 *skateboard* 7 *bat* 8 *goggles* 9 *scarf* 10 *trainers*
wrong: *suit, boots, scarf*

Station 3:
Lösungsvorschlag:
pitch: *The word for "field" in rugby.* place: *A person who wins a competition gets first …* athlete: *A person who/that does athletics.* umpire: *A person who/that controls a tennis match.* press conference: *Reporters can ask a famous person questions at a …* referee: *A person who/that controls a football match.* brakes: *The things which/that stop a car.* ice: *A famous sport from Canada is played on …* disabled: *A person who/that sits in a wheelchair is …* arrangement: *Another word for "plan".* commercial: *On TV, they show a lot of …* track: *The place which/that runners run on.*

Station 4:
kinds of sport: *hockey, badminton, cricket, rugby, tennis, athletics, baseball* place/equipment: *ice, skateboard, stick, helmet, racket, net, bat, grass pitch, oval ball, court, track, field, base* activities: *kick, pass, hit, run, carry, jump, throw, do tricks*

Station 6:
Baseball is a famous sport in the USA./A trainer is a person who helps athletes./equipment for rugby: oval ball/ball games: football, baseball, basketball, volleyball, handball/There are six players in an ice-hockey team./skateboard tricks: "Indy", "Nosegrind"/COMMERCIAL/The German word for "brake" is „Bremse".

Station 8:
a)

E	K	Z	Z	M	A	T	C	H	B	B	R	E	A	K	S	K
G	S	K	F	I	D	P	G	N	W	M	Y	J	S	C	U	S
H	R	A	I	N	R	L	J	S	J	Z	J	N	E	O	W	U
J	J	V	E	C	R	A	S	H	A	H	U	R	U	O	T	R
O	R	K	L	W	K	C	T	P	V	J	M	V	C	K	S	F
G	A	F	D	N	W	T	S	H	B	S	P	O	R	T	J	P
W	A	T	C	H	F	O	E	O	U	T	W	R	A	T	K	H
V	L	J	A	N	Y	R	G	P	U	N	D	W	S	X	S	G
Y	D	U	E	H	B	I	X	E	I	P	B	A	N	G	J	W
G	U	W	H	N	Z	O	K	O	D	S	U	R	W	Q	X	G
L	M	H	A	H	D	X	O	K	W	O	R	K	Y	E	U	A

b) *Lösungsvorschlag:*
crash: *The two cars crashed./Two horses in the race had a crash.* kick: *The player kicked the ball./He gave the ball a kick.* bang: *She banged the book on the table./There was a loud bang.* jump: *She jumped over 100 metres./Her jump was over 100 metres.* watch: *Do you watch a lot of TV?/Excuse me, what's the time? – Sorry, I don't have a watch.* rain: *I think it'll rain soon./Tomorrow evening there will be a big thunderstorm and heavy rain.*
break: *The athlete broke his leg last week./Let's have a break!* end: *How does the film end?/I don't like the end of the film.*
work: *Where do your parents work?/It is hard work to become a football star.* hope: *I hope they'll win the match./Don't lose hope. You can make it!* cook: *I'm hungry. Let's cook spaghetti./My father is a cook.* match: *Match the sentence parts./The football match was very boring.*

KV 18: English and Computing

Tip: I'm a computer word, too. Look at page 23 in your book to find more words about computers.

1 A word grid

Find 16 computer words in the grid.

E	N	G	I	N	E	H	I	C	L
M	V	K	E	M	C	N	Q	L	O
X	K	T	O	R	T	C	O	I	A
Z	I	U	A	E	E	O	A	C	D
S	S	E	R	S	D	M	B	K	K
E	S	N	M	W	G	P	A	E	T
R	E	S	U	O	G	U	I	I	W
T	G	D	S	R	H	T	B	Z	L
Y	A	Y	N	B	O	E	V	A	S
Y	P	D	S	S	E	R	D	D	A

1		9	
2		10	
3		11	
4		12	
5		13	
6		14	
7		15	
8		16	

2 A secret message from dog to dog

What is the big dog saying to the small one about the Internet? Work with a partner and find out the secret message.

A	B	C	D	E	F	G	H	I	J	K	L	M	N	O	P	Q	R	S	T	U	V	W	X	Y	Z
				20										6					11					13	

O _ _ T E _ _ _ T E _ _ E T _ O _ O _ Y
6 14 11 7 20 16 14 11 20 22 14 20 11 14 6 26 6 17 13

_ _ O _ _ _ Y O _ ' _ E _ _ O _ .
3 14 6 4 23 13 6 2 22 20 8 17 6 21

3 Teenagers and the computer

a) *How many children worked on the computer or played computer games in the year 2002? Have a guess!*

_____ % had their own computer.	_____ % used the Internet.
_____ % could use a computer at home.	_____ % liked listening to music.
_____ % (only) played games on the computer.	_____ % liked adventure games or other games.
_____ % had their own e-mail address.	_____ % never read texts on the Internet.

b) *Talk to your partner about your ideas. Compare your answers with what the teenagers really said in 2002.*

c) *Discuss what answers teenagers might give today. Check the Internet for information.*

KV 19: The world of sports

Make your own word search for one of your classmates. First fill in as many words as possible from the world of sports. Then fill in the rest of the boxes with letters. You can also draw some of the words (kinds of sports, equipment, people, games) around the box to give some hints.

_____ has found _____ (how many?) words:

_____

_____

_____

_____

_____

_____

_____

_____

_____

⟨Project⟩ English and Computing

Seite 22–23

Ziele
- Den im Lehrwerk integrierten *Skills*-Lehrgang erweitern und vertiefen
- Wortschatz zum Thema „Computer" sammeln
- Die Arbeit mit einem Textverarbeitungsprogramm kennen lernen
- *Project skills:* Informationen im Internet recherchieren
- Ein Projekt über Sportarten in den USA durchführen

Allgemeine Hinweise

Die fakultativen Projektseiten in *Green Line* 3 bieten L die Möglichkeit, Projektarbeit und Projekttechniken ab Klasse 7 schrittweise einzuführen. Medienkompetenz, fächerübergreifendes und fächerverbindendes Lernen *(cross-curricular teaching)* werden hiermit ebenso gefördert.

„Projektarbeit ist eine Form offenen Unterrichts. Der Projektbegriff ist unterschiedlich definiert und in der Fachliteratur begrifflich verschieden gefasst. Wichtig für den Erfolg ist eine wirkliche, für den Erwerb von Erfahrung geeignete Sachlage, aus der den Schülern ein echtes Problem erwächst. Viel stärker als bei allen anderen offenen Unterrichtsformen werden die Schüler an Entscheidungsfindungsprozessen beteiligt. Zu den drei wichtigsten Säulen der Projektarbeit gehören die Schülerorientierung *(learner centredness)*, die Handlungsorientierung und das soziale und kooperative Lernen. Projekte sollen nicht nur fachbezogen sein, sondern über die Fachgrenzen hinaus durchgeführt werden."
– Frank Haß (Hrsg.), *Fachdidaktik Englisch*, Stuttgart: Ernst Klett Verlag, 2006, S. 311.

Die drei Projektdoppelseiten in diesem Band zu den Themen *English and Computing, English and Biology* und *English and Geography* greifen den bilingualen Ansatz auf. Im Rahmen des Sachfachunterrichts in der Fremdsprache werden die im Zitat erwähnten Säulen der Projektarbeit berücksichtigt. Mit diesen Projektseiten sollen die S in die Projektarbeit eingeführt und die *Project skills* schrittweise erarbeitet werden: *Find information on the Internet, Make a bar chart, Give a presentation* sind Beispiele aus den Projektseiten in diesem Band.

Das wichtigste Merkmal der Projektarbeit – nämlich, dass die Schülergruppe plant, entscheidet und handelt – kann am Anfang nur mit der Hilfe von L umgesetzt werden. Die S werden nicht sofort die volle Verantwortung für ihre Projektarbeit übernehmen können. L sollte daher die Vorschläge im Schülerbuch vorstellen und gleichzeitig betonen, dass die S innerhalb des Projekts ihre Themen und die genaue Vorgehensweise frei wählen können. Vielleicht haben die S auch Änderungsvorschläge, die sich in die Projektarbeit einbringen lassen.

Schülerorientierung durch eine altersgemäße Themenwahl und Präsentation der Themen, **Handlungsorientierung** – mit zum Teil noch L-gelenkten Aktivitäten – und die authentische Nutzung von Sprache durch **soziales und kooperatives Arbeiten** in Partner- und Kleingruppen sind, wie oben dargelegt, die drei Säulen einer erfolgreichen Projektarbeit. Sie sind schon in dieser Anfangsphase deutlich zu erkennen. Die Projektseiten in *Green Line* 3 setzen den im Schülerbuch integrierten *Skills*-Lehrgang fort. Der Lehrer kann auf die *Skills* im Hauptteil des Schülerbuchs zurückgreifen, wie beispielsweise die Wörterbuchkompetenzen in Unit 1: *Using a German-English dictionary* (S. 19). Das selbstständige Lesen von Texten auf den Projektseiten wird durch die englisch-deutschen Worterklärungen (mit Lautschrift) erleichtert. Die *Vocabulary skills* helfen auch bei der Erschließung von fremden Texten im Internet. So soll im Verlauf der Arbeit mit *Green Line* der *Skills*-Lehrgang durch die Projektseiten erweitert und vertieft werden. – *But remember: Rome wasn't built in a day!*

Text	**Did you know?**	Seite 22

Ziel
- Einführung in das Projektthema
- Englisch als Kommunikationsmedium im Sachfachunterricht kennen lernen

Wortschatz *Computing, all-electronic, household*

Methodisches Vorgehen
- Zur Einstimmung lesen die S den Text in der Sprechblase und der *Did you know?*-Box.

- Anschließend überlegen sich die S in PA die Vor- und Nachteile von bilingualem Sachfachunterricht. *Why is it a good idea to speak English in other subjects? Can you think of any problems?* Die S, die bilingualen Unterricht haben, können von ihren Erfahrungen berichten. Die Ergebnisse werden an der Tafel festgehalten.

TA

> Learn new words
> More practice
> Use English to communicate
> Needn't worry about (making) mistakes
> …

Erweiterung
- Die S machen eine Liste, in welchem weiteren Sachfach sie Englisch sprechen sollten und warum.

Tipps für junge Lehrer
Die S sollten dazu ermuntert werden, englische Comics, Zeitschriften und Bücher zu lesen, Filme auf Englisch anzuschauen (DVDs mit Sprachenwahl) und bei Internetrecherchen (für Sachfächer wie Geschichte, Erdkunde etc.) auch Webseiten in englischer Sprache heranzuziehen.

STEP 1

| Üben | **Look at the keyboard** | Seite 22 |

Ziel
- Die englischen Begriffe eines *keyboard* kennen lernen
- Ein *personal vocabulary* mit *computer words* anlegen

Wortschatz *keyboard, key*

Methodisches Vorgehen
- Idealerweise sollte dieses Projekt im Computerraum stattfinden – STEPs 1 und 2 in PA oder zu dritt, da die wenigsten Schulen Computer für alle S zur Verfügung stellen können. Mehr als drei S können nicht an einem PC arbeiten.
- Wenn keine Computer vorhanden sind, können die STEPs in der Schule besprochen und als Hausaufgabe aufgegeben werden.
- Die S arbeiten die Projektseiten mit möglichst wenig L-Hilfe durch – in PA, GA oder Einzelarbeit.
- Die Ergebnisse werden im Plenum kontrolliert. Im Anschluss wird angeregt, ein *personal vocabulary* zum Thema „Computer" anzulegen: *Use your computer to make an English-German list of computer words.*

Auch als HA geeignet

Erweiterung
- Die S ergänzen ihr *personal vocabulary* fortlaufend mit neuen *computer words*.

Lösung

> 1 *at – at* 2 *return/enter – Eingabe* 3 *space bar – Leertaste* 4 *shift – Umschalttaste* 5 *control (Ctrl) – Steuerung (Strg)* 6 *hyphen – Bindestrich/Trennstrich* 7 *delete (Del) – entfernen (Entf)* 8 *colon – Doppelpunkt* 9 *question mark – Fragezeichen* 10 *slash – Schrägstrich*

Tipps für junge Lehrer
Auch wenn der Unterricht einsprachig verläuft, ist ein zweisprachiges Wörterbuch für solche Fachtermini sinnvoll. Die S sollten jedoch aufgefordert werden, im Unterricht die englischen Begriffe zu verwenden.

P ⟨Project⟩

STEP 2

Üben	**Work with a word processor**	Seite 22

Ziel
- Die Arbeit mit einem Textverarbeitungsprogramm kennen lernen

Wortschatz *word processor, instruction, file, (to) type, mystery, (to) highlight, (to) cut, position, (to) paste, Jr., international*

Methodisches Vorgehen
- Diese Aufgabe wird von den S eigenständig gelöst: *Follow these instructions.*

Erweiterung
- *Find information on the Internet about what David Beckham is doing now/has done since he joined Real Madrid in 2003. Write 3–4 sentences.*
- Alternative: Die S sammeln im Internet Informationen über einen anderen Sportler oder eine Sportlerin und spielen anschließend in GA oder im Plenum *Who is it?*. Sie geben höchstens sechs *sentence clues* vor.

Lösung
> *Who is the mystery man?*
> 1 *He was born on May 2, 1975.* 2 *He played for hours when he was a kid.*
> 3 *So he was never that good at school.* 4 *He left school when he was 16.* 5 *He went to play football for Manchester United's Jr. Team.* 6 *Two years later he played his first Premiership match.* 7 *In 1997/98 he became an English international football player.* 8 *In 2003, he went to Real Madrid.* 9 *His name is David Beckham.*

Tipps für junge Lehrer Das *Who is it?*-Spiel (Erweiterung) sollten die S in GA spielen, da auf diese Weise auch die Kontaktzeit mit Englisch erhöht werden kann. Um die Einsprachigkeit sicher zu stellen, kann ein/e S je Gruppe als Spielleiter/in bestimmt werden.

STEP 3

Üben	**Collect words for the Web**	Seite 23

Ziel
- Wörter zum Thema „Internet" sammeln
- Ein Wörterbuch benutzen

Wortschatz Siehe Lösung

Methodisches Vorgehen
- Die S bearbeiten die Aufgabe in Einzelarbeit, anschließend Vergleich mit einem/r Partner/in.
- Zur Kontrolle der Rechtschreibung können die S das *Dictionary* im Buchanhang benutzen.

TIP
Sammeln von *Internet words* für das *personal vocabulary*

TA
> When you want to go (online) you must (log on). Your computer sends your (user name) and your (password) to the server. You can use your (web browser), Internet Explorer, for example, to look at our school (website). The first page you see is the (homepage). There is a (webpage) with photos of all our teachers. You can (download) some files onto your computer. If you have a problem, you can write to me. My (e-mail address) is: webpage@dot.uk

Erweiterung
- Die S konzipieren die Aufgabe kreativ als Lückentext. Dies ist eine Aufgabe zur Differenzierung nach oben.

Lösung
> *log on, download, e-mail address, homepage, online, password, search engine, user name, web browser, website*
> (*Webpage is possible, but browser and home are then left without a partner.*)

⟨Project⟩ P

STEP 4

| Üben | **Find information on the Internet** | Seite 23 |

Ziel
- Die *Project skills* kennen lernen und anwenden
- Mit Hilfe einer Suchmaschine Informationen im Internet finden
- Informationen in einer Datei festhalten
- Computer-Begriffe auf English verstehen

Wortschatz *task, keywords, search engine, command, (to) print out, versus, Gaelic*

Methodisches Vorgehen
- Die S lesen die *Project skills*.
- In PA bzw. Einzelarbeit sollen die S – unter Zeitdruck (20 Minuten) – folgende Suchbegriffe verwenden, um mit einer Suchmaschine Informationen im Internet zu finden: 1 *British football clubs* 2 *Welsh sports* 3 *Scottish football clubs* 4 *Highland Games* 5 *Man versus Horse Marathon* 6 *Gaelic football*.
- Die Informationen werden in eine Datei getippt oder kopiert und eingefügt. Das Festhalten der Informationen in Stichwörtern ist ebenfalls Teil der *Project skills*. Die Datei wird gespeichert und ausgedruckt.
- Wenn die Schule über keinen geeigneten Computerraum verfügt, eignet sich STEP 4 auch als Hausaufgabe – ebenfalls zeitlich begrenzt!
- Die Ergebnisse werden im Plenum besprochen.

Auch als HA geeignet

Erweiterung
- Die S lösen das Kreuzworträtsel in **KV 1: Computer words.**

Lösung

Erwartungshorizont:
1 Arsenal, Chelsea, Norwich City, … 2 rugby, football 3 Glasgow Celtic, Glasgow Rangers, … 4 The Highland Games are traditional meetings with heavy events like the 'Caber toss', the 'Stone put', the 'Scottish hammer throw', the 'Weight throw', the 'Weight over the bar' and the 'Sheaf toss'. There is also music and dance and there are clan tents where you can buy traditional Scottish things. 5 This is an annual marathon race across country between runners and horses with riders which takes place in the Welsh town of Llanwrtyd Wells. The event started in 1980. 6 It's a kind of football played mainly in Ireland.

Tipps für junge Lehrer Die S sollten die Informationen, die sie im Internet finden, so umschreiben, dass die anderen S in der Lerngruppe sie verstehen: *Don't just copy and paste! You must understand it and the others in the class must understand it, too.*

Material
Kopiervorlage 1

STEP 5

| Üben | **Do a project: Sports in the USA** | Seite 23 |

Ziel
- Ein Projekt zum Thema *Sports in the USA* durchführen
- Die gelernten *Project skills* anwenden
- Kooperatives und soziales Arbeiten erleben

Methodisches Vorgehen
- Die *Project skills* aus Step 4 werden noch einmal kurz mit den S besprochen und die vier *Project steps* (siehe **KV 2: Project steps**) werden kurz erläutert. Entweder nutzt L **KV 2** als Tafelanschrieb oder die S schneiden die Teile aus und setzen ein *blackboard summary* selbst zusammen. Die Lösung heften sie in ihrem *folder* ab, nachdem sie ihr Ergebnis damit verglichen haben.
- Die S führen das Projekt im Unterricht oder zu Hause durch. In Gruppen zu viert oder zu fünft wird ein Projekt-Thema zu *Sports in the USA* ausgesucht: *a popular American sport, a sports star or a famous team.*
- In der ersten Projektstunde recherchieren die S in GA. Auf mehrere PCs verteilt suchen sie nach Informationen. Die Ergebnisse werden nach 30 Minuten

TIP
Die vier *Project steps*:
1 Collect.
2 Choose.
3 Organise.
4 Present.

P ⟨Project⟩

verglichen. *One of you must use the computer and the other(s) can take notes. Remember to write down where the information comes from – the website or webpage address.*

- Diese Recherche kann auch als Hausaufgabe durchgeführt werden. Die einzelnen S in der Gruppe vergleichen ihre Ergebnisse am Anfang der nächsten Projektstunde. Es wäre sicherlich sinnvoll, den S dann Zeit für die Recherche zu lassen.   Auch als HA geeignet
- In einer zweiten Stunde bzw. Teilstunde wird das Poster geplant. Fehlende Informationen werden ermittelt, neue Suchaufgaben werden verteilt und die grobe Gestaltung des Posters wird besprochen.
- In der dritten Stunde wird die Gestaltung mit entsprechenden Bildern und Texten fertiggestellt und das Poster im Klassenraum aufgehängt. Die S stellen ihre Poster im Plenum vor und beantworten Fragen.

Erweiterung
- Die S schreiben mit Hilfe der zuvor erarbeiteten Informationen einen kurzen Zeitschriftenartikel (10–15 Zeilen) oder eine Radioreportage (1–2 Minuten) zum Thema *Sports in the USA*.

Lösung   *Individuelle S-Antworten*

Tipps für junge Lehrer   Projektarbeit kann man „strecken", indem eine Stunde in der Woche zur Projektstunde deklariert wird.

Material
Kopiervorlage 2

KV 1: Computer words

ACROSS →
1 Suchwort
5 Leertaste
6 Umschalttaste
7 Steuerung
8 löschen
10 Passwort
14 Anweisung
18 Textverarbeitungssystem
19 Datei
20 tippen
22 einfügen

DOWN ↓
2 Suchmaschine
3 Befehl
4 Eingabetaste
6 Schrägstrich
9 herunterladen
11 Benutzername
12 (Arbeits)aufgabe
13 ausdrucken
15 einloggen
16 Tastatur
17 Taste
21 ausschneiden

ACROSS 1 search word 5 space bar 6 shift 7 control 8 delete 10 password 14 instruction 18 word processor 19 file 20 type 22 paste
DOWN 2 search engine 3 command 4 enter 6 slash 9 download 11 user name 12 task 13 print out 15 log on 16 keyboard 17 key 21 cut

KV 2: A puzzle: Project steps

Cut out the pieces of the puzzle and make a handout for: Project steps.

Project steps			
Present	Choose		1
2	Give your presentation – use English all the others can understand.	information	Collect
Put the information you want to talk about in the right order.	Organise		3
4	Find information on the Internet on 'good' websites or in a library.		Look at the information you have got. Which information is important?

Lösung:

Planung Unit 2

Übersicht

Bearbeitungszeitraum: 22 Unterrichtsstunden

Abschnitt	SB-Seiten	Ziele	Wortschatz/Grammatik & skills	WB-Übungen	CD-Tracks Kopiervorlagen Folien DVD	Gramm. Anhang (SB)
Check-in *Once upon a time …*	24–25	Epochen britischer Geschichte kennen lernen Wurzeln der britischen Nation und Kultur nachvollziehen Einem Comic Informationen entnehmen Über die eigene Haltung zu Comics sprechen	Die landeskundliche und kulturelle Kompetenz fördern Das Leseverstehen üben	S. 15/*ex.* 1, 2	Schüler-CD 1/12 Lehrer-CD 1/22, 23 KV 1, 2 Folie 4 DVD: Haunted Britain, Part A	
Language 1 *Visit the World Stage*	26–28	Das Verständnis des elisabethanischen Zeitalters vertiefen Erlaubnis, Verbote und Pflichten ausdrücken	Modalverben und ihre Ersatzformen in verschiedenen Zeitstufen kennen lernen *How to:* Sich in einem Museum zurechtfinden	S. 16/*ex.* 3–5 S. 17/*ex.* 6, 7 S. 18/*ex.* 8, 9 S. 19/*ex.* 10	Lehrer-CD 1/24 KV 3a+b Folie 5	G8, 9
Talkwise *Planning a special event*	29	Ideen für einen Schulausflug sammeln und diskutieren Eine Schulveranstaltung planen	Die Kernkompetenz „Sprechen" fördern *Useful phrases: Making suggestions*	S. 20/*ex.* 11, 12	Schüler-CD 1/13 Lehrer-CD 1/25, 26, 27	
Language 2 *Get the facts: Victorian Britain*	30–31	Das Verständnis des viktorianischen Zeitalters vertiefen Aussagen von Zeitzeugen verstehen Vorzeitigkeit und logische Zusammenhänge ausdrücken	Schlüsselbegriffe der viktorianischen Zeit Zeitenfolge *past perfect – simple past*	S. 21/*ex.* 13, 14	Lehrer-CD 1/28, 29, 30 KV 4–6 Folie 6	G10
Skills *A historical story*	32	Techniken des systematischen Leseverstehens kennen lernen und anwenden	*Reading skills:* Mit einem unbekannten Text umgehen lernen Ein Handlungsdiagramm erstellen Sammeln von *personal vocabulary*	S. 22/*ex.* 15		
Text *The diary*	33–35	Eine Erzählung mit verschiedenen Zeitebenen verstehen Die erlernten Lesetechniken anwenden und festigen Sich mit einem Text emotional auseinandersetzen	Systematik von *Reading skills* *Writing texts:* Das Ende einer Geschichte schreiben	S. 23/*ex.* 16–17	Schüler-CD 1/14–24 Lehrer-CD 1/31–41 KV 7a+b DVD: Haunted Britain, Part B	

2

Abschnitt	SB-Seiten	Ziele	Wortschatz/Grammatik & skills	WB-Übungen	CD-Tracks Kopiervorlagen Folien DVD	Gramm. Anhang (SB)
Wordwise	36	Die Herkunft englischer Wörter aus dem Französischen kennen lernen Die Bedeutung der Betonung für die Transparenz von Satzstrukturen erkennen Den persönlichen Schreibstil verbessern	Französische Lehnwörter Wortbetonung und Satzmelodie Synonyme für *to say*	S. 24/*ex.* 19	Schüler-CD 1/25 Lehrer-CD 1/42, 43, 44	
Check-out	37	Selbstkontrolle Die Lernziele der Unit 2 überprüfen	Wortschatz- und Grammatikschwerpunkte der Unit: *Useful phrases, Modal auxiliaries and their substitutes, simple past perfect* Eine Exkursion planen	S. 25/*ex.* 21–23		
⟨Text⟩ *The ruby in the smoke*	38–39	Einen Auszug aus einem historischen Abenteuerroman selbstständig erschließen Das ganzheitliche Lesen kennen lernen	Das Leseverstehen üben		Schüler-CD 1/26–29 Lehrer-CD 1/45–48 KV 8a+b	

78

Unit 2 Once upon a time ...

Hinweise

LANDESKUNDE

Roman Times

In 55 and 54 BC Julius Caesar made two expeditions to Britain to secure his provinces in Gaul. After having crossed the Medway he proceeded further inland where he met with such strong resistance from the Celtic population that he had to give up his plan to integrate the country into the Roman Republic. Because of more urgent problems in the late republic he could not afford to waste any forces.

The tribes predominantly immigrating from Belgium before 43 AD founded kingdoms and built the first fortified towns. As these belligerent tribes threatened the shipping routes along the Channel coast and additionally supported rebellious Gauls, Emperor Claudius decided on an invasion in 43 AD. In the years until 100 AD the Romans were able to expand their rule in the west as far as Wales (Anglesey/Mona) became of central importance for tin mining), in the southwest to Exeter (Isca) and in the north up to the line between the Firth of Forth and the River Clyde. London (Londinium), Chester (Castra Deva), Lincoln (Lindum), York (Eburacum), Colchester (Camulodunum), Bath (Aquae Sulis) and St. Albans (Verulamium) became important strongholds.

From 122–127 AD Emperor Hadrian had a wall built between Carlisle and Newcastle in order to defend his territory against the rebellious Picts and Scots. Some very good remains of the approx. 16ft high Hadrian's Wall with its towers and castles can still be visited today, e. g. at Housesteads (Verovicium) and Chesterholm (Vindolanda). It is clearly visible that today's road follows the line of the original wall and even sometimes touches the wall's fortifications. After the Romans had temporarily proceeded as far as the area between the Firth of Forth and the River Clyde (Antonine Wall), Hadrian's Wall was finally fortified as the northern border in 210 AD.

The third century was blessed with lasting peace which allowed towns and colonies to develop well economically. London with its approx. 25,000 inhabitants grew to be the biggest town in Britain and the centre of commerce.

Quarrels between the Roman provincial armies, which also involved the legions in Britain, as well as intensified attacks by Saxon pirates weakened the position of the Romans in the 4th century so much that they left Britain at the beginning of the 5th century. The road system designed by the Romans is still followed by some modern roads today.

Norman Times

The Normans, descendants of the Vikings, who in the course of their raids had settled along the French Channel coast, were granted Normandy in fief by the King of France as a sign of his gratitude for their acceptance of French rule. The Norman dukes were not only the most powerful French feudal lords but in this position actually held more power than the French king himself.

The Norman claim to the English throne had its origin in the marriage between Ethelred the Unready (unready = without counsel) (978–1016) and the daughter of a Norman duke. Her son Edward the Confessor (1042–1066), having grown up in Normandy, filled all important political and clerical posts with his Norman friends. With the help of a strong administration, he intended to control the English nobles, who were acting increasingly independently. However, due to a clever marriage policy, the Earl of Wessex was able to increase his family's influence. When the Earl's son Harold had fought back a Welsh attack, King Edward, who was childless, ill and had lost interest in politics, promised him the succession to the throne.

After Edward's death both Harold and William, Duke of Normandy, laid claim to the English throne. Harold, now king, was facing two threats: Norwegian troops in the north, Norman invasion in the south. On October 14, 1066 the decisive battle was fought between the English and the Normans; it was won by William the Conqueror.

William was able to secure his position quickly by connecting Anglo-Saxon institutions and peoples' law with the Norman feudal system. He consolidated his power by dividing East Anglia, Wessex, Mercia and Northumbria into counties, administered by sheriffs (who could be deposed), as well as by confiscating the estates of rebels. These were either added to the crown or given in fief to Norman followers. William ensured that these substantial estates were always in different parts of the country so as to avoid a potentially uncontrollable amount of power accumulating with one landowner. Next to the church, the king owned the biggest amount of property, and every vassal was bound to the king. The hereditary rights to the fief, however, remained untouched, which led to aristocratic dynasties forming the higher nobility. Additionally, William brought Norman clergy into England. The thus newly formed nobility distanced itself from the local population. This manifested itself particularly well in the fact that the ordinary people spoke English while the nobility spoke French and the clergy spoke Latin.

Elizabeth I (1558–1603)

Elizabeth I, daughter of Henry VIII and Anne Boleyn, was third in the royal line of succession. After her predecessor Mary Tudor had enabled Catholicism to regain influence, Elizabeth restored the church of her father. She also secured inner peace by means of low taxation and thriving trade. With a love of grandeur and ceremony, Elizabeth kept a magnificent royal court with a courtly protocol, which the courtiers were subjected to more than the monarch herself. Well into her old age she undertook costly royal visiting tours to show herself to her people and had theatre plays and other forms of amusement performed to please her guests.

Elizabeth's foreign policy was wavering and difficult to see through. Because of this and the fact that she remained unmarried, she nourished hopes of an alliance in some countries. Thus she kept them from tying bonds unfavourable for England. The country profited from frictions in Spain which was overtaxed with the task of keeping its large empire together. There were royal buccaneers such as Sir Francis Drake who satisfied the Spanish colonies' need for slaves. Philip II of Spain even tolerated attacks from English privateers as he did not want to annoy the English. He feared an alliance between England and France in the event of Mary Stuart's succession to the English throne, as her francophile policy would have been a major threat to his own country.

Elizabeth I's firm belief that Philip and Mary Stuart were plotting her assassination brought about a feud between England and Spain. After Elizabeth I had Mary Stuart executed in 1587, Philip was ready to attack England and secured financial help for an invasion from the Pope.

In 1588 the Spanish Armada was defeated due to the superior tactics of the English. As Henry VIII had already provided his ships with cannons, the English fleet was capable of firing broadsides from long distances, while the Spaniards concentrated mainly on boarding ships. When the sea battle began, Sir Francis Drake had burning ships float towards the Armada to entice them back onto the open sea, where he could cause greater damage. The Armada consisting of 130 ships was thus smashed by only 54 English ships.

The Industrial Revolution

Great Britain became the world's first industrial nation. Large deposits of coal, the availability of raw materials like cotton from the colonies, as well as the invention of the steam engine, the power machine for weaving, the mechanical loom or the 'Spinning Jenny' first changed the production process of textiles and later of other areas. Steam-powered machines made the industrial production of goods possible on a large scale. The market for these goods was secured in the colonies. Thanks to the construction of a canal system and later a network of railways goods could be transported easily from the factories to the ports. In the course of the Industrial Revolution English society changed due to the rapidly growing cities.

Victoria (1837–1901)

The rapid growth of the population in the 19th century led to the urge to expand the colonies in Canada, Australia and New Zealand at the expense of the native population. These 'white' colonies were self-governing, yet they acknowledged the British Queen as their head of state.

The British Empire, heavily based on trade, was facing growing European competition. This led to an increase in the occupation of territory and the establishment of further colonies. Seizing control at the Cape of Good Hope (1806) and invading Egypt in 1882 served the purpose of securing Britain's control of the sea-passages to India.

Check-in | **2**

STORYLINE

Zu Beginn der Unit führt Kelsey als „Historia" durch wichtige Epochen der Geschichte Großbritanniens. Bei einem Besuch bei *Madame Tussaud's* und Shakespeares *Globe Theatre* erfahren die S Näheres über das elisabethanische Zeitalter und darüber, wie man eine Klassenexkursion plant. Das Zeitalter Queen Victorias mit seinen sehr unterschiedlichen Lebensbedingungen bildet den zweiten Schwerpunkt der Unit.
Im Hinblick auf die Festigung von Fertigkeiten liegt besonderes Gewicht auf dem systematischen Leseverstehen an Hand des Haupttextes *The diary*. Hier stellt der Fund eines alten Tagebuchs die Freundschaft zwischen Chloe und Alex auf eine harte Probe, sagt es doch eine Katastrophe voraus für den Fall, dass beide gemeinsam nach Spanien fliegen.

Check-in
Seite 24–25

Ziele	• Wichtige Epochen britischer Geschichte kennen lernen
	• Wurzeln der britischen Nation und Kultur nachvollziehen
	• Einem Comic Informationen entnehmen
	• Über die eigene Haltung zu Comics sprechen

Text/Bilder **Once upon a time ...** Seite 24–25

Ziel
- Inhaltliche Grundlagen für die Unit kennen lernen
- Das Leseverstehen durch Entnehmen von Detailinformationen festigen

Wortschatz *Once upon a time ..., elephant, steel, AD, Salve!, to keep out, century, invention, wood, Valete!, heir, to attack, Norman, knight, Saxon, to hate, Bonjour, mes petits., Catholic, Protestant, gold, fave, Hasta luego!, to defeat, Elizabethan, age, poet, Romeo, wherefore art thou Romeo?, Industrial Revolution, factory, steam engine, power, workshop, empire, colony, World War II, independent, European Union*

Methodisches Vorgehen
- Kurzes Unterrichtsgespräch zum Abklären der Vorkenntnisse *(What do you know about Britain's past?)*. Hier besteht ggf. die Möglichkeit, an den Geschichtsunterricht anzuknüpfen, z. B. Mittelalter in Deutschland.
- Die Bilder des Comics werden gemeinsam gelesen, dabei Einführung der unbekannten Vokabeln.
- Anschließend benennen die S die wichtigsten Epochen. L stellt diese mittels einer *time line* auf Folie dar.
- Die S sammeln Stichpunkte zu den einzelnen Epochen; anschließend Partnerkontrolle und Vergleich der Ergebnisse im Plenum.
- Gemeinsames Lesen der *Did you know?*-Box. Die S nennen ähnliche kuriose Fakten, z. B. zur deutschen Geschichte, die sie aus dem Geschichtsunterricht oder aus Büchern kennen.

> **TIP**
> Erste Phase des Einstiegs ggf. bei geschlossenem SB

TA
> Roman Britain:
> Norman Britain:
> Elizabethan Age:
> Industrial Revolution:

Erweiterung
- Bei leistungsstärkeren Lerngruppen ist auch eine Bearbeitung in GA möglich. Jede Gruppe beschäftigt sich mit den Bildern zu einer der vier Epochen (Themen ggf. doppelt belegen). L leistet individuelle Hilfestellung und übt mit den Gruppen abwechselnd die Aussprache der neuen Vokabeln. Wichtige Stichwörter und Vokabeln zu den Epochen werden von den einzelnen Gruppen an der Tafel festgehalten.
- In einem zweiten Schritt werden die Gruppenergebnisse von einem/r oder mehreren S der Klasse präsentiert. Danach übertragen die S den TA in ihre Hefte. Aus Gründen der Zeitökonomie ist es auch möglich, jede Gruppe ihre

2 Check-in

Ergebnisse auf eine Folie schreiben zu lassen, die dann nach der Präsentation als Kopie für alle S zur Verfügung gestellt wird.
- Zur Vertiefung der landeskundlichen Informationen bearbeiten die S **KV 1: Britain and the sea** als Hausaufgabe.
- **Folie 4: Once upon a time …** stimmt auf die *Check-in*-Seiten ein.

Lösung

> *Erwartungshorizont:*
> - **Roman Britain:** *Hadrian's Wall, roads and buildings, Romans built with wood*
> - **Norman Britain:** *Battle of Hastings, Saxons against Normans, William of Normandy = King William of England, French language in England*
> - **Elizabethan Age:** *Elizabeth I, lots of ships, Francis Drake, gold and silver from Spanish ships, battle against the Armada, England won, Shakespeare*
> - **Industrial Revolution:** *James Watt, steam engine, Victoria, Empire, colonies*

Tipps für junge Lehrer

Für leistungsstärkere Gruppen ist es sicherlich spannend, die historische Chronologie gemeinsam mit „Historia" Kelsey zu erfahren. Für schwächere Lerngruppen bietet die Komplexität und abwechslungsreiche Darstellung jedoch viele Anlässe zur Ablenkung.

Material
Kopiervorlage 1
Folie 4
Ggf. Leerfolie

Üben   **1 What happened in history?**   Seite 24

Ziel
- Das Globalverständnis des Comics überprüfen
- Einzelne Epochen/Ereignisse in den chronologischen Kontext einbetten

Methodisches Vorgehen
- a) Als Hausaufgabe möglich: *Answer each question in a short text. Use your own words.*

Auch als HA geeignet

Erweiterung
- b) Die S ordnen die im Comic dargestellten Ereignisse der *time line* im hinteren Einband des SB zu. Als Hausaufgabe können die S mit **KV 2: Roman roads** exemplarisch die Bedeutung der Römer für die Entwicklung Großbritanniens nachvollziehen.

Lösung

> *Erwartungshorizont:*
> 1 *Roman Britain: The Romans were in Britain from 43 AD to the early 5th century. They built walls, roads and buildings. Parts of what they built are still there today.*
> 2 *Battle of Hastings: In this battle William of Normandy fought against King Harold of England. William won and became the new king.*
> 3 *Elizabethan Age: The time when Elizabeth I was Queen of England is called the Elizabethan Age. In this time Britain became very successful at sea.*
> 4 *Industrial Revolution: During this time there were many inventions like the steam engine and Britain became an industrial country. But this meant a lot of hard work, too, even for children.*

Material
Workbook S. 15/1
Kopiervorlage 2

Üben   **2 Listening: When is it?**   Seite 25

HV-Text

    Conversation 1
Woman 1: Oh dear. You're crying. What's wrong?
Woman 2: It's Harold. He must go to India.
Woman 1: Oh no! Why?
Woman 2: The army. Oh, I hope he gets back soon.
Woman 1: I'm sure he will, dear. You know we've got a large army there now. Britain needs our men in all of our colonies.
Woman 2: Yes, but what about the elephants and tigers – all those big animals.

Woman 1: And what about the wonderful tea? Maybe Harold will send you some of that wonderful Indian tea. He'll be back soon.

Conversation 2

Boy 1: They've opened a new shoe factory in Manchester.
Boy 2: Are you going?
Boy 1: Yes. You know there's no future for us here on the farm.
Boy 2: I know. Everything happens in the factories now.
Boy 1: I talked to Edward. You know, Edward works in the new factory.
Boy 2: And what did he say?
Boy 1: They've just changed the working hours. On Saturdays they work only ten hours.
Boy 2: What?! That's all? My dad and I work twelve hours every day on the farm.
Boy 1: I know. Me too. Factory work, here I come!

Ziel
- Einem HV-Text zielgerichtet Informationen entnehmen
- Bereits vorhandenes landeskundliches Wissen anwenden

Methodisches Vorgehen

Pre-listening:
- L und die S lesen die Höraufgabe gemeinsam, anschließend Erstellen eines *listening grid* (siehe TA).

While-listening:
- L spielt die beiden Gespräche von CD vor. Die S machen sich Notizen.

Post-listening:
- Nach zweimaligem Vorspielen Sammeln der Ergebnisse an der Tafel.

TA

	Conversation 1	Conversation 2
Age	Empire	Industrial Revolution
Information	India, large army, colonies, elephants and tigers, Indian tea	factory in Manchester, no future on farm, 'only' ten hours work on Saturdays, children work in factories

Material
s 1/12
L 1/22, 23
Workbook S. 15/2

Üben

3 Your turn: Comics

Seite 25

Ziel
- Persönliche Vorlieben bei Comics ausdrücken und begründen
- Vergleiche des Comics zu anderen Geschichtsdarstellungen ziehen

Methodisches Vorgehen
- a) Diskussion in PA, ggf. kurze mündliche Präsentation der verschiedenen Positionen in der Klasse.
- b) Bearbeitung der Aufgabe in Einzelarbeit; anschließend Sammeln der Ergebnisse an der Tafel.

TA

Comics	Books
many pictures	a few/no pictures
little text	a lot of text
funny	serious

Tipps für junge Lehrer
Die Vielfältigkeit des Materials birgt die Gefahr, sich in historischen Details zu verlieren. Die Arbeit an der Unit sollte nicht den Anspruch haben, den Geschichtsunterricht zu ersetzen.

Material
Im Anschluss an *ex. 3: Action UK! 3, Haunted Britain, Part A: Ghosts are real* sowie *Action UK! 3*, Begleitheft zu den Filmsequenzen, Unit 2 A

Language 1

Seite 26–28

Ziele
- Das Verständnis des elisabethanischen Zeitalters vertiefen
- Erlaubnis, Verbote und Pflichten ausdrücken
- Sich in einem Museum zurechtfinden

L Text	**Visit the *World Stage***	Seite 26

Ziel
- Die Ersatzformen der modalen Hilfsverben kennen lernen
- Historische und landeskundliche Kenntnisse vertiefen
- Geschlechtsspezifische Vorlieben thematisieren

Wortschatz *Briton, stage, wax, dress, to be able to, No way!, to be allowed to, modern, action, to have to*

Strukturen
- *to be able to, to be allowed to, to have to*

Methodisches Vorgehen *Pre-listening:*
- Sammeln von Vorkenntnissen zu *Madame Tussaud's*; die wenigen neuen Vokabeln der Einleitung werden hierbei semantisiert.
- L erinnert an das *Check-in* der Unit und nennt die im nachfolgenden Text wichtigen Personen: Elisabeth I., Francis Drake, William Shakespeare. Anschließend Erstellen eines *listening grid* an der Tafel.
- Die S sammeln die bereits bekannten Informationen zu den drei Personen.

While-listening:
- L präsentiert die Tonaufnahme von CD, in leistungsschwächeren Klassen bei geöffnetem SB. Mit Ausnahme der neuen Strukturen erklären sich die wenigen neuen Wörter durch Analogie mit dem Deutschen oder aus dem Kontext.
  Die S ergänzen ihre Stichwortkataloge.

Post-listening:
- Kontrolle der Ergebnisse in PA; anschließend Vergleich im Plenum.

TIP
Bei leistungsstärkeren Gruppen kann aus Gründen der Zeitökonomie auf eine vorbereitende Stoffsammlung verzichtet werden

TA

Elisabeth I	Francis Drake	William Shakespeare
wore expensive dresses, rich woman — rich country, first queen who wasn't married, had to be as strong as a man	pirate, attacked Spanish ships from the colonies in the New World, gold made England rich	writer of plays, '17th century pop star', Romeo and Juliet, plays tried to show how important England was, today: Shakespeare's Globe Theatre, workshops, open-air theatre

Material
 L 1/24

Üben **1 Read the text, and then say ...** Seite 26

Ziel
- Auf der Basis von Detailwissen eine persönliche Stellungnahme formulieren
- Persönliche Vorlieben artikulieren

Methodisches Vorgehen
- Die Aufgaben werden kurz gemeinsam gelesen. Anschließend lesen die S den Text in Einzelarbeit und machen sich Notizen zu den einzelnen Aufgaben.
- Vergleich der Ergebnisse im Plenum; L sammelt die Stichpunkte an der Tafel/auf Folie.
- Teilaufgabe 2 wurde ggf. bereits in *ex.* 1 erarbeitet.

TA
1. nice dresses, rich, strong, first queen who wasn't married
2. writer of plays, open-air theatre, Romeo and Juliet, today: Globe Theatre, kids learn about his plays in workshops

| | | | Language 1 | **2** |

> 3. A wax museum shows you what people from the past looked like. This can change what you think about them. But history is much more than this. You need to get more information.
> 4. Individuelle S-Antworten

Erweiterung
- Die S formulieren eine persönliche Stellungnahme zu den Teilaufgaben 1 oder 3. Anschließend Vergleich und Diskussion im Plenum.

Lösung
Individuelle S-Antworten

Tipps für junge Lehrer
In Verbindung mit dieser Aufgabe wäre auch eine Einführung oder Vertiefung von argumentativem Wortschatz sinnvoll. Hierbei können die *Useful phrases* auf S. 213 hilfreich sein.

Material
Ggf. Leerfolie

Üben **2 Revision: Modals** — Seite 27

Ziel
- Die Modalverben festigen als Vorbereitung für den Gebrauch in anderen Zeitstufen

TIP G 8

Strukturen
- *can, can't, must, mustn't, needn't*

Methodisches Vorgehen
- Da es sich bei dieser Aufgabe um eine Festigung bekannter Strukturen handelt, nennen die S aus Gründen der Zeitökonomie lediglich die vollständigen Sätze.

Lösung
1 *Here's a museum guide. If you want, you can ask him a question.*
2 *The faces are wax. They mustn't get too hot.*
3 *This dress is very beautiful. It must be very expensive!*
4 *Today, captains of British ships mustn't steal gold from other ships.*
5 *If your teacher says yes, we can do a workshop at the Globe Theatre.*
6 *Is Robbie Williams here? I can't see him anywhere.*
7 *I've got a map of the 'World Stage', so you needn't ask a guide.*

Tipps für junge Lehrer
Bei dieser Aufgabe ist noch einmal deutlich auf die Unterscheidung *must/mustn't/needn't* zu achten.

Material
Workbook S. 16/3

Üben **3 Find the rule** — Seite 27

Ziel
- Den differenzierten Gebrauch von *can* kennen lernen
- Die verschiedenen Zeitstufen der Modalverben systematisch darstellen

Strukturen
- *can, may, to be able to, to be allowed to, must, have to,* sowie deren Verneinungen und die verschiedenen Zeitformen

Methodisches Vorgehen
- Ein/e S liest den Text laut vor, beim Auftreten einer gesuchten Struktur rufen die S „Stop!".
- Die gefundenen Strukturen werden in Form des *grid* an der Tafel oder auf Folie zusammengetragen.

TIP
G 9
Wenn die Ergebnissicherung auf Folie erfolgt, kann diese bei *ex.* 7 ergänzt werden

TA

		Present	Past	Present perfect	Future
können	+	can	could	have been able to	will be able to
	−	can't	couldn't	have not been able to	will not be able to
dürfen	+	may	was allowed to	have been allowed to	will be allowed to

2 Language 1

		–	may not	wasn't allowed to	have not been allowed to	won't be allowed to
müssen (ex. 7)	+	must/have to	had to	have had to	will have to
		–	needn't/ don't have to	didn't have to	haven't had to	won't have to

Lösung

were they able to (Z. 1) – was he allowed to (Z. 26) – they weren't able to see (Z. 43) – you'll be able to find him (Z. 48) – maybe you'll be allowed to (Z. 50) – kids have been able to (Z. 52)

Material
Workbook S. 16/4
Ggf. Leerfolie

Üben · **4 Complete Mark's text about the Queen's pirate** · Seite 27

Ziel
- Den Gebrauch der Ersatzformen in der Vergangenheit anwenden und festigen
- Weitere Informationen zu Francis Drake kennen lernen

Strukturen
- *to be able to, to be allowed to*

Methodisches Vorgehen
- Der Text wird zunächst im Plenum besprochen und anschließend ins Heft übertragen.
- Bei leistungsstärkeren Lerngruppen kann die Aufgabe alternativ als Hausaufgabe gegeben werden.

Auch als HA geeignet

TA

he was able to cross; he was allowed to become; his ships were allowed to attack; Drake was able to finish; they were not able to defeat; people have not yet been allowed to look

Lösung · Siehe TA

Erweiterung · Folie 5: **At a museum** übt die *modals* in verschiedenen Zeitstufen.

Tipps für junge Lehrer · Das Lösen und Begründen des letzten Satzes im *present perfect* sollte besonders gelobt werden. Hier kann gut auf die Bedeutung von Signalwörtern zurückgegriffen werden.

Material
Folie 5

Üben · **5 At the Globe** · Seite 27

Ziel
- Den Gebrauch der Ersatzformen im Futur anwenden und festigen
- Weitere Details zum *Globe Theatre* kennen lernen

Strukturen
- *to be able to, to be allowed to*

Methodisches Vorgehen
- Einzelarbeit; die S formulieren ihre Antworten zunächst mündlich.
- L schreibt die Sätze an die Tafel oder auf Folie.

TA

They will be able to go to the souvenir shop.
They won't be allowed to use mobiles.
They will be able to meet the actors.
They won't be allowed to wear in-line skates.
They will be able to try on costumes.

Erweiterung
- Die S studieren zu den Skizzen ein kleines Rollenspiel ein, welches aus einem Partnerdialog zwischen L und einem/r S während einer Projektfahrt nach London besteht. Dieses könnte unter Verwendung der gleichen Strukturen auch durch andere inhaltliche Elemente erweitert werden.

Material
Workbook S. 16/5
Ggf. Leerfolie

Language 1 — 2

Üben	**6 Your turn: What can you do?**	Seite 28
Ziel	• Die neuen Strukturen im Partnergespräch anwenden	
Strukturen	• *to be able to, to be allowed to*	
Methodisches Vorgehen	• Die S formulieren in PA Sätze zu je drei Dingen, die sie früher nicht konnten oder durften bzw. die sie in der Zukunft können werden oder dürfen. • 2–3 Schülerpaare schreiben ihre Sätze zusätzlich auf Folie, um sie anschließend der Klasse zu präsentieren. • Nach Korrekturen durch die S werden ggf. weitere Fehler von L korrigiert.	**TIP** Bei leistungsschwächeren Lerngruppen schriftliche Vorentlastung als HA
TA	Individuelle S-Antworten	
Erweiterung	• Die S formulieren Antwortsätze ähnlicher Struktur auf Deutsch und setzen sie danach ins Englische um.	Auch als HA geeignet
Lösung	*Erwartungshorizont:* – *Last year I wasn't able to ride a bike. Now I can.* – *Last year I wasn't allowed to watch TV in my room. Now I am.* – *Two years ago I wasn't able to speak English. Now I can.* – *When I'm 16 I'll be allowed to go to a disco alone. I'm not yet.* – *I'll be allowed to go to bed after 12 pm when I'm 18. I'm not yet.* – *Next year I'll be able to drive a car. I can't yet.*	**Material** Workbook S. 17/6 Ggf. Leerfolie

Üben	**7 Have to**	Seite 28
Ziel	• Die verschiedenen Zeitformen von *must* und *needn't* erarbeiten • Weitere Details zum *Globe Theatre* kennen lernen	
Wortschatz	*negative*	**TIP** Der Gebrauch einer Folie hat den Vorteil einer schnelleren Kontrolle und Sicherung der Ergebnisse
Strukturen	• *to have to*	
Methodisches Vorgehen	• Die S lesen den Text auf S. 26 nochmals durch und schreiben die Formen von *must* und *needn't* in ihr Heft; alternativ unterstreichen sie die Formen auf einer vorbereiteten Folie und schreiben sie danach zur Festigung ab. Anschließend werden die neuen Formen gemeinsam in das bereits bestehende *grid* eingetragen (siehe *ex.* 3). • L hat zu b) eine Folie vorbereitet, auf der nur die vollständigen Sätze aufgeführt sind. Bei geöffnetem SB ergänzen die S die fehlenden Zeilen zunächst mündlich. Diese werden dann von L auf der Folie ergänzt und zur Sicherung von den S abgeschrieben.	
Erweiterung	• Als Hausaufgabe formulieren die S anhand der Webseite des *Globe Theatre* weitere Fragen, die dann gemeinsam beantwortet werden müssen. • KV 3a+b: **An Elizabethan puzzle** dient der Festigung des Wortschatzes und der Inhalte zum elisabethanischen Zeitalter.	HA
Lösung	a) *he didn't have to worry* (Z. 27) – *it had to be rich* (Z. 29) – *I will have to be as strong as a man* (Z. 36) – *Then we won't just have to imagine.* (Z. 55) b) 2 *He didn't have to wait long for success.* 3 *Will we have to wear warm clothes when we come to watch a play?* 4 *No, you'll have to stand, sorry.* 5 *If you want a room, you'll have to call early.* 6 *Yes, and the actors had to be careful, because people threw food at them then!* 7 *Have modern actors had to watch out for food yet?* 8 *Of course, and you don't have to worry if they walk around.*	**Material** Workbook S. 17/7, S. 18/8, 9 Kopiervorlage 3a+b Ggf. Leerfolie

2 Language 1 — Talkwise

Üben	**8 How to: Visit a museum**	Seite 28
Ziel	• Die neuen Strukturen in einem Rollenspiel anwenden • Sich in einem Museum zurechtfinden	
Wortschatz	*the following*	
Methodisches Vorgehen	• Nach einer kurzen Vorbereitungszeit spielen die S die Dialoge vor der Klasse vor.	
Erweiterung	• Zusätzlich zu den *Useful phrases* auf S. 28 gibt L weitere Hinweise, wie man sich in einem Museum zurechtfinden kann. z. B: – *First look at a map of the museum.* – *Arrange a time when you meet again.* – *Go through the museum on your own.* – *Go back to the meeting point and go off in groups of two or three.* – *Show your partner/s at least one thing you have discovered – something fantastic, horrible, etc.*	
Tipps für junge Lehrer	L sollte auch überlegen, wie die Ergebnisse eines tatsächlichen Museumsbesuches später in den Unterricht eingebracht werden könnten.	**Material** *Workbook* S. 19/10

Talkwise   Seite 29

Ziele
- Das Hörverstehen üben
- Ideen für einen Schulausflug sammeln und diskutieren
- Eine Schulveranstaltung planen

Planning a special event	Seite 29

L Üben	**1 Before you listen**	Seite 29

HV-Text

Susan: You think you're so clever, don't you? Well, I'll show you what clever is, you killer. No one can save you now!

Mr Green: The scene is much better that way, Susan. I can see that you're really trying to show what you feel. Someone has killed your brother – you're angry! Good!

Sean: Right on!

Mr Green: OK, kids. You did a good job today: I think we'll be ready to perform the show in front of the whole school next month. I'll see you all here in the hall again tomorrow.

Bill: Um, Mr Green, I've got an idea.

Mr Green: Yes, Bill, what is it?

Bill: After we've performed, can we go on a trip to see the show together in London?

Susan: Oh, that's a good idea! They say the dancers are great!

Mr Green: Hm. I think we should find out how much the tickets cost first.

Susan: Well, shall I check the prices on the Internet?

Mr Green: Yes, OK, Susan. Thanks very much. Yes, what is it, Sean?

Sean: I suggest we go by bus. That's usually cheapest.

Susan: I'm not so sure. The trains might be cheaper in the evenings. We ought to check.

Sean: Yes, OK, I'll do that and then tell you the prices.

	Susan:	Why don't we travel earlier and then we can do something else in London on the same day. What do you think?
	Mr Green:	Well, why not? Any ideas? Yes, Chloe?
	Chloe:	How about a visit to the Globe?
	Sean:	Won't that be too expensive? And I don't think we'll have time for both things.
	Chloe:	Maybe not. You're right. But we could eat somewhere nice.
	Bill:	Good idea! I know a great place near the theatre. But we ought to ask if they have a free table first.
	Chloe:	Fine. I'll do that, shall I?
	Mr Green:	Great! Well, remember to practise your texts again before tomorrow, won't you? Only three weeks until the show!

Ziel
- Ideen zu einem Bild sammeln
- Einem HV-Text zielgerichtet Informationen entnehmen

Wortschatz *making suggestions*

Methodisches Vorgehen
Pre-listening:
- a) Die S sammeln Ideen zum Bild auf S. 29. Diese werden stichwortartig an der Tafel festgehalten.

While-listening:
- L präsentiert die Tonaufnahme von CD, die S machen sich Notizen analog zu den Fragen in a).

Post-listening:
- b) Die ersten Eindrücke der S werden mit dem Inhalt des Gesprächs verglichen.

TA
school uniform, lights, poster: 'Shakespeare wrote 37 plays — How many do you ...', Shakespeare posters, one girl acts aggressively = school play

Lösung
Erwartungshorizont: class or theatre group with teacher, practising their play in the school hall

Material
◎L 1/25

Üben **2 Collect ideas for a trip** Seite 29

HV-Text Siehe HV-Text *ex. 1*

Ziel
- Ideen zur Planung eines Ausflugs sammeln
- Einem HV-Text zielgerichtet Informationen entnehmen

Methodisches Vorgehen
- a) Die S erstellen in PA eine Liste mit Ideen zur Planung eines Ausflugs. Die einzelnen Aspekte werden von L an der Tafel oder auf Folie gesammelt und von den S in ihre Hefte übertragen.
- b) Die Tonaufnahme aus *ex. 1* wird nochmals vorgespielt und die Liste anschließend ergänzt.

TA
a) transport, price, lunch + individuelle S-Antworten
b) use of Internet to find important information, best time for trip (cheap evening trains), connect other activities, distances between sights, reservations

Lösung *Siehe TA*

Material
◎L 1/26
Ggf. Leerfolie

Üben **3 Where shall we go?** Seite 29

Ziel
- Das Zusammenfügen von Textelementen üben
- Mit Hilfe von *Useful phrases* Vorschläge formulieren

2 Talkwise

Wortschatz	*suggestion, to suggest, ought to*
Methodisches Vorgehen	• a) Die Aufgabe wird mündlich bearbeitet. Ein/e S liest eine Dialoghälfte vor, diese wird von einem/r Partner/in ergänzt. • b) Nach Klärung der unbekannten Wörter formulieren die S in PA einen Dialog unter Verwendung möglichst vieler *Useful phrases*.
Erweiterung	• Der von den S vorbereitete Partnerdialog wird vor der Klasse vorgespielt, die übrigen S merken sich die Anzahl der verwendeten *Useful phrases*.

Lösung

1 I've got an idea. – Yes, what is it?
2 I think we should check the weather first. – You're right. It might rain.
3 Why don't you ask at the tourist office? – Oh, that's a good idea. I'll do that.
4 Shall I buy the tickets? – Yes, OK. Thanks very much.
5 How about lunch at a nice restaurant? – I'm not so sure. Won't that be expensive?

Üben — **Listening: A class trip to Stratford** — Workbook Seite 20

HV-Text Workbook

Narrator: Class 9JF have just finished reading a play by Shakespeare. Now they are planning a trip to Shakespeare's town, Stratford-upon-Avon.

Mrs Finley: Right, let's listen to Rachel and Tanya. What have you two found out for us?

Rachel: Well, we checked transport on the Internet. We could go by bus or by train, but the bus is cheaper, and we arrive nearer to the town centre.

Mark: Why don't we go by car? That's even cheaper.

Rachel: Don't be silly, Mark. Who's going to drive us to Stratford on a Thursday morning? And anyway, I'm not so sure that it's cheaper.

Tanya: So it's the bus then. The next topic is food.

Mark: How about lunch in a nice restaurant? There must be lots of them in a tourist place like Stratford.

Tanya: Yes, there are – but they're expensive. Would you like to pay for us all, Mark?

Boy: Very funny. We could go to a cheap snack bar.

Tanya: That's a good idea, but they're very popular – and full. That's the problem. There are so many tourists in Stratford who are poor students like us!

Mrs Finley: I suggest we take sandwiches and apples and –

Tanya: Yes, Mrs Finley is right. If we take sandwiches, we'll have more money for activities.

Rachel: Yes, activities. Shall I tell you our suggestions?

Boy: Yes, please. – What are they?

Rachel: Shakespeare first. I think we ought to visit his birthplace.

Boy: Shakespeare's birthday???

Rachel: No, his birthplace! Well, it's the house that people believe was his, but nobody is sure. We can find out more at the Visitor Centre.

Boy: Good idea. How about the theatre? Can we go and see a play?

Tanya: There are three theatres in Stratford – but we can't get any tickets. You must buy them months before.

Rachel: Next year, maybe. How about a boat trip on the River Avon? We can get rowing boats for an hour or two.

Boy: Cool! That's the best idea so far. We can have our picnic on the river or in a park. How much do the rowing boats cost?

Tanya: It doesn't say on the website. Why don't you phone the information centre and find out? I can give you the number …

Material
S 1/13
L 1/27
Workbook S. 20/11

Üben	**4 Your turn: Plan your event**	Seite 29

Ziel	• Die vorangegangenen Überlegungen in einem konkreten Projekt anwenden • Eine Schulveranstaltung planen	
Wortschatz	*open day, to prepare*	
Methodisches Vorgehen	• a) Die S bilden Gruppen und entscheiden sich für eine Aufgabe. Vor Beginn der eigentlichen Arbeitsphase formulieren sie grundlegende Planungsfragen. Diese werden auf einer Folie fixiert und zur Bearbeitung von b) auf die einzelnen Gruppenmitglieder verteilt. • b) Die einzelnen Gruppenmitglieder bereiten ihre Vorschläge in Einzelarbeit oder als Hausaufgabe vor. • c) Die Vorschläge werden in den Gruppen diskutiert. Anschließend formuliert jede Gruppe eine Projektskizze, die dann vor der Klasse präsentiert wird.	Auch als HA geeignet
Erweiterung	• Die Umsetzung der verschiedenen Arbeits- und Sozialformen dieser Aufgabe kann auch in Form eines kleinen Projektes erfolgen, an dessen Ende eine Präsentation der jeweiligen Gruppenergebnisse steht.	
Tipps für junge Lehrer	Nach Bildung der Gruppen ist es sinnvoll zu überprüfen, ob alle Themenbereiche von den Gruppen abgedeckt wurden. Dies soll eine inhaltliche Engführung oder spätere Langeweile vermeiden. Die erste Gruppenphase sollte möglichst am Ende einer Stunde erfolgen, um b) ggf. als Hausaufgabe anschließen zu können.	**Material** *Workbook* S. 20/12

Language 2

Seite 30–31

Ziele	• Das Verständnis des viktorianischen Zeitalters vertiefen • Vorzeitigkeit und logische Zusammenhänge ausdrücken

L Text	**Get the facts: Victorian Britain**	Seite 30

Ziel	• Details zur viktorianischen Epoche kennen lernen • Historische Umstände aus modernen Medien erschließen
Wortschatz	*Victorian, hot, reign, throne, raw material, empress, farmer, slum, clean, floor, government, free*
Strukturen	• *Past perfect*
Methodisches Vorgehen	• L semantisiert die nicht durch Analogie oder den Kontext zu erschließenden Wörter wie *reign, throne, raw material, empress*. • Die Namen und Lebensdaten der beiden Protagonisten werden als Überschrift an die Tafel geschrieben. Anschließend werden bereits bekannte Inhalte zu Queen Victoria gesammelt (siehe S. 25). • Der Text wird bei geöffnetem SB von CD vorgespielt und die Stichwortsammlung an der Tafel entsprechend ergänzt. • Bei leistungsstärkeren Klassen kann anschließend direkt die Sicherung des Textverständnisses durch Bearbeitung von *ex.* 1 erfolgen.
TA	Queen Victoria (1819–1901): age of the British Empire, colonies, Britain rich, long reign, cheap raw materials from the colonies, poor colonies wanted to become independent, Commonwealth

2 Language 2

> Stephen Hoskins (1810–1847): factory work, steam engine, child labour, farmer's son, life in city slums, 5:30 start of working day without breakfast, no training, simple job, had to keep machines clean, no free schools yet

Tipps für junge Lehrer — Bei der ersten Besprechung des Textes stehen die Inhalte im Vordergrund. Daher kann auf eine Einführung des *past perfect* zunächst verzichtet werden.

Material ⓞL 1/28–29

Üben 1 Look at the text
Seite 30

Ziel
- Das Textverständnis überprüfen
- Eine persönliche Vorstellung von der viktorianischen Zeit entwickeln

Methodisches Vorgehen
- Eine falsche Behauptung wird von einem/r S vorgelesen und von einem/r anderen S mit Hilfe des Textes und der Stichwortsammlung an der Tafel korrigiert.

Erweiterung
- Nach der Einführung des *past perfect*: Die S schreiben einen Partnerdialog zwischen Queen Victoria und Stephen Hoskins über die unterschiedlichen Lebensbedingungen. Als Vorbereitung hierzu kann *ex.* 1b) dienen.

Auch als HA geeignet

Lösung
a) 1 *No, she was on the throne from 1837 until 1901.*
   2 *No, Britain wanted to become rich herself.*
   3 *No, many people from the country came to work in the factories.*
   4 *No, many colonies wanted to join the Commonwealth.*
   5 *No, children were hungry because they did not have breakfast.*
b) *Individuelle S-Antworten*

Üben 2 The past perfect
Seite 31

Ziel
- Das *past perfect* kennen lernen

Wortschatz *past perfect*

Strukturen
- *Past perfect*

Methodisches Vorgehen
- a) SB geschlossen. Ein Beispielsatz aus dem Text wird an der Tafel festgehalten und die Zeitenfolge farbig gekennzeichnet.
- Die restliche Bearbeitung von Teilaufgabe a) erfolgt mündlich.
- Die Lösungssätze zu b) werden an der Tafel oder auf Folie fixiert und von den S in ihre Hefte übernommen.

TIP G 10

TA
a) When I died in 1901, <u>I had spent</u> more than 63 years on the throne.
b) 1. Many factory workers were people <u>who had worked</u> on farms, <u>so</u> they did not know what towns were like.
   2. The Empire made Britain rich <u>because the British had chosen</u> colonies which gave them cheap raw materials.
   3. On his first day in the factory <u>Stephen Hoskins had sat</u> on the floor all day, <u>so</u> his back hurt in the evening.
   4. Stephen did not go to school after work <u>because the government had not opened</u> any free schools yet.

Erweiterung
- Zur stärkeren visuellen Unterstützung kann der Text auch auf eine Folie kopiert werden, auf der die S die entsprechenden Sätze farbig unterstreichen.
- Eine inhaltliche Erweiterung zur viktorianischen Zeit ist **KV 4: Victorian education**. Darin wird der Gebrauch der Modalverben gefestigt.

Lösung	a) – Well, the Empire made Britain very rich because we had chosen colonies ... – When I became Empress of India in 1877, we had taken Australia, ... – But we had already lost the Thirteen Colonies in North America. – But after they had become independent, lots of countries which had been colonies wanted to join the Commonwealth. – Factory workers were often people from the country who had worked on farms or in small workshops before they went to the towns. – I was hungry because there had not been any bread at home for breakfast. – I hadn't done any training, so I could only do this simple job. – In the evening, after I had sat on the floor all day, my back hurt. – The government had not opened any free schools yet when I was a boy ... b) Siehe TA
Tipps für junge Lehrer	Ein besonderer Hinweis auf die unterstützende Funktion von Konjunktionen für das Satzgefüge kann das Verständnis für die Zeitenfolge erleichtern.

Material
Workbook S. 21/13
Kopiervorlage 4
Ggf. Leerfolie

Üben	**3 From fortress to museum: Simple past or past perfect?**

Seite 31

Ziel	• Die Zeitenfolge in der Vergangenheit anwenden und festigen • Den *Tower of London* kennen lernen
Wortschatz	*fortress, prison, tower*
Strukturen	• *Simple past vs. past perfect*
Methodisches Vorgehen	• L stellt zur Wiederholung die Zeitenfolge in der Vergangenheit anhand eines Beispielsatzes graphisch dar (siehe TA). • Anschließend bearbeiten die S die Aufgabe in Einzelarbeit oder als Hausaufgabe.

Auch als HA geeignet

TA	From the 13th to the 19th century people <u>had kept</u> wild animals in the Tower ... → action in the past that happened before another action in the past These animals <u>went</u> to the new zoo in 1831. → second action in the past
Erweiterung	• Die Bilder und der Text veranschaulichen die unterschiedliche Verwendung des Towers durch die Jahrhunderte. Die S bereiten ein mündliches *summary* vor, das sie anschließend im Plenum präsentieren. • An dieser Stelle ergibt sich mit **KV 5: A history quiz** auch die Möglichkeit der Wiederholung von bereits erarbeiteten historischen Details in spielerischer Form. • **Folie 6: What had happened before?** übt das *past perfect*.
Lösung	1 *went* 2 *built* 3 *had become* 4 *died* 5 *had not finished* 6 *had finished* 7 *used* 8 *had built* 9 *became* 10 *came*

Material
Workbook S. 21/14
Kopiervorlage 5
Folie 6

⊙L Üben	**4 Listening: The news at ten**

Seite 31

HV-Text	News reader: Good morning, ladies and gentlemen, you're listening to BBC Radio Empire. And now for the News at Ten. There was trouble at the palace this morning: Queen Victoria was tired because she had slept badly, and even the best tea from the colonies could not help. She stayed in bed until lunch-time and used the time to read some letters from her many fans. After she had finished the letters, the Queen got up and had lunch. Sadly, the cook was new and had made the wrong food, so the Queen shouted at her until she started to cry and ran away. One of the Queen's friends at the palace spoke of a dark day for the cook but a great day for London's

2 Language 2

shops, because after she had walked the dog, the Queen went shopping in Regent Street.

Ziel
- Die Zeitenfolge in der Vergangenheit anwenden und festigen
- Das Hörverstehen üben

Strukturen
- *Simple past vs. past perfect*

Methodisches Vorgehen
Pre-listening:
- Die S lesen die Aufgabenstellung und spekulieren über den möglichen Inhalt der *funny radio show*.

While-listening:
- Die S machen sich Notizen zur richtigen Reihenfolge der Handlungen.

Post-listening:
- Anhand ihrer Notizen formulieren die S in Einzelarbeit vollständige Sätze unter Beachtung der Zeitenfolge. Anschließend Vergleich der Ergebnisse im Plenum; dabei erklären die S den Gebrauch der Zeitformen.

TA
> The Queen was tired because she had slept badly.
> The Queen got up and had lunch.
> The Queen shouted at the cook.
> After she had walked the dog she went shopping.

Erweiterung
- KV 6: *Catch him!* übt die Vergangenheitsformen anhand eines unbekannten Textes und gibt einen weiteren Einblick in das Leben der viktorianischen Zeit.

Material
L 1/30
Kopiervorlage 6

Lösung
g), e), d), f), c), a), b)

Üben **5 Your turn: One thing after another** Seite 31

Ziel
- Die Vergangenheitsformen in einer kommunikativen Situation anwenden

Strukturen
- *Simple past vs. past perfect*

Methodisches Vorgehen
- Die S haben sich als Hausaufgabe Notizen zu witzigen oder interessanten Dingen gemacht, die sie in der Vergangenheit erlebt haben. In PA tragen sie sich diese wechselseitig vor.

Erweiterung
- In leistungsstärkeren Gruppen ist es auch möglich, dass der/die zuhörende Partner/in sich Notizen macht und dann der Klasse über die Erfahrungen des/der Anderen berichtet.

Lösung
Individuelle S-Antworten

	Skills	**2**

Skills
Seite 32

	Ziele	• Techniken des systematischen Leseverstehens kennen lernen und anwenden • Die Kenntnisse über die viktorianische Zeit vertiefen

A historical story
Seite 32

Wortschatz	*to get ready, gist, detail*

Bilder/Üben	**1 Getting ready to read**	Seite 32
Ziel	• Die eigene Erwartungshaltung als Hilfe zum Textverständnis erkennen	
Wortschatz	*pre-reading, to be about*	
Methodisches Vorgehen	• a) Die S nennen ihre Assoziationen zum Titel und zu den Illustrationen der Geschichte. Diese werden an der Tafel oder auf Folie festgehalten. • b) Die S berichten im Plenum von Geschichten und Filmen, die Vergangenes thematisieren, und tauschen sich darüber aus.	**TIP** Das Festhalten der Ergebnisse auf Folie bietet Vorteile für den späteren Unterrichtsverlauf
TA	a) diary: written personal story, secret, exciting, past pictures: (1) boy and girl (friends?) in modern clothes talking on the phone (2) man and woman in clothes from the past, talking; storm at sea, a ship which is sinking (3) boy from picture 1, excited, talking to (fighting with?) his mother in the kitchen	
Erweiterung	• Bei der Beschreibung der Bilder kann bereits auf die Bedeutung von Farben, Licht und Körpersprache für die Bildaussage eingegangen werden.	
Tipps für junge Lehrer	In a) sollten die S bewusst ermutigt werden, kreatives Raten als einen Weg zu erkennen, um sich dem Inhalt einer Geschichte zu nähern. In b) sollte bei der Nennung der persönlichen Rezeptionsgewohnheiten der S zunächst keinerlei Wertung vorgenommen werden.	**Material** Ggf. Leerfolie

Üben	**2 Reading for gist**	Seite 32
Ziel	• Ein erstes Verständnis des Textes erlangen	
Methodisches Vorgehen	• a) Die S lesen den Text in Einzelarbeit, ggf. abschnittsweise in Gruppen. • b) Die S überprüfen ihre in *ex.* 1 gesammelten Vermutungen.	
TA	Siehe ex. 1, Chloe and Alex, Gwendolyn and Timothy, a scary story about visions, problems between friends	

Üben	**3 Reading for detail**	Seite 32
Ziel	• Einem Lesetext detaillierte Informationen entnehmen • Ein Handlungsschema erstellen	
Wortschatz	*to be connected, connecting line*	
Methodisches Vorgehen	• a) + b) Die S lesen den Text in Einzelarbeit oder als Hausaufgabe noch einmal durch. • In PA fassen die S die einzelnen Abschnitte der Erzählung in jeweils 1–2 Sätzen zusammen.	Auch als HA geeignet

2 Skills

- c) Gemeinsames Erstellen der Handlungslinien an der Tafel oder auf Folie.

TIP
Sammeln von *personal vocabulary* für den *folder*

TA

Action One — Now:
A) Chloe finds diary, talks to Alex
C) Alex and Chloe discuss holiday plans
E) Chloe's mum is worried about flight
G) Chloe has gone away with her family
I) Chloe has gone to Manchester
J) Diary tells about a terrible accident that will happen; Chloe's mum is scared; Alex is angry
K) Chloe believes what the diary says and doesn't want to see Alex again; Alex is shocked

Action Two — 1878:
B) Gwendolyn talks to Timothy; first sign of something wrong
D) Timothy is able to see things that haven't happened yet
F) Timothy has the same terrible vision every day
H) Timothy has a vision about people like Gwendolyn and himself who live in another age

Now —— A —— C —— E —— G —— I —— J —— K
1878 —————— B —————— D —————— F —————— H

Erweiterung
- Ein Schülerpaar schreibt die Zusammenfassungen der einzelnen Textabschnitte auf Folienstreifen, mit deren Hilfe die Handlungslinien anschließend auf dem OHP nachvollzogen werden können.
- Alternativ kann L die Folienstreifen auch als Einstieg in die nächste Stunde selbst vorbereiten.

Material
Ggf. Leerfolie

Lösung | *Siehe TA*

Üben | **4 Thinking about the story** | Seite 32

Ziel
- Die Kenntnisse über die viktorianische Zeit vertiefen
- Die *Writing skills* anwenden und festigen

Wortschatz *close*

Methodisches Vorgehen
- a)+b) Die S bearbeiten eine der beiden Teilaufgaben als Hausaufgabe.
- Vergleich der Ergebnisse in PA; anschließend Besprechung im Plenum.

HA

TA

Life in 1878: old-fashioned names, Lord and Lady, poor family: servant girl, duty to help the family, long working days, servants' room, private tutors, servants should not be friends, candles to give light

Life today: mobile phones, boyfriend – girlfriend, jewellery/rich family, cars, holiday flight to Spain, language schools, planes

Lösung

a) *Erwartungshorizont:*
Gwendolyn *comes from a poor family and works as a servant girl for Lord and Lady Cumberland. She is sad to live without her family, but feels the duty to help them.* **Chloe** *comes from a richer family. She looks through her mother's wardrobe for jewellery to wear and talks on the phone to her boyfriend Alex.* **Timothy** *is a servant boy for Lord and Lady Cumberland and he has to do hard work.* **Alex** *is not interested in old stories and hates old names. He likes to talk to his girlfriend on the phone and to make plans for the holidays.*

| | Skills | Text | 2 |

b) **Gwendolyn:** *very poor, lonely, tired, curious, is sorry, scared, feels terrible;*
Timothy: *not boring, kind, gentle, scared;* **Chloe:** *looking for jewellery, just silly;* **Alex:** *old-fashioned name, odd/strange feelings, scared, angry, shocked*

Material
Workbook S. 22/15

Text

Seite 33–35

Ziele
- Die erlernten Lesetechniken anwenden und festigen
- Sich mit dem Thema der Erzählung emotional auseinandersetzen

S L **Text**   **The diary**   Seite 33–35

Ziel
- Einen komplizierten Handlungsverlauf verstehen
- Die systematischen *Reading skills* anwenden

Wortschatz *girlfriend, jewellery, old-fashioned, lord, lady, middle name, to joke, servant, to feed, lonely, to reply, to shine, curious, to clean, fountain, strange, odd, vision, telegram, to drown, to gasp, such, sixth sense, to continue, to nod, to wonder, ghost, great-great-grandmother, whoever, wherever, metal, flying, actually, click, line, to have no idea*

Methodisches Vorgehen
- Siehe *Skills*, S. 32

Erweiterung
- Zur Festigung der *Reading skills* ist auch das Einführen eines *Reading log* lohnend. **KV 7a+b: How to: Write a personal reading log** bietet den S dabei eine Hilfestellung.

Tipps für junge Lehrer Das Abfassen eines *Reading log* erfordert von den S sehr viel Selbstdisziplin. Es sollte ihnen daher vermittelt werden, wie wertvoll ein *Reading log* für eine eigene Stellungnahme zum Text und bei der Erarbeitung und Wiedergabe komplexer Handlungsverläufe sein kann.

Material
S 1/14–24
L 1/31–41
Kopiervorlage 7a+b

TIPPS VON MARIO RINVOLUCRI – THE ALTERNATIVE WAY

Words in my house
The diary (p. 33–35)

a) Tell each pupil to take an A 3 sheet of paper. (It is easy to stick two pieces of A 4 together.)

b) Ask each pupil to draw a large ground plan of their flat or house. (If it is a two or more storey house, tell them to choose one of the floors only.) Tell them they have five minutes to finish the drawing. They should put in as much detail, furniture etc. as they can but not, at this stage, to write on the plan.

c) Ask them to read pp. 162–163 that gives all the new words in *The diary* with explanations. Now tell them to write the words and phrases in the places they feel appropriate in the ground plan. Give some examples:

You might put **great-great-grandmother** *in a chair near the fireplace because your gran will often sit in this sort of place.*

> *You might put* **metal** *in the waste bin in the kitchen.*
>
> *You might put* **to drown** *on the table where you do your maths homework.*
>
> Tell the pupils to do their best to find appropriate places on their ground plan for all the words in the vocab list.
>
> d) When most pupils have 'classified' more than half the words stop the exercise and group them in fours. They show their plans to each other and explain why they have placed the words as they did.
>
> e) Round off the exercise by calling out a few of the words and asking who put this particular word where. Tell the pupils that placing words in a mental space is a classical memory technique which goes back at least to Ancient Greek times.
>
> *Pluses:* This sort of categorization appeals to pupils with a strong spatial intelligence and also to those of them who are divergent rather than convergent thinkers. The exercise may please some of the 'weirder' folk in your class.
> When pupils come to revise vocabulary for a test the ground plan layout is much more interesting than parallel German-English lists.
>
> *Minuses:* Some pupils find it hard to get their heads round the exercise when you first present it and have a „Quatsch!" sort of reaction. You need to help them over this stage by giving them more examples.
>
> *Acknowledgement:* This way of spatialising words is from *Vocabulary*, John Morgan et al., Oxford University Press, 2004 (2nd edition).

Üben	**1 Believe it or not?**	Seite 35
Ziel	• Eine eigene Haltung zum Lesetext formulieren	
Methodisches Vorgehen	• a) Die S sammeln, ggf. mit Beispielen aus dem Text, Argumente für ihre Position und verteidigen diese im Klassengespräch. • b) Die S sammeln eigene Ideen und Beispiele zum Thema *sixth sense* und stellen diese anschließend der Klasse vor.	Auch als HA geeignet
Tipps für junge Lehrer	An dieser Stelle sollte im Unterrichtsgespräch auch Raum für vermeintlich wenig plausible Argumente bereit gestellt werden, um die S nicht zu demotivieren. Viele nicht haltbare Positionen werden auch im S-S-Gespräch sanktioniert, allerdings nach einer lebhaften Diskussion, die an dieser Stelle durchaus wünschenswert ist.	**Material** *Workbook* S. 23/16

Üben	**2 Writing texts: Write an ending to the story**	Seite 35
Ziel	• Das Ende einer Geschichte schreiben • Stilistische Fertigkeiten vertiefen	
Wortschatz	*paragraph*	
Methodisches Vorgehen	• Die S lesen die vier Hinweise zur Aufgabe. Danach bespricht L mit der Klasse den Sinn dieses systematischen Vorgehens. • Um die Motivation der S, sich kreativ mit der Erzählung auseinander zu setzen, nicht zu schmälern, sollte auf eine Sammelphase zu den Punkten 1–4 verzichtet werden.	**TIP** Sammeln der selbstverfassten Texte im *folder*

| | | Text | Wordwise | **2** |

- Mehrere S präsentieren ihre Texte im Plenum. Anschließend wird über das beste Ende für die Geschichte abgestimmt.

Tipps für junge Lehrer Bei dieser kreativen Schreibaufgabe ergibt sich eine gute Möglichkeit, die Vielzahl der *connecting words* und ihre Funktion noch einmal zu wiederholen. Dies kann unabhängig von Punkt 3 gemeinsam geleistet und die Ergebnisse schriftlich fixiert werden.

Material
Workbook S. 23/17
Im Anschluss an *ex.* 2: *Action UK!* 3, Haunted Britain, Part B: *The Green Lady* sowie *Action UK!* 3, Begleitheft zu den Filmsequenzen, Unit 2 B

Wordwise
Seite 36

Ziele
- Die Herkunft englischer Wörter aus dem Französischen kennen lernen
- Die Bedeutung der Betonung für die Transparenz von Satzstrukturen erkennen
- Den persönlichen Schreibstil verbessern

Üben **1 French words in English** Seite 36

Ziel
- Französische Wörter im Englischen kennen lernen
- Synergieeffekte beim Fremdsprachenerwerb erkennen

Methodisches Vorgehen
- Die S bearbeiten Teilaufgabe a) zunächst in PA. L hat eine Folie vorbereitet, auf der in der rechten Spalte die französischen Wörter aufgelistet sind. Möglich wäre an dieser Stelle auch eine Strukturierung der Wortpaare, z. B. nach solchen, die orthographisch keine Unterschiede aufweisen.
- Die S nennen die jeweiligen englischen Entsprechungen und die Tabelle wird komplettiert. Sie kann später durch Hinzufügen weiterer Wortpaare ergänzt werden.
- Zusätzlich schreiben die S jeweils ein Wortpaar auf große Karteikarten oder auf ein Flipchart, um die Parallelen im Klassenraum zu visualisieren.
- Anschließend werden die Wortpaare ausgesprochen und auf Unterschiede in der Aussprache eingegangen.

> **TIP**
> Zusammenarbeit mit dem Fach Französisch

TA

English	French	English	French
actor	acteur	to excuse	excuser
grandparents	grands-parents	to repeat	répéter
family	famille	dialogue	dialogue
visitor	visiteur	history	histoire
cousin	cousin	problem	problème
to arrive	arriver	music	musique
to change	changer	theatre	théâtre
departure	départ	station	station
to dance	danser	different	différent

Erweiterung
- Die S suchen selbstständig nach weiteren Parallelen mit dem Französischen. Diese Aufgabe eignet sich auch gut als Hausaufgabe.

Auch als HA geeignet

2 Wordwise

	• In Zusammenarbeit mit der Französisch- (Latein-, Spanisch-) Lehrkraft kann angeregt werden, umgekehrt beim Lernen von Vokabeln auf den Gebrauch im Englischen einzugehen.	**Material** Ggf. Leerfolie Karteikarten, Flipchart
Lösung	*Siehe TA*	

Üben | **2 Sounds: Sentence stress** | Seite 36

HV-Text Identisch mit SB-Text

Ziel
- Die Bedeutung der Wortbetonung für die Satzaussage erkennen
- Regeln für die Wortbetonung im Satz verstehen

Wortschatz *stress, to stress*

Methodisches Vorgehen
- Vorspielen der Satzbeispiele von CD; die S stellen Vermutungen an zu Regelmäßigkeiten bei unbetonten Wörtern.
- Die S versuchen, sich durch lautes Sprechen der Wortbetonung zu nähern, und überprüfen diese bei einem erneuten Vorspielen der Satzbeispiele.

Lösung
b) 1 *Maybe* you'll be *allowed* to *go* to the *Globe* Theatre *while* you're in *London*.
2 *I think* we *ought* to *phone* the *tourist* office *before* we go.
3 The *government* had *not* opened any *free* schools *yet* when *I* was a *boy*.
4 *Gwendolyn's parents* have *sent* her to *work* as a *servant* girl for *some rich people*.

Tipps für junge Lehrer Es sollte darauf geachtet werden, dass die S sich keine falschen Intonationsmuster antrainieren. Bei größeren Schwierigkeiten mit der Betonung sollte frühzeitig auf die Korrektur durch die CD zurückgegriffen werden.

Material L 1/42

Üben | **Listening: Sounds – Sentence stress** | Workbook Seite 24

HV-Text Workbook Identisch mit WB-Text

Material
S 1/25
L 1/43
Workbook S. 24/19

Üben | **3 Improve your style** | Seite 36

Ziel
- Den persönlichen Schreibstil verbessern

Methodisches Vorgehen
- Die S lesen still den Text *The diary* (S. 33–35) noch einmal durch und sammeln schriftlich Alternativen zum Verb *to say*.

Auch als HA geeignet

Erweiterung
- Neben den Alternativen für die Einleitung von direkter Rede können auch kommunikative Floskeln und Äußerungen des Erstaunens in den Dialogen herausgearbeitet werden.

Lösung
1 *"I was looking for some jewellery,"* Chloe explained to Alex.
2 *"That is funny,"* Gwendolyn laughed.
3 *"It's always the same,"* Timothy answered.
4 *"The Spanish are leaving,"* the man gasped.
5 *"Romeo, Romeo wherefore art thou Romeo?"* Juliet asked Romeo.
6 *"You can work in the factory,"* the man shouted.

Weitere Varianten von 'to say' im Text: to smile, to reply, to nod

| | | | Wordwise | 2 |

⊙L Song **4 ⟨A Song: Greensleeves⟩** Seite 36

HV-Text

Alas, my love, you do me wrong,
To cast me off discourteously.
And I have loved you so long,
Delighting in your company.

Chorus:
Greensleeves was all my joy,
Greensleeves was my delight,
Greensleeves was my heart of gold,
And who but my lady Greensleeves.

I have been ready at your hand,
To grant whatever you would crave,
I have both wagered life and land,
Your love and good-will for to have.

Chorus

Well, I will pray to God on high,
that thou my constancy mayst see,
And that yet once before I die,
Thou wilt vouchsafe to love me.

Chorus

Ziel
- Ein bekanntes englisches Volkslied kennen lernen

Wortschatz *Alas, to do wrong, to cast off, discourteously, for, to delight in, company, joy, delight, and who but …*

Methodisches Vorgehen

Pre-listening:
- Die S lesen die erste Strophe und den *chorus* und stellen Vermutungen an, worum es in dem Lied gehen könnte. L führt ggf. unbekannte Vokabeln ein.

While-listening:
- Das Lied wird von CD vorgespielt. Die S machen sich Notizen zur Stimmung und zum Inhalt.

Post-listening:
- Vergleich der Ergebnisse in PA; anschließend Besprechung im Plenum.

Erweiterung
- Ggf. kann an dieser Stelle bereits auf die Ähnlichkeit einiger Wörter mit der modernen Ausdrucksweise eingegangen und so bereits früh Berührungsängste mit der Sprache der Shakespeare-Zeit vermieden werden.

Tipps für junge Lehrer Die Stimmung des Liedes sollte im Vordergrund stehen. Eine vollständige Analyse des Inhaltes würde die S dieser Altersstufe sicherlich überfordern.

Stationenlernen Im Anschluss an *Wordwise* kann das Stationenlernen durchgeführt werden (**Kopiervorlagen 9–14**). Der Arbeitsbericht hierzu findet sich als **KV 17** bei Unit 1. Für die Standbilder in **Station 1: Frozen Pictures (KV 9)** können L oder die S eine Digitalkamera mitbringen, um die Geschichte von Romeo und Julia anschließend als Fotostory präsentieren zu können.

> **TIP**
> Für die Standbilder (Station 1) Digitalkamera mitbringen

Material
⊙L 1/44
Kopiervorlagen 9–14
Kopiervorlage 17 (Unit 1)

2 Check-out

Check-out — Seite 37

Ziele • Die Lernziele der Unit in Selbstkontrolle überprüfen

Üben | **1 Complete Gwendolyn's diary** — Seite 37

Ziel • Die Ersatzformen der Modalverben in verschiedenen Zeitstufen festigen

Strukturen • *to have to, to be able to, to be allowed to*

Methodisches Vorgehen
• L weist eingangs auf G 9 hin, die S schlagen ggf. im Grammatikanhang nach.
• Die S lösen die Aufgabe schriftlich in Einzelarbeit; anschließend Selbstkontrolle oder Vergleich der Ergebnisse in PA.

TIP G 9

Lösung *Siehe SB S. 214*

Material Workbook S. 25/21

Üben | **2 Plan a class trip** — Seite 37

Ziel
• Die *Useful phrases* zur Formulierung von Vorschlägen anwenden und festigen
• Eine Exkursion planen

Methodisches Vorgehen • Die S bearbeiten die Aufgabe in Einzelarbeit; anschließend Selbstkontrolle oder Vergleich der Ergebnisse in PA.

Lösung *Siehe SB S. 214*

Material Workbook S. 25/22

Üben | **3 Retell Chloe and Alex's story** — Seite 37

Ziel
• Wesentliche Inhalte einer Erzählung wiedergeben
• Die Zeitenfolge in Satzgefügen erkennen

Strukturen • *Simple past vs. past perfect*

Methodisches Vorgehen
• L weist eingangs auf G 10 hin.
• Die S lösen die Aufgabe schriftlich in Einzelarbeit; anschließend Selbstkontrolle oder Vergleich der Ergebnisse in PA.

TIP G 10

Erweiterung • In leistungsstärkeren Lerngruppen kann diese Aufgabe in Form einer schriftlichen Nacherzählung eingesetzt werden, wobei die S auf den korrekten Gebrauch der Zeitenfolge auch im mündlichen Englisch hingewiesen werden sollten.

Auch als HA geeignet

Lösung *Siehe SB S. 214*

Material Workbook S. 25/23

Üben | **4 Your turn: Plan a visit to the museum** — Seite 37

Ziel • Eine Exkursion planen

Methodisches Vorgehen • Die S bearbeiten die Aufgabe in Einzelarbeit oder als Hausaufgabe; anschließend Vergleich in PA und Präsentation der Vorschläge im Plenum.

Auch als HA geeignet

Lösung *Siehe SB S. 214*

Dictation

A letter home from a Roman soldier

Dear wife,

Our ship started to cross the sea between France and England at six o'clock in the morning. We landed on the British coast at the small town of Dover. Our great Emperor Claudius first invaded Britannia in 43 AD. Britannia is quite a small island, but it is very pretty. It is also in an important corner of our great Empire. We travelled by horse to Londinium on a good road. It is a wonderful city with hot baths and churches and libraries. Tonight we are going to the theatre to see a new play. I eat very well. Thank you for the warm socks. I will need them! I don't know when I can come home. Maybe next year. I'll write again soon.

Your husband Julius.

⟨Text⟩

Seite 38–39

Ziele	• Einen adaptierten Auszug aus einem Roman selbstständig erschließen • Das ganzheitliche Lesen kennen lernen • Das *creative writing* üben

 Text ⟨**The ruby in the smoke**⟩   Seite 38–39

Ziel
- Einen Auszug aus einem Jugendroman selbstständig erschließen
- Vermutungen über den weiteren Verlauf der Handlung anstellen

Wortschatz Annotationen S. 38–39

Methodisches Vorgehen

Pre-reading:
- Die S betrachten die Bilder auf S. 38–39 sowie den Titel und stellen Vermutungen über den Inhalt der Geschichte an (Hinweise: *ruby, beware*, ängstliche Blicke, gedeckte Farben).
- Die S lesen den Einführungstext und erschließen selbstständig unbekanntes Vokabular durch die Annotationen oder das *Dictionary* im Buchanhang.
- Anschließend überprüfen die S anhand des Einführungstextes die von ihnen zuvor angestellten Vermutungen zum Inhalt der Geschichte.

While-reading:
- Die S lesen die Geschichte als Hausaufgabe und fassen die Handlung in Stichworten zusammen.
- Alternative: Die Geschichte wird von CD präsentiert. Bei leistungsschwächeren Lerngruppen kann der Text hierbei in Sinnabschnitte gegliedert werden.

Post-reading:
- Die S überprüfen ihr Textverständnis durch Bearbeitung von **KV 8a: The ruby in the smoke**.
- Anschließend sprechen die S zunächst mit einem/r Partner/in und dann in Kleingruppen über eine mögliche Fortführung der Geschichte.
- Jede Gruppe schreibt ihre Ideen in Stichpunkten auf Folie; anschließend Präsentation im Plenum.

Erweiterung
- Mit **KV 8b: The ruby in the smoke**, *ex.* a), sollen die S für die besondere Bedeutung von Adjektiven für die Textaussage sensibilisiert werden. Eigene Beispiele können beliebig ergänzt werden.

2 ⟨Text⟩

- In **KV 8b**, *ex.* b), werden die S zum kreativen Schreiben angeregt. Dabei sollten sie auf die zuvor gesammelten Adjektive zurückgreifen.

Material
⊙s 1/26–29
⊙L 1/45–48
Kopiervorlage 8a+b
Ggf. Leerfolie

Lösung

> *Negativ konnotierte Adjektive: grey, sad, cold, brown, empty, old, untidy, unhappy, thin, strange, dark, scared, surprised, evil, terrible, bad*
> *Positiv konnotierte Adjektive: familiar, young, strong, quick, small*

!

TIPPS VON MARIO RINVOLUCRI – THE ALTERNATIVE WAY

From writing to reading
The ruby in the smoke (pp. 38–39)

a) Before the pupils work on this text write the following words on the board (the words are atmospheric ones taken from the first 35 lines of the text):

grey	scared	empty	old	thin
brown	careful	untidy	sad	
not large	cold	too big	untidy	sad

b) Ask each pupil to write five short sentences and to include between one and three of the above words in each of their sentences. Tell the pupils that the sentences can tell a story or they can equally well be separate. Look over people's shoulders and help with vocabulary and grammar.

c) Ask the pupils to get up, move about the room and read their sentences to each other.

d) Read lines 1–36 of the passage as atmospherically and dramatically as you can. The pupils listen with their eyes shut.
Play them the CD of the same lines. They listen with their eyes shut.
Now ask them to read the text for themselves.

Pluses: The active, creative writing phase opens pupils up to the power of these very simple, descriptive words. It prepares them to be receptive in both listening and reading.

Minuses: You may feel iffy about reading the lines yourself. For sure, your English may not be as 100 % native sounding as the voices on the CD, but the students are learning English from you. The book and the CDs are psychologically secondary in your pupils' minds to the fully human, three-dimensional reality of Herr/Frau X, their English teacher, i.e. you.

⟨Freiarbeit⟩

Ziele
- Einen Text selbstständig erschließen
- Durch das Schreiben eines *summary* die *Writing skills* festigen
- Einen fiktionalen Text in einen Comic übertragen

Methodisches Vorgehen
- Die S lesen zunächst in Einzelarbeit den Auszug aus einem Tagebuchroman und wandeln diesen anschließend in einen Comic mit sechs Bildern um (siehe **KV 15a+b: Once upon a time**). Sollten einzelne S mehr als sechs Bilder für ihren Comic benötigen, so kann **KV 15b** vervielfältigt werden. Ergänzt wird jedes Bild durch ein oder zwei erläuternde Sätze, die im Ganzen eine Zusammenfassung der Geschichte ergeben.
- Anschließend schneiden die S die einzelnen Bilder des Comics aus und mischen diese. Der/die Partner/in hat nun die Aufgabe, die Bilder in die richtige Reihenfolge zu bringen. Die Arbeit mit den eigenen Produkten sowie der Rätselcharakter der Aufgabe wirken auf die S grundsätzlich motivierend.

Erweiterung
- Den S kann neben dem Text *Factory hands* der Text *The ruby in the smoke* (S. 38–39) zur Umwandlung in einen Comic zur Wahl gestellt werden.
- Um binnendifferenziert zu arbeiten, können anschließend Partner/innen zusammengebracht werden, die verschiedene Geschichten bearbeitet haben. Dies erschwert die Rekonstruktion, stellt aber gleichzeitig eine größere Herausforderung für leistungsstärkere S dar.
- Zur Leseförderung kann den S der zu Grunde liegende Tagebuchroman *Mill Girl* oder andere Tagebuchromane aus der Reihe *My Story* (hg. von *Scholastic Children's Books*), die eingangs der Unit angesprochene historische Themen aufgreifen, empfohlen werden.

TIP
Der Zeitrahmen für die Freiarbeit umfasst zwei Unterrichtsstunden inkl. HA

Lösung

Erwartungshorizont:
1. *Eliza and her family are in Manchester/ in front of a mill.*
2. *Eliza is given a diary by her teacher./ Eliza is writing into her diary.*
3. *Eliza is talking to her parents./ Eliza is in bed and pretends to sleep. Her mother is talking to her./ Eliza is standing sadly in front of the school/in her classroom.*
4. *The father is working in the loud and airless mill.*
5. *Eliza is doing housework.*
6. *The family is visiting Michael./ The mother says she will never send Eliza to the mill.*
7. *Eliza is worried about something./ Eliza watches her parents keeping something from her.*
8. *Eliza is unhappy about going to the mill./ You can see a pair of hands working at the mill.*

Material
Kopiervorlage 15a+b
Schere, Bleistift, Buntstifte

KV 1: Britain and the sea

The sea has always been important for Britain. Invaders¹ came to Britain and people from Britain took other countries with the help of their ships. Look at the map. Match the ships with the dates on the time line and write the date plus the ship's number in the map.

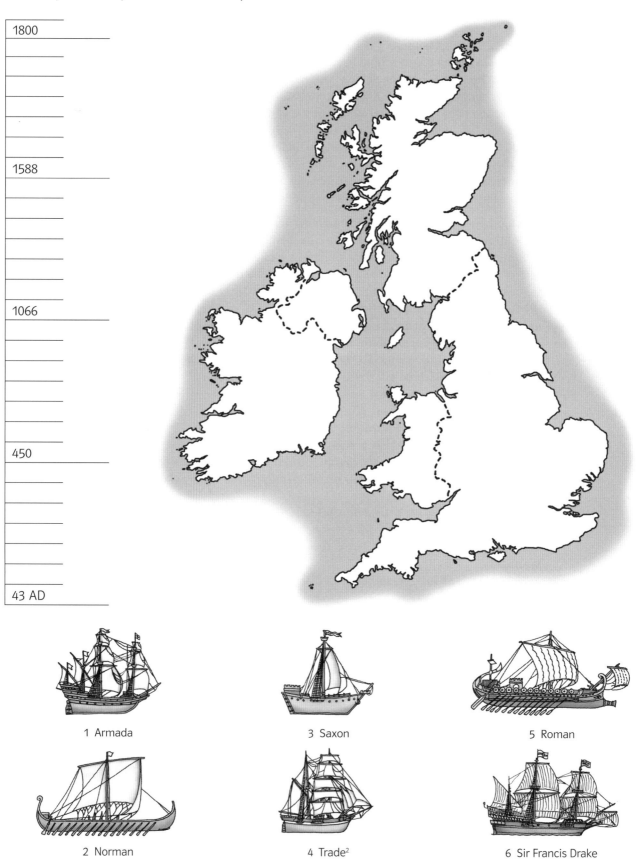

1 Armada   3 Saxon   5 Roman

2 Norman   4 Trade²   6 Sir Francis Drake

¹**invader** [ɪnˈveɪdə] = Eroberer • ²**trade** [treɪd] = Handel

Lösung: 43 AD – 5; 450 – 3; 1066 – 2; 1588 – 1 + 6; 1800 – 4

KV 2: Roman roads

The Romans were the first people who built real roads in Britain. They built them in a direct line from one point to the next, even over hills, because they wanted to reach all parts of the Empire with their soldiers quickly. Today you can still see parts of these Roman roads.
Look at the three Roman roads at the bottom of the page and draw them on the map. Find out which cities of modern Britain are on or near these roads. Use an atlas or the Internet. Maybe you can also find out why the Romans started to build castles there.

1 Watling Street

Dover to London, through the Midlands north of Birmingham to Chester

2 Ermine Street

London to Lincoln to York, up to Scotland

3 Fosse Way

Exeter to Lincoln, crossing Watling Street east of today's Birmingham

KV 3a: An Elizabethan puzzle (Partner A)

a) *Look at the puzzle on the left.
Your partner has the same grid – but without the words. You must help him/her to find them. First say what kind of word it is (noun, verb, …).*

Example: "Number one is a noun. It is a person who attacks ships."

If he/she can't guess, give him/her another tip or the first letter of the word.

b) *Now look at the puzzle on the right. Your partner has the same grid – but with the words. He/she will help you to find them.*

USEFUL PHRASES
It means the same as …
It's the opposite of …
It sounds the same as …
This was the person who …
This is a thing which …
I'm looking for two words …

1	P	I	R	A	T	E			
2	D	E	F	E	A	T			
3	N	E	W		W	O	R	L	D
4	S	T	R	O	N	G			
5	D	R	E	S	S				
6	G	L	O	B	E				
7	A	C	T	I	O	N			
8	R	O	M	E	O				
9	P	R	O	T	E	S	T	A	N	T
10	O	P	E	N	-	A	I	R	
11	P	O	E	T					
12	F	A	M	O	U	S			

GREEN LINE 3

KV 3b: An Elizabethan puzzle (Partner B)

a) *Look at the puzzle on the left. Your partner has the same grid – but with the words. He/she will help you to find them.*

USEFUL PHRASES
It means the same as …
It's the opposite of …
It sounds the same as …
This was the person who …
This is a thing which …
I'm looking for two words …

b) *Now it's your turn to help your partner with the words.*

Example: "Number one: This is a verb. It describes what the Spanish king did to England with his ships."

If your partner can't guess, give him/her another tip or the first letter of the word.

1	A	T	T	A	C	K			
2	G	O	L	D					
3	C	O	L	O	N	I	E	S	
4	D	R	A	K	E				
5	S	T	A	G	E				
6	Q	U	E	E	N				
7	S	H	A	K	E	S	P	E	A	R	E
8	A	C	T	O	R	S			
9	W	O	R	K	S	H	O	P	
10	P	O	P	U	L	A	R		
11	C	L	E	V	E	R			
12	I	M	A	G	I	N	E		

GREEN LINE 3

KV 4: Victorian education

a) The school day

Hello, I'm Vicky, I'd like to tell you about our school day and the rules we have to follow. You must know that our teachers are very strict. When we don't follow the rules, they hit us on the hand with a ruler or we must stand in the corner. Here are some of the rules:

1. Pupils must stand up to answer questions.
2. Pupils must wait until they are allowed to speak.
3. Pupils must call their teachers "Madam" or "Sir".
4. Pupils must stand up when the teacher enters the room.
5. Pupils must use their right hand when they write.
6. Boys needn't learn needlework[1].
7. Good pupils get prizes.
8. Pupils must not put their hands up until the teacher tells them to do so.
9. Pupils must not ask questions.
10. Children who are late or behave badly are hit on the hand with a ruler.

Decide for each rule if you think it's good (+) or bad (−). Compare the rules with the situation at your own school. What is different today? Write 3–4 sentences. Use your exercise book.

b) How to behave

There are lots of mistakes you can make when you visit someone. This is what my mum told me before we first went to Sir William:

Remember
1. to speak in a gentle voice.
2. to leave when the person you visit is wearing clothes for going out.
3. not to speak or act angrily.
4. to say kind things.
5. to control yourself.

It is wrong
6. to look around the room.
7. to look at your watch when you are visiting someone.
8. to walk around the room when you wait for the person you are visiting.
9. to play with anything in the room.
10. to say anything about another visitor who has just left the room.

Write down the rules the way Vicky's mother would have told them to her. Use modals.

Example: You should speak in a gentle voice.

[1]**needlework** ['niːdlwɜːk] = Handarbeit

Lösung: 2 You must/have to leave when the person you visit is wearing clothes for going out. 3 You mustn't speak or act angrily. 4 You should say kind things. 5 You must/have to control yourself. 6 You mustn't look around the room. 7 You mustn't look at your watch when you are visiting someone. 8 You mustn't walk around the room when you wait for the person you are visiting. 9 You're not allowed/you mustn't play with anything in the room. 10 You mustn't say anything about another visitor who has just left the room.

KV 5: A history quiz

Play this game with your partner. If you get to a box with a question and you answer it correctly, you can throw the dice[1] again.

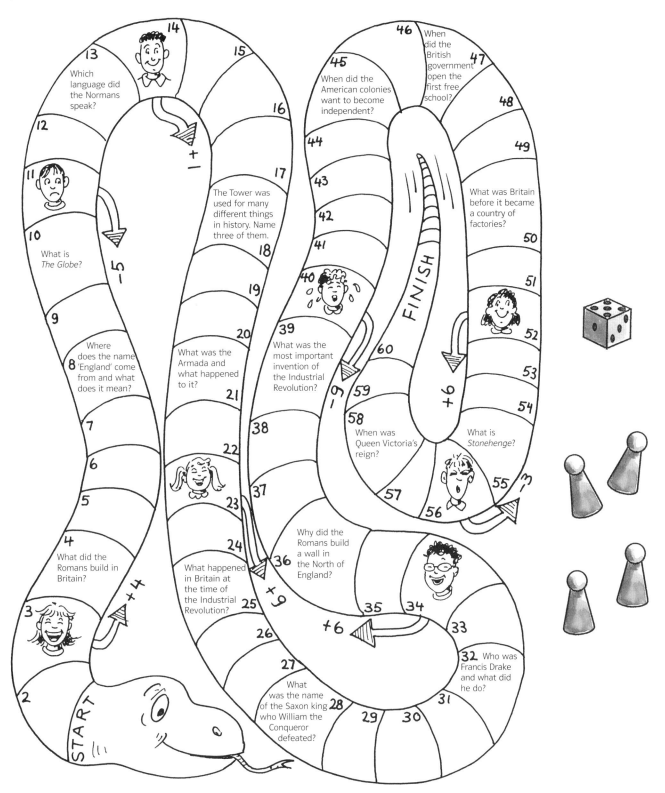

[1]**dice** [daɪs] = Würfel

Lösung: 4 *Walls, roads and buildings.* 8 *The Angles gave England its name: It means 'Land of the Angles'.* 10 *William Shakespeare's theatre in London.* 13 *French.* 18 *Fortress, royal palace, prison, museum, zoo.* 21 *130 Spanish ships which attacked England. England defeated the Armada in 1588.* 25 *All over Britain they built factories with machines and steam engines.* 28 *Harold.* 32 *He was the "Queen's pirate" and defeated the Spanish Armada.* 36 *They wanted to keep the Scots out of their empire.* 39 *The steam engine.* 45 *In 1776.* 47 *In 1870.* 50 *A country of farms.* 55 *A famous stone ring from the times of the earliest people in Britain.* 58 *1837–1901.*

KV 6: Catch him!

Charlie Peace was born in 1832. His father had worked hard in a coal mine[1] before he had an accident. Because Charlie wasn't good at school, he started to work in a factory when he was 13.
Soon after that Charlie had an accident at work and hurt his leg badly. He spent a year in hospital and never got a real job again although he was good at many things.
Peace was a great acrobat although he had hurt his leg. As a child he had taught himself how to play the violin and he was a very good actor. All of these things later helped him to run away from the police.
Charles Peace was a thief. And a very good one. This was his new job. He broke into houses, stole everything he could find and sold it later.
One day, after the police had surprised him in bed, Peace used his skills as an acrobat to get through a window that was open only six inches[2]. When Peace ran away, the police were waiting for him outside.
Another day, when the police was chasing him, Peace went into a boys' boarding school and he told them, "I'm an actor". After he had performed Shakespeare almost all day, the police had gone and Peace went home. When he was 44 years old, Peace looked very different, so when the police made a poster of him in 1876, it said that he was 55 to 60 years old.

a) *Read the text and underline the sentences in the past perfect.*
b) *Now answer the following questions. Use your exercise book.*
   1. Why did Charlie start to work in a factory?
   2. What was Charlie good at although he had hurt his leg?
   3. How did Charlie learn how to play the violin?
   4. Why were these things important for Charlie?
   5. How did he get away from the police at the boarding school?

c) *What happened to Charles Peace later in his life? Match the sentences:*

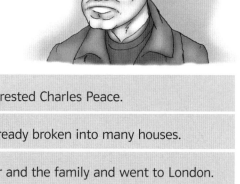

1. Because Charlie had fallen in love with a woman,	A. so they arrested Charles Peace.
2. Then after he had said goodbye to his wife,	B. he had already broken into many houses.
3. He had even changed his name	C. he left her and the family and went to London.
4. When the police finally got him in 1878,	D. he killed the woman's husband.
5. His girlfriend had told the police his real name	E. and called himself Thompson.

d) *Look for more information about Charles Peace on the Internet.*

Lösung: a) *His father had worked hard; he had hurt his leg; he had taught himself; the police had surprised him; after he had performed Shakespeare* b) 1 *Because he wasn't good at school.* 2 *He was a great acrobat.* 3 *He taught himself.* 4 *Because they helped him to run away from the police.* 5 *He performed Shakespeare all day.* c) 1D; 2C; 3E; 4B; 5A

¹coal mine ['kəʊl maɪn] = Kohlebergwerk • ²inch [ɪnʃ] = Zoll (= 2,54 cm)

KV 7a: How to: Write a personal reading log

When you read a longer text, it can be like travelling through a story. When we travel, a map can help us to find our way. When we read a text, it is helpful to write down what we think of it. This is called a log, like a log book written by the captain of a ship.

What are the rules for writing a personal reading log? First you look at the first part of the text and write down in a few sentences what happens. Then you write in the box in the middle what you personally think about this part of the story and what information you get about the people. Finally, you write down any questions you have in the box on the right. At the end of your log you will know a lot more about the text and you can always have a look at your log when you talk about the text with your classmates.

Write your personal reading log for 'The diary' (page 33–35).

Part	What happens?	What do I think of it?	Questions
A	Chloe has found a Victorian diary and tells her friend Alex about it. They talk about old-fashioned Victorian names. Gwendolyn's diary tells us that she is from a poor family and has to work for Lord and Lady Cumberland. She feels very lonely, but she has already found a friend in the house, Timothy.	Diaries are good to tell us something about the past. I think Alex is right. Clarence is a terrible name. At the beginning the story is sad, because Gwendolyn is not at home with her family. I don't like sad stories.	Where does my own name come from? Do I like it? How was the year 1878 different from today? Will Gwendolyn always be sad at the Cumberlands' house?
B	Gwendolyn works long days. Timothy thinks that life with the Cumberlands is boring. Gwendolyn likes to be with Timothy. Other people may not like it that they are together and talk a lot.	I would not like to have to work as a servant.	Are boys and girls in the Cumberlands' house not allowed to talk to each other?
C	Alex tells Chloe that he has heard enough about boring people.	I think Alex is not very nice to Chloe.	How do I like the story about Gwendolyn and Timothy?
D	Something is wrong with Timothy. He can see things in the future.	I don't believe that people can see things in the future.	What other things will Timothy tell us about?

© Ernst Klett Verlag GmbH, Stuttgart 2008. Alle Rechte vorbehalten.
ISBN 978-3-12-547143-6

GREEN LINE 3

KV 7b: How to: Write a personal reading log

E			
F			
G			
H			
I			
J			
K			

KV 8a: The ruby in the smoke

a) *"The year is 1872". What do you remember about this time? Write sentences in your exercise book. These words can help you:*

Victoria	workshops	colonies	Empire	India
revolution	inventions	raw materials	tutors	servant girl

b) *Read the text on page 38 again and then look at the following sentences. Are they right, wrong, or not in the text. Tick ✔ the right box and correct the sentences which are wrong.*

		right	wrong	not in the text
1	Mr Higgs gives Sally some important information.			
2	She has to go to a house near the river Thames.			
3	It is a grey November morning.			
4	Sally does not like to walk along the grey river so she takes a cab.			
5	The house does not look nice.			
6	After she has rung a bell, an old man opens the door.			
7	He has a thin face and fine eyes.			
8	He is even more scared than Sally.			
9	Major Marchbanks was a good friend of Sally's parents.			
10	Sally asks the man about "The Seven Blessings".			

c) *Read the text on page 39 again. Then close your book and finish the sentences. Use your own words.*

1. "I have an enemy," Major Marchbanks says, "_____."

2. He hides with Sally in the garden because _____.

3. Major Marchbanks gives Sally _____.

4. Suddenly a woman warns them and says, "_____."

5. At the door Major Marchbanks tells Sally, "_____."

6. When Sally walks back to town, _____.

Lösung: b) 1 *Wrong (Mr Higgs dies when Sally asks him about the strange message.)* 2 *Right* 3 *Not in the text* 4 *Wrong (She decides to save money and walks to the house.)* 5 *Right* 6 *Wrong (The man opens the door before she rings the bell.)* 7 *Right* 8 *Right* 9 *Not in the text* 10 *Right*

© Ernst Klett Verlag GmbH, Stuttgart 2008. Alle Rechte vorbehalten.
ISBN 978-3-12-547143-6   GREEN LINE 3

KV 8b: The ruby in the smoke

a) *Read the text on page 38 again and write down all the adjectives you can find. Write the adjectives which you think have a positive meaning on the left side of the house and those which you think have a negative meaning on the right side. There are many more negative adjectives in the story than positive ones. Do you know why? Write down some more positive and negative adjectives which are not in the text.*

fine

grey

b) *Choose one of the following topics and write a short paragraph in your exercise book. Use adjectives from your list.*

What do you think are "The Seven Blessings"?
or
What do you think is in the brown package Major Marchbanks gives to Sally?

KV 9: Stationenlernen Unit 2 (Wordwise)

Station 1: Frozen pictures[1]

a) *Read the following sentences about Romeo and Juliet. Work in small groups (3–4 pupils) and translate the sentences.*

b) *Discuss how you can do a 'frozen picture' for each sentence. Don't forget the body language (face, arms, …)!*

c) *Choose five sentences and do a 'frozen picture' in your group.*

A In Verona there are two families who have hated each other for years.
B One day the Capulet servants start a fight with the Montague servants in the streets of Verona.
C At the Capulets' party Romeo sees Juliet and falls in love with her.
D After the party, Romeo risks his life and climbs up the balcony[2] to Juliet's bedroom.
E Romeo and Juliet marry in the cell[3] of Lawrence, the priest.
F Juliet's cousin Tybalt kills Romeo's best friend in a fight.
G Romeo is angry and sad and kills Tybalt.
H Juliet talks to the priest who tells her to take something which makes her fall asleep.
I Romeo sees Juliet, thinks that she is dead and kills himself.
J Juliet wakes up, sees Romeo and kills herself, too.

Station 2: The character box

a) *Work with a partner. Decide on ONE character for each of you: Romeo or Juliet.*

b) *Draw small objects that tell your partner something about the character in your character box.*

c) *Describe to your partner the objects in your character box and say why you have chosen them.*

  Example: The priest Lawrence: church, candle, song book, …

Character box for _____

[1]**frozen picture** [ˌfrəʊzn ˈpɪktʃə] = Standbild • [2]**balcony** [ˈbælkəni] = Balkon • [3]**cell** [sel] = Klosterzelle

KV 10: Stationenlernen Unit 2 (Wordwise)

Station 3: In Shakespeare's times

a) *Cut out the cards with the verbs in grid 2.*

b) *Read the sentences in grid 1 and decide which verb fits which sentence. Put the cards with the verbs on the table in the correct order. What do you see in the picture? (It is a place where they performed plays in Shakespeare's times.)*

c) *Fill in the correct verbs in grid 1.*

Grid 1

As soon as Romeo and Juliet _____ at the party …	Romeo and Juliet _____ in secret[1] because …	After Tybalt _____ Romeo's best friend …	When Romeo _____ the country …	After Juliet _____ from her sleep …
↓	↓	↓	↓	↓
… they _____ that they loved each other.	… their families _____ each other for a long time.	… Romeo _____ Tybalt.	… Juliet _____ the priest for help.	… she _____ that Romeo was dead.

Grid 2

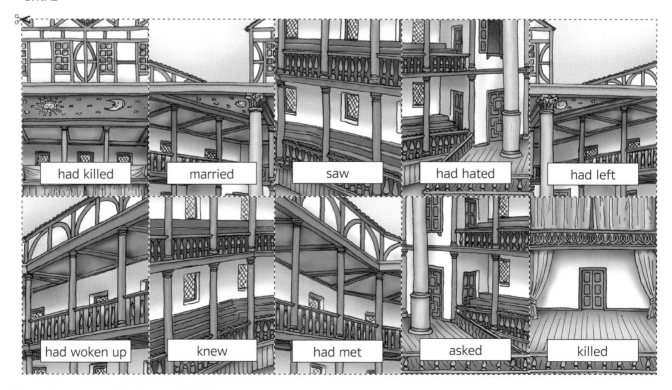

| had killed | married | saw | had hated | had left |
| had woken up | knew | had met | asked | killed |

[1] **(to) do sth in secret** [ɪn ˈsiːkrət] = etw. heimlich tun

KV 11: Stationenlernen Unit 2 (Wordwise)

Station 4: Write a poem

Create a short poem about Romeo and Juliet. Write it in your folder.
This is how it works:

1. first line: a noun
2. second line: two adjectives
3. third line: a group of three words
4. fourth line: a sentence with four words
5. last line: a noun

Verona | cold | sword | fights | out
Romeo | take | Tybalt | death | your | dark

Station 5: A game

Play this game with a partner or in small groups (3–4 pupils).
Take turns and move forward. When you come to a square¹ with a sentence about Romeo and Juliet, form three sentences about what the people could say in this situation. If the sentences are correct, you can stay on the square. If not, you must go back one square. The person who gets to "Finish" first is the winner. Good luck!

START ↓ Miss a turn. →	A street fight. Somebody is shouting. →	Romeo sees Juliet for the first time. He asks his friend questions about her.	Juliet talks to Romeo. She doesn't know who he is.	You can only move on if you get a "six". ↓
Romeo sees how Tybalt kills his best friend.	The priest helps Romeo and Juliet and they get married in secret².	Go back 4 squares.	Juliet is on the balcony and talks to Romeo.	Juliet's nurse³ tells her who Romeo is. ←
↓ Romeo and Juliet meet for the last time. →	Move forward 1 square. →	Romeo sees Juliet who is asleep.	Go back three squares.	The families want to become friends because they both have lost their child. ↓ **FINISH**

• ²**(to) do sth in secret** [ɪn ˈsiːkrət] = etw. heimlich tun   ¹**square** [skweə] = Spielfeld   • ³**nurse** [nɜːs] = Kindermädchen; Amme

GREEN LINE 3

KV 12: Stationenlernen Unit 2 (Wordwise)

Station 6: A comic

a) *Look at the pictures and read the sentences. What are the people saying? Write in your exercise book.*

b) *Think of three more scenes and draw them in the boxes.*

The Capulet family and the Montague family are enemies.

1. Two Capulet servants and two Montague servants are fighting.

2. Lady Capulet tells Juliet that she must marry.

3. At a big party in the Capulets' house Romeo sees Juliet for the first time.

4. The party is over but Romeo sees Juliet on her balcony[1].

5. Romeo and Juliet marry in secret[2].

6. Romeo doesn't want to fight with Tybalt.

7. Romeo's friend starts a fight.

8. Romeo's friend is dead.

9. Romeo and Tybalt fight and Romeo kills Tybalt.

10.

11.

12.

[1]**balcony** ['bælkəni] = Balkon • [2]**(to) do sth in secret** [ɪn 'siːkrət] = etw. heimlich tun

KV 13: Stationenlernen Unit 2 (Wordwise)

Station 7: Act the scene!

a) *Read the following situations in groups. Decide which one you like best.*

b) *Write a script[1] for the situation. You need a person who tells the story, too!*

c) *Read the story in your group. Use your voices carefully!*

d) *Act the scene in front of the class. Have fun!*

In the Capulets' house	The party in the Capulets' house
– Lady Capulet – Juliet – nurse[2] Lady Capulet tells Juliet that she must marry. Juliet does not want to. The nurse tries to talk to her, too.	– Romeo – Romeo's friend Mercutio – Juliet At the party, Romeo sees Juliet for the first time. He talks to his friend and later to her.
The fight	**The end**
– Romeo – Romeo's friend Mercutio – Tybalt Tybalt wants to fight, but Romeo doesn't. Tybalt kills Romeo's best friend Mercutio. Romeo kills Tybalt. He knows what that means. He must leave the country.	– Lord Capulet – Lady Capulet – Lord Montague They see the dead bodies and promise to be friends.

✂--

Station 8: Secret messages

What did Juliet say to Romeo? Fill in the letters in sentence 2 with the help of sentence 1.
Maybe you know the sentence already.
Who finishes first?

1: Romeo:

"W h o   i s   t h a t   b e a u t i f u l   g i r l?"
 20 10 1   2 19   18 10 5 18   6 4 5 3 18 2 9 3 15   11 2 17 13

2: Juliet:

17 1   4 1   17 1   4 1   20 10 4 17 4 9 1 17 4   5 17 18

18 19 1 3   17 1   4 1

[1] **script** [skrɪpt] = Regiebuch • [2] **nurse** [nɜːs] = Kindermädchen; Amme

GREEN LINE 3

KV 14: Stationenlernen Unit 2 (Wordwise)

Station 9: What happened then?

a) *Look at the verbs. Think of the story of Romeo and Juliet and find the right order.*

b) *Tell the story in your own words. Write it in your exercise book. Use the simple past. Use connecting words to improve your style.*

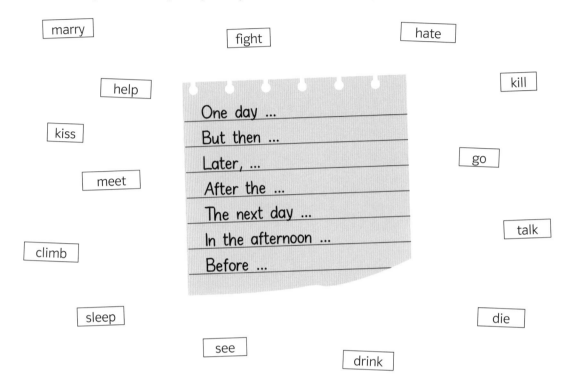

Station 10: Another word for 'say'

Read the sentences and match the verbs in the box (one for each sentence). Use the past tense.

shout   ask   explain   say happily   tell   reply   gasp   wonder

1. "Who's that beautiful girl?" Romeo _____ .
2. "Oh, no! He's dead," Juliet _____ .
3. "Juliet, you're almost fourteen," Lady Capulet _____ , "it's time to marry."
4. "Does she really love me?," Romeo _____ .
5. "Oh Lawrence, please help me!" "Don't worry, I have a plan," the priest _____ .
6. "Now we must learn to love and not to hate," Lord Capulet _____ .
7. "Look over there: This is Juliet, the only Capulet daughter. She's thirteen and very rich," a friend _____ Romeo.

Lösungen zu den Stationen

Station 2
Lösungsvorschlag: Juliet: *a picture of Romeo, a beautiful rose from the garden, a love poem*
Romeo: *a picture of Juliet, a sword, a ring for Juliet*

Station 3
had met/knew; married/had hated; had killed/killed; had left/asked; had woken up/saw
The picture shows Shakespeare's Globe Theatre in London.

Station 4
Verona
Cold, dark
Romeo fights Tybalt
"Take out your sword!"
Death

Station 6
Lösungsvorschlag: a) 1 Servant 1: *We are going to kill you!* Servant 2: *Wait until we get you!* 2 *Juliet, you're old enough now. It's a good time to marry.* 3 R: *I want to kiss you!* J: *But I don't know you!* 4 R: *Let's get married.* J: *You know that we can't get married! Our families hate each other!* 5 *Are you ready?* 6 T: *Take out your sword, Romeo!* R: *I don't want to fight!* 7 *Fight with me, not with Romeo!* 8 *What have you done? He's dead!* 9 *You killed my friend, now you have to die!*

Station 8
2 *"Romeo, Romeo, wherefore art thou Romeo?"*

Station 9
Lösungsvorschlag: *hate – see – go – talk – kiss – climb – help – marry – fight – kill – meet – drink – sleep – die*

Station 10
1 *asked* 2 *gasped* 3 *said happily* 4 *wondered* 5 *replied* 6 *explained* 7 *told*

KV 15a: Once upon a time

Factory hands

It is 1842, the time of the Industrial Revolution. Thirteen-year-old Eliza Helsted lives in Manchester with her parents and her sister Emmy. The girls go to school, their parents work at the mill, a large factory where they make cotton. Her brother William has died in an accident at the mill.

Read the text. You don't have to understand every word. If you like, you can use a dictionary to look up some of the words.

Saturday 23rd April 1842
I've been wondering what to do with this book since Miss Croom gave it to me yesterday. She says I must practise my writing in it but I don't think she'll mind if I begin a diary. I can practise my writing and write down everything I think and feel. I'm hoping it'll be a real friend. I have never had anything this nice before. But best of all are the words Miss Croom has written on the first page:

To Eliza Helsted. For excellent progress. April 1842.

Miss Croom says I'm her best pupil. I'm looking forward to telling Father what she said and seeing how proud he is!

Wednesday 27th April 1842
It's late but I must tell you although I almost cannot write the words. I MUST LEAVE SCHOOL. Emmy, too. Not that she minds. She doesn't care about it as I do and danced round the room when Mother told us. Father wouldn't even look at me. He just looked at the floor, holding his hat in his hands when he told me that there's no money for it. I didn't say a word. Just went upstairs. I didn't want them to see how much I minded. Mother came upstairs later but I turned my face away and pretended to sleep. "I'm sorry, Eliza," she said softly, "But think about it. You're thirteen now. Most girls have left school and are working long before that. You're lucky to learn how to keep the house." I knew that what she said was true but I didn't care. I just wanted her to go. Feel too upset to write more.

Monday 2nd May 1842
This afternoon Mother went down to the mill with Father's lunch as usual. I hated going into that spinning room, and Father never stopped working when I went in – just took his tea from me with a smile. He doesn't like the machines to stop more than necessary. The more he spins the more he will earn. I'd not want to wait long there either – that room is so hot and airless and thick with the smell of oil. The windows are often shut so that you cannot breathe in there in the summer. And the noise! All those machines! I can't believe it's worse in the weaving shed but Father says it is, and that's why Mother is so deaf now.

Monday 9th May 1842
Little Michael was injured at the mill this afternoon. Mr Brigham said the machine banged into him. Too tired to see it, Mr Brigham cried. Mr Brigham said he could have been killed and that he was lucky only his arm was hurt, but I had to turn away and sit down when I saw it. It reminded me of William. "Never again will a child of mine work at that place. *Never*," I heard Mother say to herself. Her words made me so glad. I couldn't bear to work at the mill.

Friday 20th May 1842
Feeling a bit worried today. I think that something is kept from me.

Saturday 21st May 1842
Something terrible has happened. I almost cannot write the words. I MUST START WORKING AT THE MILL ON MONDAY. "You said I never …," I cried to Mother. "Where must I work?" I asked angrily. The room was so quiet that I could hear myself breathe. "In the carding room. They need more hands." I wasn't Eliza any more, just a pair of hands. Factory hands.

(adapted from Sue Reid, *Mill Girl. The diary of Eliza Helsted, Manchester, 1842–43*, London: Scholastic Children's Books, 2002, pp. 8–9, 31–33, 39–40, 52–54)

a) *Read the story. Then draw and write a comic about it with six pictures. Write one or two sentences for each picture. You can use speech bubbles, too.*

b) *Cut out the pictures and mix them. Give them to your partner. Let him/her find the right order.*

KV 15 b: Once upon a time

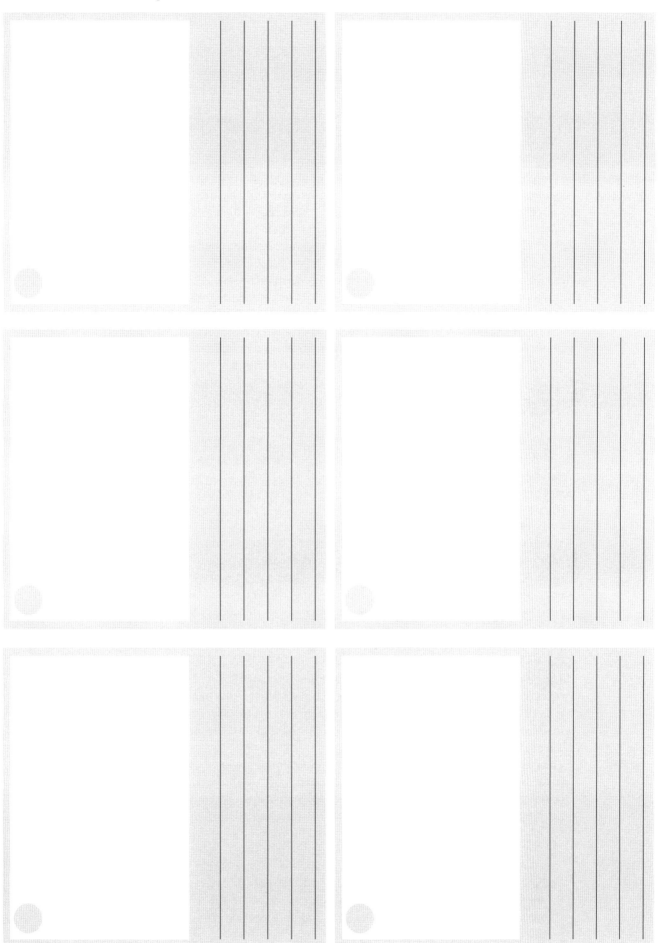

⟨Revision for tests⟩ Unit 1–2

Seite 40–41

Ziele
- Vorbereitung auf Standardprüfungen
- Die Modalverben und ihre Ersatzformen anwenden
- Einen Leserbrief schreiben
- Einen Ausflug planen
- Die Techniken des systematischen Leseverstehens anwenden

Allgemeine Hinweise

Die Einführung und das Üben von Strukturen und Fertigkeiten erfolgt auch in *Green Line* 3 in den *Language*-Teilen der Units. Weitere Übungsmöglichkeiten gibt es in den *Revision*-Aufgaben jeder Unit, auf den *Check-out*-Seiten und – als drittes „Sicherheitsnetz" – in den *Revisions*.

Die *Revisions* sind Unit-übergreifend und dienen der Sicherung des Grundwissens. So werden wichtige strukturelle und kommunikative Pensen vorangegangener Units wiederholt. Die *Revisions* sollen den S verdeutlichen, welche Stärken, aber auch Schwächen sich bezüglich ihrer Grammatikkompetenz und ihrer Kommunikationsfähigkeit an diesem Punkt erkennen lassen.

Die methodische Vorgehensweise sollte so ausgerichtet sein, dass wesentliche Teile der Aufgaben von den S eigenständig bearbeitet werden, um so einerseits die Selbstständigkeit zu fördern und andererseits mögliche Wissenslücken zu schließen. Die Aufgaben sollten daher einzeln oder thematisch passend zueinander bearbeitet werden. Die Korrektur kann im Klassenverband, aber auch eigenständig oder in PA erfolgen. Die Aufgaben in den *Revisions* sollten nicht als Grundlage für eine Benotung eingesetzt werden.

LANDESKUNDE ZU EX. 5

The facts about the **Great Fire of London** are simple: The fire started in Pudding Lane, in a baker's shop owned by Thomas Farriner – who was the King's baker. His maid failed to put out the ovens at the end of the night. The heat created by the ovens caused sparks to ignite Farriner's wooden home. In her panic the maid tried to climb out of the building, but she failed. She was one of the few victims of the fire.

Once it had started, the fire spread quickly. The city was basically made of wood and in September everything was dry. Strong winds aroused the flames. Despite evidence to the contrary, the Lord Mayor was not too concerned by what he was told. "A woman could piss it out," was his apparent comment when he was told that the fire was a cause for concern.

In 1665, during the Great Plague, King Charles II had fled London. Many would have liked to have done the same and so only few criticised the King when he left for the countryside. In September 1666, however, he stayed in London and took charge of the operation to save the city. His plan was to create fire-breaks. This required knocking down undamaged buildings to starve the fire. In addition, Charles ordered that navy rations stored in docks in the East End should be given to those who had fled the city.

The heat created by the fire was so great that the lead roof of the old St Paul's Cathedral melted. Many saw the lead flowing down the streets. It is said that many pigeons lost their lives as they refused to leave their nests and they plummeted into the fire as their wing feathers got burned. But the actual human casualty rate was remarkably low with possibly only five people having died in the fire.

The greatest fear the authorities had was that the flames might cross the River Thames and set fire to the southern parts of the city. If it could be kept north of the river, however, the authorities could claim a victory. Finally, the weather came to their assistance. The wind, which before had helped the fire spread, turned on itself and drove the flames back into what had already been burned. The fire had nothing more to ignite and finally died down.

The Great Fire burned down 84 churches and the old St Paul's. However, it also destroyed the filthy streets associated with the Great Plague. The Fleet, a 'tributary' that flowed into the Thames, was nothing more than an open sewer associated with disease and poverty. The fire effectively boiled the Fleet and sterilised it. Slums were simply burned away. In this sense, the fire did London a favour and it was now up to the city's authorities to re-build and re-plan the city. The responsibility for this was given to Sir Christopher Wren.

⟨Revision A⟩ R

> As with the Great Plague of 1665, a great deal of information we have about the Great Fire comes from Samuel Pepys who kept a diary of the event. He wrote: "September 2nd: Jane [his maid] comes and tells us that she hears that above 300 houses have been burned down by the fire … poor people staying in their houses as long as till the very fire touched them, and then running into boats or clambering from one pair of stairs by the waterside, to another … I saw a fire as one entire arch of fire above a mile long: it made me weep to see it. The churches, houses are all on fire and flaming at once, and a horrid noise the flames made and the cracking of the houses."
> For more information check:
> http://www.historylearningsite.co.uk/great_fire_of_london_of_1666.htm

Üben   **1 Mixed bag: Mixed tenses**   Seite 40

Ziel
- Verschiedene Zeitformen wiederholen und festigen
- Die Ersatzformen der Modalverben anwenden
- Eine eigene Stellungnahme unter Verwendung der Modalverben formulieren

Strukturen
- Verschiedene Zeitformen, *to have to, to be able to, to be allowed to*

TIP
G 1–3, 9

Methodisches Vorgehen
- L weist auf den Grammatikanhang hin, falls die S eine Hilfestellung brauchen. Dies gehört zur eigenständigen Wiederholungsarbeit für eine Prüfung.
- Die S bearbeiten die Aufgabe in Einzelarbeit; anschließend Vergleich mit einem/r Partner/in. Problemfälle können im Plenum besprochen werden.

Erweiterung
- L stellt den S eine weitergehende Aufgabe zum Text: *What should Debbie do? Tell us your opinion.* Die S sollten aufgefordert werden, bei ihren Antworten die Modalverben und deren Ersatzformen zu verwenden.

Auch als HA geeignet

Lösung
> 1 *is surfing*   2 *is doing*   3 *is downloading*   4 *is*   5 *will be able to wear*
> 6 *has already started*   7 *had to wear*   8 *don't have to show*   9 *weren't allowed to play*   10 *were*   11 *looks*   12 *is playing*   13 *will not be able to win*
> 14 *are*   15 *did not have to try*   16 *won*   17 *starts*   18 *will have to leave*
> 19 *remembers*   20 *is coming*   21 *will be*   22 *am not*

Tipps für junge Lehrer
Die S sind häufig verunsichert, wenn Lückentexte unterschiedliche Lösungsmöglichkeiten anbieten. In den Lücken 2, 12 und 20 sollte das *present progressive* zur Wiedergabe der Zukunft verwendet werden, um die neue Struktur im Vergleich zum *going to future* zu festigen (siehe G 3). L sollte den Unterschied im Plenum noch einmal deutlich machen.

TIP
G 3

Material
Workbook S. 26/1

Üben   **2 A reader's letter: Do you agree?**   Seite 40

Ziel
- Einen Leserbrief schreiben
- Die *Useful phrases: Agreeing and disagreeing* anwenden

Methodisches Vorgehen
- L erinnert an *Talkwise* S. 12 und die *Useful phrases* und macht deutlich, dass solche Redewendungen auch in der Schriftsprache verwendet werden können.
- Die S machen sich Notizen zum Thema *sixth sense* und schreiben ihren eigenen Leserbrief. Anschließend werden mehrere Leserbriefe im Plenum vorgestellt.

TIP
Useful phrases
S. 12

Auch als HA geeignet

Erweiterung
- Die S tauschen sich in Kleingruppen über ihre Leserbriefe aus.

Lösung
> *Erwartungshorizont:*
> I was really interested in your article about the 'sixth sense'. That's what I think, too. I'm sure some people have visions and you cannot use science to explain everything. Some really strange things happen, so I agree when you say that some people have got a 'sixth sense'.

R ⟨Revision A⟩

Tipps für junge Lehrer	L kann ein Stimmungsbild abrufen, indem er die S fragt, wer wie Laura denkt und wer eine gegenteilige Meinung vertritt. Zwei Leserbriefe können zusätzlich auf Folie geschrieben und als Impuls für eine Diskussion in der Klasse verwendet werden. So werden die *Useful phrases* weiter vertieft.	**Material** *Workbook* S. 26/2 Ggf. Leerfolie
Üben	**3 Plan a trip to a sports event**	Seite 40
Ziel	• Einen Ausflug planen • Die *Useful phrases: Making suggestions* anwenden	**TIP** *Useful phrases*, S. 29 Alternativ auf bereits bekannte Themen zurückgreifen
Methodisches Vorgehen	• L schreibt als Impuls die Überschrift „Berlin-Marathon" an die Tafel. Die S sammeln Ideen dazu in einem kurzen *brainstorming*. • L weist auf *Talkwise* S. 29 hin: *Planning a special event*. In Einzelarbeit sammeln die S Ideen für einen Ausflug zum Berlin-Marathon und verfassen anschließend einen Dialog. • Alternative: Die S schreiben ihre Dialoge in PA, lernen sie zu Hause auswendig und präsentieren sie gemeinsam vor der Klasse. • L kann auch ein anderes Thema wählen, wenn dies für die Lerngruppe sinnvoller erscheint.	Auch als HA geeignet
Erweiterung	• Die S erklären, wie sie eine Internetrecherche zum Thema „Berlin-Marathon" durchführen würden. Hier sollten sie ihre Kenntnisse aus dem *Project: English and Computing* nutzen.	
Lösung	*Erwartungshorizont:* You: How about a trip to Berlin to watch the Marathon? Your partner: Good idea! We could go to the sports shop in town. They often have information about trips to marathons. A friend of my dad's ran in New York last year. You: Yes, we can do that, but why don't we check the Internet, too? Just put Berlin and marathon in the search engine. I'm sure we'll find something. Your partner: Shall I try to find a map of the race? You: We'll have to find a good place to stand so we can see the runners when they come. Your partner: I'm going to town with Mum tomorrow. I'll go to the sports shop – and we can use the Internet right now!	
Tipps für junge Lehrer	Es ist immer eine gute Idee, auf bereits besprochene Themen zurückzugreifen, um Inhalte bzw. sprachliche Mittel umzuwälzen (siehe Erweiterung). Außerdem sollte L sich die Freiheit nehmen, das Thema einer Aufgabe zu ändern, wenn es sinnvoll erscheint. Bei dieser Aufgabe könnte der geplante Besuch eines Bundesligaspiels auf die S motivierend wirken.	**Material** *Workbook* S. 26/3
Üben	**4 Make a word web: Sport**	Seite 40
Ziel	• Den Wortschatz zum Thema „Sport" wiederholen und vertiefen	
Methodisches Vorgehen	• L bespricht mit der Klasse, welche beiden *words* oder *phrases* als Überschriften dienen sollen (Beispiel siehe TA). • Die S schreiben die Wörter aus der Box auf Papierschnipsel und ordnen sie in PA oder Kleingruppen den beiden Überschriften zu. Anschließend bilden sie weitere Untergruppen für das *word web*. Wenn ein Wort zwei oder mehreren Untergruppen zugeordnet werden kann, sollten weitere Papierschnipsel mit diesem Wort beschriftet werden. • Anschließend werden die Ergebnisse an der Tafel festgehalten.	
TA	with a ball tennis, Wimbledon, court, umpire, racket football, referee, goal, kick, field	

⟨Revision A⟩   R

> **without a ball**
> athletics, track, athlete, race, 400 metres, marathon
> swimming, pool, water, goggles
> Winter Olympics, snow, ski jump

Erweiterung
- Die S ergänzen das *word web* durch sechs (oder mehr) Vokabeln zum Thema „Sport", z. B. *baseball, bat, match, ice hockey, ice, sticks*.

Lösung *Siehe TA*

Tipps für junge Lehrer Die S sollten dazu ermuntert werden, *word webs* zu einem Thema als effektive Möglichkeit des Vokabellernens zu nutzen. In den Units 1 und 2 eignen sich hierzu die Themen „Sport" und „Geschichte".

Text/Üben **5 London, 1666**   Seite 41

Ziel
- Die erlernten Lesetechniken anwenden und festigen
- Eigene Ideen zu einer Geschichte sammeln
- *Writing texts:* Das Ende einer Geschichte schreiben

> **TIP**
> *Reading skills*, S. 32

Methodisches Vorgehen
- L weist auf die *Skills*, S. 32 hin und fasst die vier Hauptschritte als TA zusammen. Die S erläutern kurz die einzelnen Schritte.
- Anschließend bearbeiten die S die Aufgaben in Einzelarbeit – siehe Tipps für junge Lehrer. Die Aufgaben können als Hausaufgabe fertig gestellt werden.

Auch als HA geeignet

TA
> **Reading skills**
> 1. Getting ready to read
> 2. Reading for gist
> 3. Reading for detail
> 4. Thinking about the story

Lösung
a) about what happened in London in 1666 (title); a big fire, people running away from it (picture)
b) **Who?** Sam, his master, Mr Fenton, and their families
   What? Fire starts in baker's house in Pudding Lane; more than 13,000 houses burn down; only six people die; people go to the country; Sam wants to leave London and find his family
   When? Very early on September 2, 1666
   Where? In London – London Bridge, St Paul's Cathedral, the Tower of London and the Thames can be seen in the picture
c) his family: because he loves them; Mr Fenton: because he gives him a job; Sam wants to find his family, but he will lose his job if he leaves
d) Mr Fenton: has an arrangement with Sam's parents, Sam needs to learn a job (shoemaker); needs Sam's help (to build a new house)
   family: Sam loves his family; just wants to know if they are safe; they might need his help
e) Erwartungshorizont: Sam stays with his master, Mr Fenton. His family knows where he is, so he must wait until they come back to London. He can't really do anything and mustn't risk his job and his future – although he is very unhappy about it.

Tipps für junge Lehrer Einzelarbeit muss auch geübt werden! Daher sollten Fragen der S vor der Beschäftigung mit dem Text beantwortet werden. Auch das Lesen der Arbeitsaufträge gehört in diese Phase. Dies ist gleichzeitig eine Vorbereitung auf Standardprüfungen: *Read the questions first, think, make notes – and then start to write.* Während der Einzelarbeit gilt die Regel: Absolute Ruhe! Die S sollten auch eine Zeitvorgabe erhalten, um möglichst effektiv arbeiten zu können.

Material
Workbook S. 27/4

Planung Unit 3

Übersicht

Bearbeitungszeitraum: 22 Unterrichtsstunden

Abschnitt	SB-Seiten	Ziele	Wortschatz/Grammatik & skills	WB-Übungen	CD-Tracks Kopiervorlagen Folien DVD	Gramm. Anhang (SB)
Check-in *Living together*	42–43	Über bekannte Fernsehserien sprechen Über das eigene Familienleben berichten	Wortfeld *family life*	S. 28 / ex. 1–4	Schüler-CD 1/30 Lehrer-CD 2/1–4, 5, 6 KV 1a–c Folie 7	
Language 1 *Sunday lunch*	44–45	Eine Familiendiskussion verstehen	Die *self*-Pronomen und *each other* verwenden	S. 29 / ex. 5–7 S. 30 / ex. 8	Lehrer-CD 2/7	G11, 12
Talkwise *Meet halfway*	46	Einen Kompromiss schließen Streitgespräche verstehen und beurteilen	Useful phrases: *Finding a compromise*	S. 31 / ex. 10–12	Schüler-CD 1/31 Lehrer-CD 2/8–9, 10 DVD: A working day, Part A	
Language 2 *Chatroom messages*	47–48	Einen Internet-Chat verstehen Ratschläge erteilen	Theoretisch erfüllbare Bedingungen mit *if-clauses type 2* ausdrücken Regelfindung: *Tenses in if-clauses type 1* R: *If-clauses type 1*	S. 32 / ex. 13–15 S. 33 / ex. 16, 17	KV 2–4	G13
Language 3 *A letter to an agony aunt*	49	Über Beziehungsprobleme lesen und sprechen Über entscheidende Ereignisse im eigenen Leben berichten	Nicht erfüllbare Bedingungen mit *if-clauses type 3* ausdrücken Regelfindung: *If-clauses types 1–3*	S. 34 / ex. 18, 19	Folie 8 DVD: A working day, Part B	G13
Skills *Telephone messages*	50	Telefonnachrichten auf einem Anrufbeantworter verstehen Nachrichten hinterlassen und annehmen	*Listening skills*: Anrufbeantworter Useful phrases: *Telephone messages*	S. 35 / ex. 20–22	Lehrer-CD 2/11–13 KV 5	
Text *Home alone*	51–53	Einen Sketch lesen und verstehen	*How to*: Ein Theaterstück aufführen Das Wortfeld *family life* erweitern *Writing texts*: Ein Theaterprogramm erstellen	S. 36 / ex. 23–26	Schüler-CD 1/32–36 Lehrer-CD 2/14–18 KV 6–8 Folie 9	
Wordwise	54	Den Wortschatz der Unit umwälzen und vernetzen Personen beschreiben Die Wortwahl in einem Song untersuchen	*Adjectives and their opposites* Word stress	S. 37 / ex. 27	Lehrer-CD 2/19, 20 KV 9, 10	

Abschnitt	SB-Seiten	Ziele	Wortschatz/Grammatik & skills	WB-Übungen	CD-Tracks Kopiervorlagen Folien DVD	Gramm. Anhang (SB)
Check-out	55	Selbstkontrolle Die Lernziele der Unit 3 überprüfen	Wortschatz- und Grammatikschwerpunkte der Unit: *Useful phrases, self-pronouns* und *each other, if-clauses types 1-3*	S. 38/*ex.* 30–32		
⟨Text⟩ *A series of unfortunate events*		Einen Auszug aus einem Roman eigenständig erschließen		S. 39	Schüler-CD 1/37 Lehrer-CD 2/21	

Unit 3 Living together

Hinweise

LANDESKUNDE

The Harry Enfield Show is a British sketch show starring Harry Enfield and Paul Whitehouse. It was first broadcast on BBC Two in 1990. One of the regular characters included in the show is Kevin, a teenager like every other teenager, who ruins his parents' lives with his refusal to do anything. Kevin hates his parents, he is lazy, he wants to do his own thing and he never listens to others.

The Royle Family is a popular British television sitcom, which ran for three series between 1998 and 2000. The series is known for its simple production and realistic portrayal of working-class family life at the turn of the millennium. It deals with the lives of the Royles, a working class family in Manchester. Every episode takes place in the family home. Mum, Dad, and their two adolescent children, Denise and Antony, mostly sit in front of the TV in their living room, smoking, talking and bantering.

The Waltons is an American television series (1972–1981) which is set in the 1930's and 1940's, during the Great Depression, continuing through to World War II. The show is about the life of the Walton family, who have their home in the Blue Ridge Mountains of Virginia. John and Olivia Walton, the parents, live with their seven children and John's parents on Walton's Mountain. The story of the family's life is told through the eyes of John-Boy, the eldest son, who dreams of attending college and becoming a famous writer. Many people still remember the signature scene which closed almost every episode: The family house lies in darkness, but there is one light in an upstairs window. Through voice-overs, two or more characters have a very short, often humorous conversation. Then they say goodnight to each other.

Starting out as a family cartoon on TV on January 14, 1990 *The Simpsons* is the longest-running primetime animated TV series in history. So far the show has aired more than 400 episodes in 19 seasons and *The Simpsons Movie*, a feature-length film, was released worldwide on July 26, 2007. The show is a parody of the 'Middle American' lifestyle. The Simpsons live in the fictional town of Springfield which is inhabited by a wide range of different characters. The title family consists of
- Homer Simpson who works as a safety inspector at the local nuclear power plant. He is a man who loves his family and will do anything to prove that.
- Marge, his wife, who tries to keep peace in her family. She is a loving mother and homemaker, but has briefly tried out a number of careers outside the home (e.g. police officer, anti-violence activist).
- Bart, a 10-year-old provocateur, who is the eldest child and only son of Homer and Marge. Bart's interests include skateboarding, comic books, video games and terrorizing Lisa.
- Lisa, an intelligent and precocious 8-year-old girl, who is wise beyond her years. She plays the saxophone and is the vegetarian member of the family.
- Maggie, the baby of the family, who conveys a wide range of emotions via her pacifier-sucking noises.

STORYLINE

Im Mittelpunkt der Unit steht die Begegnung mit den Pattersons, einer Familie mit drei heranwachsenden Kindern im Teenageralter. Das tägliche Familienleben ist durch typische Probleme gekennzeichnet. Die beiden Töchter/Zwillinge haben häufig Streit; der Sohn kommt sonntags nicht aus dem Bett und die Eltern stehen zwischen zwei Generationen. Auf der einen Seite müssen sie mit der Erziehung der Kinder klar kommen, die eine kurze Abwesenheit der Eltern für eine unerlaubte Party im Elternhaus nutzen. Andererseits müssen sie sich aber auch um den hilfsbedürftigen Großvater kümmern, der nicht mehr alleine und ohne Betreuung leben kann.

| | | Check-in | **3** |

Check-in

Seite 42–43

Ziele
- Den individuellen Wortschatz erweitern: Wortfeld *family life*
- Sich über bekannte Fernsehsendungen austauschen
- Über das eigene Familienleben berichten

Text/Fotos **Living together** Seite 42–43

Ziel • Über beliebte TV-Sendungen sprechen

Wortschatz *to meet, wise, to brush one's teeth, or, pip, to grow, to eat up, crust, to go curly, to marry, bad luck, hat, to tell a lie, lie, (not) any more, vegetarian, to split up, to get on, to behave, twin, to drive someone crazy, selfish, to tidy (up), 2L8 (= too late), UR (= you are), I don't care!, microwave, frozen, Brussels sprout, DIY (= Do-it-yourself)*

Methodisches Vorgehen
- SB geschlossen. L erkundigt sich zur Einstimmung nach aktuellen Fernsehsendungen, die die S gerne bzw. regelmäßig sehen. Die S nennen entsprechende Sendungen und beantworten kurz in 1–2 Sätzen die Frage: *What is the show about?*
- L lässt – falls bisher nicht genannt – die Namen einiger angloamerikanischer TV-Serien nennen, die auch bei uns bekannt sind und leitet anschließend zu den Szenenfotos im SB über: *Let's look at some scenes from British and American TV shows.*

 L Üben **1 Listening: Favourite TV shows** Seite 42

HV-Text
Dialogue 1
Girl: Harry Enfield's show is on tonight on cable.
Boy: I've seen it so many times.
Girl: He does some great characters. My favourite is Kevin the teenager. He reminds me of you!
Boy: What do you mean, he reminds you of me?
Girl: He's always angry, and he always says "I hate you!" to his parents.
Boy: Oh, yeah – I know how he feels! But he changes, doesn't he? Something happens and he becomes the perfect son.
Girl: Yeah, but that's only a dream, remember?

Dialogue 2
Girl: I'd like to watch *The Royle Family* tonight.
Boy: The royal family? So you're a fan of Prince William, are you? Or is it Harry?
Girl: No, not the real royal family. I mean *The Royle Family*. 'Royle' with an 'e' at the end.
Boy: Oh, yeah, that. I've never watched it. What's it about?
Girl: Well, it's about a family from the north of England. Mum, Dad, their daughter Denise and the son Anthony. But nothing happens in the show. All the action takes place in the living room, and they just sit around all day and watch TV.
Boy: Sounds like most British families. Boring!
Girl: I know, but it's really, really funny.

Dialogue 3
Girl: American families on TV are different, aren't they?
Boy: What's that old American show about that big family with hundreds of children? The oldest boy is called something like John-Boy.
Girl: Oh, you mean *The Waltons*! They only have seven children, not hundreds!

3 Check-in

Boy: Everything is always so perfect. Good night, John-Boy! Good night, Elizabeth!
Girl: I know. They're so nice to each other all the time. Not like in real life.
Boy: But Grandpa Zeb is a bit like our grandpa. Hard on the outside, but with a soft heart.

Dialogue 4

Boy: I think *The Simpsons* is like a real American family.
Girl: Really? I've never seen it. Isn't there a woman with big blue hair?
Boy: That's Marge, the mother. She and Homer have three children – Bart, Lisa and the baby. Bart says things like "Eat my shorts" and "Don't have a cow, man!".
Girl: "Eat my shorts"?
Boy: Yes, it's like "Get lost" or something. And Lisa always says, "If anyone needs me, I'll be in my room."
Girl: Sounds just like our sister when she's fed up. But why "Don't have a cow, man!"?
Boy: That's because Lisa doesn't eat meat. It all started when they went to a zoo and Lisa saw some sheep …

Ziel
- Die Bildbeschreibung üben
- Kurze Gespräche über englische und amerikanische Familienserien verstehen und auswerten

Wortschatz *scene, in*

Methodisches Vorgehen

Pre-listening:
- a) SB geöffnet; Arbeit im Plenum oder in PA (*Think-Pair-Share*-Methode). Die S beschreiben nacheinander die vier Szenenfotos und stellen Vermutungen darüber an, worum es in diesen TV-Sendungen geht. Hierbei sollen Ideen zum Themenbereich *family life* entwickelt und der Wortschatz reaktiviert bzw. erweitert werden (→ ggf. zweisprachige Wörterbücher einsetzen).
- Zusammentragen der Ergebnisse im Plenum. Themenrelevanter Wortschatz wird von den S in ihrem *folder* gesammelt.

While-listening:
- b) L leitet von der Aussage der Szenenfotos zur Thematik des HV-Textes über. Die S legen ein Lösungsraster für ihre Notizen an.
- L präsentiert die Tonaufnahme zweimal, die S machen sich Notizen. Vergleich der Lösungen im Plenum. Hierbei soll zugleich überprüft werden, welche Aspekte, die in a) genannt wurden, auch in der Tonaufnahme erwähnt werden.

Post-Listening:
- c) kann nach einer kurzen Sammlungsphase (z. B. *mindmap*) zur Übung von Kurzvorträgen vor der Klasse (*a one-minute talk*) genutzt werden. Nach einer angemessenen Vorbereitungszeit wird ggf. durch Losentscheid festgelegt, wer seine TV-Familie und deren Probleme im Plenum vorstellt.

> **TIP**
> Bei der Bildbeschreibung auf die Verwendung des *present tense (progressive/simple)* achten

> Auch als HA geeignet

Erweiterung **Did you know?**
- L schreibt die folgenden Fragen auf eine Folie:
    1. *How many hours did mothers spend in the kitchen in the 1950s?*
        a) *seven* b) *ten* c) *thirteen*
    2. *How many hours do mothers spend in the kitchen today?*
        a) *six* b) *eight* c) *ten*
    3. *How many British children live with just one parent?*
        a) *one in four* b) *one in ten* c) *one in twenty*
    4. *How many hours do British children between four and 15 years old watch TV a week?*
        a) *nine* b) *seventeen* c) *twenty-one*
    5. *How many of these hours are children's TV?*
        a) *four* b) *five* c) *six*

Check-in 3

- Die S beraten über die richtigen Antworten mit einem/r Partner/in oder in Kleingruppen. Vergleich mit den Angaben im SB. Für jede richtige Antwort gibt es einen Punkt. Anschließend vergleichen die S die Zahlen mit ihren eigenen Erfahrungswerten.

Lösung

Conversation	Name of TV show	What about?
1	Harry Enfield Show	family with teenage son (Kevin: always angry, but changes)
2	The Royle Family	family from the North of England, no action – sit in living room + watch TV
3	The Waltons	American family, seven children → not like real life/always too nice
4	The Simpsons	real American family (Marge, Homer, Bart, Lisa, baby = Maggie), say funny things, sound like 'real' people

Erweiterung: 1c); 2a); 3a); 4b); 5b)

Tipps für junge Lehrer
Es empfiehlt sich in diesem Zusammenhang, die *family words (father, mother, uncle, niece, cousin, etc.)* zu wiederholen bzw. zu ergänzen. L festigt hierbei Aussprache und Orthographie (z. B. *aunt, daughter, son*).

Material
L 2/1–4
Ggf. Leerfolie, Wörterbücher

Üben   **2 The Pattersons**   Seite 43

Ziel
- Die Bildbeschreibung üben
- Einfachen persönlichen Mitteilungen/Notizen Informationen entnehmen

Wortschatz *each other*

Methodisches Vorgehen
- L schreibt die Bildüberschrift *Meet the Pattersons* an die Tafel, die S öffnen die Bücher und lassen das Foto 1–2 Minuten stumm auf sich wirken.
- „Blitzlicht": Nach kurzer Bedenkzeit äußert sich jede/r S zu der im Foto dargestellten Situation (nur **1–2 Sätze** pro S!). Die Aufforderung, sich zu äußern, kann durch die Weitergabe eines Symbols (hier vielleicht eine Fernbedienung für TV/DVD o. Ä.) unterstützt werden. Die Einzeläußerungen werden weder von L noch von den Mitschülern kommentiert.
- Zusätzlicher Wortschatz wird bei Bedarf durch L eingeführt, erläutert und an die Seitentafel geschrieben.
- Anschließend gemeinsames Lesen der Fragen im SB und Klären des konkreten Arbeitsauftrags. Weiteres Vorgehen nach der *Think-Pair-Share*-Methode:
  - Der Textsorte (persönliche Mitteilung/Notiz/Hinweis) entsprechend lesen die S die sieben Texte zuerst still in Einzelarbeit.
  - Bearbeitung des konkreten Arbeitsauftrags in PA.
  - Vergleich der Ergebnisse mit anderen Schülerpaaren.
  - Vorbereitung der Rückmeldung an das Plenum.
- Die Besprechung der Ergebnisse erfolgt im Plenum. L hält die S dazu an, ihre Aussagen mit Zitaten aus den Texten zu belegen.
- Alternativ kann die schriftliche Auswertung der Kurztexte auch in die Hausaufgabe verlagert werden.

> **TIP**
> Die Kernpunkte der Schülerbeiträge sollten von den S in *keywords* schriftlich festgehalten werden, da sie Grundlage des Partnergesprächs in *ex. 3* sind

Auch als HA geeignet

Erweiterung
- KV 1a–c: **The Pattersons**: L hängt die ggf. auf DIN A3-Format vergrößerten und laminierten Fotos im Klassenraum auf. Die S schauen sich die Fotos der Reihe nach an und lassen sie einige Zeit auf sich wirken. Danach wählt jede/r S für sich ein Bild aus und notiert seine Ideen dazu auf einem Blatt Papier (Gedanken, Gefühle, Assoziationen, Stimmungen, usw., aber keine konkreten Hinweise auf die abgebildeten Personen!). L sammelt die Zettel ein, mischt sie und

verteilt sie neu an die S. Diese lesen die Notizen und versuchen eine Verbindung zu einem der Fotos herzustellen. Die S hängen die Notizzettel zu den Fotos, die ihrer Meinung nach am ehesten zu den Notizen passen. Diskussion der Ergebnisse im Plenum.
- **Folie 7: Feelings** übt das Beschreiben von Gefühlen im Allgemeinen sowie im Hinblick auf das Zusammenleben in der Familie anhand von Fotos.

Lösung *Individuelle S-Antworten*

Material
Workbook S. 28/1, 2
Kopiervorlage 1a–c
Folie 7

> **!**
>
> **TIPPS VON MARIO RINVOLUCRI – THE ALTERNATIVE WAY**
>
> **Family sayings**
> **Meet the Pattersons** (Grandpa Patterson's wise words, p. 43)
>
> a) In preparation, think of some of the wise things your parents and grandparents said to you. Just to get you thinking, here are some of the childhood injunctions I remember:
>
> My German Nan: „Morgen, Morgen, nur nicht heute, sagen alle faulen Leute."
> My mother: „Lift your feet up – shoe leather costs money!"
> My father: „Mario, distraction will be your ruin …"
>
> Forget mine and prepare three or four wise dicta you remember from your childhood.
>
> b) In class write these up on the board, high in the top left hand corner. Ask pupils to come and write parental injunctions from their family up on the board. Tell the pupils to write these in English if they can and if not in German. Fill the board with this wisdom!
>
> c) With the help of the pupils translate all the utterances that are in German into English. Rub the German sentences out as you go along.
>
> d) Group the pupils in fours to decide which of the sayings on the board they would feel happy exposing their own children to. Ask them to choose the three they feel most appropriate for the next generation.
>
> e) Have the board wiped clean. Ask each group to write up the three sayings they are happy to pass on to the next generation.
>
> *Pluses:* In this activity pupils draw on powerful language from their home environment. This naturally comes in mother tongue and so the language challenge is to re-render it in English. In the exercise deep, emotive language from home is 'transformed' into middle-distance English, thus making the target language a bit more emotionally real and close.
>
> *Minuses:* Some introverted pupils feel embarrassed in this sort of activity – don't press them. If they don't want to contribute family sayings they can 'pass'.

Üben   **3 Your turn: Family life**   Seite 43

Ziel
- Das Familienleben der Lehrbuchfamilie mit der eigenen Erfahrungswelt vergleichen

Methodisches Vorgehen
- Die S vergleichen zunächst jede/r für sich das, was sie bisher über die Pattersons erfahren haben (siehe *keywords ex.* 2) mit ihrer eigenen Familie und sam-

| | | Check-in | Language 1 | 3 |

meln ihre Ergebnisse in einer einfachen Liste: *What is different?/What is the same?*
- Die S besprechen ihre Ideen mit einem/r Partner/in.
- Abschließende Gesprächsrunde im Plenum.

Lösung | *Individuelle S-Antworten*

Material
Workbook S. 28/3

◉s ◉L **Üben** | **4 Listening: A telephone message** | Seite 43

HV-Text Cleaning lady:
Hello, er … it's me. I don't know if you remember me, but I'm the lady who does the cleaning for your father. Anyway, I had a bit of a shock when I went to his house this afternoon. He was sitting in front of the TV in a cold room. He hadn't eaten anything that day, and he hadn't shopped for two days. I made him a hot bath and a nice cup of tea. Then I went shopping for him. But it's not really my job to do that, Mr Patterson, and I thought you should know. I'm worried about your father, Mr Patterson. So could you call me back, please? My number is 01753 529564. Thank you and bye.

Ziel
- Einer Telefonnachricht zielgerichtet Informationen entnehmen

Wortschatz *telephone, cleaning lady, answerphone*

Methodisches Vorgehen
Pre-listening:
- L lenkt die Aufmerksamkeit der S auf *Grandpa Patterson* und fordert sie auf, sich in einem kurzen *brainstorming* Gedanken über den Großvater zu machen. Mögliche Leitfragen: *How old is he? Where does he live? Could there be any problems? etc.*

While-listening:
- a) L präsentiert die Tonaufnahme zweimal, die S machen sich Notizen *(key-words only!)*. Vergleich der Lösungen erst in PA, dann im Plenum.

Post-listening:
- b) Diese anspruchsvolle Aufgabe (Differenzierung nach oben) wird im Plenum bearbeitet. Die S entwickeln mündlich mögliche Lösungsstrategien, die gemeinsam diskutiert werden.

Lösung
Message from cleaning lady: had a bit of a shock
- *Grandpa sitting in front of TV in the cold living room; not eaten that day; not shopped for two days*
- *made him a hot bath and tea; went shopping → not her job*
- *worried; asks Mr Patterson to call her back*

Material
◉s 1/30
◉L 2/5, 6
Workbook S. 28/4

Language 1

Seite 44–45

Ziele
- Die Form und Funktion der Reflexivpronomen kennen lernen
- Eine Familiendiskussion verstehen

◉L **Text** | **Sunday lunch** | Seite 44

Ziel
- Ein Gespräch am Mittagstisch verstehen

3 Language 1

Wortschatz *to enjoy oneself, himself, to help oneself (to), themselves, to decide, yourself, extra, to stand, myself, yourselves, to get dressed, old people's home, to relax, ourselves*

Strukturen
- *Reflexive pronouns*

Methodisches Vorgehen
- Der Textsorte entsprechend kann der Dialog als kombinierter Hör-/Leseverstehenstext behandelt werden. Zuerst SB geschlossen, Einsatz der Tonaufnahme von CD. Anschließend kurzes *brainstorming* anhand der *wh-questions*.
- Dann SB geöffnet, die S lesen leise mit.
- L und die S erstellen gemeinsam eine Liste der wichtigsten Informationen zu jeder Person, die in einer Tabelle festgehalten werden (siehe TA).
- Die S fassen die Ergebnisse mündlich zusammen. Als schriftliche Hausaufgabe listen sie die Probleme auf, die es in der Familie Patterson gibt.

TA

Mrs Patterson	
Mr Patterson	
Amy	
Mel	
Jake	

Erweiterung
- Zur Vorbereitung auf den Textschwerpunkt der Unit und die anschließende *How to*-Übung können die S in Vierergruppen eine kurze szenische Umsetzung dieser typischen Familiensituation einüben. Nach Möglichkeit lernen die S ihren Text auswendig; leistungsschwächere S dürfen eine *cue card* verwenden, um Texthänger zu vermeiden.
- Alternativ bereiten die S in GA eigene Rollenspiele zu ähnlichen Familiensituationen vor; anschließend Präsentation der Rollenspiele vor der Klasse.

Material
L 2/7

Üben **1 Funny or not?**   Seite 44

Ziel
- Über typische Situationen im Familienalltag sprechen
- Die eigene Meinung darlegen und begründen

Methodisches Vorgehen
- a) + b) sollten sofort im Anschluss an die Präsentation und die Besprechung des Dialogtextes bearbeitet werden, d. h. die neue Grammatik *(reflexive pronouns)* wird erst in *ex.* 2 angesprochen.
- a) Die S tauschen sich im freien Gruppengespräch über typische Familiensituationen aus.
- Die anspruchsvolle Teilaufgabe b) wird nach dem Gruppengespräch im Plenum weiter vertieft.

Erweiterung
- Alternativ kann b) zur Textproduktion (hier: eigene Stellungnahme) genutzt werden: Nach Beendigung der GA bzw. der Besprechung im Plenum verfasst jede/r S einen ersten Entwurf (*first draft*); darauf folgt *peer editing* in Dreier-/ Vierergruppen. Die Reinschrift erfolgt als Hausaufgabe.

Lösung | *Individuelle S-Antworten* |

Tipps für junge Lehrer In b) lässt sich gut die „Methode 66" anwenden: Die Lerngruppe wird so aufgeteilt, dass jeweils sechs S sechs Minuten lang über eine Frage/ein Thema sprechen (hier: *What do you think of the Pattersons?*). Durch die Begrenzung der Zeit und der Gruppengröße wird ein gewisser Erwartungsdruck erzeugt, der die S dazu bringen soll, rasch zur Sache zu kommen. Der Vorteil liegt darin, dass alle S zu

Wort kommen können und die Redeangst im Vergleich zum Plenum meist deutlich reduziert ist.

Üben	**2 What do the Pattersons say?**	Seite 44
Ziel	• Erste Bewusstmachung der *reflexive pronouns*	
Strukturen	• *Reflexive pronouns*	
Methodisches Vorgehen	• Gemeinsames Lesen des Beispiels im SB. Dann schriftliche Bearbeitung in Einzelarbeit und Partnerkontrolle. Ergebnissicherung im Plenum unter Einbeziehung der *Grammar*-Box auf S. 45.	Auch als HA geeignet
	• Die Aufgabe kann auch zuerst mündlich im Unterricht und dann schriftlich als Hausaufgabe bearbeitet werden.	
Lösung	1 *"Everyone can help themselves to vegetables."* 2 *"Then help yourself to extra sprouts."* 3 *"I'll make myself a sandwich."* 4 *"I've just hurt myself with this knife!"* 5 *"Do it yourself, Jake! This isn't a hotel, you know."*	

Üben	**3 *Myself* or *me*?**	Seite 45
Ziel	• Eine Regel für die Verwendung der Reflexivpronomen erkennen und anwenden	
Wortschatz	*reflexive, herself, to turn off, itself*	
Strukturen	• *Reflexive pronouns vs. personal pronouns*	**TIP** G 11
Methodisches Vorgehen	a) Zunächst überlegt jede/r S die Lösung in Einzelarbeit. Dann Besprechung und Ergebnissicherung im Plenum. Die S formulieren eine einfache Regel für die Verwendung der Reflexivpronomen. Erst danach wird im Grammatikanhang nachgelesen.	
	• Im Anschluss sollte unmittelbar Teilaufgabe b) zur Überprüfung und Festigung mündlich in PA bearbeitet werden; anschließend Vergleich im Plenum.	
	• In leistungsschwächeren Lerngruppen kann b) auch als schriftliche Hausaufgabe bearbeitet werden.	Auch als HA geeignet
Lösung	b) 1 *me* 2 *herself* 3 *herself* 4 *himself* 5 *herself* 6 *me*	**Material** *Workbook* S. 29/5

!

TIPPS VON MARIO RINVOLUCRI – THE ALTERNATIVE WAY

Quantification dictation
Myself or *me*? (p. 45)

a) Dictate the sentences below to the class. Each pupil should complete the sentence writing in the age which was true for them. Have one average-level pupil do his/her dictation on the board.

1. I could feed myself by around the age of ... (read with rising intonation)
2. I was able to get dressed by myself when I was ... (check that everybody remembers to quantify)
3. I could go to the toilet on my own by the time I was ...
4. I could read to myself by ...
5. I began to do up my car seat belt myself when I was ...
6. They allowed me to cross the road by myself when I got to around ...
7. My parents let me go to school on my own at something like ...
8. I taught myself to swim at ...

3 Language 1

> b) Group the pupils in fours to share those first moments of independence!
>
> c) Get the class to help correct the pupil's text on the board.
>
> *Pluses:* This little autobiographical trip helps make the use of 'myself' more grounded and real. Anchoring the language in the teenagers' own experience is one way of ensuring fast and deep learning.
>
> *Minuses:* Any personalisation runs the risk, with a few pupils, of feeling invasive.
>
> *Acknowledgement:* This technique comes from *Dictation Many Ways*, Paul Davis et al., Cambridge University Press, 1986.

Üben	**4 Reflexive in German, not in English**	Seite 45
Ziel	• Vom deutschen Sprachgebrauch abweichende, nicht reflexive Verben erkennen und anwenden	
Wortschatz	*to call*	
Strukturen	• *Reflexive verbs (German) vs. non-reflexive verbs (English)*	
Methodisches Vorgehen	• a) Die S bearbeiten die fünf Sätze in Einzelarbeit. Besprechung im Plenum und Vergleich mit dem deutschen Sprachgebrauch. • b) In PA formulieren die S weitere Sätze unter Verwendung der übrigen sechs Verben; Partnerkontrolle. Anschließend werden zu jedem Verb einige Beispielsätze im Plenum abgerufen. • Eine schriftliche Bearbeitung kann für die Hausaufgabe vorgesehen werden.	Auch als HA geeignet
Erweiterung	• Pantomime: Ein/e S führt eine Tätigkeit vor, die im Deutschen mit einem reflexiven Verb ausgedrückt wird. Die Mitschüler erraten die Tätigkeit und entscheiden, ob das englische Verb ebenfalls reflexiv ist, z. B.: *Are you washing yourself?/Are you getting dressed?/Have you hurt yourself?*	
Lösung	a) 1 *They (Jake and Miriam) split up (last night).* 2 *She (Amy) has decided to become a vegetarian.* 3 *He (Jake) hasn't got dressed yet.* 4 *At lunch he (Jake) should sit down first.* 5 *He (Jake) is in a hurry because he is meeting his friends in ten minutes.* b) *Individuelle S-Antworten*	**Material** *Workbook* S. 29/6

Üben	**5 *Themselves* or *each other*?**	Seite 45
Ziel	• Den unterschiedlichen Gebrauch von *themselves* und *each other* kennen lernen	
Strukturen	• *themselves vs. each other*	
Methodisches Vorgehen	• Die S erschließen eigenständig den Unterschied in der Verwendung von *themselves* und *each other* anhand der *Tip*-Box im SB. L verweist auf G 11 und G 12 im Grammatikanhang. • Alternativ kann L den Unterschied auch mit Hilfe eines Handspiegels und eines Schülerpaares, das entsprechend vor der Klasse agiert, anschaulich darstellen: *Paula and Charlotte are looking at themselves – and now they are looking at each other.*	**TIP** G 11, 12
Erweiterung	• Die S bilden in Einzelarbeit oder PA weitere Satzpaare. Hierzu dürfen sie das *Dictionary* im Buchanhang nutzen, um geeignete Verben zu finden. Auch als Hausaufgabe möglich.	Auch als HA geeignet

| | | Language 1 | Talkwise | 3 |

| **Lösung** | 1 *The twins are taking a photo of themselves.* 2 *The twins are looking at each other angrily.* 3 *The twins are shouting at each other loudly.* 4 *The twins are doing their homework themselves.* 5 *The twins are looking at themselves./They are enjoying themselves.* |

Material
Workbook S. 29/7

| **Üben** | **6 Stress the subject in a sentence** | Seite 45 |

Ziel
- Die *reflexive pronouns* zur Betonung des Subjekts in einem Satz verwenden

Strukturen
- *Reflexive pronouns*

TIP
G 11c)

Methodisches Vorgehen
- Zu Beginn spielt L, ggf. mit zwei eingeweihten S, eine kurze Szene vor, die aus der Klassensituation heraus die Funktion des Reflexivpronomens am Ende eines Satzes verdeutlicht. Dann gemeinsames Lesen von G 11c).
- Bei dieser Aufgabe ist eine mündliche Bearbeitung ausreichend; sie kann auch in PA durchgeführt werden.

Erweiterung
- PA: Analog zu den Sätzen im SB formuliert jede/r S fünf Sätze, auf die ein/e Partner/in unter Verwendung eines Reflexivpronomens reagieren kann; z. B. *My sister can feed the dog today. – No, you must/should do it yourself.*

| **Lösung** | 2 … *myself.* 3 … *told me herself.* 4 … *build it ourselves!* |

Material
Workbook S. 30/8

Talkwise

Seite 46

Ziele
- Streitgespräche in der Familie verstehen und beurteilen
- Mit Hilfe von *Useful phrases* einen Kompromiss schließen

| **Üben** | **Meet halfway** | Seite 46 |

Wortschatz *to meet halfway*

Methodisches Vorgehen
- Die folgenden drei Aufgaben bilden ein in sich geschlossenes Lernarrangement zum Bereich „Hören/Sprechen" und sollten deshalb unbedingt im Zusammenhang bearbeitet werden.

| **Üben** | **1 Before you listen** | Seite 46 |

Ziel
- Mündliche Aussagen auf ihre Wirkung hin untersuchen und kategorisieren

Wortschatz *to feel sorry for, difference*

Methodisches Vorgehen
- SB geschlossen. L schreibt die Überschrift *Meet halfway* an die Tafel. Die S überlegen in PA, was hier gemeint sein könnte. L: *With a partner, discuss what this phrase means and try to find situations in which people might use it.* Die S vergleichen ihre Ideen im Plenum.
- L fasst die Ergebnisse zusammen und lenkt die Aufmerksamkeit auf den Aspekt des richtigen bzw. angemessenen Sprachgebrauchs in Konfliktsituationen.
- a) + b) L teilt die Klasse in zwei Gruppen ein. Die S der Gruppe A suchen alle „richtigen" *(right way)* und die der Gruppe B alle „falschen" *(wrong way)* Tipps heraus und notieren sie in einer Tabelle (siehe TA). Anschließend Vergleich mit einem/r S derselben Gruppe.

3 Talkwise

- Jede/r S sucht sich eine/n Partner/in aus der jeweils anderen Gruppe. Die S besprechen ihre Listen und diskutieren ggf. Überschneidungen. Anschließend ergänzen sie ihre Tabellen. Ein Schülerpaar kann auf einer Folie arbeiten, die bei der abschließenden Besprechung der Lösungen im Plenum auf den OHP gelegt wird.

TA

Right way	Wrong way
– Ask what the other person thinks. – Show you understand what the other person feels. – Explain your feelings or ideas. – Stay cool. – Show you are listening. – Be polite. – Be positive before you say what you really think. – Walk away if someone gets aggressive.	– Get angry. – Shout. – Always agree with the other person. – Cry – then the other person will feel sorry for you. – Say "You always ..." or "You never ..." a lot.

Erweiterung
- Die S ergänzen die beiden Listen mit eigenen Ideen.

Lösung   a) *Siehe TA*

Material Ggf. Leerfolie

Üben 2 Listening: Right way / wrong way   Seite 46

HV-Text

Dialogue 1

Kim: Why can't I go to Sarah's party?
Dad: Because I said you can't.
Kim: But why? It's not fair!
Dad: Because it's too late. You know the rules. You have to be home by ten.
Kim: Why ten? That's when most parties start! Anyway, all my friends are going. Mum, tell Dad ... !
Mum: No, Dad and I agree. We don't care what your friends do. You're only thirteen!
Kim: Yes! I'm thirteen. This is a party for teenagers, and that's why it's on Saturday night.
Dad: When you're eighteen you can do what you want. But while you're still at school, late nights are not a good thing.
Kim: So I have to sit in my room on a Saturday night while my friends are having fun? I can't do homework non-stop. Anyway, there's no school on Sunday. I can get up late.
Dad: Kim, you're not going to that sort of party, and that's that.
Kim: What do you mean by 'that sort of party'?
Mum: Listen. Sarah's parents are away next weekend. Do they know about the party?
Dad: What? This is news to me! You mean Sarah's parents won't be there?
Kim: Sarah's older sister will be there.
Mum: Oh, no, not her! She's only 17, but she behaves like, well, you know what I mean.
Kim: No, I *don't* know what you mean.
Mum: Sarah will invite older boys. She'll invite men! So 'no' means 'no'!
Kim: OK, so I can't go. Great! I saved my pocket money so I could buy some new clothes for this party, and now I can't wear them.
Mum: That's your problem.
Kim: I can't believe what I'm hearing. Why are you ALWAYS so mean? You HATE me! I'll have a boring Saturday night in my room. Fine. I'm going to practise right NOW!

| | | Talkwise | 3 |

Dialogue 2

Jill: Dad, can we talk about this party on Saturday?
Dad: A party? I don't know anything about it. Tell me.
Jill: Well, you know my friend Katie? It's her party and she's invited me. All my friends will be there, too.
Dad: I see. And what sort of a party will it be?
Jill: Just a normal teenage party. A bit of music, dancing, food, you know. It'll be fun.
Dad: And when is it? What time on Saturday, I mean.
Jill: It starts at ten, and goes on till late.
Dad: Hm. Ten sounds a bit late to me. Ah … here's your mum. What do you think about this? Jill wants to go out on Saturday night. A party at her friend's house.
Mum: Yes, she told me. How do you feel about it?
Dad: Well, I don't mind parties, but it's very late.
Jill: It is Saturday night, Dad. There's no school the next day.
Dad: You've got a point, but if you were out all night, we'd worry about you. There'll be lots of other parties – I really don't think you should go to this one.
Mum: Dad's right, Jill. Ten o'clock is very late to go out for the evening.
Jill: Do you remember that film I went to last month? That finished at midnight.
Dad: That's true, but I was there to pick you and your friend up in the car.
Jill: OK. I've got an idea. If I went to the party at ten, then you could pick me up at midnight. It would be like when I went to the cinema. And my phone would be on all the time, so you can call me if you need to.
Dad: You've worked it out already, haven't you, young lady?
Jill: Well I know it's a bit late, but this way I can be at the party, and you won't have to worry.
Mum: Hm, maybe we can meet halfway.
Jill: Please say yes! Please!
Dad: Well, all right. It's a deal.

Ziel	• Einem HV-Text zielgerichtet Informationen entnehmen
Methodisches Vorgehen	*Pre-listening:* • L leitet zur Thematik der Dialoge über: *Well, you all know that sometimes parents and children have different ideas about what is right or wrong. …* Ein/e S liest den Arbeitsauftrag zu a) laut vor. • Die S erstellen ein *listening grid* zu den vier Hörträgen im SB (siehe TA). *While-listening:* • L präsentiert die Tonaufnahme von CD. Hierbei empfiehlt es sich, die beiden Dialoge separat zu bearbeiten. Die S hören aufmerksam zu und machen sich Notizen im *listening grid*. • Nach erneutem Anhören der Dialoge organisieren die S ihre Notizen in PA. *Post-listening:* • Abschließend Besprechung im Plenum. L oder die S füllen das Lösungsraster an der Tafel/auf Folie aus. • b) Diskussion der Frage im Plenum.

> **TIP**
> In leistungsschwächeren Lerngruppen das Lösungsraster vorgeben

TA

	Dialogue 1	Dialogue 2
What?	go to her friend's party	go to party at her friend's house
How?	only 13 = too young, parents not at home	don't mind parties but think it's very late, think they'd be worried

Why?	all her friends are going	Saturday night = no school the next day, went to a film that finished at midnight
Parents?	say no	say yes

Lösung *Siehe TA*

Material
L 2/8–9
Ggf. Leerfolie

S L **Üben**

Listening: A family problem

Workbook Seite 31

HV-Text Workbook

Mother: I've decided! This family is going to get fit!
Son: Fit, Mum?
Mother: Yes. We're not fit enough.
Father: Who?
Mother: All three of us, Mike. You, too. You're the worst. You're overweight.
Son: Yes, Dad. You said it yourself the other day!
Father: Thank you, Ben!
Mother: I think we should do an activity regularly together, as a family. The problem when you try to keep fit alone is that it's easy just to think – you know – oh, I don't feel like it today. But if the activity is part of our family routine, we'll do it.
Son: I think it sounds like fun.
Father: OK, I suppose we can try it. What kind of activity were you thinking of, Diana?
Mother: I thought we could jog in the park.
Father: Jog in the park, eh? Hm.
Mother: What's wrong with the idea? It's a good, cheap way to get fit, isn't it? I mean, you only need trainers to do it. What do you think, Ben?
Son: Sorry, Mum, but I think it sounds boring. And it's no fun to jog in the rain.
Father: Maybe we could all go swimming together. Is it OK to get wet in a swimming pool, Ben?
Son: Very funny, Dad!
Father: We can also walk to the swimming pool because it's so near. That's healthy, too.
Mother: You're right. And we all enjoy swimming. But the swimming pool is often very full. And then you can't swim because other people are in your way all the time.
Son: That's true. I remember I was there once when you couldn't move!
Father: OK, so what's your suggestion, Ben?
Son: Let's think – I know! Why don't we ride our bikes to get fit? In good weather, of course! But a bike ride is more fun than jogging round the park. At least you aren't looking at the same trees all the time.
Mother: He's got a point. You go further on a bike, so you can visit different places.
Father: I think you two have forgotten how many hills there are around here – too many hills! I'll never be able to get up them on a bike.
Son: Because you're overweight!
Mother: Oh dear, it isn't easy to find an activity we all like. Come on. We have to decide how we're going to get fit. I'm not going to give up …

Material
S 1/31
L 2/10
Workbook S. 31/10

Üben

3 Role play: Meet halfway

Seite 46

Ziel • Einen Kompromiss schließen

Wortschatz *to earn, I see., to mind, You've got a point.*

144

	Talkwise	Language 2	**3**

Methodisches Vorgehen	• a) Die S ordnen die *Useful phrases* den beiden Listen zu. Einzelarbeit; anschließend Partnerkontrolle. Die S ergänzen ggf. die beiden Listen mit eigenen *Useful phrases*. • b) Die S wählen mit einem/r Partner/in eine der im SB vorgegebenen Situationen; leistungsstärkere S denken sich eigene Konfliktsituationen aus. Die Schülerpaare erstellen ihre Dialoge anhand der Vorgaben und bereiten zur Erleichterung des freien Sprechens ggf. *cue cards* vor, auf die jedoch nur zentrale Stichworte und keine ganzen Sätze notiert werden. Einstudieren in PA; anschließend Präsentation der Dialoge im Plenum.	
Lösung	a) A: *Can we talk about …?, What do you think …?, How do you feel about …?, I've got an idea …/Maybe …, A + B: alle Useful phrases möglich* b) *Individuelle S-Antworten*	**Material** Workbook S. 31/11, 12 Im Anschluss an *ex.* 3: *Action UK!* 3, A working day, Part A: *Chasing Pete* sowie *Action UK!* 3, Begleitheft zu den Filmsequenzen, Unit 3 A
Tipps für junge Lehrer	Da aus Zeitgründen in der Regel nur wenige S das Rollenspiel im Plenum präsentieren können, spielen sich je zwei S gegenseitig das Rollenspiel vor. So kommt jeder S zum Zug und in der Kleingruppe ist es oft einfacher, die Leistung der Mitschüler/innen zu beurteilen und konstruktiv Kritik zu üben. Hilfreich kann hier ein Beobachtungsbogen (*assessment sheet*) sein. Auf diesem Weg lässt sich auch festlegen, welche Paare ihr Rollenspiel noch einmal im Plenum vorstellen.	

Language 2

Seite 47–48

> **Ziele**
> • Einen Internet-Chat verstehen
> • Gesetzmäßigkeiten bei der Bildung von Konditionalsätzen Typ II erkennen und anwenden
> • Ratschläge mit Hilfe von Konditionalsätzen Typ II erteilen

Text	**Chatroom messages**	Seite 47
Ziel	• Über Chatrooms sprechen	
Wortschatz	*type, to chat, to turn into, to get rid of, junk, to wish, jealous (of), especially*	
Tipps für junge Lehrer	L sollte vorab klären, inwieweit hier mit Blick auf die Lerngruppe eine weitere kritische Betrachtung von *chatroom activities* sinnvoll sein könnte. Einen lesenswerten Einstieg in die Thematik bietet die „Internet-Fibel für die Grundschule. Unterrichtsmaterialien zu Themen der Internetsicherheit" (http://www.secure-it.nrw.de/_media/pdf/schule/UM_Grundschule_einzel.pdf). Weitere Unterrichtshinweise und Links finden sich bei der Bundesprüfstelle für jugendgefährdende Medien (http://www.bundespruefstelle.de/bmfsfj/generator/bpjm/die-bundespruefstelle,did=53124.html).	
Üben	**1 Sort the messages**	Seite 47
Ziel	• Einen Chatroom-Dialog rekonstruieren	
Methodisches Vorgehen	• L erläutert die Aufgabenstellung. Bearbeitung der Aufgabe in Einzelarbeit oder PA. • In der gemeinsamen Besprechung im Plenum sortieren die S vorbereitete Folienstreifen mit den Chateinträgen auf dem OHP. Zwei leistungsstärkere S fassen Amys Problem und die Antwort von Tess in eigenen Worten mündlich zusammen.	

3 Language 2

| Lösung | B – G – E – H – F – C – A – D | Material
Ggf. Leerfolie |

| Üben | **2 Match the parts** | Seite 47 |

Ziel
- Das Textverständnis durch Zusammenfügen von *if-clause* und *main clause* überprüfen
- Eine Regel zu den *if-clauses type 2* finden

Wortschatz *probably, to translate*

Strukturen
- *If-clauses type 2*

TIP
G 13

Methodisches Vorgehen
- a) Die S bilden die Konditionalsätze durch Kombination der Satzhälften und tragen sie nach *if-clause* und *main clause* getrennt in eine Tabelle ein (siehe TA).
- b) Die S markieren die Verbformen mit unterschiedlichen Farben und benennen die Zeiten. L führt den Begriff *conditional* für die Zeit im *main clause* ein.
- L weist auf die Besonderheit in Satz 6 hin (*If I were you, … → advice*).
- Die Übersetzung der Sätze kann als schriftliche Hausaufgabe erfolgen.

TA

if-clause	main clause
If Tess <u>knew</u> Jake and Mel,	she <u>wouldn't want</u> brothers or sisters.
If Mel and Amy <u>had</u> their own bedrooms,	they <u>wouldn't fight</u> so much.
If they <u>used</u> the hobby room as a bedroom,	they'<u>d have</u> to get rid of some junk.
If Amy <u>had</u> a bigger room than Mel,	Mel <u>would be</u> jealous.
If Mel and Amy <u>tried</u> to build another wall,	it <u>would</u> probably <u>fall</u> down again.
If I <u>were</u> you, Amy,	I'<u>d talk</u> to my sister about the idea first.
↓	↓
simple past	conditional (would + infinitive)

Lösung
a) 1 + c)   2 + e)   3 + a)   4 + f)   5 + d)   6 + b)
b) Siehe TA

Tipps für junge Lehrer
In leistungsschwächeren Lerngruppen können die Bestandteile des Konditionals I (und später des Konditionals II) als visuelle Hilfe auf eine Wandzeitung (= Stück von einer Tapetenrolle) geschrieben und im Klassenzimmer aufgehängt werden.

Material
Workbook S. 32/13
Ggf. Tapetenrolle

TIPPS VON MARIO RINVOLUCRI – THE ALTERNATIVE WAY

Grammar letter – the so-called '2nd conditional'
Chatroom messages (p. 47)

a) To introduce the new grammar, write your pupils a 'grammar letter' about how you would feel and react if you belonged to the other gender group. Your letter might start:

Dear Everybody,
I am sitting at my computer and wondering how things would be if I was a man/a woman, instead of a woman/a man. How would the world look to me? Would people seem different to me? If I were a man/woman I would probably …

Give yourself temporarily to the fantasy and complete a short personal letter to your pupils. Copy the letter so each person gets one.

b) Give out your letter in class. The pupils read it silently.

c) Use the board to explain how this structure works.

d) Ask the pupils to work on their own and write you a letter in which they talk about how they would feel as the other sex. Take in the letters.

e) In the next class go through any mistakes they have made with the target structure.

Variations: You can use the 'grammar letter' technique to present virtually any structure to the class. It is important that your letter really is a letter to the pupils and not just a grammar presentation text. The pupils need to learn something mildly interesting about you and your world. 'Grammar letter' is a generic technique that works across levels.

Pluses: Personalised presentation of structures makes this phase of the lesson much less dry than when you use impersonal texts for the same purpose. Your pupils would have to be anaesthetized not to be interested in you as a person.

Minuses: At first writing 'grammar letters' can mop up too much of your out-of-lesson, professional time. I would suggest that if you take more than 15–20 minutes to create your letter, then this is a technique to bypass.

There is a danger that you may stock-pile 'grammar letters' and end up using the same texts year after year. If the technique begins to taste stale to you, the pupils will pick up on it. They have terrifyingly accurate noses.

Acknowledgement: This activity comes from *Humanising your Coursebook*, ed. Mario Rinvolucri, Delta Publishing, 2002.

Üben	**3 Amy on chat**	Seite 47

Ziel
- Die *if-clauses type 2* anwenden und festigen

Wortschatz on chat

Strukturen
- *If-clauses type 2*

Methodisches Vorgehen
- a) + b) Bearbeitung in Einzelarbeit oder schriftlich als Hausaufgabe.

Auch als HA geeignet

Erweiterung
- Zur weiteren Übung und Festigung kann **KV 2: What would happen if …?** eingesetzt werden.
- Differenzierung nach oben: Leistungsstärkere S können sich zusätzlich eine ähnliche Minigeschichte überlegen, in der Ursache und Wirkung mit Hilfe von Konditionalsätzen ausgedrückt wird.

Lösung
a) 1 *lent* 2 *broke* 3 *would try* 4 *didn't know* 5 *would not need* 6 *was* 7 *was not able to* 8 *would have*
b) *Individuelle S-Antworten*

Tipps für junge Lehrer Die Bearbeitung von Teilaufgabe b) lässt sich so erweitern, dass die S nach der Besprechung der schriftlichen Hausaufgabe zur Ergebnissicherung einen Kurzvortrag *(a one-minute talk)* erarbeiten und diesen dann weitgehend spontan in Kleingruppen oder im Plenum halten.

Material
Workbook S. 32/14
Kopiervorlage 2

3 Language 2

Üben	**4 Imagine!**	Seite 48
Ziel	• Die *if-clauses type 2* anwenden und festigen	
Wortschatz	*purse, comma*	
Strukturen	• *If-clauses type 2* (nachgestellter Hauptsatz)	
Methodisches Vorgehen	• a) L schreibt den Beispielsatz an die Tafel und lässt die Verbformen in Haupt- und Nebensatz von den S unterschiedlich farblich markieren. Ein/e S erklärt zur Wiederholung, wie die *if-clauses type 2* gebildet werden. Anschließend bearbeiten die S die Aufgabe in Einzelarbeit schriftlich; dann Partnerkontrolle bzw. kurze Besprechung im Plenum. • b) Kurze Phase mit Partnergespräch. Die S unterhalten sich entweder mit dem/der Sitznachbarn/in oder bewegen sich für ca. fünf Minuten frei durch die Klasse und sprechen mit möglichst vielen Mitschülern/innen.	**TIP** G 13
Erweiterung	• *Conditional chain*: L gibt einen *if-clause type 2* vor, z. B. *"If I had enough money, I would spend my summer holidays in Canada"*. L fordert einen S auf, den Hauptsatz aufzugreifen und davon ausgehend einen neuen *if-clause type 2* zu bilden, z. B. *"If I spent my summer holidays in Canada, I would go to the Rocky Mountains first"*. Die Kette wird fortgesetzt, bis alle S einmal an der Reihe waren. • Anschließend kann **KV 3: A personality test** eingesetzt werden. Bearbeitung als schriftliche Hausaufgabe möglich.	Auch als HA geeignet
Lösung	a) 2 *If I found £ 1 in the park, I'd pick it up and keep it.* 3 *If I found someone's purse at school, I'd give it to a teacher.* 4 *If I got too much change from a shop assistant, I'd tell him/her about it.* 5 *If I won £ 10,000, I'd save half and buy a boat with the other half.*	**Material** Workbook S. 32/15 Kopiervorlage 3
Üben	**5 Would you ever do this?**	Seite 48
Ziel	• Die *if-clauses type 2* anwenden und festigen	
Strukturen	• *If-clauses type 2* (vorangestellter Hauptsatz)	
Methodisches Vorgehen	• Schriftliche Bearbeitung der Aufgabe in Einzelarbeit; anschließend Partnerkontrolle und Vergleich der Ergebnisse im Plenum. Hierbei werden die zugrunde liegenden Grammatikregeln wiederholt.	Auch als HA geeignet
Lösung	*Erwartungshorizont:* – *I would only read my best friend's diary if he/she asked me to do it.* – *I would only do a bungee jump if I got € 1,000,000 for it.* – *I would only eat cat food if I were a cat.* – *I would only paint my face green if you painted your face blue.* – *I would only learn to speak Chinese if I had to live in China for some time.* – *I would only travel to Alaska if my friends came with me.* – *I would only spend € 1000 on clothes if my parents gave me the money.*	**Material** Workbook S. 33/16
Üben	**6 Your turn: Give advice**	Seite 48
Ziel	• Einen Ratschlag erteilen	
Wortschatz	*advice, difficult*	
Strukturen	• *If I were you, I'd …*	

		Language 2	**3**

Methodisches Vorgehen	• a) L erläutert die Verwendung von *If I were/was you …* bei geöffnetem SB (→ *Tip*-Box). Für leistungsschwächere S kann L auch ein Beispiel mit konkretem Klassenbezug an die Tafel schreiben (z. B. *Look at that. The floor is quite dirty. If I were you, I'd clean it after the lesson.*) und so diese Besonderheit im Sprachgebrauch veranschaulichen. • Die S bearbeiten die Aufgabe schriftlich in Einzelarbeit; anschließend Partnerkontrolle oder Besprechung der Ergebnisse im Plenum. • b) Die S notieren analog zu den Vorgaben in a) weitere „Problemsituationen" und erfragen dann mündlich Rat von einem/r Partner/in. Jedes Paar trägt abschließend das beste Beispiel im Plenum vor. Weitere Sätze (→ Problemstellung + Ratschlag) können in der Hausaufgabe selbstständig gebildet werden.	**TIP** G13b) L weist darauf hin, dass *advice* ein *collective noun* ist und somit keine Pluralform bildet (→ *some advice/pieces of advice*) Auch als HA geeignet

Lösung

Erwartungshorizont:
a) 1 *If I were you, Amy, I'd show her some recipes on the Internet.*   2 *If I were you, Mel, I'd tell her to ask me first.*   3 *If I were you, Jake, I'd go to bed earlier.*   4 *If I were you, Mel, I'd ask her not to do that.*   5 *If I were you, Mel, I'd talk with them about your problem.*   6 *If I were you, girls, I'd discuss this problem with your parents.*

Üben   **7 Revision: If-clauses type 1**   Seite 48

Ziel   • Die *if-clauses type 1* wiederholen und festigen

Strukturen   • *If-clauses type 1*

Methodisches Vorgehen	• Ein/e S liest den Beispielsatz im SB laut vor. L überträgt den Satz an die Tafel und entwickelt gemeinsam mit den S das Tafelbild. Die S benennen die unterschiedlichen *tenses*, die Verbformen werden an der Tafel unterstrichen bzw. farblich markiert. • Die S bearbeiten die Aufgabe schriftlich in Einzelarbeit. Ergänzend sollten v. a. leistungsschwächere S auch hier die Verbformen unterschiedlich farblich markieren. Vergleich im Plenum. • Ein/e S formuliert noch einmal zusammenfassend, was bei der Bildung von Konditionalsätzen Typ I zu beachten ist.	**TIP** Ggf. kann auch der zweite Satz gemeinsam gelöst und an die Tafel geschrieben werden

TA

If-clauses type 1	
if-clause	main clause
If you <u>don't brush</u> your teeth three times a day, If you <u>eat</u> apple pips, ↓ simple present	they <u>will</u> all <u>fall</u> out. a tree <u>will grow</u> in your stomach. ↓ will future

Erweiterung   • KV 4: **A busy family** bietet eine weitere Übungsmöglichkeit auf anspruchsvollem Niveau. Die S können hier unter Verwendung der zu übenden Struktur kurze Dialoge schreiben, einüben und vorspielen.

Lösung

– *If you eat apple pips, a tree will grow in your stomach.*
– *If you don't eat up your crusts, your hair won't get curly.*
– *If you sing at the table, you'll marry a crazy person.*
– *If you put a hat on a bed, that will be bad luck.*
– *If you tell a lie, your nose will grow.*

Material
Workbook S. 33/17
Kopiervorlage 4

3 Language 2

Üben	8 ⟨A poem: I wish⟩		Seite 48

Ziel • Ein Gedicht unter Berücksichtigung formaler Kriterien schreiben

Wortschatz *wish*

Methodisches Vorgehen
- Diese fakultative Aufgabe kann zuerst in Einzelarbeit, dann in PA als *peer editing* durchgeführt werden.
- Erscheint eine Bearbeitung der Aufgabe aus Zeitgründen oder mit Blick auf die Klassensituation nicht möglich, kann der Schreibauftrag als freiwillige Hausaufgabe für interessierte S gestellt werden. Gelungene Texte werden im *folder* abgeheftet, aber nach Möglichkeit auch der Klasse zugänglich gemacht (Vorlesen im Plenum/Wandzeitung).

Auch als HA geeignet

TA
```
I wish I were _____ (+ adjective)
But I am _____ (+ adjective)
I wish I _____ (+ action)
But I _____ (+ negative)
I wish ...
```

Erweiterung
- An dieser Stelle können für interessierte S weitere Möglichkeiten und Wege zum Verfassen eigener kurzer Gedichte angeboten werden. Die S schreiben ihre Texte selbstständig in Frei- oder Vertretungsstunden bzw. zu Hause. L oder kleine „Schüler-Redaktionskonferenzen" lesen und editieren: Gelungene Gedichte werden den Mitschülern/innen zugänglich gemacht.
- Unter dem Titel *Time machine* begeben sich die S auf Zeitreisen in die Vergangenheit oder in die Zukunft. L gibt den Anfang des Gedichts vor:
   If I had a time machine, …
- Darüber hinaus lassen sich andere, für jede Zielgruppe passende Gedichtanfänge dieser Art finden, z. B.:
   If I were invisible, …
   If I were a teacher for a day, …
   If I played in the Bundesliga, …
   If I were a rich girl/boy, …
- http://ettcweb.lr.k12.nj.us/forms/wish.htm: Hier können die S online ein *Instant wish poem* schreiben und ausdrucken oder als Anhang einer E-Mail verschicken.

Auch als HA geeignet

Lösung *Individuelle S-Antworten*

Tipps für junge Lehrer Dieses recht einfach strukturierte Gedicht kann v. a. für leistungsstärkere S gut für ein systematisches Schreibtraining (*texts as models for my own texts*) genutzt werden. Eingangs liest L das Gedicht bei geschlossenem SB laut vor (*Listen and enjoy the poem.*). Anschließend bei geöffnetem SB kurzes Gespräch über den Inhalt. Gemeinsame Erarbeitung des Gedichtaufbaus im Unterrichtsgespräch (→ gleichmäßiger Wechsel des Satzanfangs: *I/But*, steter Wechsel der Verbformen: *wish – were/could … – present form of be/can*). Hinweis auf die Variation in den letzten beiden Zeilen. Das Gerüst für den Gedichtanfang kann L an die Tafel/auf Folie schreiben. Die S füllen die Lücken und schreiben dann in Anlehnung an das Modell weiter, wobei sich die Wünsche auch auf andere Personen/Dinge beziehen dürfen und die Abfolge individuell verändert werden kann. Die so entstehenden Gedichte werden möglichst auswendig gelernt und in Gruppen/im Plenum vorgetragen.

Stationenlernen Im Anschluss an *Language* 2 kann das Stationenlernen durchgeführt werden (**Kopiervorlagen 11–17**). Der Arbeitsbericht hierzu findet sich als **KV 17** bei Unit 1.

Material
Kopiervorlagen 11–16
Kopiervorlage 17 (Unit 1)
Ggf. Leerfolie
Poster, Filzstifte für Wandzeitung

Language 3

Seite 49

Ziele
- Kurze Texte über Beziehungsprobleme lesen und verstehen
- Nicht erfüllbare Bedingungen ausdrücken
- Regeln für die Bildung und die Verwendung der Konditionalsätze Typ I–III formulieren
- Über wichtige Ereignisse im eigenen Leben berichten

Text **A letter to an agony aunt** Seite 49

Ziel
- Einem Text zielgerichtet Informationen entnehmen

Wortschatz *agony aunt, boyfriend, to go out with, to go crazy, secret, to listen to*

Methodisches Vorgehen

Pre-reading:
- SB geschlossen. Falls vorhanden blättert L ein Exemplar einer britischen/amerikanischen Jugendzeitschrift durch und kommentiert dabei, welche Art von Artikeln dort abgedruckt sind. Bei der Leserbriefseite hält L inne und erläutert im Gespräch mit den S ausführlich, was eine *agony aunt* ist. L schreibt den Begriff an die Tafel.
- Die S nennen typische Probleme bzw. Konfliktsituationen, in denen Jugendliche solche Briefe schreiben, um sich Rat zu holen. Sammeln der Beiträge an der Tafel.

While-reading:
- SB geöffnet. L leitet zum Text über: *Let's read Linda's letter to the agony aunt of TEEN BUZZ magazine and try to find out what her problem is. Read the text and make notes.*
- Die S lesen (= *skimming*) Marys Brief und machen sich Notizen; die Antwort der *agony aunt* sollte vorher zugedeckt werden. Anschließend Vergleich im Plenum und Ergänzung des Tafelbildes.
- Die S formulieren mündlich Ratschläge, die eine Kummerkastentante in diesem Fall geben könnte. Anschließend gemeinsames Lesen der Antwort. Ein/e S liest laut vor. Ergänzung des TA.

Letter to an agony aunt can be about:
- problems with parents
- no friends
- problems with a/the best friend
- problems at school
- personal problems (hair, weight, etc.)
- …

Linda's problem is:
- best friend Tina not talking to her/doesn't know what to do
- told Tina that her boyfriend had other girls → got angry
- Linda talked to her mum → contacted Tina's parents (Luke = secret boyfriend!) → Tina not allowed to see Luke again/must stay at home on Saturday

Mary's advice:
- did the right thing/real friend
- but: stories really true?
- more careful with words
- Tina will find out for herself if Luke is really that bad

Üben **1 Complete the sentences** Seite 49

Ziel
- Bewusstmachung der *if-clauses type 3*

3 | Language 3

Strukturen	• *If-clauses type 3*
Methodisches Vorgehen	• Ein/e S liest den Beispielsatz laut vor; L schreibt ihn an die Tafel oder auf Folie.
	• Nachdem die S ein weiteres Beispiel für einen *if-clause type 3* im Text gefunden haben, notiert L diesen Satz, leicht verändert, ebenfalls an der Tafel und leitet die Bildung des *conditional perfect (would + have + past participle)* gemeinsam mit den S ab.
	• Schriftliche Bearbeitung in Einzelarbeit oder PA; Vergleich der Ergebnisse im Plenum.

TIP
G 13 c
Die Bildung des *past perfect* sollte ins Tafelbild aufgenommen werden

TA

> If Linda <u>hadn't told</u> her sister ..., they <u>wouldn't have split up</u>.
> If Linda <u>hadn't said</u> anything, Tina <u>wouldn't have been</u> so angry with her.
>   ↓   ↓
>   past perfect   conditional perfect
>   had + past participle   would + have + past participle

• Abschließend benennen die S die Konditionalsätze in Marys Antwort (*if-clauses type 3*: *If you hadn't said anything, you wouldn't have been a real friend./If you had been more careful with your words, maybe Tina would have listened to you.*; *if-clause type 1*: *If the boy is as bad as you say, she'll soon find out herself.*)

Erweiterung
• Differenzierung: Leistungsstärkere S können anhand der Textinformation selbstständig weitere Konditionalsätze bilden, während L den schwächeren S ggf. Hilfestellung gibt. Beispiele:
– *If Linda's mum hadn't told them, Tina's parents wouldn't have found out about Tom.*
– *If Linda had known it was a secret, she wouldn't have told her mum.*
– *If Tina's parents hadn't heard about Luke from Linda's mother, Tina wouldn't have had to stay at home last Saturday.*

Lösung
> 2 *If Linda hadn't told her mum about Tina, Linda's mum wouldn't have told Tina's parents.* 3 *If Linda hadn't said anything to Tina, she wouldn't have got angry with her/she wouldn't have run out of the room.* 4 *If Linda had been more careful with her words, maybe Tina wouldn't have been so angry with her.*

Material
Workbook S. 34/18
Ggf. Leerfolie

Üben **2 Find the rule** Seite 49

Ziel	• Regeln für die Bildung und den Gebrauch der *if-clauses type 1–3* formulieren
Strukturen	• *If-clauses type 1–3*
Methodisches Vorgehen	a) Schriftliche Bearbeitung in Einzelarbeit oder PA. Die S übertragen die Tabelle ins Heft, lesen die Texte noch einmal durch und tragen die gesuchten *tenses* (siehe TA) ein. Ein leistungsstärkeres Schülerpaar erhält eine vorbereitete Folie und trägt hier die Lösungen in die Tabelle ein.
	b) Ergebnissicherung anhand der Folie. Abschließend formulieren die S einfache Regeln für die Verwendung der Konditionalsätze.
	• Erst danach vergleichen die S ihre Regelformulierungen mit den Erläuterungen im Grammatikanhang (G 13). L weist besonders auf die *English summary* auf S. 140 unten hin.

TIP
G 13

Type	verb form in if-clause	verb form in main clause
1	simple present	will + infinitive
	If I <u>go</u> to bed late tonight,	I <u>will be</u> tired tomorrow.
2	simple past	would + infinitive
	If I <u>went</u> to bed late every night,	I <u>would be</u> tired all the time.

Language 3

	past perfect	would + have + past participle
3	If I <u>had gone</u> to bed earlier last Monday,	I <u>would not have been</u> tired on Tuesday.

Erweiterung
- Jede/r S überlegt sich einen *if-clause* und schreibt ihn auf ein Karteikärtchen oder einen Spickzettel. Es bleibt den S überlassen, ob sie *type 1, type 2* oder *type 3* für ihren Satzanfang auswählen. In der Folge interagieren möglichst alle S einmal miteinander, wobei die Unterrichtsorganisation von den räumlichen Gegebenheiten abhängig sein wird.
- Steht ausreichend Raum zur Verfügung, empfiehlt sich die Methode des „Kugellagers" *(Double circle)*. Die S bilden zwei Kreise. Die S im Innenkreis nennen ihrem Gegenüber den vorbereiteten Satzanfang, z. B. *If our teacher left the classroom now, …* Der/die S im Außenkreis bildet spontan einen inhaltlich passenden und grammatisch korrekten Hauptsatz. Kontrolle durch den/die Partner/in im Innenkreis. Die S im Außenkreis bewegen sich dann im Uhrzeigersinn weiter. In der nächsten Runde werden die Rollen getauscht.
- Alternativ gehen die S durch den Klassenraum und befragen sich gegenseitig. Auch hier empfehlen sich meist zwei Durchgänge mit vorher festgelegten Rollen.
- **Folie 8: What if?** übt die *if-clauses type 2 and 3*.

Lösung   *Siehe TA*

Material
Folie 8
Ggf. Leerfolie,
Karteikarten

Üben   **3 Your turn: Your story**   Seite 49

Ziel
- Über persönliche Ereignisse und deren Folgen berichten
- Die *if-clauses type 3* anwenden und festigen

Strukturen
- *If-clauses type 3*

Methodisches Vorgehen
- Hier handelt es sich um einen recht anspruchsvollen Arbeitsauftrag, der den S ein hohes Maß an Reflexion abverlangt und der die Bereitschaft, sich zu Privatem zu äußern, voraussetzt. Aus diesem Grund empfiehlt sich eine schriftliche Bearbeitung in der Hausaufgabe, wobei die Benutzung eines zweisprachigen Wörterbuches anzuraten ist.
- L weist die S darauf hin, dass hier auch „alltäglichere Ereignisse" und deren Folgen beschrieben werden können.

Erweiterung
- Mit veränderten Arbeitsaufträgen können **KV 2** und **KV 4** an dieser Stelle als weiteres Übungsmaterial genutzt werden.

Lösung   *Individuelle S-Antworten*

Tipps für junge Lehrer   Bei dieser Aufgabe sollte Wert darauf gelegt werden, dass leistungsstärkere S nicht nur Einzelsätze, sondern einen zusammenhängenden Text schreiben.

Material
Workbook S. 34/19
Kopiervorlagen 2, 4
Im Anschluss an
ex. 3 Action UK! 3,
A working day,
Part B: *A London rickshaw driver*
sowie *Action UK!* 3,
Begleitheft zu den Filmsequenzen,
Unit 3 B

3 Skills

Skills
Seite 50

 Ziele
- Über persönliche Kommunikation sprechen
- Telefonnachrichten verstehen
- Das Wortfeld „Telefonieren" erweitern und vertiefen
- Eine Telefonnachricht hinterlassen und annehmen

Text	**Telephone messages**	Seite 50

Ziel • Über persönliche Kommunikation sprechen

Wortschatz *difficult*

Methodisches Vorgehen
- Zu Beginn der Stunde schreibt L das Wort *TELEPHONE* in die Mitte der aufgeklappten Tafel und führt dann mit den S ein einleitendes *brainstorming* durch. Die S äußern spontan Gedanken und Vorstellungen, die sie mit dem Begriff verbinden. L notiert zentrale Stichworte an der Tafel *(cluster/mindmap)*.
- Anschließend leitet L zu *ex.* 1 über.

Üben	**1 Answerphones**	Seite 50

Ziel • Eine persönliche Stellungnahme abgeben

Wortschatz *voice mail*

Methodisches Vorgehen
- Einstieg über die „Blitzlicht"-Methode: Wenn möglich sitzen die S im Kreis. Nach kurzer Vorbereitung in Einzelarbeit gibt jede/r S eine persönliche Stellungnahme zu der Eingangsfrage ab (nur **1–2** Sätze pro S!). Eine kurze Diskussion kann sich anschließen, die Einzeläußerungen werden jedoch nicht kommentiert.
- L leitet zu *ex.* 2 über.

Lösung | *Individuelle S-Antworten* |

ⓛ **Üben**	**2 Listening: Understand a message**	Seite 50

HV-Text

Dialogue 1

Woman: Hello. The person you are calling can't take your call at the moment. If you'd like to leave a message with your name and phone number, please speak after the tone.

Mel: Hi, this is Mel calling. I've got a message for Kim. Kim, I'm trying to call Charlie Parker, you know, from Year 10, but he never answers his mobile. If you've got his home phone number, maybe you could text me on my mobile, or just call me back. My number is 01753 529464 – but you know that already, don't you?

Dialogue 2

Woman: Hello. The person you wish to speak to is not available at the moment. Please leave a message with your name and phone number after the tone.

Jane: Hi, this is Jane with a message for Ben. I need Penny's new e-mail address. If you've got it, could you call me back at my home phone number? The number is 0173 23432. Hope to hear from you soon. Bye!

Dialogue 3

Tom: Hi, you've got Tom Watson's mobile number. I'm afraid I can't take your

Skills 3

>> call right now, but if you leave your name and number after the beep, I'll get back to you as soon as I can.
> Pete: Hi, Tom. This is Pete here. I'm just calling to say that I've lost Amy Patterson's phone number. Do you have it? Could you call me back or e-mail me? Thanks a lot.

Ziel
- Einem Hörtext zielgerichtet Informationen entnehmen

Wortschatz *caller, to contact*

Methodisches Vorgehen

Pre-listening:
- SB geschlossen. L bereitet die S kurz auf die Situation der HV-Texte vor: *You are going to listen to three short messages from an answerphone. Be careful: There are six different speakers – three recorded voices on the answerphone and three callers.*
- Die S sammeln Ideen, welche Nachrichten normalerweise auf einem Anrufbeantworter hinterlassen werden; L oder ein/e S schreibt die Ideen an die Tafel/auf Folie.
- SB geöffnet. Die S lesen den Arbeitsauftrag und fertigen ein einfaches Lösungsraster für ihre Notizen an (siehe TA).

While-listening:
- L präsentiert die drei *phone messages* zuerst ohne Unterbrechung von CD, dann einzeln nacheinander mit jeweils einer kurzen Pause, damit die S Stichworte notieren können.
- In einem dritten Durchgang werden alle drei *phone messages* noch einmal hintereinander vorgespielt; die S vervollständigen bzw. korrigieren ihre Notizen.
- Vergleich und Diskussion der Notizen in PA. Ein Schülerpaar erhält eine Folie mit Lösungsraster für die gemeinsame Kontrolle im Plenum.

Post-listening:
- Siehe *ex.* 3

> **TIP**
> In leistungsschwächeren Lerngruppen sollte die CD mehrfach gestoppt werden, damit die S ausreichend Zeit haben, ihre Notizen im Lösungsraster einzutragen

TA

Who phoned?	Who is it for?	Message?	Contact?
Mel	Kim	wants Charlie Parker's (Year 10) home phone number	text on mobile/call back
Jane	Ben	needs Penny's new e-mail address	call back at home phone number
Pete	Tom	wants Amy Patterson's phone number	call back/e-mail

Lösung *Siehe TA*

Material
L 2/11–13
Ggf. Leerfolie

Üben

3 Leave a message

Seite 50

Ziel
- Eine Telefonnachricht hinterlassen

Wortschatz *to leave, to take a call, tone, I'm afraid*

Methodisches Vorgehen
- Schriftliche Bearbeitung in Einzelarbeit; anschließend Partnerkontrolle. Die Partner/innen besprechen, welcher ihrer Lösungstexte der Bessere ist.
- Mehrere Schülerpaare tragen ihre Ergebnisse im Plenum vor: Ein/e S liest den Ansagetext, der/die andere S die Nachricht.

Lösung

> *Erwartungshorizont:*
> Hi, Don. This is Jake here. I'm just calling to say that I've left my skateboard helmet at your house. If you've found it, could you call me back or e-mail me? Thanks a lot.

3 Skills

Tipps für junge Lehrer Kurze Texte wie die Ansage im SB eignen sich gut als Grundlage für eine Aufgabe, die die Fertigkeit zum Rekonstruieren von Texten schult. Hierbei handelt es sich um eine Methode, die ähnlich schon von Benjamin Franklin genutzt wurde, um seine *Writing skills* zu verbessern:
- L liest den Text im normalen Sprechtempo eines Anrufbeantworters vor. Die S hören aufmerksam zu und versuchen, den Inhalt der Ansage zu verstehen.
- L liest den Text im gleichen Tempo noch einmal vor. Die S notieren sich *keywords* und *phrases*.
- Austausch der Notizen mit einem/r Partner/in und erste Textrekonstruktion.
- Die S bilden zuerst Vierer-, dann Sechser- oder Achtergruppen (abhängig von der Klassengröße), die sich jeweils auf einen Text einigen. Ein/e S übernimmt die Rolle der/des Schreibers/in.
- Vergleich und Bewertung der Texte anhand des Genauigkeitsgrads im Plenum. Diese Aufgabe kann auch als Wettbewerb durchgeführt werden. Sieger/in ist, wer den Text mit den wenigsten Abweichungen vorlegt. Der Schwierigkeitsgrad kann erhöht werden, indem es auch für Rechtschreibfehler Minuspunkte gibt.

Material
Workbook S. 35/20

Üben

4 Role play: A phone message

Seite 50

Ziel
- Eine Telefonnachricht annehmen
- *Useful phrases* sammeln und anwenden

Wortschatz *to be in*

Methodisches Vorgehen
- Die S erstellen in PA ein kurzes Telefongespräch unter Berücksichtigung der *Useful phrases*. Zur Vorbereitung und Wortschatzfestigung kann **KV 5: Quadromino: Telephone messages** eingesetzt werden. Als Hausaufgabe lernen die S ihre Rolle auswendig; unsichere S können für das Vorspielen vor den Mitschülern *cue cards* anfertigen. In der Folgestunde erfolgt die Präsentation der kleinen Spielszenen zunächst in Gruppen (6–8 S). In jeder Gruppe wird das beste Telefongespräch durch Abstimmung ausgewählt und abschließend im Plenum präsentiert. Auch hier kann ggf. ein/e „Sieger/in" durch Abstimmungsentscheid ermittelt werden.

TIP
Beim Vorspielen sitzen die S Rücken an Rücken und benutzen ihre ausgeschalteten Handys

HA
Material
Workbook S. 35/21, 22
Kopiervorlage 5

Lösung *Individuelle S-Antworten*

Text — 3

Text
Seite 51–53

Ziele
- Einen Sketch lesen und verstehen
- Ein Theaterstück aufführen
- Ein Theaterprogramm erstellen

 Text **Home alone** — Seite 51–53

Ziel
- Einen Sketch inhaltlich erfassen

Wortschatz
Home alone., cast, Shut up!, witch, costume, grumpy, to manage (to do sth), on one's own, talk, to make a decision, decision, to get in the way, to make sure, mask, First things first., doorbell, What's going on?, guy, one by one

Methodisches Vorgehen
- Ausgehend von der Überschrift *Home alone* und dem Foto im SB sammeln die S Ideen, worum es in dem kurzen Theaterstück gehen könnte. Der Textsorte entsprechend wird der Text dann zuerst als Tonaufnahme präsentiert.
- L verteilt vorab **KV 6: Home alone** oder gibt die *wh-questions* und die Anzahl der Szenen an der Tafel vor. SB geschlossen; L spielt die Tonaufnahme vor. Die S machen sich während des Hörens Notizen.
- Die S vergleichen und besprechen ihre Ergebnisse mit einem/r Partner/in.
- SB geöffnet. L spielt die Tonaufnahme noch einmal vor. Die S lesen mit und kontrollieren ihre Ergebnisse.

Erweiterung
- **Folie 9: Home alone** reaktiviert das Textverständnis anhand von Bildern.

Tipps für junge Lehrer
Vor Bearbeitung des Textes können die S zunächst aufgefordert werden, in PA eine kurze Bildbeschreibung zu verfassen. Mögliche Leitfragen: *Who is in the photo? What are the people doing? How do they feel? What is their problem?*

Material
S 1/32–36
L 2/14–18
Kopiervorlage 6
Folie 9

Üben **1 Talk about the play** — Seite 53

Ziel
- Über ein Theaterstück diskutieren

Wortschatz *to react*

Methodisches Vorgehen
- a) „Bienenkorb"/*Buzz group*: Ein/e S liest den Arbeitsauftrag laut vor. Anschließend erhalten die S zehn Minuten Zeit, in Kleingruppen (3–5 S, im Idealfall 4 S) die beiden Fragen miteinander zu besprechen und zu einem gemeinsamen Ergebnis zu gelangen. Jede Gruppe bestimmt vorab einen/ eine Sprecher/in, der/die während der Besprechung Notizen macht und diese anschließend im Plenum präsentiert. Kontroverse Arbeitsergebnisse werden ggf. gegenüber gestellt und gemeinsam diskutiert.
- b) Diese anspruchsvollere Aufgabe kann in der Hausaufgabe vorbereitet werden. Hierzu notieren die S *keywords/phrases* auf einem Spickzettel (*cue card*).
- c) Offenes Unterrichtsgespräch; die S äußern sich spontan.

Auch als HA geeignet

Erweiterung
- Differenzierung nach oben: *Write a different ending for the sketch.*

Lösung | *Individuelle S-Antworten*

Tipps für junge Lehrer
Diese Aufgabe eignet sich für ein weiteres Verfahren des kooperativen Lernens. Vergrößern Sie hierfür **KV 7: Place mat** auf DIN A3-Format. Die Klasse wird dann idealerweise in Vierergruppen aufgeteilt und jede Gruppe erhält eine Kopie des „Platzdeckchens". Jedes Gruppenmitglied schreibt seine Gedanken zum Arbeitsauftrag in seinen Schreibbereich des Arbeitsblattes. Nach der anschließenden Diskussion verständigt sich die Gruppe auf eine gemeinsame Lösung, die in der Mitte des Blattes aufgeschrieben wird.

Material
Workbook S. 36/23, 24
Kopiervorlage 7

3 Text Wordwise

Üben	**2 How to: Put on a play**		Seite 53

Ziel • Eine Theateraufführung planen und durchführen

Wortschatz *to put on (a play), director, props (pl.), lights (pl.), programme, actress, rehearsal, to rehearse, curtain, audience, to applaud*

Methodisches Vorgehen
- Zur Vorbereitung wird der Text szenenweise von CD vorgespielt. Die S achten bevorzugt auf Aussprache und Intonation. Anschließend üben die S in Gruppen (6–8 S) das laute Lesen in verteilten Rollen.
- L bespricht mit den S die Vorgehensweise und legt einen konkreten Arbeits- und Zeitplan fest. Bei der Gruppenbildung sollten die S berücksichtigen, dass für eine erfolgreiche Aufführung nicht nur Schauspieler/innen benötigt werden. Hierbei bietet **KV 8: Let's put on a play!** eine sinnvolle Hilfestellung. In dieser Phase sollte auch die Arbeitsgruppe bestimmt werden, die das Programmheft erstellt (vgl. *ex.* 3).
- Anschließend bereiten die S in GA eine Aufführung des Sketches vor. Sie schreiben den jeweiligen Rollentext heraus und üben das laute Sprechen, falls möglich mit CD. Als längerfristige Hausaufgabe werden die Rollentexte auswendig gelernt.
- Den Abschluss der Arbeit bildet eine Aufführung des Theaterstücks, nach Möglichkeit in einem größeren Rahmen (z. B. Schulfest, Tag der Offenen Tür, Elternabend).

TIP
Aus Zeitgründen ist es auch denkbar, dass jede Gruppe nur eine Szene des Stücks für eine mögliche Aufführung vorbereitet

Material
Workbook S. 36/25
Kopiervorlage 8

Üben	**3 Writing texts: Write an interesting programme for the play**		Seite 53

Ziel • Ein Theaterprogramm erstellen

Wortschatz *author*

Methodisches Vorgehen
- Die in *ex.* 2 bestimmte Arbeitsgruppe erstellt ein Programmheft, wenn möglich am Computer, das vervielfältigt und zur Aufführung verteilt wird.
- Wird das Theaterstück nicht aufgeführt, erstellen die S anhand der Leitfragen im SB eine Art „Programmzettel" für eine imaginäre Aufführung.

Lösung | *Individuelle S-Antworten* |

Material
Workbook S. 36/26

Wordwise

Seite 54

Ziele
- Adjektive zur Personenbeschreibung systematisieren
- Die Aussprache schulen
- Die Wortwahl in einem Songtext untersuchen

Üben	**1 Describing people**		Seite 54

Ziel • Adjektive zur Beschreibung von Personen systematisieren und festigen

Methodisches Vorgehen
- a) + b) können als vorbereitende Hausaufgabe schriftlich bearbeitet werden.
- Nach der Besprechung in der Folgestunde wird die anspruchsvollere Teilaufgabe c) im Plenum bearbeitet. Die S suchen auch hier Wortpaare zur Beschreibung der Pattersons, die sie ihren Listen hinzufügen.

Auch als HA geeignet

Erweiterung	Differenzierungsmöglichkeit: • Zur weiteren Festigung und Übung der Adjektive zur Personenbeschreibung kann für schwächere S **KV 9: Adjective memory** eingesetzt werden. Es wird nach den bekannten Regeln des Memory gespielt. • Leistungsstärkere S bearbeiten **KV 10: Describing people**.	**TIP** Durch Beispiele verdeutlichen, dass viele Adjektive sowohl Gefühle/ Zustände als auch das Aussehen beschreiben

Lösung

What people *are* like:	What people *look* like:
tall – short, grumpy – happy, slow – fast, boring – interesting, healthy – ill, cool – nervous, quiet – loud, wise – silly, calm – excited, bad – good, kind – selfish, shy – aggressive, rich – poor, strong – weak	cool – nervous, bad – good, strong – weak, crazy – normal, …

Tipps für junge Lehrer
Zum Abfragen und Festigen der Vokabeln (hier der paarweise zugeordneten Adjektive) kann auch bei dieser Aufgabe die Methode des „Kugellagers" *(Double circle)* eingesetzt werden. Hierzu bilden die S einen Innen- und einen Außenkreis, die einander zugewandt sind. Jede/r S hat ein Gegenüber. Die Zufallspartner befragen sich gegenseitig (hier z. B. *What is the opposite of strong?*). Nach angemessener Zeit bewegen sich die Kreise in entgegengesetzter Richtung. Alternativ dazu kann sich auch nur der Außenkreis um eine Position weiterbewegen. Jede/r S hat damit eine andere Person als Gesprächspartner/in. L legt vorab fest, wie viele „Gesprächsphasen" es geben soll.

Material
Workbook S. 37/27
Kopiervorlagen 9, 10

Üben   2 Sounds: Word stress   Seite 54

HV-Text departure – government – message – commercial – antique – relax – rehearsal – themselves – colony – decision – official – laptop – compare – swimsuit – assistant – audience – answerphone

Ziel • Die Aussprache schulen

Wortschatz *official*

Methodisches Vorgehen
- SB geöffnet. L erläutert die Aufgabenstellung.
- L spielt die Tonaufnahme vor. Die S lesen leise mit.
- L spielt CD ein zweites Mal ab. Die S markieren die betonte Silbe mit einem Bleistift.
- L schreibt das Lösungsraster an die Tafel. Vier S kommen nach vorne; je ein/e S ist für eine Spalte zuständig. Die Mitschüler/innen lesen die im SB vorgegebenen Wörter laut vor; die S an der Tafel entscheiden, in welche Spalte das jeweilige Wort eingetragen werden muss. Die betonte Silbe wird unterstrichen. Anschließend übertragen die S das Lösungsraster in ihre Hefte.
- Erneutes Vorspielen der Tonaufnahme. Die S sprechen im Chor, in Gruppen und einzeln nach.

TA

xX	Xx	xXx	Xxx
mistake	feeling	politeness	telephone
antique	message	departure	government
relax	swimsuit	official	colony
themselves	laptop	rehearsal	audience
compare		commercial	answerphone
		decision	
		assistant	

3 Wordwise

Erweiterung	• Die S finden für jede Rubrik fünf weitere Wörter (auch als Hausaufgabe möglich).	Auch als HA geeignet
Lösung	*Siehe TA*	
Tipps für junge Lehrer	Zur Aussprachesschulung können die S mit den in der Aufgabe vorgegebenen Wörtern schriftlich Unsinnsätze bilden, die sie anschließend laut vorlesen, z. B. *The assistant in the red swimsuit made the mistake to compare my laptop with an antique answerphone while I talked to the government on my telephone.*	**Material** ⊚ L 2/19

> **!**
>
> **TIPPS VON MARIO RINVOLUCRI – THE ALTERNATIVE WAY**
>
> **The elastic band word stress exercise**
> **Sounds: Word stress** (p. 54)
>
> a) Put all the words from *ex.* 2 up on the board. Give the pupils a rubber band each. Demonstrate what they are going to do: Say 'answerphone' and as you say it take an elastic band with two hands and pull your hands away from each other big time for the stressed syllable and give two little pulls for the two unstressed syllables. For 'laptop' you give two equal strength pulls.
>
> b) Have all the pupils standing facing you with elastic bands at the ready.
>
> Run through all the words on the board, saying them loudly yourself and leading the elastic banding. They pull their bands and shout the words.
>
> Say the words again but do not model the actions. They do the actions and repeat the words.
>
> *Pluses:* Chaz's activity gets people up and moving, and in a linguistically purposeful way. It only takes between five and eight minutes and it appeals to people with both musical and kinaesthetic intelligences.
>
> *Minuses:* The game may at first seem a bit childish to some mid-teenagers.
>
> *Acknowledgement:* I learnt this technique from Chaz Pugliese, the *Pilgrims Teacher Training* DOS.

⊚ L Song	**3 ⟨A song: Shiny happy people⟩**	Seite 54
HV-Text	Identisch mit SB-Text	
Ziel	• Das Hörverstehen üben • Einen Songtext analysieren	
Wortschatz	*shiny, crowd, ground, silver, to sound, to express*	
Methodisches Vorgehen	*Listening comprehension:* • L bereitet die S auf die Thematik des Songs vor, ohne die qualifizierenden Adjektive *shiny* und *happy* zu erwähnen: *You are going to listen to a pop song now. It is about 'people'. Listen carefully and try to remember as many words and sentences from the text as you can.* • SB geschlossen. L spielt den Song von CD vor. Die S nennen spontan alle Wörter, an die sie sich erinnern. • L spielt den Song ein zweites Mal vor. Die S schreiben die Wörter, die sie ganz	

| | Wordwise | Check-out | **3** |

sicher verstanden haben, in ihr Heft. Vergleich im Plenum; L sammelt die Beiträge an der Tafel. Auf dieser Grundlage äußern die S weiter gehende Vermutungen, worum es in dem Song geht.
- SB geöffnet. Die S lesen den Text und überprüfen die Richtigkeit des TA. Klären von Verständnisfragen. Falls von den S gewünscht: nochmaliges Anhören des Songs.

Working with the text:
- L macht deutlich, dass es bei Songtexten und Gedichten einige Gemeinsamkeiten gibt. Hierbei können die Begriffe *rhyme/alliteration/repetition* als Kategorien für die folgende Arbeit am Text eingeführt bzw. reaktiviert werden.
- Die S bearbeiten a) schriftlich in Einzelarbeit oder PA. Kontrolle im Plenum; L sammelt die Ergebnisse an der Tafel.
- Anschließend mündliche Bearbeitung von Teilaufgabe b) im Unterrichtsgespräch.
- L weist interessierte S auf die *Free Section*, S.120–122, hin.

TA

rhymes:	around/ground
alliteration:	meet me; take ... town; happy ... holding hands
repetitions:	people; shiny; happy; love me/them; hands; take it

Lösung

a) *Siehe TA*
b) *Erwartungshorizont:* **being happy** – *shiny, happy, laughing, flowers, gold, silver, shine;* **love** – *happy, meet, people, love, flowers, gold, silver, shine, holding hands;* **being sad** – *cry*

Material
L 2/20

Check-out

Seite 55

Ziele • Die Lernziele der Unit in Selbstkontrolle überprüfen

Üben **1 Reflexive pronouns** Seite 55

Ziel • Die *reflexive pronouns* in Abgrenzung zu *each other* anwenden

Strukturen • *Reflexive pronouns vs. each other*

TIP
G 11, 12

Methodisches Vorgehen
- L weist eingangs auf G 11 und G 12 hin.
- Die S bearbeiten die Aufgabe in Einzelarbeit; anschließend Selbstkontrolle bzw. Überprüfung durch eine/n Partner/in.

Lösung *Siehe SB S. 214*

Material
Workbook S. 38/30

Üben **2 Put in the correct verb form** Seite 55

Ziel • Die *if-clauses type 2* und *type 3* wiederholen und anwenden

Strukturen • *If-clauses types 2 and 3*

TIP
G 13

Methodisches Vorgehen
- a) + b) L weist eingangs auf G 13 hin; die S schlagen ggf. im Grammatikanhang nach. Die S lösen die beiden Teilaufgaben in Einzelarbeit schriftlich. Anschließend Selbstkontrolle bzw. Überprüfung durch eine/n Partner/in.

161

3 Check-out

Lösung	*Siehe SB S. 214*	**Material** *Workbook* S. 38/31, 32

Üben	**3 On the phone**	Seite 55
Ziel	• Eine Telefonnachricht für eine/n Freund/in hinterlassen	
Methodisches Vorgehen	• Die S überlegen sich ein kurzes Telefongespräch in PA. • Nach einer angemessenen Übungszeit spielen die S ihr Telefongespräch anderen Schülerpaaren vor.	
Lösung	*Siehe SB S. 215*	

Üben	**4 Good advice**	Seite 55
Ziel	• Einem/r Freund/in Ratschläge erteilen	
Methodisches Vorgehen	• Die S erstellen anhand der Vorgabe und der Hilfen im SB ein kurzes Rollenspiel in PA.	
Lösung	*Siehe SB S. 215*	

Dictation

Dear Mary,

I need your advice! I have this problem with my parents. I am a rock music fan and I like going to concerts. So every time there is a good concert I ask my parents if I can go but they always say no because I am not good enough at school. But if my twin sisters wanted to go to a party next Saturday they would always say yes. The girls always get what they want – it's just so unfair. Please don't tell me to talk to my parents because they won't listen anyway. So what can I do?

Jake

⟨Text⟩

Workbook Seite 39

Ziele
- Einen adaptierten Auszug aus einem Roman eigenständig erschließen
- Die bewusste Lenkung des/der Lesers/Leserin in einem Erzähltext kennen lernen

Text/Üben ⟨A series of unfortunate events⟩ Workbook Seite 39

Wortschatz Annotationen S. 39

Methodisches Vorgehen

Pre-reading:
- Die S lesen den kursiv gedruckten Einführungstext. Unbekanntes Vokabular wird durch die Annotationen oder ein Wörterbuch erschlossen.
- L stellt einführende Fragen: *Before you listen to and read the text, think about books or films with happy endings. What would you have to change to turn them into stories with sad endings? Which do you prefer: happy or sad endings?*

While-reading:
- L leitet zur Lektüre des Textes über. Präsentation von CD, die S lesen leise mit. Während des Hörens/Lesens unterstreichen die S in verschiedenen Farben, was im Text über die drei Baudelaire-Kinder ausgesagt wird.
- Die S lesen den Text noch einmal durch und erschließen unbekannten Wortschatz durch die Annotationen. Sie fertigen eine Tabelle an, in der sie die zuvor unterstrichenen Aussagen über die Hauptfiguren sammeln. Anschließend Partnerkontrolle.

Post-reading:
- Die Aussagen aus dem Text werden im Plenum zusammengetragen und von L an der Tafel/auf Folie festgehalten.
- L stellt weitergehende Fragen zum Text: *Now that you have listened to the beginning of the story: What do you think will happen to the children? The books are called 'A series of unfortunate events': What unfortunate events can you think of? Look at your grid again: How will the three children manage to get out of difficult situations?*

TA

Violet	Klaus	Sunny
– the eldest of the three	– the middle child	– the youngest
– likes to skip rocks	– the only boy	– an infant
– fourteen years old	– likes to examine creatures in tide-pools	– very small for her age, scarcely larger than a boot
– right-handed	– twelve years old	– has four big sharp teeth
– likes inventing and building strange devices	– wears glasses which make him look intelligent	– likes to bite things
– when she's thinking hard, her long hair is tied up in a ribbon to keep it out of her eyes	– reads a lot of books and remembers a lot of the information	– can't really speak
		– most people don't understand her

Erweiterung
- Um den S die Lenkung des/der Lesers/Leserin zu verdeutlichen, stellt L die Frage, wie es dem Autor gelingt, neugierig auf den weiteren Fortgang der Geschichte zu machen: *Look at the text again. Find words or phrases which the author uses so that we want to read more.*
- Die S markieren in PA die entsprechenden Stellen am Rand. Anschließend Besprechung der Ergebnisse im Plenum.

Lösung

While-reading: Siehe TA
Post-reading: Individuelle S-Antworten
Erweiterung: **it was gray and cloudy** (Z. 10): The weather often goes with what happens in a story. – **to do what they liked** (Z. 16): We know that the beach is

empty, but we want to find out what the children like to do there. – **that mysterious figure** *(Z. 60): We want to know who the figure is.* – **the children saw with relief** *(Z. 65): Now we know it's not so bad. But what does he want?* – **some very bad news** *(Z. 73): We want to know what the bad news is.* – **have perished** *(Z. 74): Mr Poe doesn't know how to say this, so he uses very difficult language. Then he uses simpler words to make sure the children know what he is talking about. We also want to know what he means.*

Material
◎S 1/37
◎L 2/21
Ggf. Leerfolie

⟨Freiarbeit⟩

Ziele
- Telefonnachrichten lesen und verstehen
- Anhand von Telefonnachrichten unterschiedliche Stimmungen beschreiben
- Eine Telefonnachricht verfassen
- Eine Gruppendiskussion vorbereiten und durchführen

Strukturen *If-clauses type 1 and 2*

Methodisches Vorgehen
- **KV 17a: Look who's talking!** Die S ordnen die Telefonnachrichten den Ihnen aus Unit 3 bekannten Personen zu und schließen aus dem Inhalt der Nachrichten auf die Stimmung der einzelnen Anrufer/innen. Sprachliche Hilfen bieten die Adjektive auf S. 54, *ex. 1*.
- Die S verfassen eine eigene Telefonnachricht für ein Mitglied der Familie Patterson und lesen sie ihrem/ihrer Partner/in vor. Der/die S muss erraten, wer die Nachricht auf dem Anrufbeantworter der Pattersons hinterlassen hat, und welche Stimmung aus der Nachricht und der Stimmlage der Anrufer/innen deutlich wird. Anschließend Rollentausch.
- **KV 17b: Look who's talking now!** Die S bereiten in GA mit Hilfe der Rollenkarten eine Diskussion zwischen den verschiedenen Mitgliedern der Familie Patterson vor. Die Vorschläge auf den Rollenkarten sollen ergänzt und in der Diskussion glaubwürdig vertreten werden. Methodische und sprachliche Hilfen bietet *Talkwise*, S. 46. Die anschließende Präsentation wird von der Klasse mit Hilfe der Rollenkarten arbeitsteilig evaluiert.

TIP
Der Zeitrahmen für die Freiarbeit beträgt 2–3 Stunden inkl. HA

Erweiterung
- **KV 17a:** Die S können ihre Nachrichten auf Band oder auf einen Anrufbeantworter sprechen und der Klasse vorspielen. Diese muss den/die Anrufer/in erraten.
- **KV 17b:** Die Diskussion kann als Theaterstück oder durch Notizen zu den einzelnen Rollen als spontane Diskussion vorbereitet werden.

Lösung

KV 17a: *a)* A *Mel and Amy*   B *Mr and Mrs Patterson*   C *Jake*
b) + c) Individuelle S-Antworten
KV 17b: *Individuelle S-Antworten*

Materialien
Kopiervorlage 17a+b
Ggf. Wörterbücher, Aufnahmegerät

KV 1a: The Pattersons

KV 1b: The Pattersons

KV 1c: The Pattersons

KV 2: What would happen if …?

The Clarks (Mr and Mrs Clark, their daughters Sarah and Laura, their son Peter, and Laura's mice Biscuit and Cheese) are moving to their new house. Peter is sitting in his room. He is listening to his new CD. But he knows he must help the others.

Say what would happen if Peter did not help the others. Write ten if-clauses.

Start like this: If Peter didn't help the others, his father would be very angry. If Mr Clark was angry, he …

Lösung: … would shout at Peter. If he shouted at Peter, Laura would drop the box. If Laura dropped the box, it would open. If the box was open, Biscuit and Cheese would run into Sarah's room. If Sarah saw the mice, she would fall off the chair. If she fell off the chair, she would hurt her arm. If Sarah hurt her arm, she would cry for help. If she cried for help, Mrs Clark would run into her room. If Mrs Clark ran into Sarah's room, she would fall over Laura. If she fell over Laura, she would shout. If Mrs Clark shouted, Mr Clark and Peter would come to Sarah's room, too.

KV 3: A personality test

a) *Do this personality test with your partner. First choose the right verb from the top box on the left to complete sentences 1–4. Be careful with the tense!*

b) *Think of possible sentences for a) and b) in 3 and 4.*

c) *Find two possible situations and sentences for 5 and 6.*

meet see find come	**Personality test** What kind of person are you?
1. If your best friend _____ to school wearing exactly the same T-shirt as you, …	a) you would laugh about it with him or her. ☐ or b) you would be very unhappy and keep your jacket/pullover on all day. ☐
2. If you _____ that someone was stealing something from a sports bag at school, …	a) you would tell it to a teacher. ☐ or b) you would behave as if you didn't see it. ☐
3. If you _____ a nice boy/girl in a chatroom, …	a) _____ ☐ or b) _____ ☐
4. If you _____ a purse in the playground with 50 euros in it, …	a) _____ ☐ or b) _____ ☐
5. _____	a) _____ ☐ or b) _____ ☐
6. _____	a) _____ ☐ or b) _____ ☐

d) *Now do your partner's test. Talk about your results.*

Lösung: 1 came 2 saw 3 met 4 found

3 Kopiervorlagen

KV 4: A busy family

a) Look at the picture. What is happening in each room? Write the sentences in your exercise book.

b) What might the people say? Write complete if-clauses (type 1) and use the correct tense.

Lösung: a) 1 Kids are dancing in the room upstairs. 2 The grandmother is sitting in her bed. 3 The dog is barking. 4 The mother is coming into her son's room. Her son is reading on his bed. 5 The boy and the girl in the living room are watching TV and doing their homework at the same time. 6 The girl in the kitchen is eating lots of food. Her father is looking for something to eat.

GREEN LINE 3

KV 5: Quadromino: Telephone messages

Cut out the grid and match the parts so that you get 'Useful phrases'.

it for me, please? bye. Can I speak Hope to hear	me back, please? Just a moment,	I'll get a pen. speak to … Can I take	you tell her that …? Could he/she call I've got a
repeat that, please? again later.	You're welcome. I'm sorry, I didn't	message for … he's busy. I'd like to Could you spell	to say that … in at the moment. You can phone
Bye. Yes, please. Could Could you call	I help you? Sorry, he/she isn't	name and address. This is … Hello, how can	from you soon. me at … I'll phone
this is … speaking. Thanks and I'm just calling	understand your name. Thanks I'll give you my	me back, please? a lot. I' m afraid Hello/Hi,	a message? to …, please? Could you

Lösung:

You're welcome. I'm sorry, I didn't	Bye. Yes, please. Could Could you call	you tell her that …? Could he/she call I've got a	me back, please? Just a moment,
understand your name. Thanks I'll give you my	me back, please? a lot. I' m afraid Hello/Hi,	message for … he's busy. I'd like to Could you spell	I'll get a pen. speak to … Can I take
name and address. This is … Hello, how can	this is … speaking. Thanks and I'm just calling	it for me, please? bye. Can I speak Hope to hear	a message? to …, please? Could you
I help you? Sorry, he/she isn't	to say that … in at the moment. You can phone	from you soon. me at … I'll phone	repeat that, please? again later.

ISBN 978-3-12-547143-6

KV 6: Home alone

What's happening?
Listen carefully and make notes (keywords only!).

Scene 1:

Who?	
Where?	
When?	
What?	
Why?	

Scene 2:

Who?	
Where?	
When?	
What?	
Why?	

Scene 3:

Who?	
Where?	
When?	
What?	
Why?	

Scene 4:

Who?	
Where?	
When?	
What?	
Why?	

Scene 5:

Who?	
Where?	
When?	
What?	
Why?	

KV 7: Place mat

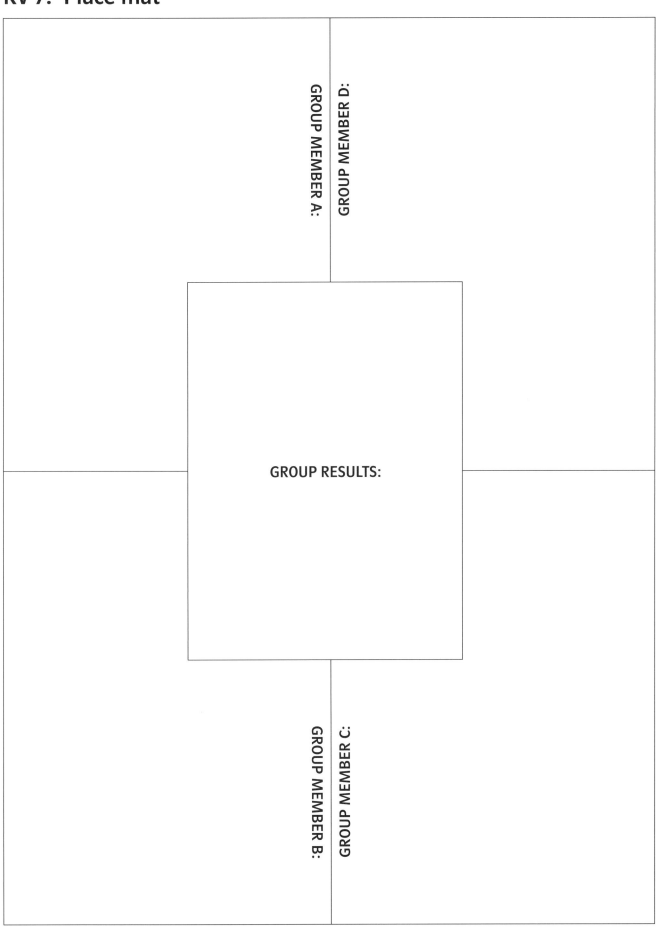

KV 8: Let's put on a play!

Group members	Who?	Jobs?/Equipment?/Things to organise?	When?	Comments?
Director + assistant				
Actors				
Prompter[1]				
Lights and sound				
Props				
Costumes/make-up				
Programme				
Video				

[1] **prompter** [ˈprɒmtə] = Souffleur, Souffleuse

KV 9: Adjective memory

Cut out the cards and mix them. Find the opposites. You can play alone, with a partner or in groups of three or four.

tall	short	grumpy	happy	slow	fast
healthy	ill	boring	interesting	cool	nervous
quiet	loud	wise	silly	bad	good
kind	selfish	shy	aggressive	rich	poor
strong	weak	calm	excited	crazy	normal
young	old	fantastic	horrible	thin	overweight
tiny	big	gentle	scary	brilliant	terrible

KV 10: Describing people

a) *Cut out an interesting picture of **a person you do not know** from a magazine. Stick the picture on the worksheet.*

b) *Look at the picture for some minutes and think about the person. What does he/she look like? What do you think he/she is like? How does he/she feel?*

c) *Fill in words which describe the person.*

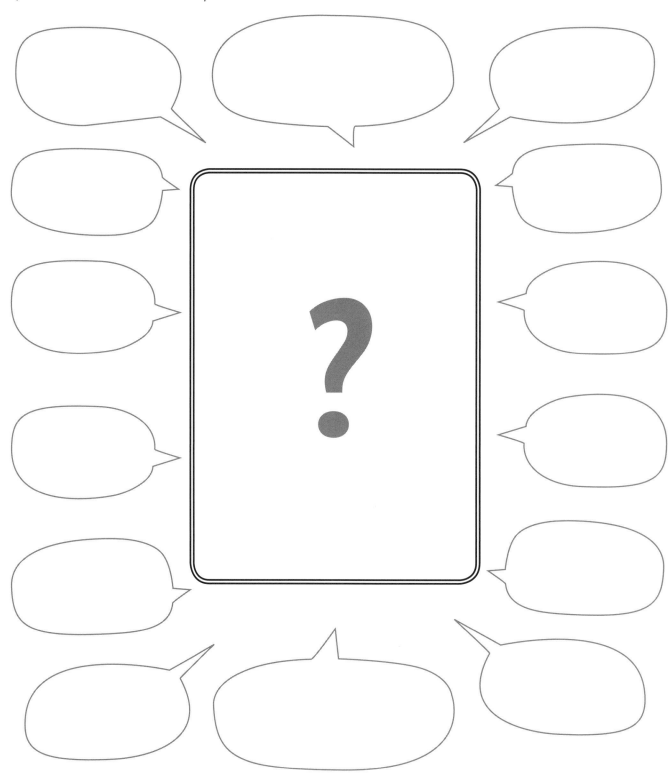

d) *Write a short text (100–150 words) about this person in your exercise book.*

KV 11: Stationenlernen Unit 3 (Language 2)

Station 1: More than words

Often you can see how people are or how they feel when you look in their faces.

| happy | angry | scared | excited | cool |
| grumpy | sad | shy | nervous | |

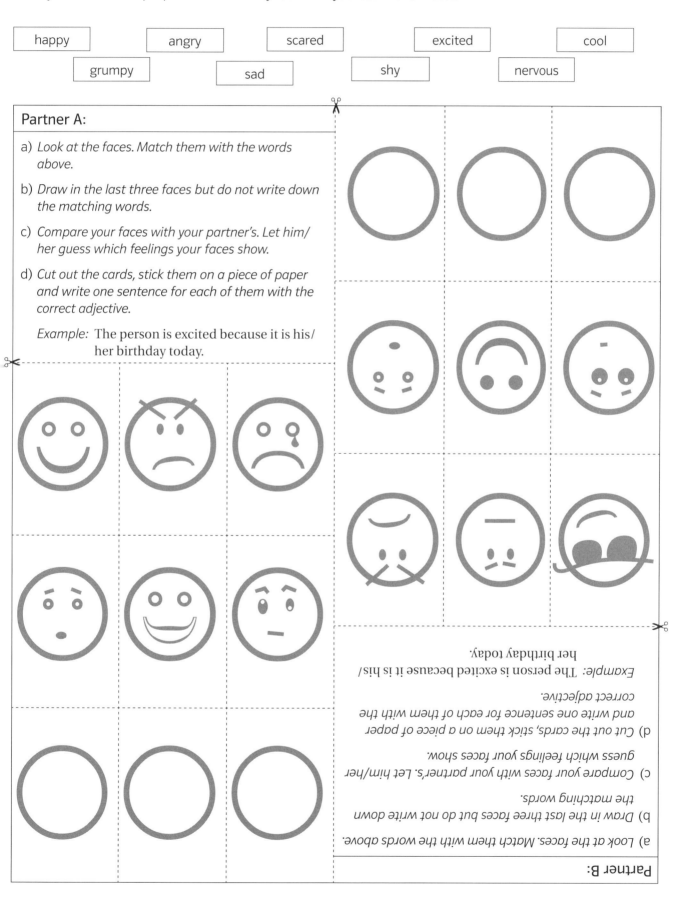

Partner A:

a) Look at the faces. Match them with the words above.

b) Draw in the last three faces but do not write down the matching words.

c) Compare your faces with your partner's. Let him/her guess which feelings your faces show.

d) Cut out the cards, stick them on a piece of paper and write one sentence for each of them with the correct adjective.

Example: The person is excited because it is his/her birthday today.

Partner B:

a) Look at the faces. Match them with the words above.

b) Draw in the last three faces but do not write down the matching words.

c) Compare your faces with your partner's. Let him/her guess which feelings your faces show.

d) Cut out the cards, stick them on a piece of paper and write one sentence for each of them with the correct adjective.

Example: The person is excited because it is his/her birthday today.

KV 12: Stationenlernen Unit 3 (Language 2)

Station 2: If …

Finish the sentences and compare them with your partner's.

1. If I were my English teacher, I _____
2. If someone on the bus was aggressive, I _____
3. If I felt hurt, I _____
4. If I were my parents, I _____
5. If someone needed help after an accident, I _____
6. If _____

Station 3: A game

a) *Read the phrases on the cards. Make sure you understand them.*
b) *Cut out the cards, put them face down on the table and mix them.*
c) *The first player takes a card, reads the phrase and acts it – without words, of course! The others guess what the phrase is. Take turns.*

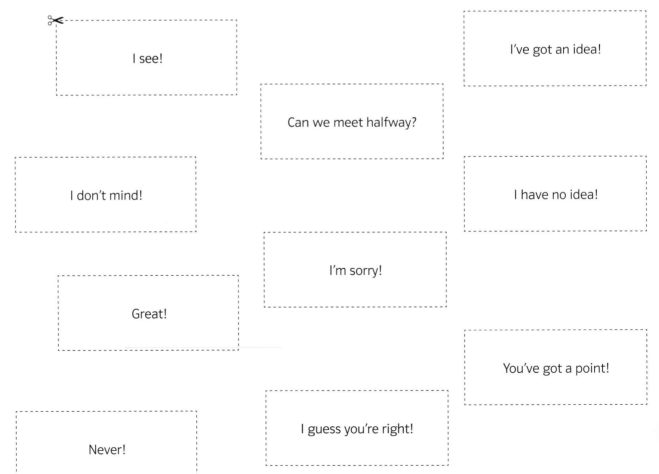

I see!		I've got an idea!
Can we meet halfway?		
I don't mind!		I have no idea!
	I'm sorry!	
Great!		You've got a point!
Never!	I guess you're right!	

KV 13: Stationenlernen Unit 3 (Language 2)

Station 4: Useful phrases

a) *Draw the following grid in your exercise book:*

b) *Read the phrases and fill in the grid.*

Great!	I know, but …	Maybe, …	I don't want to …	I'm hurt because …
OK, fine!	That's true, but …	I see!	I know!	I'm worried that …
I don't mind, but …	I'm angry that …	You've got a point, but …		I don't like it!
I'm sorry, but …	I understand, but …	I'm sad that …		I guess you're right!

Station 5: Cheer up[1] your friend!

a) *Cut out the cards, put them face down on the table and mix them. Make sure that you understand them.*

b) *Take one card and read it. Think of a sentence to cheer up your partner. The phrases in the boxes can help you. Take turns.*

| Don't worry! | Cheer up! | Come on, … | It can't be as bad as that … | Try again! |
| Maybe … | Hey, look, why don't you …? | If you look at it this way, … | | I see what you mean, but … |

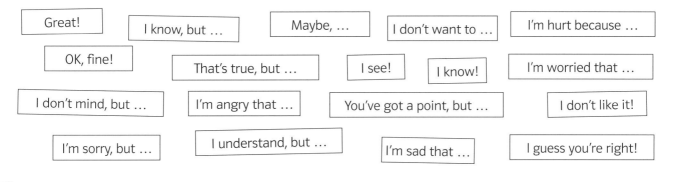

[1] **(to) cheer sb up** [tʃɪərˌʌp] = jmdn. aufmuntern

KV 14: Stationenlernen Unit 3 (Language 2)

Station 6: Give advice!

a) *Imagine your friend needs your advice. He/she has got different problems. Think of six more problems and write keywords in the empty boxes.*

b) *Start the game: The first player throws the dice¹. He/she moves to the box with the correct number, reads out the keywords and forms a sentence/gives advice. If the sentence is correct, cross out the problem. Take turns!*

Example: sister spends lots of time in bathroom: If I were you, I'd get up earlier.

⚀	⚁	⚂	⚃	⚄	⚅
		Dad is very strict			teacher often calls parents
Mum wants lots of help in the house	brother uses mobile		parents don't want to buy pet	sister spends lots of time in bathroom	

✂ ....

Station 7: Meet halfway!

a) *Look at the words in the grid. Think of a dialogue between a brother and a sister who discuss a problem and meet halfway. Choose five or more words from the grid.*

b) *Write the dialogue in your exercise book.*

c) *Compare your dialogue with a partner's.*

talk	angry	true
understand	meet	forget
sorry	mind	maybe

¹**dice** [daɪs] = Würfel

KV 15: Stationenlernen Unit 3 (Language 2)

Station 8: Sort it out!

a) *Look at the picture. A lot of people are in trouble. What are their problems? Take notes about the different situations.*

b) *Imagine these people manage to sort out their problems. Write down for each situation what they might say in the end (1–2 sentences).* Example: I guess you're right, let's try again!

c) *Work with a partner. Take turns to match the sentences with the situations.*

Station 9: Different feelings

a) *Read the dialogue with a partner.*

b) *Choose one adjective for A and one for B:*

| angry | surprised | nervous |
| shy | cool | ... |

c) *Now read the dialogue the way an angry, surprised … person would speak. Finish the dialogue.*

d) *Read your dialogue to the class.*

A: When can we meet again?

B: You decide, you're the boss.

A: What about tomorrow?

B: Fine!

A: _____

B: _____

…

KV 16: Stationenlernen Unit 3 (Language 2)

Station 10: Planning a holiday trip

a) *Work in groups of four. Imagine you are a family and you are planning your summer holidays. Cut out the cards and decide who is who in the group.*

b) *Each of you: Think of reasons why you would like to do what is written on the card.*

c) *Take turns to tell each other what you would like to do.*

d) *As a group, decide on what to do for the holidays. Meet halfway. The phrases on page 46 in your book will help you.*

Mother

name: Mary
age: 39
job: teacher
hobbies: reading books about other countries

idea for holidays:
tour through another country

Father

name: Peter
age: 43
job: doctor
hobbies: fishing

idea for holidays:
holiday flat at a lake

Daughter

name: Tina
age: 14
hobbies: chatting, music, disco

idea for holidays:
beach holiday

Son

name: Tom
age: 10
hobbies: riding a bike, football

idea for holidays:
adventure park

Lösungen zu den Stationen

Station 1
A: 1 *happy* 2 *angry* 3 *sad* 4 *scared* 5 *excited* 6 *nervous*; B: 1 *cool* 2 *grumpy* 3 *angry* 4 *shy* 5 *happy* 6 *scared*

Station 2
Lösungsvorschlag: 1 *… wouldn't give my pupils any homework.* 2 *… would get off the bus.* 3 *… would tell the person who hurt me.* 4 *… wouldn't be so strict.* 5 *… would try to help.* 6 *… I had a lot of money, I would live in a big house.*

Station 4
☺: *I see!; OK, fine!; Great!; I guess you're right!; I know!* 😐: *I know, but …; I don't mind, but …; That's true, but …; I understand, but …; I'm sorry, but …; You've got a point, but …; Maybe …* ☹: *I'm angry that …; I'm worried that …; I don't like it!; I don't want to …; I'm hurt because …; I'm sad that …*

Station 7
Lösungsvorschlag: S: *Hi, David. Can we talk?* B: *Forget it! Get out of my room!* S: *I'm sorry, but …* B: *Sorry? You used my mobile without asking me and now it's broken!* S: *I can understand that you're really angry. I'll save my pocket money and buy you a much cooler one, I promise!* B: *And what should I do until then?* S: *Maybe you can use mine?* B: *OK! Although I don't like it, it's old …*

KV 17a: Look who's talking!

a) *This afternoon three people have tried to call the Pattersons, but the family is not at home. Guess which family members the messages are for.*

b) *Look at the messages again. Think about how the people's voices might sound and find adjectives to describe them. The adjectives on page 54 in your book can help you.*

c) *Choose one member of the Patterson family and write a telephone message someone left for him/her. Use the Useful phrases on page 50 in your book. Read the message to your partner and let him/her guess which family member the message is for.*

Hello, this is the Pattersons' answerphone. We are not at home, so we can't take your call at the moment. Please leave a message for us after the tone, and we'll call you back soon. Bye.

A.

Hi, _____. This is Katie. Sorry, but I can't come to your party tonight, although I'd really love to. Monster parties are fun! My parents have gone out, and nobody can take me to your house. What is more, I haven't finished working on my biology project yet. Hope I can come to your next party! See you at school on Monday. Bye!

B.

Good afternoon, _____. This is Mrs Clay speaking. I help your father in the house. Well, I would like to talk to you about him. I'm a bit worried, you see, and I'm not sure whether he can look after himself and live on his own any longer. He forgets a lot of things. He doesn't want to move and live in an old people's home. Please call me at 01753 529564. Thank you. Have a nice evening. Goodbye!

C.

Hello, this is a message for _____. I got your twelve or so messages on my mailbox, thank you very much. I'm only calling to tell you not to phone me again. I'm fed up with it. You treated me badly. It's over.

D.

KV 17b: Look who's talking now!

The twins love to phone their friends, write texts or e-mails and visit chatrooms. This is why they would like to have their own line and phone number. The family is discussing what would happen if they had their own line.
In a group of six pupils give a role card to every group member and prepare a discussion. What do the role cards tell you about the family members?
The tips and Useful phrases on page 46 in your book can help you. Use if-clauses.

Role cards

Mrs Patterson	Mr Patterson
thinks … – the twins shouldn't spend too much time on the phone – the phone bill would be too high because the twins would talk on the phone for hours – they wouldn't spend enough time on their homework …	thinks … – a new line is too expensive – the phone should only be used for short messages and information – people who talk on the phone for a long time are terrible …
Mel	**Amy**
– wants her own line because her friends have one, too – doesn't want others to listen when she is on the phone – thinks Grandpa and Jake shouldn't have their own line because … …	– wants to share a line with Mel – thinks it would be fun to share a line with her twin – the family should get a flat rate anyway …
Jake	**Grandpa**
thinks … – he as the older brother should have his own line first – with his own line he could have talked to Miriam in his own room and she would still be his girlfriend …	thinks … – when he was young, children didn't even have their own rooms and they "survived", too – children don't need their own phone number – if he moves in with the Pattersons, he should have his own line …

⟨Project⟩ English and Biology

Seite 56–57

Ziele
- Den im Lehrwerk integrierten *skills*-Lehrgang erweitern und vertiefen
- Essgewohnheiten in anderen Ländern kennen lernen
- Das Erstellen von Balkendiagrammen als neues *Project skill* einüben
- Ein Projekt über gesunde Ernährung durchführen

STEP 1

	Look at breakfast in different countries	Seite 56

Text/Üben

Ziel
- Essgewohnheiten in anderen Ländern kennen lernen
- Erfahrungen mit Essgewohnheiten in anderen Ländern austauschen
- Den individuellen Wortschatz durch *food words* erweitern

Wortschatz cereal, sausage, porridge, Japanese, soup, Mexican, Swedish, butter, jam

Methodisches Vorgehen
- L führt die S in das Thema ein, indem er/sie vom englischen Frühstück im letzten Urlaub (oder vom Frühstück in einem anderen Land) erzählt und dabei die Begleittexte zu den Bildern in STEP 1 vorentlastet. Nach dem Einführungssatz zur Aufgabe: *People from different countries …* fährt L mit *For example, when I was in … I …* fort.
- Die S lesen die Texte in Einzelarbeit, betrachten die Bilder und beschriften **KV 1: Breakfast in different countries** mit neuen und bereits bekannten Vokabeln.
- a) + b) Die S besprechen die Aufgaben in GA. Jede Gruppe fasst anschließend ihre Gespräche im Plenum kurz zusammen.

Erweiterung
- Die S sammeln die *food words* für ihren *folder*.

Lösung *Individuelle S-Antworten*

Tipps für junge Lehrer Wenn der Englischunterricht in der ersten Stunde liegt, könnte L mit den S „gesund" frühstücken. Die S schreiben ihre mitgebrachten Frühstückszutaten – *breakfast foods* – auf Englisch an die Tafel und berichten, was sie sonst zu Hause essen würden: *Let's see what you've got. Do you eat anything other than this at home?* Die dabei aufkommenden neuen Vokabeln werden ebenfalls an die Tafel geschrieben. Die S erstellen eine *mindmap* zum Thema *A German breakfast*, das sie in STEP 2 verwenden können. Deutsch-englische Wörterbücher wären an dieser Stelle hilfreich.

Material
Kopiervorlage 1
Ggf. Wörterbücher

STEP 2

	Find out about your own breakfast	Seite 56

Üben

Ziel
- Sich mit den eigenen Essgewohnheiten auseinandersetzen
- Eine *mindmap* zu den *breakfast foods* erstellen

Methodisches Vorgehen
- Die S bilden zwei Gruppen – Mädchen und Jungen getrennt – und sammeln ihre Frühstückszutaten auf Moderations- bzw. Karteikarten – eine Karte für jede Zutat. Den S sollten dabei deutsch-englische Wörterbücher zur Verfügung gestellt werden (mindestens ein Wörterbuch pro Gruppe).
- Am Ende der ersten GA-Phase halten die Gruppen auf jeder Karte (oben rechts) fest, wie viele S die jeweilige Zutat zum Frühstück essen.

- Im Plenum werden die Kategorien für die Frühstückszutaten festgelegt: *fruit, cereal, bread, milk products, …*
- Die S fertigen in ihrer Gruppe mit den zuvor gesammelten *breakfast foods* eine *mindmap* an zum Thema *Our breakfast*. Je ein oder zwei S einer Gruppe kleben dabei die Karten als *mindmap* auf ein Poster. Die beiden Poster werden anschließend an der Tafel bzw. an der Wand aufgehängt.
- Als Hausaufgabe können die S nach dem vorgegebenen Muster in **KV 1** eine kurze Präsentation zu einem für sie typischen Frühstück vorbereiten, z. B. mit einem/r beschrifteten Foto/Zeichnung und einem kurzen Begleittext.

HA

Auch als HA geeignet

Material
2 Poster, Moderations- bzw. Karteikarten, Filzstifte, Klebstoff
Ggf. Wörterbücher

Erweiterung
- Die S vergleichen die Essgewohnheiten der Mädchen und der Jungen in der Klasse in einem kurzen Text oder als Dialog (evtl. für eine Radiosendung). Der Text kann als Hausaufgabe und der Dialog in PA während des Unterrichts verfasst werden.

Tipps für junge Lehrer
Die Visualisierung von Ergebnissen spielt eine wichtige Rolle. Die S sollten dazu angehalten werden, auf den Kärtchen in Druckschrift zu schreiben und den vorhandenen Platz ausnutzen.

STEP 3

Üben	**Make a bar chart**	Seite 56

Ziel
- Ein Balkendiagramm erstellen
- Ergebnisse in Balkendiagrammen beschreiben und vergleichen

Wortschatz *bar chart, survey, x-axis, y-axis*

Methodisches Vorgehen
- Die S lesen die Arbeitsaufträge in den *Project skills*. Anhand der *mindmaps* in STEP 2 entscheiden die S im Plenum, welche *breakfast foods* sie für den Vergleich zwischen Jungen und Mädchen wählen (höchstens fünf). Als Hausaufgabe werden die beiden Balkendiagramme erstellt.
- Für die Arbeit mit den Balkendiagrammen werden zunächst *Useful phrases: Describing and comparing bar charts* an der Tafel gesammelt (siehe TA).
- Mit Hilfe der *Useful phrases* vergleichen die S die Essgewohnheiten der Mädchen und der Jungen in der Klasse. Auch diese Aufgabe eignet sich als Hausaufgabe.

HA

TIP
Useful phrases sammeln

Auch als HA geeignet

TA

> Useful Phrases: Describing and comparing bar charts
> The bar chart shows …
> In the bar chart, you can clearly see that …
> Most of the girls/boys eat … for breakfast, but only … girls/boys say they do.
> On the one hand … is most popular with the girls/boys, but on the other hand the girls/boys like … best.
> Only a few girls/boys eat … , but a lot of girls/boys do.
> Both the girls and the boys …

Erweiterung
- Die S können ihre Ergebnisse auch vergleichen, indem sie die beiden Säulen zu einem *breakfast food* nebeneinander stellen. Alternativ wäre ein Balkendiagramm für die gesamte Klasse denkbar (siehe Vorschlag im SB).

Lösung | *Individuelle S-Antworten* |

Tipps für junge Lehrer
Um selbstständig arbeiten zu können, sollten die S Wörterbücher benutzen und/oder mit dem *Dictionary* im Buchanhang arbeiten.

Material
Grafikpapier
Ggf. Wörterbücher

P ⟨Project⟩

STEP 4

Text/Üben	**Look at food and its contents**	Seite 57

Ziel
- Das eigene Frühstück unter gesundheitlichen Gesichtspunkten überprüfen
- Fächerübergreifendes Denken fördern

Wortschatz *contents (pl), to contain sth, fat, protein, carbohydrate, mineral, vitamin, fibre*

Methodisches Vorgehen
- L und die S lesen den Text und die Aufgabenstellung gemeinsam durch. Anschließend tragen die S die zuvor erarbeiteten Ergebnisse (*breakfast foods in our class* und *breakfast foods in …*) in das Diagramm in **KV 2: A healthy breakfast?** ein.
- Bei Problemfragen bietet sich *cross-curricular teaching* an. Die S klären offene Fragen mit ihrem/r Biologie-Fachlehrer/in.
- Danach diskutieren die S in PA, ob sie ihr Frühstück für gesund halten, und ob in anderen Ländern das Frühstück gesünder ist. Ihre Meinung sollten sie anschließend im Plenum begründen können.
- Ggf. kann L hier die *Fish-Bowl*-Methode statt einer Plenumsdiskussion anwenden. Eine kleine Gruppe diskutiert und die anderen Mitglieder der Lerngruppe hören zu und machen sich Notizen.
- Die Ergebnisse sollten anschließend in einem Text zusammengefasst werden. Interessanter wäre es, ein Interview zu schreiben, indem ein/e Experte/in die Ist-Situation beschreibt und dann eine Empfehlung für ein gesünderes Frühstück gibt.

Auch als HA geeignet

Erweiterung
- Die S stellen mit Bildern aus Zeitschriften ein Werbeplakat für ein gesundes Frühstück zusammen. Hierzu sollten sie sich *advertising slogans* ausdenken und in ihr Plakat integrieren.

Lösung | *Individuelle S-Antworten*

Tipps für junge Lehrer Die S sollten lernen, offene Sachfragen durch eigene Recherchen zu beantworten oder sie mit ihren Fachlehrern/innen zu erörtern.

Material Kopiervorlage 2

STEP 5

Text/Üben	**Do a project: Healthy food**	Seite 57

Ziel
- Ein Projekt zum Thema *healthy food* durchführen
- Die gelernten *Project skills* anwenden
- Kooperatives und soziales Arbeiten erleben

Wortschatz *campaign, information stand*

Methodisches Vorgehen
- L und die S lesen den Text und die Aufgabenstellung gemeinsam durch.
- Im Sinne der Schülerorientierung sollte das Planungsgespräch im Plenum sehr offen gestaltet werden. Welches Projekt könnten die S in ihrer Schule durchführen? Wenn keine Projektwoche geplant ist, welche weiteren Möglichkeiten gibt es für die S? Ein Informationsstand auf dem Schulhof oder in der Schulkantine? Berichte in der Schülerzeitung? Ein eigenes *leaflet*, das die S auf dem Schulhof bzw. in anderen Englisch-Klassen verteilen? Wie könnte eine *healthy food campaign* in der Schule tatsächlich aussehen? Welche Aufgaben fallen an? Welche S interessieren sich für welche Aufgaben? Diese Fragen werden mit L im Plenum besprochen.

TIP
Wichtig bei der Planung eines Projektes: Einteilung der Gruppen, Aufgaben, *deadlines*

⟨Project⟩ P

- Die Projektplanung wird von L geleitet und an der Tafel oder auf einem Poster visualisiert: Termine, Aufgaben, Gruppenmitglieder. Das Projekt kann sich über einige Wochen verteilen, indem bestimmte Tage als Projekttage deklariert werden (Terminplanung, *deadlines*).
- In GA werden die einzelnen Gruppenaufgaben im Detail besprochen und die Aufgaben innerhalb der Gruppe verteilt.
- Nach der Gruppenarbeitsphase wird überlegt, wie die einzelnen Ergebnisse in das Gesamtprojekt eingegliedert werden können.

Erweiterung
- Eine der Gruppen könnte die Arbeit mit einer Videokamera aufnehmen und eine kurze Filmdokumentation der Projektarbeit erstellen. Die Präsentation der Arbeit in der Klasse oder an einem Elternabend bietet eine zusätzliche Motivation.

Lösung *Individuelle S-Antworten*

Tipps für junge Lehrer Dieses Projekt eignet sich hervorragend für eine (klassenübergreifende) Schulprojekt-Woche, aber auch im Schulalltag gibt es vielfältige Möglichkeiten, die drei Säulen der Projektarbeit in einer Englisch-Klasse zu praktizieren: Schülerorientierung, Handlungsorientierung sowie soziales und kooperatives Arbeiten.

Material
Ggf. Poster, Videokamera

KV 1: Breakfast in different countries

a) *Look at the pictures of breakfasts in different countries and name the breakfast foods in the pictures with new words and words you already know. Page 56 in your book can help you.*

b) *Write a short text (3–4 sentences) about breakfast in Germany. The texts on page 56 in your book can help you.*

KV 2: A healthy breakfast?

a) *What do the boys and girls in your class eat for breakfast? Write the names of the breakfast foods in the diagram. Then do the same thing for breakfast foods in another country.*

b) *Which is the healthiest breakfast? Say why. Ask your biology teacher if you need help.*

Planung Unit 4

Übersicht

Bearbeitungszeitraum: 22 Unterrichtsstunden

Abschnitt	SB-Seiten	Ziele	Wortschatz/Grammatik & skills	WB-Übungen	CD-Tracks Kopiervorlagen Folien DVD	Gramm. Anhang (SB)
Check-in *The UK on the move*	58–59	Städte und Regionen in Großbritannien kennen lernen Fotos beschreiben und vergleichen Regionale sprachliche Besonderheiten unterscheiden Die eigene Region vorstellen	Wortfeld „Landschaften, Städte und Gebäude beschreiben"	S. 40/ex. 1–3	Schüler-CD 1/38–43 Lehrer-CD 2/22–27, 28–33 KV 1a+b Folie 10	
Language 1 *Welsh relatives*	60–61	Über den Umzug in eine neue Stadt und die Bedeutung von Familie und Freunden sprechen	Wortfelder „Umzug" und „Familie und Freunde" *The definite and the indefinite article* *Adjectives used as nouns* *How to:* Neue Bekanntschaften machen R: *Possessive pronouns*	S. 41/ex. 4, 5 S. 42/ex. 6–8	Lehrer-CD 2/34 KV 2 DVD: Cultural differences, Part A	G14, 15
Talkwise *Dealing with problems*	62	In Problemsituationen sprachlich adäquat reagieren	*Useful phrases:* Helping and apologizing	S. 43/ex. 9, 10	Lehrer-CD 2/35, 36 KV 3	
Language 2 *Up North*	63–65	Eine pakistanische Familie kennen lernen Über Liverpool und die Beatles sprechen	Wortfeld „Sinneswahrnehmungen" *Adjectives after certain verbs* *Future perfect* R: *Adjective or adverb?*	S. 44/ex. 11, 12 S. 45/ex. 13, 14 S. 46/ex. 15, 16	Schüler-CD 1/44 Lehrer-CD 2/37, 38, 39, 40 KV 4, 5 DVD: Cultural differences, Part B	G16, 17
Skills *Factual texts*	66	Lesetechniken zum Erschließen von Sachtexten kennen lernen Einem Sachtext gezielt Informationen entnehmen	*Reading skills:* Einen Sachtext lesen	S. 47/ex. 17	KV 6a+b	
Text *Changing places*	67–69	Sachtexte eigenständig erschließen Die erlernten Lesetechniken anwenden	*Skimming* und *scanning* Eine Internetrecherche durchführen *Writing texts:* Eine Reiseempfehlung	S. 48/ex. 18–20	Schüler-CD 2/1–3 Lehrer-CD 3/1–3 Folie 11	

Abschnitt	SB-Seiten	Ziele	Wortschatz/Grammatik & skills	WB-Übungen	CD-Tracks Kopiervorlagen Folien DVD	Gramm. Anhang (SB)
Wordwise	70	Den Wortschatz der Unit wiederholen und festigen Die Aussprache schulen Wortbildungsregeln erkennen/wiederholen	Pluralwörter Aussprachregeln Wortbildung	S. 49/ex. 22, 23	Schüler-CD 2/4 Lehrer-CD 3/4, 5 KV 7, 8	G18
Check-out	71	Selbstkontrolle Die Lernziele der Unit 4 überprüfen	Wortschatz- und Grammatikschwerpunkte der Unit: *Useful phrases, the definite and the indefinite article, adjectives after certain verbs*	S. 50/ex. 24–26		
⟨**Text**⟩ *Benny and Omar*	72–73	Einen Auszug aus einem Jugendroman eigenständig erschließen Über Probleme und Chancen von Auswanderung sprechen	Wortfelder „Reisen" und „Landschaften und Städte beschreiben"		Schüler-CD 2/ 5–8 Lehrer-CD 3/ 6–9 KV 9, 10	

Unit 4 The UK on the move

Hinweise

LANDESKUNDE

Manchester, approx. 486,000 inhabitants, is the third largest city in the UK. It was the world's most important industrial city and the international centre of textile manufacture and cotton spinning and played a central role in the Industrial Revolution. During this period the canal system grew, and Manchester became one end of the world's first intercity passenger railway. Today Manchester is one of the UK's centres of arts, media, higher education and commerce and one of Europe's most modern cities. It is famous for its music scene, and the annual music festival 'In The City' is regarded by the global music community as the premier new music event in the world which has helped launch the careers of bands like Oasis, Radiohead, Suede, Elastica, Coldplay, The Darkness, Doves, Foo Fighters and many more. Manchester is also famous for its two Premiership football clubs, Manchester United and Manchester City. Manchester United's Old Trafford ground is the largest club football ground in the UK with a capacity of 76,000, and England's only UEFA-rated 5-star stadium. For more information check: http://www.visitmanchester.com and http://www.manchester.gov.uk

Windsor, the royal city, is a suburban town and tourist destination 21 miles west of the city of London. It is best known as the site of **Windsor Castle.** Windsor Castle, one of three official residences of the Queen, is the largest occupied castle in the world and it has been a royal home and fortress for over 900 years. Situated north of Windsor Castle is the King's College of Our Lady of Eton, commonly known as Eton College or just Eton, a public school (privately funded and independent) for boys, founded in 1440 by King Henry VI. Eton is one of the most exclusive schools in the world. 18 former prime ministers attended the school. The school dress dates from the 1850s; pupils still wear black tailcoats and waistcoats and pin-striped trousers. For more information check: http://www.windsor.gov.uk/attractions/attract_index.htm

Liverpool, approx. 448,000 inhabitants, is the fifth largest city in the UK. It was built across a ridge of hills rising up to a height of around 230 feet (70 metres) above sea-level at Everton Hill, on the River Mersey. In 2004 Liverpool's waterfront was declared a UNESCO World Heritage site, reflecting the city's importance in the development of the world's trading system and dock technology. The docks are central to Liverpool's history, with the best-known being **Albert Dock**: the first enclosed, non-combustible dock warehouse system in the world and built in cast iron, brick and stone. Liverpool possesses the largest national museum collection outside of London. It is also home to Europe's oldest Chinatown.
Liverpool is famous for being the birthplace of The Beatles, and 'The Beatles Story' is the only museum in the world that is entirely Beatles-themed. Liverpool FC and Everton are Premiership football clubs. Liverpool's well-known ground is called Anfield Road. Liverpool's inhabitants are referred to as Liverpudlians or Scousers, Scouse (originally a sailor's dish) being synonymous with the Liverpool accent. In 2007, the city celebrated its 800th anniversary, and in 2008 it holds the European Capital of Culture title. For more information check: http://www.visitliverpool.com and http://www.beatlesstory.com

Wales is located in the south-west of Great Britain and is bordered by England to the east, the Bristol Channel to the south and the Irish Sea to the west and north. Wales is the largest principality in the world, it covers an area of 20,000 sq km, 250 km north to south, and 200 km east to west. Two thirds of the population of Wales live in the valleys and coastal plain of the south, with a further significant population concentration in the north-east. The remaining areas in Mid Wales, the south-west and west are predominantly rural and characterised by hilly and mountainous terrain. There are 732 miles of unspoilt beaches, coves and rugged cliffs to explore, and over 400 castles and ancient monuments to visit. In Wales there are more castles per sq mile than in any other country in Western Europe!
Wales is often referred to as 'the land of song', being particularly famous for harpists, male voice choirs, and solo artists. The official languages in Wales are English and Welsh. Wales is officially bilingual and Welsh is now a compulsory language up to GCSE level for all pupils. Head of state is

the British monarch, currently Queen Elizabeth II (since 1952). Executive power is derived with the Queen and exercised by the Parliament of the United Kingdom at Westminster, with some powers devolved to the National Assembly for Wales in Cardiff. The most popular sports in Wales are football and rugby. For more information check: http://www.visitwales.co.uk

North Wales comprises the island of Anglesey, the Llŷn peninsula and the Snowdonia mountain range, together with the catchment areas of the Rivers Conwy, Clwyd and Dee. The area is mostly rural with many mountains and valleys. This, in combination with its coast (on the Irish Sea), has ensured that tourism is the principal industry. You can visit castles and stately homes, art galleries, craft centres, museums or explore the rugged coastline. Snowdonia National Park, with Snowdon, Wales' highest mountain, is a popular area for climbing, canoeing, sailing, quad biking or walking. There is also high-tech industry in this region – Airbus set up a wing factory at Broughton in Flintshire. During the Industrial Revolution and still today slate has been quarried in Noth Wales. Farming, which was once the principal economic force in the area, is now much reduced in importance. For more information check: http://www.nwt.co.uk/html/thingstoseeanddo.htm

South Wales borders England and the Bristol Channel to the east and south, and Mid Wales and West Wales to the north and west. South Wales incorporates the capital city of Cardiff and the cities of Newport and Swansea. The area also includes the South Wales Valleys and the Brecon Beacons National Park. During the Industrial Revolution coal, copper, iron, silver, lead, and gold were mined in South Wales. This changed the landscape considerably. By the 1830s, hundreds of tons of coal were being transported by barge to the ports of Cardiff and Newport. In the 1870s, coal was transported to these docks by rail networks. Today you can visit the National Waterfront Museum in Swansea to find out more about that period in Welsh history. From the early 1970s, the Welsh economy faced massive restructuring with large numbers of jobs in traditional heavy industry disappearing and being replaced gradually by new ones in light industry and in services. Today, Cardiff is the largest city in Wales and serves as a major centre of culture, sport and history in the UK. Cardiff Castle is one of Wales' leading tourist attractions, dating from the arrival of the Romans in the first century AD. After the Norman Conquest, the Castle's Keep was built and a number of medieval fortifications and dwellings followed.
Each year there is The National Eisteddfod of Wales, a festival of Welsh music which can be traced back to 1176 when Lord Rhys held a grand gathering at his castle in Cardigan, to which poets and musicians from all over the country had been invited. A chair at the Lord's table was awarded to the best poet and musician, a tradition that prevails in the modern-day National Eisteddfod. South Wales is also famous for its beautiful beaches, among them the beach at Rhossili on the Gower Coast. For more information check: http://www.south-wales.org.uk

Reading, approx. 143,000 inhabitants, is located some 66 km west of central London on a low ridge between the Rivers Thames and Kennet. The University of Reading is ranked as one of the UK's 10 most research-intensive universities and as one of the top 200 universities in the world. Established as an extension college of Christ Church, Oxford, in 1892, it received a Royal Charter in 1926, the only university to do so between the two World Wars. Reading has a well-known rowing club which takes part in summer races on the Thames against other rowing clubs. For more information check: http://www.reading-guide.com

Leicester, approx. 285,000 inhabitants, is located in the east Midlands, on the River Soar and at the edge of the English National Forest. Major industries in Leicester today include food processing, hosiery, knitwear, engineering, electronics, printing and plastics. The city centre is mainly Victorian with some later developments, which have usually been integrated in smoothly. The city plays host to an annual Pride Parade (Leicester Pride), a Caribbean Carnival (the largest in the UK outside London), the largest Diwali celebrations outside of India (the ethnic background of 30% of the population of Leicester is Asian), the largest comedy festival in the UK (Leicester Comedy Festival), and the award-winning music festival Summer Sundae with the connecting Summer Sundae Fringe festival. For more information check: http://www.goleicestershire.com

Starry Magazine is an online magazine which features celebrity interviews, movie and music reviews, contests and more. For more information check: http://www.starrymag.com

4 Check-in

Bhangra, in the traditional sense, is a folk dance and not a music form. It is a fusion of music, singing and the beat of the *dhol* drum, single-stringed instruments called the *ektara*, the *tumbi*, and an instrument reminiscent of an enlarged pair of tongs called *chimta*. The accompanying songs are small couplets written in the Punjabi language called *bolis*. They relate to harvest celebration, love, patriotism or current social issues.

STORYLINE

Im Mittelpunkt der Unit stehen das Kennenlernen verschiedener Städte und Regionen des UK und der Umzug in eine andere Stadt. Die Internetseite *VISIT BRITAIN Kids* stellt verschiedene Städte/Regionen des UK vor und veranstaltet ein Gewinnspiel, bei dem es einen Aufenthalt bei einer Gastfamilie in einer anderen Stadt/Region zu gewinnen gibt. Dies soll es den Jugendlichen ermöglichen, das Leben dort probeweise kennen zu lernen.

Shirin Khan ist bereits vor einem Jahr von Manchester nach Swansea gezogen, da ihr Vater hier einen Job als Ingenieur gefunden hat. Sie hat in Rhona Williams eine Freundin gefunden, die ihr die Stadt gezeigt hat und die sie um ihre große pakistanische Familie beneidet. Als Shirins Familie ihrer Tante Zeba beim Umzug hilft, lädt sie Rhona ein, ihre Familie kennen zu lernen. Rhona staunt über die Größe der Familie, das asiatische Essen und die Sprache (Punjabi). Shirins Cousin Tariq beantwortet ihre Fragen und erzählt ihr von Manchester. Zusammen mit Shirins englischer Mutter machen die beiden Mädchen einen Ausflug nach Liverpool, wo sie die *Beatles Story* und *Albert Dock* besichtigen.

VISIT BRITAIN Kids veröffentlicht unterdessen die Erfahrungsberichte dreier Gewinner. Wayne aus London verbrachte eine Woche in Swansea. Er wunderte sich über die bilingualen Straßenschilder und schwärmt von dem wunderschönen *Gower Beach*, dem *National Waterfront Museum* und dem *Swansea Leisure Centre Skatepark*. Michael aus Leicester war für eine Woche in Liverpool und amüsiert sich über den Akzent der Bewohner. Seine Highlights waren eine Fahrt mit der Fähre über den River Mersey, die Besichtigung der *Williamson Tunnels* und des Fußballstadiums *Anfield Road*. Auch Rhona hat gewonnen und durfte für eine Woche nach Reading, wo sie zunächst wegen ihres walisischen Akzents ausgelacht wurde. Sie mochte die Open-Air-Festivals und fand die Musik wesentlich besser als die ihres Freundes, der in einem traditionellen walisischen Chor singt. Rhona war begeistert von dem modernen Schwimmbad, und ihre Austauschpartnerin nahm sie mit zum Rudern. Im Sommer würde sie gerne noch einmal zurückkommen, um das berühmte Ruderrennen zu sehen.

Check-in
Seite 58–59

Ziele	• Städte und Regionen des UK kennen lernen
	• Verschiedene Varianten des Englischen hören und unterscheiden
	• Die eigene Region vorstellen

Text/Fotos	**The UK on the move**	Seite 58–59

Hinweis Die S können an dieser Stelle ihr Wissen aus den vorherigen Bänden oder ihr Allgemeinwissen über Städte und Regionen des UK reaktivieren und einbringen (vgl. *Green Line* 1, Unit 4, 6 und *Green Line* 2, Unit 2, 6).

Ziel • Städte und Regionen des UK kennen lernen

Wortschatz *to be on the move, on average, to move (house), perhaps, exchange, region, industry, cult, birthplace, recently, facelift, landscape, Welsh, to be proud (of), regional, culture, wing, coal mine, heavy industry, male voice choir, to exist*

Methodisches Vorgehen
• Zunächst Betrachtung der Karte vorne im SB: *These are the British Isles. Do you know any other terms?* Die Begriffe *United Kingdom, Great Britain* und *England* werden an der Tafel festgehalten. Mit Hilfe der Karten auf S. 170 werden die Unterschiede erläutert.

> **TIP**
> Die Folie kann später wieder verwendet und ergänzt werden

196

Check-in 4

- SB geschlossen. L fragt die S, welche Städte und Regionen des UK sie bereits kennen. Mit Hilfe einer Wandkarte werden diese in **Folie 10: The British Isles** eingetragen. Parallel dazu werden die Beiträge in einer Tabelle an der Tafel festgehalten. Die S ergänzen ihr Wissen über die jeweiligen Städte/Regionen mündlich.
- L ergänzt ggf. die Städte *Manchester*, *Windsor* und *Liverpool*, sowie die Regionen *North* und *South Wales* auf der Folie und in der Tabelle und fragt Vorwissen der S dazu ab.
- L erläutert den Kontext der *Check-in*-Seite *(VISIT BRITAIN Kids* = Internetseite für Kinder und Jugendliche, hier: Preisausschreiben für einen Austausch innerhalb des UK) und führt in diesem Zusammenhang bereits die Vokabeln *to move (house), on the move, exchange* ein. Dann leitet L zur Betrachtung des *Check-in*-Textes über: *Let's find out more about these cities/regions …*
- Die S lesen den Text und betrachten die Fotos.
- Die neuen Vokabeln werden im Textzusammenhang eingeführt bzw. erschließen sich den S über die (dem Deutschen ähnliche) Schreibweise *(region, industry, cult, coal)*.
- Neue Informationen werden in der Tabelle ergänzt.

TA

Great Britain: England, Scotland, Wales
The United Kingdom: England, Scotland, Wales and Northern Ireland

Countries	Regions	Cities
England	North-West England, …	London, Greenwich, Birmingham, Manchester, Windsor, Liverpool, …
Scotland	Highland, …	Aberdeen, Edinburgh, …
Wales	North Wales, South Wales, …	Cardiff, Swansea, …
Northern Ireland	…	Belfast, …

Erweiterung
- L zeigt Folien oder Dias mit weiteren Fotos der im SB vorgestellten Städte/Regionen.
- **KV 1a+b: A trip around the UK:** Die S lernen in GA spielerisch das UK kennen. Die KV kann auch am Ende der Unit 4 oder zwischendurch eingesetzt werden.

Tipps für junge Lehrer Es fördert das Interesse der S, wenn sie ihr Vorwissen aus früheren Units reaktivieren und bereits vorhandenes landeskundliches Allgemeinwissen einbringen können. Gleichzeitig werden landeskundliche Kenntnisse umgewälzt und bleiben länger im Gedächtnis.

Material
Kopiervorlage 1a+b
Folie 10
Wandkarte
Ggf. Dias

Üben | **1 Find the information** | Seite 58

Ziel
- Fotos beschreiben und vergleichen
- Sehenswürdigkeiten nach Interesse ordnen und mit dem/r Partner/in vergleichen

Wortschatz *contrast, less*

Methodisches Vorgehen
- a) ist eine Fortführung des methodischen Vorgehens zum *Check-in*-Text.
- b) kann mündlich im Plenum oder schriftlich in Einzelarbeit mit anschließender Partnerkontrolle bearbeitet werden. Nützliche Vokabeln zum Be-

4 Check-in

schreiben von Landschaften/Städten/Gebäuden werden an der Tafel festgehalten.
- c) Vor Bearbeitung der Aufgabe sollte die *Did you know?*-Box gelesen werden. Anschließend erstellen die S die beiden Listen in Einzelarbeit.
- d) In der PA-Phase ist es wichtig, dass die S ihre Auswahl begründen. Hier bieten sich für stärkere S gute Differenzierungsmöglichkeiten an. L sollte abschließend einige Beispielsätze an der Tafel festhalten. Bei schwächeren Lerngruppen kann es hilfreich sein, bereits vor Bearbeitung der Aufgabe einen Beispielsatz anzuschreiben, der dann als Muster dient.

TIP
In leistungsschwächeren Klassen ggf. Steigerung der Adjektive wiederholen (*Green Line* 2, S. 137/138, G 9, 10)

Statt der Karte im Buch bietet sich auch eine Folie/Wandkarte an, um die Aufmerksamkeit der S sicher zu stellen

TA

b) Talking about …

Landscapes	Cities	Buildings
flowers, green, a lot of trees/forests, lake, hills, the sea/a river, …	city centre, streets, parks, museums, houses, underground, …	modern, old-fashioned, tall, castle, church, office buildings, museum, …

d) Examples:
I would like to visit Liverpool. I want to see the stadium of Liverpool FC.
I wouldn't want to go to North Wales because I would have to climb mountains there.

Lösung b) *Siehe TA* c) + d) *Individuelle S-Antworten*

Tipps für junge Lehrer L sollte in der PA-Phase sicherstellen, dass die S nicht lediglich ihre Listen austauschen, sondern ihre Auswahl differenziert begründen.

Material
Workbook S. 40/1

2 Listening: Regional voices   Seite 59

HV-Text a) **Dialogue 1**

Ted: Welcome to another of our programmes about the regions of the UK. We wanted to find out what people in the UK think about their own region. So we sent our reporter Silvia Benn round the country, and here's what she found out. First she went to Swansea, the second largest city in Wales.
Silvia: Excuse me, I'm from Gamma Radio. I'd like to ask you a question.
Man: OK, go ahead.
Silvia: What is typical of Wales for you?
Man: Oh, I don't know. There are so many things. Um … Well, there's the language, of course – and the way we speak English. The English often say we sing when we talk!
Silvia: Do you sing – oh, I mean: Do you *speak* Welsh?
Man: No, not very much. I learned it at school, of course. I can say 'Bore da'. That's 'Good morning'. But I don't think many people speak Welsh as their first language today.
Silvia: Well, about a quarter of Welsh people do speak the language, you know.
Man: Really? It's that many, is it?
Silvia: Most of them live in North Wales, not here in the south. What about music and singing?
Man: Yes, singing is typically Welsh. We're very proud of that here.
Silvia: Do you like singing?
Man: Yes, I do, but only in a big rugby crowd, you know what I'm saying? We've got some great Welsh singers. But I don't think you've heard of them in England.

Silvia: Oh yes, we have! We know lots of Welsh singers and stars. But let's get back to you. Are there any places or things which are important for your Welsh identity?

Man: Well, I love the landscape – especially the mountains. We've got a beautiful country, you know. There aren't any mountains in England.

Silvia: Well, some places in the Lake District in northern England aren't much smaller than Snowdon in North Wales, you know. I often feel there's a kind of competition between Wales and England.

Man: Yes, maybe you're right about that. The English often think they're better than the Welsh. But we've got the best music, and the best rugby players!

Silvia: Well, thank you for your time and …

Dialogue 2

Silvia: Today I'm in the town of Reading, not far from London, and my first interview is coming up. Excuse me, I'm from Gamma Radio. Have you got a moment?

Girl: Oh, hello.

Silvia: Tell me, are you English?

Girl: Yes, I am. I live here in Reading.

Silvia: Are you proud of that?

Girl: Um – I don't know, I never really thought about it … But, yes, I *am* proud of it.

Silvia: Now, English isn't the same thing as British, is it? What's so special for you about your identity as an English girl?

Girl: I can only talk about this part of England, the south. We've got everything here. We've got all these new buildings, see? And if you look around, you'll kind of see lots of people; they're shopping, sitting in cafés … The rest of Britain isn't like that.

Silvia: You could be wrong there. I know some really exciting cities in Scotland and Wales which look the same – and in other parts of England, too.

Girl: Well, maybe – but they're kind of all so far from London. And that's where it's happening, isn't it? All the big shows, the concerts, sport type things … You can get to London in forty minutes, so you're close to the Channel Tunnel and Europe, aren't you?

Silvia: What about other, older aspects of English traditions and culture?

Girl: Well, kind of – I like the small towns and villages with their pretty houses and gardens. I like the landscape here, too. It looks green and rich and friendly.

Silvia: Is it the same in the North of England, too?

Girl: Oh no! I've never been there, but I should think it's all dirty and industrial, and it rains all the time, and …

Dialogue 3

Silvia: For my last report I've come to the North-West of England, to Manchester. Well, it's not raining at the moment, and I've got a young man with me who looks very happy. Tell me, is it so terrible to live in the North-West?

Male Youth: No, why should it be?

Silvia: Some people think everything is dirty and sad here.

Male Youth: Well – maybe it was like that sixty years ago, like. But things have changed, haven't they?

Silvia: The Industrial Revolution started in the North of England. Is it still part of your culture and tradition here?

Male Youth: Oh, I reckon – yeah. You can see a lot of the old buildings. Some factories are museums now – or flats for people with money. And people here are still proud of all the inventions, like. So, dirty and sad? No way.

Silvia: But in modern times the North hasn't kept up with the South.

4 Check-in

Male Youth: Oh aye, you're right there. When the old industries stopped, there was nothing else here. But the North is coming back up again, like – look at all the music from round here. That's something to be happy about, isn't it?

Silvia: Apart from the industrial tradition, what else is important to you for your cultural identity?

Male Youth: Well, we've got mountains and that. And I like the way people talk here, too. That's *my* English!

Silvia: Thank you, I've enjoyed our conversation. Now back to Ted in the studio.

Ted: Many thanks, Silvia. By the way – we've checked that rain. It *does* rain more in Manchester than in London. But not that much!

b) **One**

Man: Yes, singing ('singin'') is typically Welsh. We're very proud of that here ('yuhr').

Man 2: Yes, singing is typically Welsh. We're very proud of that here.

Man: Yes, I love the landscape – especially the mountains. We've got a beautiful ('boodiful') country, you know.

Man 2: Yes, I love the landscape – especially the mountains. We've got a beautiful country, you know.

Two

Girl: Well, maybe – but they're kind of all so far from London. And that's where it's happening ('‘apnin''), isn't it ('innit')?

Woman: Well, maybe – but they're all so far from London. And that's where it's happening, isn't it?

Girl: Oh no! I've never been there, but I should think it's all dirty ('dir'y') and industrial, and it rains all the time, and …

Woman: Oh no! I've never been there, but I should think it's all dirty and industrial, and it rains all the time, and …

Three

Male Youth: And people here (''ere') are still proud of all the inventions, like. So, dirty ('dirteh') and sad? No way.

Man: And people here are still proud of all the inventions. So, dirty and sad? No way.

Male Youth: But the North is coming back up again, like – look at all the music from around here. That's something ('summat') to be happy (''ap-peh') about, isn't it ('i'ntit')?

Man: But the North is coming back up again – look at all the music from around here. That's something to be happy about, isn't it?

Ziel
- Regional geprägtes Englisch verstehen

Methodisches Vorgehen

a) *Pre-listening:*
- L: *You are going to hear a radio programme of Gamma Radio about regions in the UK. A reporter, Silvia Benn, interviews people from three different regions of Britain. Make a listening grid in your exercise books before you listen to the programme.* (siehe TA)

While-listening:
- Die S machen sich Notizen zu den drei Interviewpartnern.

Post-listening:
- Die S vergleichen ihre Notizen. Anschließend gemeinsames Ausfüllen der Tabelle an der Tafel/auf Folie. L kann ggf. Zusatzfragen zum Hörtext stellen: *How many people speak Welsh in Wales?* (a quarter) *What does the girl think about the North of England?* (dirty, rains a lot) *Where does it rain more, in London or in Manchester?* (Manchester)

b) *Pre-listening:*
- L: *We will now listen to parts of the interview again. This time I want you to listen to the language. What words do the people say differently to the other speakers you hear? Write the words in the grid.*

While-listening:
- Die S machen sich Notizen in ihre Hefte.

Post-listening:
- Die S beantworten nach dem Beispiel im Buch, welche Wörter von den Interviewpartnern verschieden ausgesprochen werden. Diese werden in das *grid* aus Aufgabe a) eingetragen.

TA

	Man	Girl	Male youth
Region/city	South-West Wales, Swansea	South England, Reading	North-West England, Manchester
What they like about their region	– the English say they sing when they speak – the best music – the best rugby-players – the landscape (mountains)	– new buildings – not far from London – close to the Channel Tunnel and Europe – small towns and villages around	– the city changed – factories are now museums – the music – the mountains – the way people talk
Words they say differently	singing, here, beautiful	happening, isn't it, dirty	here, dirty, something, happy, isn't it

Erweiterung
- Die S hören den Originaltext aus Aufgabe a) erneut an und versuchen, weitere Wörter herauszuhören, deren Aussprache sie anders gelernt haben.
- Besonders gute S können auch versuchen, umgangssprachliche Formulierungen herauszuhören.

Lösung
a) + b) *Siehe TA*
Erweiterung: hello, thought, forty, houses, be, sad
umgangssprachliche Formulierungen: you know what I'm saying?, like, see?, oh aye, ...

Material
◎ s 1/38–43
◎ L 2/22–27, 28–33
Workbook S. 40/2
Ggf. Leerfolie

Tipps für junge Lehrer
Die HV-Texte sollten zweimal abgespielt werden, um den S die Möglichkeit zu geben, ihre Notizen zu ergänzen.

Üben   **3 Your turn: Your region**   Seite 59

Ziel
- Über die eigene Region berichten

Methodisches Vorgehen
- Unter dem Eindruck der Dialoge aus *ex. 2* und mit Hilfe der *Check-in*-Texte erstellen die S unter Berücksichtigung der in Aufgabe a) genannten Kategorien eine Liste *(mindmap)* mit Aspekten, die sie im Hinblick auf ihre Region erwähnenswert finden.
- Anschließend tauschen sich die S in GA oder im Plenum über ihre Aufzeichnungen aus, begründen dabei ihre Auswahl und ergänzen ggf. weitere Aspekte.

Erweiterung
- Ausgehend von dieser Aufgabe können die S in GA Werbebroschüren für ihre Region erstellen. Informationen finden sie u. a. im Internet oder in der Touristeninformation ihrer Stadt. Sie können kurze Texte zu Einwohnerzahl, Lage, Geschichte, Sehenswürdigkeiten, Sprache, Kultur, usw. verfassen und diese durch Fotos o. Ä. ergänzen.

TIP
Englischsprachige Prospekte der Heimatstadt mitbringen

Auch als HA geeignet

4 Check in — Language 1

- Alternativ oder ergänzend zu obigem Vorschlag sammeln die S *curious facts* (vgl. *Did you know?*-Box, S. 58) über ihre Region, die anschließend im Plenum vorgestellt werden. Zusätzlich können die S eine *Top 10* ihrer *curious facts* erstellen.

Lösung | *Individuelle S-Antworten*

Material Workbook S. 40/3

Language 1

Seite 60–61

Ziele
- Eigene Stellungnahmen formulieren
- Regeln zum Gebrauch des bestimmten und unbestimmten Artikels erkennen und anwenden
- Die Verwendung von Adjektiven als Nomen kennen lernen
- Eine Unterhaltung mit einer neuen Bekanntschaft führen

 Text | **Welsh relatives**

Seite 60

Ziel
- Über die Themen „Umzug in eine andere Stadt" und „Bedeutung von Familie und Freunden" sprechen
- Das Hör- und Leseverstehen üben

Wortschatz *abstract, article, relative, engineer, firm, the poor, tea, friendship, I'd rather, bilingual, a pair of, taste, to be into sth, awful*

Strukturen
- *Definite and indefinite article, adjectives used as nouns*

Methodisches Vorgehen
- SB geschlossen. L fragt die S, wer von ihnen bereits in eine andere Stadt umgezogen ist. Die S erzählen im Plenum von ihren Erfahrungen und nennen Gründe für den Umzug (z. B. neue Arbeitsstelle der Eltern, neues Haus, etc.). Diese werden an der Tafel festgehalten.
- Daran anknüpfend stellt L die Frage, was den S bei der Eingewöhnung in der neuen Umgebung geholfen hat/helfen würde (Freunde, Familie, Beitritt in einen Verein, etc.). Anschließend leitet L zum Text im SB über.
- Die neuen Vokabeln werden aus dem Zusammenhang erschlossen und ggf. durch weitere Beispielsätze ergänzt.
- Nach dem ersten Hören/Lesen des Dialogs stellt L mehrere Fragen zum Textverständnis (z. B. *Why did Shirin's family move to Swansea? Why does Rhona suddenly love Welsh lessons? Where did Rhona meet her new boyfriend? etc.*)
- Die Bewusstmachung der neuen Grammatik soll erst in *ex.* 2 erfolgen.

TA
```
Reasons to move:        What helps you to feel at home in a new city?
– new job               – new friends
– bigger house          – your family
– ...                   – joining a club ...
```

Erweiterung
- Die S überlegen sich *Right or wrong?*-Sätze in Einzelarbeit; anschließend werden diese von einem/r Partner/in korrigiert (z. B. *Rhona's boyfriend plays hockey./Shirin is an only child./Shirin's father works as a doctor./…*).

Tipps für junge Lehrer Schülerorientierung ist essentiell für guten Unterricht, deshalb sollten die S so oft es geht eigene Erfahrungen einbringen können. Beim Thema Umzug/neue Freundschaften bietet sich dies sehr gut an.

Material L 2/34

Language 1 | **4**

❗ TIPPS VON MARIO RINVOLUCRI – THE ALTERNATIVE WAY

Sentences to paragraphs as pre-reading activity
Welsh relatives (p. 60)

a) With books shut and before studying the passage dictate:
I miss my aunts and uncles. (line 8)
Now tell the pupils to write the next two short sentences they imagine.
Tell them to read the three sentences on their page to their neighbours.

b) Dictate: *They work on projects for the poor.*
Tell the pupils to write the next two short sentences they imagine.
Again they share what they have written with people near them.

c) Repeat the above with this sentence: *Do you remember that guy we saw?*

d) Dictate: *The music he listens to is awful.*
Tell the pupils to imagine the two sentences that come **before** this one.
They compare their texts with those of their neighbours.

… and now books open for the reading …

Pluses: The pupils go from modest creative writing into having a look at the whole text. Before they meet the text they have already imaginatively 'domesticated' a bit of it.

Minuses: The writing takes 20–30 minutes and some colleagues will find this too long as a lead-in to reading.

Üben	**1 Friends or family?**	Seite 60
Ziel	• Eine eigene Stellungnahme formulieren	
Methodisches Vorgehen	• L sammelt *Useful phrases* an der Tafel (Verweis auf *Talkwise*-Seiten der Units 1 und 3). Diese können durch weitere *phrases* ergänzt werden. • Die S machen sich zunächst in Einzelarbeit Notizen und diskutieren anschließend mit Hilfe der *Useful phrases* in PA die Fragen im SB. L erweitert die Aufgabenstellung ggf. um den Zusatz: *Give reasons and examples*.	**TIP** Wiederholung *Useful phrases* Unit 1 (S. 12) und Unit 3 (S. 46)

TA

```
Useful phrases: Giving opinions
I think …
I don't think …
In my opinion …

You want to say: Yes!          You want to say: No!
I agree.                        I don't agree.
You're right.                   Sorry, but you're wrong.
Exactly!                        Don't be silly!

You agree, but not on everything
You've got a point, but …
That's true, but …
I know, but …
```

4 Language 1

Üben | **2 Find the rule** | Seite 60

Ziel
- Regeln zum Gebrauch des bestimmten und unbestimmten Artikels erkennen und anwenden

Wortschatz *abstract, definite, indefinite, love*

Strukturen
- *Definite and indefinite article*

Methodisches Vorgehen
- Die Vokabel *abstract* wird mit Hilfe der *Tip*-Box auf S. 60 eingeführt. L weist auf die unterschiedliche Betonung im Deutschen und im Englischen hin. Gleiches gilt für *article*. Die Bedeutung von *definite* und *indefinite* ergibt sich aus der Aufgabenstellung.
- a) Schriftliche Bearbeitung in Einzelarbeit, leistungsstärkeren S kann L eine Folie geben, auf der sie die gefundenen *abstract nouns* untereinander auflisten. Kontrolle an der Tafel oder über die Folie.
- b) Die S ergänzen ihre Liste mit den *abstract nouns* um zwei weitere Spalten. In die mittlere Spalte werden jetzt Sätze zu den *abstract nouns* mit bestimmtem Artikel und in die rechte Spalte ohne bestimmten Artikel eingetragen. Wenn keine passenden Beispielsätze im Text vorkommen, werden diese durch eigene Beispielsätze ergänzt. Anschließend versuchen die S mündlich, eine Regel zur Verwendung des bestimmten Artikels zu formulieren.
- c) Die S schreiben jeweils vier weitere Sätze zu den *abstract nouns* aus a).
- L verweist auf den Grammatikanhang (G 14a), der gemeinsam gelesen wird. Neben den *abstract nouns* werden hier die Besonderheiten des bestimmten Artikels bei Verkehrsmitteln und Mahlzeiten eingeführt. Die S suchen auch hierzu Beispiele im Text und ergänzen die Tabelle mit eigenen Beispielsätzen.
- Abschließend wird das Tafelbild durch die Regel für die Verwendung des bestimmten Artikels ergänzt.

TIP
G 14 a

Auch als HA geeignet

TA

	The definite article	
Abstract nouns	With a definite article	Without a definite article
work	The work he did in Manchester was boring.	A firm here had work for him.
friendship	The friendship we have is very important.	Friendship is important.
life	The life I live is fantastic.	Life got harder.
love	He is not the love of my life.	It must be love!
music	A lot of the music he listens to is awful.	He's into music.
Transport	With a definite article	Without a definite article
bike	Look at the red bike over there!	He goes to work by bike.
bus	I met him on the bus into town.	When I visit my grandmother I usually go by bus.
Meals	With a definite article	Without a definite article
lunch	I didn't like the lunch he cooked for us yesterday.	I met him after lunch.

↓ ↓ ↓

With some nouns (abstract nouns, transport, meals) you use the definite article differently in English and in German.

Language 1 | **4**

> In English we use the definite article
> – when we talk about certain things or people.
> – when we can describe the noun by an of-phrase or a relative clause.
>
> We don't usually use the definite article when we talk about things or people in general.

Material
Workbook S. 41/4
Ggf. Leerfolie

Lösung
a) + b) *Siehe TA*
c) *Individuelle S-Antworten*

Üben — **3 Talk about people you know** — Seite 61

Ziel
- Die Regel zum Gebrauch des bestimmten Artikels anwenden
- Die Verwendung des unbestimmten Artikels in Abweichung vom Deutschen kennen lernen

Strukturen
- *Definite and indefinite article*

TIP G 14b

Methodisches Vorgehen
- Nach Besprechung von G 14b und der *Tip*-Box auf S. 61 Ergänzung des Tafelbildes aus *ex. 2*.
- Die S bearbeiten *ex. 3* in Einzelarbeit. Anschließend Kontrolle im Plenum.

TA
> **The indefinite article**
> We use the indefinite article when we talk about a person's job or for special phrases.

Lösung
> *Erwartungshorizont:*
> *My mother is a baker. She goes to work by train. She reads the newspaper at breakfast.*
> *My sister is a doctor. She goes to work by bike. She goes shopping after lunch.*

Tipps für junge Lehrer
Hier bietet sich eine Differenzierungsmöglichkeit für leistungsstärkere S an. Diese können eigene Sätze bilden. Beispiel: *My grandmother is a star. She goes to work by helicopter. She plays in great movies at night and sleeps after breakfast.*

Material
Workbook S. 41/5

Üben — **4 You can use some adjectives as nouns** — Seite 61

Ziel
- Die Verwendung von Adjektiven als Nomen kennen lernen und anwenden

Strukturen
- *Adjectives used as nouns*

TIP G 15

Methodisches Vorgehen
- Vor Bearbeitung von *ex. 4* sollte L noch einmal auf den Text *Welsh relatives* verweisen und Zeile 13–15 an die Tafel schreiben: *They work on projects for **the poor** in Pakistan, …*
- L erklärt mit Hilfe von G 15 die Regeln zum Gebrauch von Adjektiven als Nomen.
- Die S bearbeiten *ex. 4* in Einzelarbeit.

TA
> **Adjectives used as nouns**
> They work on projects for <u>the poor</u> in Pakistan.
>
> We use <u>the + adjective</u> when we talk about a group of people.
> (the poor = all poor people)

Erweiterung
- PA: Jeder S schreibt vier Adjektive auf, und der/die Partner/in bildet Sätze wie in Aufgabe b).

4 Language 1

• An dieser Stelle bietet sich auch **KV 2: The definite and the indefinite article** zur Wiederholung des Gebrauchs des bestimmten und unbestimmten Artikels an.

Auch als HA geeignet

Lösung

a) 1 *Doctors help the sick.* 2 *People sometimes collect money for the poor.* 3 *Reporters like to interview the famous.* 4 *DJs are very popular with the young.* 5 *We can learn a lot from the old.* 6 *People are often jealous of the rich.*
b) *Individuelle S-Antworten*

Tipps für junge Lehrer

Der Hinweis auf G 15 ermöglicht ein gezieltes Nachschlagen im Grammatikanhang des SB. Dies kann für schwächere S von Vorteil sein, wenn die Grammatik in der Klasse einsprachig behandelt wird.

Material
Workbook S. 42/6
Kopiervorlage 2

Üben | **5 How to: Meet new people** | Seite 61

Ziel
• Eine Unterhaltung mit einer neuen Bekanntschaft führen

Methodisches Vorgehen
• L führt in die Kommunikationssituation ein: *Imagine you meet someone new after a film at the cinema or at a party. You want to start a conversation. How can you start? What would you like to know about the other person?*
• An der Tafel/auf Folie werden *Useful phrases* in einem *brainstorming* gesammelt und durch die Beispiele aus dem SB ergänzt.
• Die S befragen sich gegenseitig und versuchen möglichst viel über den/die Partner/in herauszufinden.
• Als Hausaufgabe überlegen die S, wie die Unterhaltung weitergehen bzw. wie man ein weiteres Treffen arrangieren könnte. Diese Sätze werden in der nächsten Stunde im TA/auf Folie ergänzt.

> **TIP**
> Sammeln von *Useful phrases* für den *folder*

 HA

TA

> Useful phrases: Meeting new people
>
> How to start a conversation:
> Hi, haven't we met before?
> Hello. I like your sunglasses!
> Hi, we've just seen the same film.
> It was cool, wasn't it?
> ...
>
> Questions you can ask:
> Did you enjoy the film?
> Do you live near here?
> Do you like pizza/spaghetti ...?
> What's your favourite film/music?
> ...
>
> How to go on:
> Would you like to have a drink?
> Shall we dance?
> Would you like to go swimming/in-line skating/... next weekend?
> ...

> **TIP**
> Um den TA auch in der nächsten Stunde nutzen und erweitern zu können, bietet sich eine Folie an

Erweiterung
• Jeder S stellt den/die Partner/in im Plenum vor.
• Alternative: Nach dem Vorbild des aus dem Fernsehen bekannten „Speed-Dating" werden Tische im Klassenraum so verteilt, dass sich je zwei S an einem Tisch gegenüber sitzen. Jedes Paar hat drei Minuten Zeit, sich kennen zu lernen (Signal). Danach wechselt eine/r der S zum nächsten Tisch. Am Ende entscheidet sich jede/r S für den/die Partner/in, mit dem/der er/sie die meisten Gemeinsamkeiten hatte.

Tipps für junge Lehrer

Die oben skizzierte Alternative sollte man nur in Lerngruppen mit einer guten Klassengemeinschaft ausprobieren, da ansonsten S in eine Außenseiterrolle gedrängt werden könnten.

Material
Workbook S. 42/7
Ggf. Leerfolie

| | | | Language 1 | Talkwise | **4** |

Üben	**6 Revision: Possessive pronouns**	Seite 61

Ziel	• Die *possessive pronouns* wiederholen und festigen
Strukturen	• *Possessive pronouns*
Methodisches Vorgehen	• Zunächst Wiederholung der *possessive pronouns* im Plenum, ggf. TA. • Anschließend Bearbeitung der Aufgabe in Einzelarbeit.

TIP
Green Line 2,
G 29 (S. 150)

TA

Possessive determiners + nouns	Possessive pronouns
Is that my book?	No, it's mine.
I thought that was your book.	No, that's yours!
Let's watch his videos.	Yes, his are always great!
Is this her map?	No, hers is over there.
Here are our sandwiches.	No, wait — they are ours.
Are these your pens?	Or are yours in the bag?
Do you like their ghost stories?	No, theirs aren't scary.

We use possessive pronouns when we don't want to repeat the noun.

Material
Workbook S. 42/8
Im Anschluss an
ex. 6: *Action UK!* 3,
Cultural
differences, Part A:
Greg in love sowie
Action UK! 3,
Begleitheft zu den
Filmsequenzen,
Unit 4 A

Lösung   1 *mine*   2 *yours*   3 *his*   4 *ours*   5 *theirs*   6 *hers*

Talkwise
Seite 62

Ziele	• In Problemsituationen sprachlich angemessen reagieren

Üben	**Dealing with problems**	Seite 62

Wortschatz   *helping, apologizing, dealing with problems, to deal with*

⊚L Üben	**1 Listening: Shall I do that for you?**	Seite 62

HV-Text
Shirin: Hello Mr Williams. Oh, what have you done to your arm?
Gavin: I broke it. I fell on it while I was playing rugby. I hurt my foot, too.
Shirin: Poor you! Oh, can I help you with that rucksack? It must be hard when you can only use one arm.
Gavin: Oh, would you do that? That's very kind of you, Shirin. It's not far to our house now.
Shirin: No problem. Right, I've got it now.
Gavin: You were on your way into town, weren't you? You'll miss your bus because of me.
Shirin: I'll get the next one. Oh, am I walking too fast for you?
Gavin: Sorry, it's my foot. I'm very slow, I know. Could you go a bit more slowly?
Shirin: Sure. Just take your time. You're doing fine.
Gavin: Right, here we are!
Shirin: Shall I open the front door for you? You can't do it with one hand.
Gavin: No, it's OK, thanks. Susan's at home, so I can just ring the bell. You go off to town now. And thanks a lot, Shirin. You've been a great help.
Shirin: You're welcome, Mr Williams. Bye!

4 Talkwise

Ziel	• Einen Dialog zu einer Problemsituation verstehen • Hilfe anbieten und annehmen
Wortschatz	*Take your time.*
Methodisches Vorgehen	*Pre-listening:* • a) L führt mit Hilfe des Bildes in die Situation ein. Die S beschreiben Rhonas Vater und stellen Spekulationen an, welches Problem er haben und wie Shirin ihm helfen könnte. In diesem Zusammenhang werden die neuen Vokabeln eingeführt: *Describe the picture. Don't hurry, you can take your time. Mr Williams has got a problem. What is it? How can he deal with his problem? How can Shirin help him?* *While-listening:* • Die S vergleichen den Inhalt des Dialoges mit den von ihnen angestellten Vermutungen. *Post-listening:* • Die S beantworten die Fragen in Aufgabe a). • Ergänzung: L stellt Verständnisfragen zum HV-Text: *How did Mr Williams break his arm? What happened to his foot? Where did Shirin want to go before she met Mr Williams?* • b) An der Tafel/auf Folie werden *Useful phrases* gesammelt (siehe SB). • Anschließend hören die S den Dialog erneut an und ergänzen weitere Satzbausteine.
TA	**Useful phrases: Helping** You want to help someone / Someone helps you Can I help? / That's very kind of you. Shall I ... ? / Could you ... for me? Just take your time ... / You've been a great help ... Can I help you with ...? / Would you ... ? No problem. / That's very kind of you. You're welcome. / Thank you.
Lösung	a) Mr Williams broke his arm and hurt his foot. He has problems to carry his rucksack with just one hand. Shirin takes his rucksack and carries it for him. Ergänzung: Mr Williams fell on his arm while he was playing rugby. He hurt his foot, too. Shirin wanted to go into town by bus. b) Siehe TA
Tipps für junge Lehrer	Die Tandemaufgabe im *Workbook* bietet den S die Gelegenheit, das Gelernte in PA und nicht im Plenum anzuwenden, dadurch werden Hemmschwellen abgebaut. Tandemaufgaben bieten darüber hinaus den Vorteil, dass die S auf die Informationen ihres Gegenübers angewiesen sind und so authentische Kommunikationssituationen entstehen.

Material
L 2/35
Workbook S. 43/9
Ggf. Leerfolie

Üben	**2 Work with a partner**	Seite 62
Ziel	• Einen Dialog schreiben	
Methodisches Vorgehen	• Die S verfassen in PA Dialoge zu einer der vorgegebenen Situationen. • Differenzierungsmöglichkeit: Leistungsstärkere S können eigene Situationen erfinden.	
Erweiterung	• **KV 3: Helping and apologizing**, Teilaufgabe a), bietet gute Differenzierungsmöglichkeiten. Leistungsschwächeren S können *Useful phrases* an die Hand gegeben werden, leistungsstärkere S können die vorgegebenen Dialoge kreativ ausgestalten.	

		Talkwise	4

- *Act it out:* Mehrere Schülerpaare spielen ihre Dialoge vor.

Lösung | *Individuelle S-Antworten*

Material
Kopiervorlage 3

Üben 3 Listening: Sorry!   Seite 62

HV-Text

Shirin: Hi, Rhona! Have you been shopping?
Rhona: Yes, I've just bought a CD.
Shirin: I hope the lyrics aren't in Welsh!
Rhona: Don't be so critical, Shirin. I told you: I like Welsh now. Anyway, my new CD is really brilliant modern music – just with Welsh lyrics.
Shirin: That's OK, then. Much better than all those Welsh folksongs …
Rhona: Shirin …
Shirin: People who sing that kind of song in Welsh must be real idiots! What's the matter?
Rhona: Er … Shirin, this is my boyfriend, David. He sings in a traditional Welsh choir. They've won prizes at the Eisteddfod.
David: Hello, Shirin.
Shirin: Oh no … ! Rhona, I had no idea … I – I'm terribly sorry, David. I didn't recognise you without your glasses!
David: Never mind. It's OK.
Shirin: You must think I'm very rude.
Rhona: It wasn't very nice, Shirin.
Shirin: I didn't mean to hurt your feelings, honestly! I …
David: You don't need to go red, Shirin.
Shirin: But it's so embarrassing!
Rhona: I tried to tell you.
Shirin: I wish I'd never said it.
David: Let's just forget it, OK?
Shirin: Oh, Rhona, I don't know what …

Ziel
- Einen Dialog zu einer peinlichen Situation verstehen
- Entschuldigungen aussprechen und annehmen

Wortschatz *to apologize, I didn't mean to … , rude, Never mind!*

Methodisches Vorgehen

Pre-listening:
- a) L führt in *ex.* 3 ein: *Sometimes we do or say something embarrassing. If you are polite, you apologize afterwards. That means you say sorry, because you didn't mean to say something that is not polite but rude. Hopefully, the other person is not really angry and says: Never mind! That means: Forget about it. Let's listen to a conversation between Shirin and Rhona. What does Shirin say and why is she sorry?*

While-listening:
- Die S hören den Dialog an und finden Antworten auf die oben genannten Fragen.

Post-listening:
- Die S beantworten die Fragen im Plenum.
- b) An der Tafel/auf Folie werden *Useful phrases* gesammelt (siehe SB).
- Anschließend hören die S den Dialog erneut an und ergänzen weitere Satzbausteine.

4 Talkwise

TA

> **Useful phrases: Apologizing**
>
> | You want to apologize | Someone apologizes to you |
> |---|---|
> | I apologize … | Never mind./No problem./Don't worry. |
> | I'm terribly sorry … | Be more careful next time. |
> | I didn't mean to be rude. | It's OK. |
> | I had no idea … | You don't need to go red. |
> | I'm terribly sorry. | Let's just forget it. |
> | I didn't mean to hurt your feelings. | |
> | I wish I'd never said it. | |

Material
◎ L 2/36
Workbook S. 43/10
Ggf. Leerfolie

Lösung
a) *Shirin says that people who sing songs in Welsh must be real idiots. She is sorry because Rhona's new boyfriend sings in a Welsh choir.*
b) *Siehe TA*

Üben

4 Role play: An embarrassing situation

Seite 62

Ziel
- Die *Useful phrases* anwenden
- Einen Dialog verfassen und vorspielen

Methodisches Vorgehen
- a) L teilt die Klasse in Dreier- bzw. Vierergruppen ein.
- Gemeinsames Lesen der Arbeitsanweisung und ggf. Klären von Fragen.
- In GA verfassen die S einen Dialog zur vorgegebenen Situation.
- Die S spielen ihre Dialoge vor.
- Differenzierungsmöglichkeit: Leistungsstärkere S können eigene Situationen erfinden.
- b) Die S erzählen peinliche Situationen, die sie aus Zeitschriften oder aus dem Fernsehen kennen. Natürlich dürfen sie auch von eigenen Missgeschicken berichten.
- Eine solche Aufgabe benötigt Vorbereitungszeit, d. h. die S sollten sich zunächst Notizen machen. Jede/r S schreibt zehn zentrale Begriffe auf einen Zettel, die ihm/ihr beim Vortragen helfen sollen.

> **TIP**
> Die S sollten zum Einüben ihrer Dialoge den Klassenraum verlassen, um ungestört arbeiten zu können

Auch als HA geeignet

Erweiterung
- **KV 3: Helping and apologizing**, Teilaufgabe b), bietet gute Differenzierungsmöglichkeiten. Schwächeren S können *Useful phrases* an die Hand gegeben werden, stärkere S können die vorgegebenen Dialoge kreativ ausgestalten.
- Alternativ können die S auch einen Comic zu einer peinlichen Situation zeichnen. Jede/r S erhält anschließend den Comic eines/r Mitschülers/in und muss diesen verschriftlichen.
- L kann auch einen DVD- oder Videoausschnitt mit einer peinlichen Situation zeigen, allerdings ohne Ton. Die S schreiben anschließend die dazu passenden Dialoge.
- In Jugendzeitschriften gibt es oft eine Foto-Love-Story. Auch hier finden sich peinliche Situationen. L entfernt den Text aus den Sprechblasen und lässt die S neue Dialoge schreiben.

Lösung

Individuelle S-Antworten

Tipps für junge Lehrer
Bei GA müssen die Arbeitsanweisungen klar sein. Stehen diese nicht im SB, sollte man sie noch einmal schriftlich an der Tafel fixieren. Zudem sollte man den S einen festen zeitlichen Rahmen vorgeben. Die Zeitangabe, wann die S fertig sein müssen, sollte ebenfalls an der Tafel stehen.

Material
Kopiervorlage 3

| | | Language 2 | 4 |

Language 2

Seite 63–65

Ziele	• Einen Text zu einem pakistanischen Familienessen lesen und verstehen
	• Die Unterscheidung von Adjektiven und Adverbien wiederholen
	• Den Gebrauch von Adjektiven nach bestimmten Verben erkennen und anwenden

Material
Kopiervorlagen 11–15
Kopiervorlage 17 (Unit 1)

Stationenlernen Vor oder nach *Language* 2 kann das Stationenlernen durchgeführt werden (**Kopiervorlagen 11–15**). Der Arbeitsbericht hierzu findet sich als **KV 17** bei Unit 1.

 Text **Up North** Seite 63

Ziel
• Das Leben einer pakistanischen Familie kennen lernen
• Das Hör- und Leseverstehen üben

Wortschatz *up North, Asian, curry, to smell, to taste, Punjabi, to sound, to seem, exhibition*

Strukturen • *Adjectives after certain verbs*

Methodisches Vorgehen
• Die S schlagen die Karte vorne im SB auf. L: *Rhona and Shirin live in Manchester. Can you show me Manchester on the map?* Die S zeigen auf Manchester. L: *Manchester is in the North of England. People say it's up North.* L legt das Bild von S. 63 auf Folie auf. Die S beschreiben das Photo, und L erläutert in diesem Zusammenhang die neuen Vokabeln: *This is Shirin's family. They are from Pakistan, they are Asian. They speak Punjabi. The food is Asian, too. It smells nice and tastes good* (L zeigt dabei auf die Nase und macht eine Bewegung mit dem Mund.). *They often eat curry.*
• L präsentiert den Text von CD, die S lesen leise mit.
• Anschließend lesen die S den Text mit verteilten Rollen. Die Vokabeln *to sound, to seem, exhibition* werden aus dem Zusammenhang erschlossen.

TIP
Karte im SB-Umschlag

Erweiterung
• Exkurs: *Asians in Britain.* L erläutert, dass es in Großbritannien sehr viele asiatische Familien gibt, vor allem im Norden Englands, zum Beispiel in Manchester oder Bradford. Sie tragen zur multikulturellen Vielfalt Großbritanniens bei, indem sie ihre Traditionen, ihr Essen, ihre Musik, usw. in die westliche Gesellschaft einbringen. Gerade die zweite Generation der asiatischen Einwanderer steht aber manchmal auch zwischen den Kulturen. Um diese Probleme aufzuzeigen und den S ein vielschichtigeres Bild asiatischer Familien in Großbritannien zu vermitteln, bietet sich der Film *Bend it like Beckham* an. Dieser kann ab Klasse 7 (mit Untertiteln) eingesetzt werden.

Material
⊙L 2/37

Üben **1 Read the text and say…** Seite 63

Ziel • Das Textverständnis überprüfen

Methodisches Vorgehen • Die S bearbeiten *ex.* 1 in Einzelarbeit. Anschließend Kontrolle im Plenum.

Lösung
1 *They have come to help Aunt Zeba to move house.*   2 *The Asian food looks unusual to Rhona.*   3 *She is surprised because some of Shirin's older relatives speak a language she cannot understand.*   4 *Tariq's mother gets angry when Tariq answers a question in English and not in Punjabi.*   5 *Liverpool is famous for The Beatles.*   6 *The girls have to be at the 'Beatles Story' exhibition at 5 o'clock.*   7 *Individuelle S-Antworten.*

Material
Workbook S. 44/11

4 Language 2

Üben	**2 Revision: Adjective or adverb?**	Seite 63
Ziel	• Den Gebrauch von Adjektiven und Adverbien wiederholen und festigen	
Strukturen	• *Adjectives and adverbs*	
Methodisches Vorgehen	• Gemeinsames Wiederholen der Regeln im Plenum, Erstellen eines TA als Hilfestellung. • Anschließend bearbeiten die S *ex.* 2 in Einzelarbeit. • Vergleich im Plenum. Dabei sollte auch die Bildung der Adverbien *happily* und *carefully* gesondert thematisiert werden.	**TIP** Vgl. *Green Line* 2, G 27 (S. 148)

TA

Adjective	or adverb?
Mr Williams is a careful driver. He is very careful. Adjectives describe nouns. Adjectives follow the verb <u>to be</u>.	He drives carefully. Adverbs describe a verb. We build adverbs by adding –ly. There are some irregular adverb forms (e.g. <u>well</u>) which you have to learn!

Lösung	1 *regularly* 2 *great* 3 *excitedly* 4 *famous* 5 *new* 6 *nervous* 7 *scary* 8 *well* 9 *happily* 10 *carefully* 11 *lucky*	**Material** *Workbook* S. 44/12

Üben	**3 Verbs with adjectives**	Seite 64
Hinweis	In leistungsstärkeren Lerngruppen empfiehlt es sich, Teilaufgabe d) vor Teilaufgabe c) zu besprechen (Differenzierung nach oben).	
Ziel	• Die Verwendung von Adjektiven nach bestimmten Verben kennen lernen und anwenden	
Strukturen	• *Adjectives after certain verbs*	
Methodisches Vorgehen	• a) Mit Verweis auf *ex.* 2 und den dort erstellten TA suchen die S Adverbien im Text S. 63. • b) In einem zweiten Schritt suchen die S im Text Adjektive, die ein Verb beschreiben. • d) Bewusstmachung: Durch die strukturierte Anordnung (siehe TA) erkennen die S bereits unterschiedliche Verbgruppen, die durch Adjektive beschrieben werden. Die Regelfindung erfolgt durch Impulsfragen. L: *Which other verb do you know which needs an adjective?* (Ergänzung des Verbs *to be* an der Tafel) • L: *What kinds of verbs are described by adjectives?* Verweis auf *Grammar*-Box und *Tip*-Box im SB. Die S erkennen, dass es sich hier um Verben handelt, die Sinneswahrnehmungen und Zustände beschreiben. L ergänzt TA. • Anschließend bearbeiten die S Teilaufgabe c) in Einzelarbeit.	**TIP** G 16 Auch als HA geeignet

TA

Adverbs describing a verb		Adjectives describing a verb
say quietly eat hungrily tell her excitedly speak well	senses	look unusual smell good taste good sound great look sad

| | Language 2 | 4 |

```
                    ⎡ feel hungry
         condition  ⎢ seem happy
                    ⎢ feel good (better)
                    ⎣ be happy

                    ⎡ get angry
         „werden"   ⎣ become famous
```

Verbs which describe a sense or condition are followed by an adjective.
The verbs to get and to become (= werden) are followed by an adjective.

Lösung
a) + b) + d) *Siehe TA*
c) 1 *interesting* 2 *slowly* 3 *cold* 4 *terrible* 5 *angry* 6 *good*
    7 *patiently* 8 *good* 9 *horrible* 10 *hungrily* 11 *wicked* 12 *quickly*

Tipps für junge Lehrer
Eine frühzeitige Bewusstmachung erleichtert die Bearbeitung von Teilaufgabe c). Gleichzeitig fordert dieses Verfahren der Regelfindung die leistungsstärkeren S.

Material
Workbook S. 45/13

Üben   **4 ⟨A game: Sixth sense⟩**   Seite 64

Ziel
- Die neue Grammatik spielerisch einüben

Strukturen
- *Adjectives after certain verbs*

Methodisches Vorgehen
- Spielverlauf nach Arbeitsanweisung im SB.
- Nach der ersten Runde übernimmt jeweils ein/e S die Rolle von L. Weitere Kategorien könnten sein: *It smells nice/awful. It tastes good/horrible/funny. It looks unusual/funny/ugly. It sounds terrible/nice. …*

Lösung   *Individuelle S-Antworten*

Üben   **5 Your turn: A new situation**   Seite 64

Ziel
- Die neue Grammatik im Gespräch anwenden
- Über ein persönliches Erlebnis berichten

Strukturen
- *Adjectives after certain verbs*

Methodisches Vorgehen
- a) L ruft die Situation im Text S. 63 in Erinnerung: *Rhona is visiting her friend Shirin and meets the rest of her family. How does she feel about the new faces, the food, the different language etc.?* Die S machen sich in Einzelarbeit Notizen. Anschließend Vergleich im Plenum. Dabei sollte darauf geachtet werden, dass die S die neue Grammatik anwenden. Ggf. muss L nachfragen: *What did the food taste like?* etc.
- b) Ausgehend von Rhonas Erlebnis machen sich die S Notizen zu einer Situation, in der sie etwas Ähnliches erlebt haben. Anhand dieser Notizen berichten sie anschließend (möglichst frei) ihrem/r Partner/in davon.

Erweiterung
- Anhand von **KV 4: Adjectives after certain verbs** können die S die neue Grammatik üben. Gleichzeitig erfahren sie etwas über die indische Küche, die in Großbritannien sehr beliebt und verbreitet ist. So wurde z. B. *Chicken Tikka Masala* 2001 zum inoffiziellen britischen Nationalgericht erklärt.

Material
Workbook S. 45/14
Kopiervorlage 4

Lösung   *Individuelle S-Antworten*

4 Language 2

Üben	**6 Tariq's week**	Seite 65
Ziel	• Das *future perfect* kennen lernen und anwenden	
Wortschatz	by, Bhangra, reply	
Strukturen	• *Future perfect*	
Methodisches Vorgehen	• L führt in Tariqs Situation ein: *Tariq is moving house tomorrow. He is nervous and he thinks about what will be. Let's read about it.*	**TIP** *Green Line* 2, G 30–32
	• Die neuen Vokabeln werden zunächst aus dem Textzusammenhang erschlossen. Zur Erläuterung der Bedeutung von *by* anschließend gemeinsames Lesen der Box auf S. 172.	
	• **Vor** der Einführung des *future perfect* wird an dieser Stelle das *will future* wiederholt (siehe *Green Line* 2, G 30–32)	
	• Bewusstmachung: L schreibt aus dem Text die Formen des *future perfect* an die Tafel. *There is a new tense in this text. Can you explain what Tariq expresses by using this tense? How do we form it?*	**TIP** G 17
	• Nach der Besprechung des Beispiels im SB formulieren die S zwei Sätze zu jedem Bildpaar aus *ex.* 6.	Auch als HA geeignet

TA

```
                 The future perfect
we will have moved  ⎫
we will have lost   ⎬  Handlung ist in der Zukunft abgeschlossen
I won't have found  ⎪
Shirin will have gone ⎭

We form the future perfect: will/won't + have + past participle
```

Erweiterung	• Die S zeichnen weitere Bildpaare für die restlichen Wochentage und beschreiben diese. Auch als PA möglich: Die S tauschen ihre Bildpaare aus und beschreiben jeweils die des/der Partners/Partnerin.	Auch als HA geeignet
	• **KV 5: The future perfect – Moving house** festigt die neue Grammatik und bietet in Teilaufgabe b) gute Differenzierungsmöglichkeiten nach oben, da die Schüler hier frei formulieren können.	
Lösung	1 *He'll get his pocket money on Monday. By the end of the week he'll have spent it all.* 2 *He'll borrow a lot of books from the library on Tuesday. By the end of the week he won't have read any of them.* 3 *He'll buy a new CD on Wednesday. By the end of the week he'll have lost it.* 4 *He'll write an e-mail to Shirin on Thursday. By the end of the week he'll have got a reply from her.*	**Material** *Workbook* S. 46/15 Kopiervorlage 5

ⓛ Üben	**7 Listening: The Beatles Story**	Seite 65
HV-Text	Female announcer: This is the first part of an audio tour to the 'Beatles Story'. When the second part begins, go into the next room of the exhibition.	
	Male narrator: In the 1950s lots of new and exciting things were happening in Britain. There was a new youth and music culture in Liverpool, which because of the busy docks had close links with America. Young men from the boats came and went in the city on the River Mersey, bringing with them a new kind of music: rock and roll.	
	In 1957 Paul McCartney and John Lennon, who were both already active in the Liverpool music scene, met at a church event, and started a band. George Harrison joined the band soon after, followed by Pete Best, their original drummer. The	

Language 2 — 4

group called themselves 'The Quarrymen' and began to play concerts around the City. The band had a few different names before they decided on 'The Beatles'.

The group played for a while in Hamburg, Germany, and then at the Cavern Club in Liverpool, a record producer from London heard them and liked them a lot. They agreed to make a record together for a record firm in London. Beatlemania was going to begin! 'The Beatles' didn't start to perform their music for their own record firm – Apple – until 1968.
'The Beatles' recorded their first single 'Love Me Do' after Ringo Starr had taken Pete Best's place on the drums. The record got to Number 17 in the charts. Their second single 'Please Please Me' was the first of many which got to Number 1. Beatlemania arrived in America in 1964, when 73 million people watched the band on Ed Sullivan's famous TV show.

At the end of the 1960s Apple started to have money problems, and the members of the band began to have arguments. In 1969 two of 'The Beatles' married: Paul to Linda Eastman and John to Yoko Ono, his second wife. The band split up in 1970 when Paul said he wanted to work alone. The Beatles story finally ended in 1975, five years before John Lennon died in an attack in New York on the 8th of December 1980.

Ziel	• Das Hörverstehen üben • Informationen über die Beatles erhalten
Wortschatz	*audio*
Methodisches Vorgehen	• a) SB geschlossen. L zeigt Folien/Photos/Filmausschnitte zu den Beatles und spielt dazu im Hintergrund einige ihrer Lieder ab. • Die S erstellen eine *mindmap* mit ihrem Vorwissen über die Beatles; Vergleich an der Tafel/auf Folie. *Pre-listening:* • b) Gemeinsames Lesen der *introduction* und der Multiple-Choice-Fragen. *While-listening:* • Die S beantworten die Fragen im SB. *Post-listening:* • Vergleich der Ergebnisse in PA.
TA	The Beatles English band from Liverpool members: John Lennon, Paul McCartney, George Harrison, Ringo Starr songs: Yesterday, Let it be, Can't buy me love, Hey Jude, Yellow Submarine etc. …
Lösung	a) Individuelle S-Antworten (siehe TA) b) 1b, 2a, 3b, 4a, 5c
Tipps für junge Lehrer	Wann immer es möglich ist, sollte zur Förderung der Motivation authentisches Material zur Anschauung eingesetzt werden.

TIP
The Beatles Anthology von den Beatles und Geoff Wonfor (DVD – 2003)

Beatles-Spielfilm *Help!* (Neuauflage von EMI und Apple auf DVD – 2007)

Material
L 2/38
Fotos/Musik/Filmausschnitte
Ggf. Leerfolie

S L **Üben** **Listening: After The Beatles Story** Workbook Seite 46

HV-Text Workbook	Rhona: Wow, that was great! Shirin: Cool, wasn't it? Imagine, The Beatles were the first boy band! Did you see how wild their fans were about them – they even cried at their concerts! Rhona: I guess they also went crazy about their looks. I think their hair looked cool, don't you? Shirin: Yeah, it's wicked! It must have been terrible for the fans when John Lennon was killed. He's definitely the most famous Beatle.

4 Language 2

Rhona: I'm not sure, I think Paul McCartney is more famous – he worked alone after the band split up, didn't he?
Shirin: Hm, I don't know. Anyway, so there were John and Paul, the two lead singers. What were the other two guys' names again?
Rhona: George Harrison, he played lead guitar. And Ringo Starr, the drummer.
Shirin: Oh yes, that's it. I really liked some of their songs. 'Yellow Submarine' and 'Yesterday' are cool, don't you think?
Rhona: Hm, my favourite songs are 'She Loves You' and 'Michelle'. And the thing I liked best about the museum was that you could actually look at so many original things, like John Lennon's glasses and George Harrison's first guitar.
Shirin: And the big yellow submarine and all the photos of the band members! We must tell my mum how good the museum is. Come on, let's see what they have in the souvenir shop …

Material
S 1/44
L 2/39
Workbook S. 46/16

Song   **8 ⟨A song: I wish I was back in Liverpool⟩**   Seite 65

HV-Text

I wish I was back in Liverpool. Liverpool Town where I was born,
Where there ain't no trees, no scented breeze, no fields of waving corn.
But there's lots of girls with peroxide curls, and the black-and-tan flows free.
There's six in a bed by the old Pierhead. And it's Liverpool Town for me.

T'is seven long years since I wandered away to sail the wide world o'er,
Me very first trip on an old steamship that was bound for Baltimore.
I was seven days sick and I just couldn't stick that bobbing up and down,
So I told them, Jack, you'd better turn back for dear old Liverpool town.

Chorus

We dug the Mersey Tunnel, boys, way back in thirty-three,
Dug an 'ole in the ground until we found an 'ole called Wallasey.
Then the foremen cried: Come on outside, the roof is falling down!
Well, I'm telling ya', Jack, we all swam back to dear old Liverpool town.

Chorus

There's every race and colour of face, there's every kind of name,
But the pigeons on the Pierhead, they treat you all the same.
And if you walk up Upper Parliament Street, you'll get faces black and brown,
And I've also seen them orange and green in dear old Liverpool town.

Chorus

Text: Stan Kelly, © Heatside Music Ltd.; Rudolf Slezak Musikverlag GmbH, D-22089 Hamburg

Ziel
- Das Hörverstehen anhand eines authentischen Popsongs schulen
- Kreatives Schreiben üben

Wortschatz   *ain't (= isn't/aren't), scented, breeze, waving, corn, peroxide, curl, to flow*

Methodisches Vorgehen
- Die S hören den Song zweimal an und versuchen den Inhalt auch ohne Kenntnis der unbekannten Vokabeln zu verstehen.
- Anschließend gemeinsames Lesen des Liedtextes und Sammeln von Aspekten, die der Sänger an Liverpool mag (*was born there, pretty girls, …*).
- Erweiterung: Die S verfassen einen Liedtext über ihre Heimatstadt.

Material
L 2/40
Im Anschluss an ex. 8: *Action UK!* 3, Cultural differences, Part B: *The Curry Mile and more* sowie *Action UK!* 3, Begleitheft zu den Filmsequenzen, Unit 4 B

		Skills **4**

Skills
Seite 66

> **Ziele**
> - Lesetechniken zum Erschließen von Sachtexten kennen lernen und anwenden
> - Einem Sachtext gezielt Informationen entnehmen

Text   **Factual texts**   Seite 66

Wortschatz   *factual text, research*

Methodisches Vorgehen
- In *Green Line* 2, Unit 7, haben die S gelernt, wie Überschriften und Bilder helfen können, einen Sachtext zu verstehen. Dieses Wissen sollte vor Bearbeitung dieser Seite noch einmal abgerufen werden.

TIP
Green Line 2, Unit 7 (S. 98)

Üben   **1 Skimming**   Seite 66

Ziel
- Einen Text überfliegen lernen *(skimming)*
- Schlüsselwörter markieren und als Orientierungshilfe nehmen

Wortschatz   *skimming, to skim, to concentrate, keyword*

Methodisches Vorgehen
- L gibt die Übersetzung von *factual text, skimming* und *research* vor. Das Verb *to concentrate* sollte den S durch seine Ähnlichkeit mit dem Deutschen keine Schwierigkeiten bereiten. Eine Semantisierung des unbekannten Vokabulars sollte nur im Notfall vorgenommen werden. Die S sollen lernen, einen Text zu überfliegen, d. h. sich auf das Wesentliche zu konzentrieren und Vokabeln aus dem Gesamtzusammenhang zu erschließen.
- a) Die S lesen den Text im SB und notieren sich mögliche *keywords*.
- b) Anhand der *keywords* fassen die S das Thema des Textes kurz zusammen.
- Anschließend erläutern die S, nach welchen Kriterien sie die Schlüsselwörter markiert haben. L markiert auf Folie sinnvolle Schlüsselwörter und macht deutlich, dass es nicht darum geht, möglichst viel zu unterstreichen.

TIP
Text S. 66 auf Folie

Lösung
> a) *Erwartungshorizont:* Reading, town, 'must-see', place to live and work, regional centre, computer technology, high-tech jobs, modern buildings, international firms, city centre shops, hotels, water, rowing, houseboats, fishing, Rivermead Leisure Complex, sports, concerts, festivals, near London, 40 minutes by train
> b) The text is about Reading, which is a town near London. It's the regional centre in the UK's 'Silicon Valley' and it offers lots of jobs and activities.

Tipps für junge Lehrer   Eine Alternative zum Notieren der *keywords* wäre, dass sich jede/r S zu Beginn des Schuljahres eine Folie und einen abwaschbaren Folienstift zulegt. Diese Folie wird dann bei Bedarf über die Texte im SB gelegt, so dass markiert und angekreuzt werden kann, ohne in das SB zu schreiben.

Material
Ggf. Leerfolie

Üben   **2 Scanning**   Seite 66

Ziel
- Einen Sachtext gezielt auf Informationen hin untersuchen

Wortschatz   *scanning, to scan, topic, a must-see, conference, dinner, leisure, on land, during (+ noun), motorway*

Methodisches Vorgehen
- Der Unterschied zwischen *skimming* und *scanning* wird anhand der unterschiedlichen Aufgabenstellungen in *ex.* 1 und *ex.* 2 erarbeitet.
- Die S beantworten die Fragen in *ex.* 2, anschließend erörtern sie, wie sie dabei vorgegangen sind. Eine große Hilfestellung bieten auch hier die in *ex.* 1 gesammelten *keywords*.

217

4 Skills

Lösung | a) *no* b) *yes* c) *no* d) *yes* e) *no* f) *yes*

Üben | **3 Collect information** | Seite 66

Ziel
- Einen Text nach inhaltlichen Kategorien untersuchen
- Eine Inhaltsangabe verfassen

Methodisches Vorgehen
- a) Anhand der Informationen und Schlüsselwörter aus *ex.* 1 und *ex.* 2 wird im Plenum eine Liste mit Themen erstellt, die im Text angesprochen werden.
- Die S suchen in PA Informationen zu den einzelnen Themen im Text und fassen diese in Schlagwörtern zusammen.
- b) Anschließend verfassen die S anhand der gesammelten Informationen eine Inhaltsangabe des Textes.

TA

> Reading
> location: 40 miles from London, 40 minutes by train or one hour by bus on the M4
> jobs: computers, high-tech jobs, international firms, shops
> leisure: rowing, shopping, fishing, Rivermead Leisure Complex, sports
> music scene: concerts, festivals
> day trips from Reading: go to London for a concert or a shopping trip

Erweiterung
- Anhand von **KV 6a+b: Reading skills** wenden die S die neu erworbenen *skills* auf einen weiteren Sachtext an und üben diese mit einer Tandemaufgabe.

Lösung
a) *Siehe TA*
b) *Individuelle S-Antworten*

Tipps für junge Lehrer | Bevor die S Teilaufgabe b) bearbeiten, sollten die Grundregeln einer Inhaltsangabe wiederholt werden. Ggf. kann man diese auf einem Lernplakat festhalten, das für alle gut sichtbar in der Klasse aufgehängt wird.

Material
Workbook S. 47/17
Kopiervorlage 6a+b

Üben | **4 ⟨Write an e-mail⟩** | Seite 66

Ziel
- Eine E-mail schreiben

Methodisches Vorgehen
- Sammeln von *Useful phrases* zum Schreiben einer E-Mail an der Tafel.
- Die S nutzen ihre Informationen aus *ex.* 3 und die *Useful phrases*, um Debbie in einer E-mail Tipps für ihren Besuch in Reading zu geben.

TA

> How to write an e-mail/a personal letter
> Dear …
> How are you?
> Thank you for your letter. It was nice to hear from you.
> Yours …/Love …
>
> How to give tips for a city trip
> … is famous for …/known for …
> There is/are …
> When you go to …, I'd suggest you …/I think you should …
> You must visit …
> Have a look at …

Erweiterung
- Die S verfassen eine E-Mail über den eigenen Besuch in einer englischen Stadt.

Lösung | *Individuelle S-Antworten*

			Text	**4**

Text

Seite 67–69

Ziele	• Einen Sachtext eigenständig erschließen
	• Die erlernten Lesetechniken anwenden
	• Eine Internetrecherche durchführen

⊚s ⊚L Text/ Fotos	**Changing places**	Seite 67–69
Wortschatz	*changing places, It's a pity., accent, to get tired of, interactive, across, for laughs, waterfront, weird, crowd, to cheer, to try out, to make fun of, quite, to hang out (with)*	**Material** ⊚s 2/1–3 ⊚L 3/1–3

Üben	**1 Before you read**	Seite 67
Ziel	• Die Bildbeschreibung üben	**TIP**
	• Das *skimming* als Lesetechnik anwenden und festigen	*Ex.* 1b) und *ex.* 2 knüpfen an die auf S. 66 trainierten *Reading skills* an. L sollte vorher noch einmal auf die Definitionen von *skimming* und *scanning* hinweisen
Methodisches Vorgehen	• a) Die S beschreiben die Fotos im SB bzw. auf **Folie 11: Changing places** und begründen, welche Orte ihnen am besten gefallen.	
	• b) L erinnert an den Wettbewerb der Internetseite *VISIT BRITAIN Kids*: *Three winners had the chance to visit another part of Britain. Here they talk about their 'holidays'. Find out which places they visited and write down what you already know about these places.*	
Lösung	a) Individuelle S-Antworten	
	b) 1 Wayne visited Swansea. Michael visited Liverpool. Rhona visited Reading.	
	2 Individuelle S-Antworten	
		Material Folie 11

Üben	**2 Collect more information**	Seite 67
Ziel	• Einen Text und dessen Wortschatz eigenständig erschließen	
	• Einen Text nach inhaltlichen Kategorien untersuchen	
Methodisches Vorgehen	• Der Wortschatz des Textes kann aus dem Zusammenhang erschlossen werden. L weist allerdings auf die Aussprache von *interactive* und *weird* gesondert hin.	
	• Die S fertigen eine Tabelle an (siehe TA) und suchen die passenden Informationen im Text. Sie kennzeichnen positive (+) und negative (-) Aspekte. Sammeln der Ergebnisse an der Tafel/auf Folie.	

TA

	Swansea	Liverpool	Reading
Language	Welsh accent and signs (funny) + most people speak English —	Liverpool accent (funny) +	people don't speak BBC English +/–
People		nice girls + aggressive football fans —	richer than Swansea +/– made fun of her Welsh accent —
Leisure activities	café on the hill + National Waterfront Museum +	vistors' sightseeing tour +	leisure pool + rowing +

4 Text

	Swansea Leisure Centre Skatepark +	Ferry across the Mersey +	visiting Windsor +
Historic places		Williamson Tunnels +	Windsor Castle +/-
Culture		The Beatles (for old people) — Football at Anfield Road +	open-air rock and folk festivals +
Nature	The Gower Coast (the beach at Rhossili) +		Thames +/-

Erweiterung
- Zur Überprüfung des Textverständnisses kann L ergänzende Fragen stellen: *Why was Wayne disappointed* (Vokabel erklären) *when he arrived in Swansea? (The shops were the same as in London.) Why didn't Wayne stay longer at the beach? (He got tired of the fresh air and it was cold.) Wayne doesn't like museums. Why did he go to the National Waterfront Museum? (Because his exchange partner wanted to go.) What did Rhona like about the leisure pool? (It had a lot of extras.) Rhona's arms and shoulders hurt. What happened? (She went rowing.) What does Rhona mean when she talks about all the rubbish in the tourist shops? (The expensive souvenirs that they sell in the shops.)*
- Alternative: Die S überlegen Fragen zum Text und beantworten diese in PA.

Lösung *Siehe TA*

Material
Workbook S. 48/18, 19
Ggf. Leerfolie

Üben 3 ⟨Would you like to live there?⟩ Seite 68

Ziel
- Einen Wunsch äußern und begründen

Methodisches Vorgehen
- Anhand der Notizen aus *ex.* 1 und 2 diskutieren die S in PA, an welchem Ort sie gerne leben würden.

Lösung *Individuelle S-Antworten*

Tipps für junge Lehrer L sollte sich hierbei bewusst zurücknehmen und nur bei groben sprachlichen Fehlern eingreifen. Dadurch erhalten die S die Möglichkeit zum experimentellen Umgang mit Sprache ohne Leistungsdruck.

Üben 4 Writing texts: Your "top three places" Seite 68

Ziel
- Eine Internetrecherche durchführen
- Einen Text über ein Urlaubsziel in Großbritannien verfassen

Wortschatz *search engine, at least*

Methodisches Vorgehen
- Die S erstellen zunächst in GA eine *mindmap* zu Städten und Regionen in Großbritannien, die sie aus den bisherigen Units oder aus eigener Erfahrung kennen. Eine große Wandkarte kann als Erinnerungsstütze dienen.
- a) Anschließend fertigt jede/r S eine Liste mit Aktivitäten an, die er/sie im Urlaub/ in der Freizeit gerne macht. Aus dieser Liste wählt er/sie drei Aktivitäten aus und überlegt, welche Stadt/Region in Großbritannien sich dafür am besten eignen würde. Die Karte vorne im Buch bietet Anhaltspunkte, da hier zusätzlich besondere Merkmale der jeweiligen Regionen aufgeführt sind.

TIP
Für die Internetrecherche:
www.visitbritain.co.uk

	Text	**Wordwise**	**4**

- b) Mit Hilfe des Internets suchen die S einen geeigneten Urlaubsort. Als Ausgangsseite bietet sich http://www.visitbritain.co.uk an.
- c) L verweist auf die *Reading skills* auf S. 66.
- d) Die S machen sich mit Hilfe der im SB aufgeführten Aspekte Notizen zu den *top three places* an dem von ihnen ausgewählten Urlaubsort.
- Abschließend verfassen die S anhand ihrer Notizen einen Text über ihre *top three places*. Die Texte im SB können dazu als Vorlage dienen.
- e) In leistungsschwächeren Lerngruppen bietet es sich an, die Texte im SB vor dem Schreiben eigener Texte auf *Useful phrases* hin zu untersuchen.

TIP
Hinweis auf *Reading skills*, S. 66

TA

```
Useful phrases to talk about holiday places and plans
I expect ...                         I like/don't like ...
The whole place is ...               It must be funny to ...
I can't wait to ...                  I want to ...
If I went to ..., I would ...        It doesn't cost much.
I would enjoy ...                    People seem to be ...
There is/there are ...               In the summer they have ...
I will be able to ...                I'd like to see that ...
I can have a look at ...             It's a good place to ...
It's a good way to meet people.
I found out a lot about the city from ...
In the guidebook/on the website it says that ...
```

- Die S übertragen die Liste mit den *Useful phrases* in ihren *folder* und ergänzen sie durch weitere Vokabeln zur Beschreibung ihrer Lieblingsorte.

Lösung
a)-d) *Individuelle S-Antworten*
e) *Siehe TA*

Material
Workbook S. 48/20
Ggf. Wandkarte

Wordwise

Seite 70

Ziele
- Den Wortschatz der Unit wiederholen und festigen
- Aussprache und Hörverstehen üben
- Die Umformung von Nomen in Adjektive üben

Üben **1 Mixed bag: An interesting idea** Seite 70

Ziel
- Den Wortschatz der Unit wiederholen

Methodisches Vorgehen
- Die S ergänzen die fehlenden Wörter; bei Schwierigkeiten können ihnen die Texte der Unit weiterhelfen.

Erweiterung
- KV 7: **Bingo** wiederholt ebenfalls den Wortschatz der Unit.

Lösung
1 *who* 2 *exchange* 3 *interesting* 4 *region* 5 *house* 6 *winners* 7 *visited* 8 *found* 9 *fun* 10 *sound* 11 *stay* 12 *rather* 13 *exciting*

Material
Kopiervorlage 7

Üben **2 Singular or plural?** Seite 70

Ziel
- Die Regel zu den *pair words* kennen lernen und anwenden

4 Wordwise

Strukturen	• *Pair words*	
Methodisches Vorgehen	• Gemeinsames Lesen der Arbeitsanweisung und des Beispiels im SB. Anschließend ergänzen die S die fehlenden Wörter in Einzelarbeit/PA.	**TIP** G 18
Lösung	*pairs of trousers, pairs of jeans, pairs of glasses, pair of goggles, pair of shoes, pairs of socks*	**Material** Workbook S. 49/22

ⓁÜben 3 Sounds: One sound makes a difference — Seite 70

HV-Text	1 price 2 bad 3 dog 4 men 5 boat	
Ziel	• Unterschiede in der Aussprache ähnlich geschriebener Wörter erkennen	
Methodisches Vorgehen	• a) Anhand des Beispiels im SB wird den S die Bedeutung der richtigen Aussprache eines einzelnen Lauts bewusst gemacht. Anschließend spielt L die Wörter in Aufgabe a) zweimal vor. Die S notieren sich, welches Wort sie hören. Kontrolle im Plenum. • b) Zum Üben von Aussprache und Hörverstehen erfolgt Teilaufgabe b) in PA.	**TIP** Lautschrift wiederholen
Erweiterung	• **KV 8: Wordwise**, Teilaufgabe a), übt ebenfalls Aussprache und Hörverstehen.	**Material** Ⓛ 3/4 Kopiervorlage 8
Lösung	*1b), 2a), 3a), 4b), 5a)*	

ⓈⓁ Üben Listening: Sounds and spellings — Workbook Seite 49

HV-Text Workbook	Narrator: 1 women; 2 quite; 3 gist; 4 love; 5 earn; 6 average; 7 cult; 8 cool; 9 curry	**Material** Ⓢ 2/4 Ⓛ 3/5 Workbook S. 49/23

Üben 4 Make adjectives — Seite 70

Ziel	• Die Umformung von Nomen in Adjektive üben	
Methodisches Vorgehen	• Die Aufgabe ist Differenzierung nach oben. Gemeinsame Besprechung der Arbeitsanweisung und der Beispiele, anschließend Einzelarbeit.	
Lösung	*milky, eventful, painful, helpful, regional, traditional, cultural, industrial*	
Erweiterung	• Die S bilden Sätze mit den zuvor gebildeten Adjektiven. • **KV 8: Wordwise**, Teilaufgabe b), greift das Thema *word formation* auf.	**Material** Kopiervorlage 8

			Check-out	4

Check-out
Seite 71

Ziele	• Die Lernziele der Unit in Selbstkontrolle überprüfen

Üben	**1 With or without *the*?**		Seite 71
Ziel	• Die Regel zum Gebrauch des bestimmten Artikels anwenden		
Strukturen	• *The definite article*		
Methodisches Vorgehen	• Die S bearbeiten *ex.* 1 in Einzelarbeit. Anschließend Selbstkontrolle bzw. Überprüfung durch eine/n Partner/in.		**TIP** G 14 a
Lösung	*Siehe SB S. 215*		**Material** *Workbook* S. 50/24

Üben	**2 *The, a/an*, or no article?**		Seite 71
Ziel	• Die Regel zum Gebrauch des unbestimmten Artikels anwenden		
Strukturen	• *The indefinite article*		
Methodisches Vorgehen	• Die S bearbeiten *ex.* 2 in Einzelarbeit. Anschließend Selbstkontrolle bzw. Überprüfung durch eine/n Partner/in.		**TIP** G 14 b
Lösung	*Siehe SB S. 215*		

Üben	**3 Adjective or adverb?**		Seite 71
Ziel	• Die Regel zum Gebrauch von Adjektiven und Adverbien anwenden		
Strukturen	• *Adjectives and adverbs*		
Methodisches Vorgehen	• Die S bearbeiten *ex.* 3 in Einzelarbeit. Anschließend Selbstkontrolle bzw. Überprüfung durch eine/n Partner/in.		**TIP** G 16
Lösung	*Siehe SB S. 215*		**Material** *Workbook* S. 50/26

Üben	**4 Your turn: What can you say?**		Seite 71
Ziel	• In Problemsituationen sprachlich angemessen reagieren		
Methodisches Vorgehen	• Die S bearbeiten Aufgabe a) und b) in Einzelarbeit oder PA. • Ggf. Vorspielen mehrerer Dialoge.		**TIP** *Useful phrases*, S. 62
Lösung	*Individuelle S-Antworten; Erwartungshorizont siehe SB S. 215.*		
Tipps für junge Lehrer	Teilaufgabe b) bietet gute Differenzierungsmöglichkeiten für leistungsstärkere S. Schwächere S können sich an den *Useful phrases* S. 62 orientieren.		

4 Check-out ⟨Text⟩

Dictation

Hi, my name is Sharon. My birthplace is London but we recently moved house, because my father found a new job as an engineer. His new firm is in Manchester. That's up North. A lot of Asian people live here. And you can eat curry everywhere. There are lots of leisure activities: I'm into pop music and Manchester has got a great music scene. You can hang out with friends at the department stores, go to the cinema, or if you get tired of the city you can go to Liverpool, which is not far away. In Liverpool you can do lots of exciting things. Maybe you want to visit the Beatles Story, a museum about the famous band. Or, if you are a football fan, go to a match at Anfield Road. The Liverpool accent is called the 'Scouse' accent. It sounds quite funny! Still, I'd rather live in Wales or in Scotland. Never mind! On average we move house every two years. I can wait …

⟨Text⟩ Seite 72–73

Ziele	• Einen adaptierten Auszug aus einem Jugendroman eigenständig erschließen
	• Über Chancen und Probleme von Auswanderung sprechen
	• Einen Brief/Tagebucheintrag verfassen

 Text ⟨Benny and Omar⟩ Seite 72–73

LANDESKUNDE

Tunisia, officially the Tunisian Republic, is a country situated on the Mediterranean coast of North Africa. It is bordered by Algeria to the west and Libya to the south-east. Around 40 % of the country is composed of the Sahara desert, with much of the remainder consisting of particularly fertile soil and a 1,300 km coastline. The official language in Tunisia is Standard Arabic. Sfax is a Mediterranean port on the Gulf of Gabes, 270 km to the south-east of Tunis. With a population of 340,000 (in 2005) it is Tunisia's second largest city and an industrial centre for processing phosphates.

Wortschatz Annotationen S. 72/73

Methodisches Vorgehen *Pre-reading:*
- SB geschlossen. L fragt die S, was diese aus dem Urlaub oder aus den Medien bereits über Tunesien wissen. Sammeln allgemeiner Informationen.
- L leitet mit der Frage, wie man nach Tunesien kommt, zu Bennys Geschichte über: *Benny went by plane, too. It was a long journey …*
- Zunächst bearbeiten die S **KV 9: Benny's flight to Tunisia**. Sie beschreiben Bennys Reise von England nach Tunesien und wiederholen den Wortschatz zum Thema *travelling*. Vergleich im Plenum.
- Anschließend hören die S den kursiv gedruckten Einführungstext von CD. Fragen zum Textverständnis: *Why does Benny have to move to Tunisia? (His dad has to go and work there, otherwise he will lose his job.) Where do they live in Tunisia? (In Marhaba, a village near the city of Sfax.) What do you think a 'walled camp' is? (There is a wall around the village.)*
- Zur weiteren Einstimmung auf den Text bearbeiten die S folgenden Arbeitsauftrag: *Imagine you had to move to Tunisia. Write down the three most important things you would take with you and explain why. Then discuss your choice with your neighbour.*

> **TIP**
> KV 9 greift Wortschatz aus *Green Line* 2, Unit 7 auf

⟨Text⟩ **4**

- Die S einigen sich in PA auf drei Gegenstände, die sie nach Tunesien mitnehmen würden. Sie präsentieren und begründen ihre Auswahl im Plenum. Beispiele: *a dictionary (language problems), sun lotion (lots of sun), swimsuit (beaches), …*

While-reading:
- L: *You have thought of some problems already. Let's see what happens to Benny and his family.* L präsentiert den Text von CD, die S lesen leise mit. Anschließend lesen sie den Text erneut und erschließen unbekannten Wortschatz mit Hilfe der Annotationen/dem Wörterbuch.

Post-reading:
- L leitet zur Bearbeitung von **KV 10: Tunisia** über: *After what you have heard from Mr Khayssi, would you like to live in Tunisia? Why not?*
- Die S bearbeiten **KV 10**, Teilaufgabe a). Schwächere S nehmen den Text im SB und die Annotationen zu Hilfe.   Auch als HA geeignet
- L leitet zur Bearbeitung von **KV 10**, Teilaufgabe b), über: *There are not only dangers in Tunisia. Mr Khayssi exaggerated* (Vokabel einführen). *When Benny meets Omar he gets to know the real Tunisia.* Die Aufgabe bietet gute Differenzierungsmöglichkeiten und fördert das freie Schreiben. Schwächeren S können ergänzend Vokabeln an die Hand gegeben werden.

Erweiterung
- Ausgehend vom letzten Satz der Geschichte (*This was a pity because Benny was allergic to mosquitoes.*) schreiben die S einen Brief aus dem Krankenhaus an Bennys ehemalige Schulkameraden. Der Brief sollte Bennys bisherige Erlebnisse in Tunesien beinhalten und Hinweise aus dem Text aufgreifen (z. B. dass Benny zur *factory* fahren musste, dass die Krankenschwester dort kein Englisch verstand, usw.). Alternativ ist auch ein Tagebucheintrag möglich.
- Ausgehend vom Text (Z. 94: *He pulled himself out of the chair and went for a sleep.*) können die S auch aufschreiben, was Benny in seiner ersten Nacht in Tunesien träumt.

Lösung | *Individuelle S-Antworten*

Material
◎ s 2/5–8
◎ L 3/6–9
Kopiervorlagen 9, 10

Tipps für junge Lehrer Die Vorschläge zum methodischen Vorgehen sollten als Anregung und nicht als Pflichtübung gesehen werden. Die Erweiterungsaufgaben schulen das Nacherzählen.

4 Kopiervorlagen

KV 1a: A trip around the UK

Play this game with three or more people. First cut out the picture cards. Put the cards face down on the table. Sort them as in the example on the right.

You need a dice[1] and each player should have a coloured piece of paper to move from one square[2] to the next. Take turns to throw the dice and move.

If you get to a white square, read the text. Then look at one of the picture cards. If the picture matches the text and you can name the place, you can keep the picture card. If the picture doesn't match the text, you must put it back on the table. If you get to a grey square, follow the instructions. The winner is the one with the most cards.

[1] **dice** [daɪs] = Würfel • [2] **square** [skweə] = Spielfeld

Lösung: A21 … Cliffs   B1 … Scotland, Wales and Northern Ireland   C13 … its wild landscape of mountains and lakes   D17 the Channel Tunnel   E7 Windsor   F3 … coast(line)   G19 … sheep   H15 Heathrow   I5 Liverpool   J11 Manchester   K9 … rowing   L23 … South Wales

226   GREEN LINE 3

KV 1b: A trip around the UK

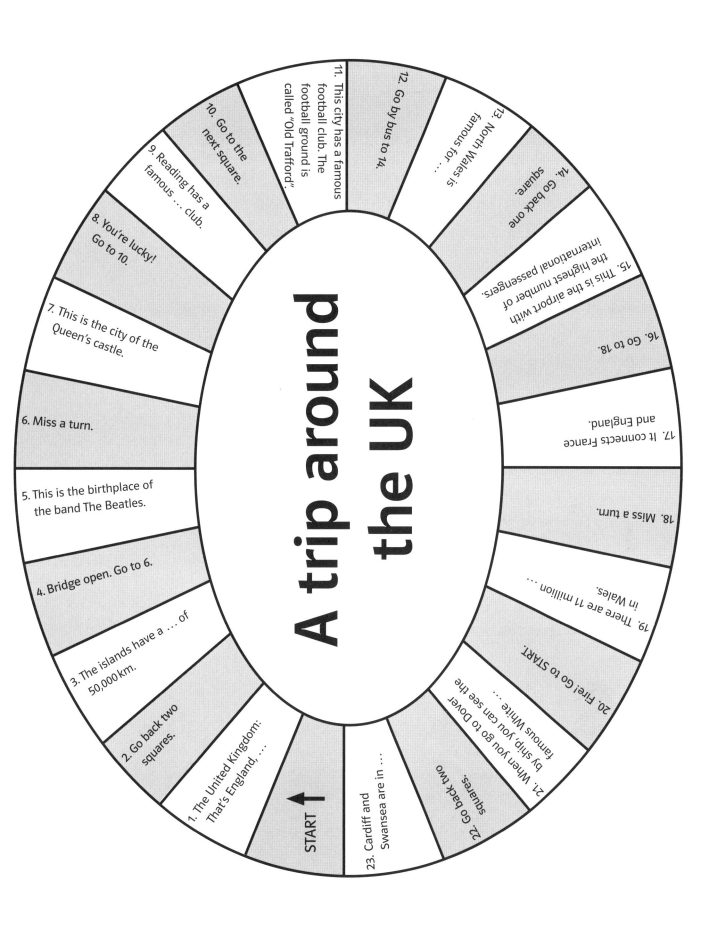

KV 2: The definite and the indefinite article

a) *Girls' talk*

*Rhona and Shirin are talking about Rhona's new boyfriend. Fill in the definite article **the** where it is needed.*

1. Shirin: So, tell me all about it! Have you finally found _____ love?
2. Rhona: Come on, he's not _____ love of my life, but he's nice.
3. Shirin: Where did you meet?
   Rhona: It was _____ luck. We met on _____ bus into town.
4. Shirin: What happened next?
   Rhona: We went to the cinema and had _____ dinner together.
5. Shirin: I bet[1] _____ dinner he cooked was perfect. But what did you do after that?
6. Rhona: We listened to _____ music and he played me some of _____ music he likes.
7. Shirin: Nothing else? _____ life is too short to wait too long until you kiss someone.
8. Rhona: Don't be so curious! I only say: I'll always remember _____ time we spent together …
9. Shirin: And what about people like me? _____ sad and _____ lonely? *(She laughs.)*
10. Rhona: _____ friendship we have is more important to me than any boy.

b) *Boys' talk*

*Fill in the indefinite article **a/an** where it is needed.*

1. Boy: Hey, you missed the goal! You want to be _____ rugby player?
2. David: Sorry, boys. I was thinking about something else. I met _____ girl on the bus and …
3. Boy: What are you talking about? Is this _____ excuse?
4. David: I really like her. She wants to become _____ doctor and she thinks I've got _____ great taste and …
5. Boy: This is _____ important game for us. Concentrate now! Didn't you buy _____ new pair of trainers last Friday? Now is the time to use them!
6. David: I've got _____ headache. I think I'll go home.
7. Boys: Look at him! He is _____ real lovefool[2] … *(They laugh.)*

[1] **(to) bet** [bet] = wetten • [2] **lovefool** [ˈlʌvfuːl] = verliebter Trottel

Lösung: a) 1 -- 2 the 3 -- ;the 4 -- 5 the 6 --;the 7 -- 8 the 9 the; the 10 the
b) 1 a 2 a 3 an 4 a; -- 5 an; a 6 a 7 a

KV 3: Helping and apologizing

a) *Work with a partner. Look at the pictures. All of these people have got a problem and you want to help them. What can you say? What do they say? Write the dialogues in your exercise book.*

USEFUL PHRASES
Can I help you? Shall I …?
Just take your time.
That's very kind of you.
Could you … for me?
You've been a great help.
You're welcome.

b) *Work with a partner. What would the people say in these situations? Write down the dialogues.*

1. You spill¹ some coke over your friend's new pullover.
2. You say in a loud voice that the food is bad while the waitress is standing behind you.
3. A woman talks unkindly about her friend's boyfriend.

4. You ride your bike too fast. A car almost hits you.
5. You told your best friend you had to do your homework and you couldn't play football with him. Then he meets you and your new girlfriend.

USEFUL PHRASES
I apologize. I'm terribly sorry …
I didn't mean to be rude.
I had no idea …
I didn't mean to hurt your feelings.
I wish I'd never said that.
Never mind.
No problem.
Don't worry.
Be more careful next time.
Let's just forget it.

¹**(to) spill** [spɪl] = (ver)schütten

KV 4: Adjectives after certain verbs

a) *Collect some adjectives for these verbs and write them in your exercise books.*

| smell | sound | taste | seem | look | feel |

Example: to smell: great, awful, …

b) *The Khans like to eat out on Sundays. They always go to their favourite curry place, 'The Bombay Hut'. One day they take Rhona with them. Rhona is the only non-Indian person at the restaurant. Write down what she thinks.*

Wow, I've never been to an Indian restaurant before! I feel _____!

Rhona: "The food looks _____! Everything smells _____. I hope it tastes _____. The music is

Indian, too, it sounds _____. Shirin seems _____, maybe we should order soon …"

c) *Look at the menu of 'The Bombay Hut'. Try to guess what the different kinds of food are. What would you like/ wouldn't you like? Explain your opinion and write it in your exercise book. You can use the words from a).*

Example: I wouldn't like garlic[1] naan. It smells awful.

BOMBAY HUT

Appetizers:
Vegetable Samosa
Garlic Naan

Soups:
Chicken Soup
Lentil Soup

BOMBAY HUT

Main Dishes:
Tandoori Shrimps
Lamb Curry
Rice and Peas
Aloo Gobi
Chicken Tikka Masala

BOMBAY HUT

Desserts:
Kheer

Drinks:
Soft Drinks
Mango Juice
Indian Tea
Lassi

d) *Work with a partner. One of you is the guest and the other one is the waiter/the waitress. Now order your meal at 'The Bombay Hut'. Write a dialogue in your exercise book.*

[1] **garlic** ['gaːlɪk] = Knoblauch

KV 5: The future perfect – Moving house

a) *Aunt Zeba and her five sons are moving house. Aunt Zeba has made a list with things she needs to do. But by the end of the week she won't have done all of them. Write down what she will have done and what she won't have done.*

- pack everything into boxes ✓
- call for a big van
- turn off washing machine ✓
- make sandwiches ✓
- find garage key
- say goodbye to neighbours ✓
- clean bathroom
- buy cat food ✓
- check bills ✓
- relax for an hour
- …

1. She will have packed everything into boxes.

b) *Think of reasons why Aunt Zeba won't have done some of the things on her list.*

Example: She won't have called for a big van because she will have asked her neighbour to put the boxes in his car.

Lösung: a) 2 She won't have called for a big van. 3 She will have turned off the washing machine. 4 She will have made sandwiches. 5 She won't have found the garage key. 6 She will have said goodbye to the neighbours. 7 She won't have cleaned the bathroom. 8 She will have bought cat food. 9 She will have checked the bills. 10 She won't have relaxed for an hour.

© Ernst Klett Verlag GmbH, Stuttgart 2008. Alle Rechte vorbehalten.
ISBN 978-3-12-547143-6

GREEN LINE 3

KV 6a: Reading skills (Partner A)

Britain has more than 2,500 miles of coast. Some of it is flat, but in many places there are high cliffs. Because Britain is an island, enemies have always found it very difficult to conquer[1] Britain. The last person who did this was William the Conqueror. He and his men came to Britain on ships from France in 1066. William won a battle at Hastings on the south coast and became King of England. Today, of course, it is easier to get to Britain. You can go by ferry or plane, or through the Channel Tunnel.

1 Talking about the pictures

With your partner: Describe and compare the pictures of the sea/coast.

2 Skimming

a) *Look through the text quickly. Do not read every word. Concentrate on keywords. Mark the keywords with a coloured pen.*

b) *Now tell your partner in one or two sentences what your text is about.*

3 Scanning

a) *Look at the text again. Do not read every word. Is there any information about these things? Tick the correct boxes.*

changes in the sea	☐	ways of travelling to Britain	☐	battle	☐
sea industries	☐	Britain's coast	☐	day trips	☐

b) *Tell your partner about the things in a). Then find out about the other things from your partner.*

[1] **(to) conquer** [ˈkɒŋkə] = erobern

Lösung: 3a) Britain's coast, battle, ways of travelling to Britain

KV 6b: Reading skills (Partner B)

The sea still plays a big role in the lives of many British people. Fishing and North Sea oil are important industries. And because the coast is never more than seventy miles away, it is easy to go to the seaside for a day trip or a holiday. People who live close to the sea know that it often changes. Sometimes it is calm and then it is safe to play in the waves. But there are storms, too, and the wind and the rain can make the sea rough[1] and dangerous. Even in good weather there are always strong tides[2] around the British coast.

1 Talking about the pictures

With your partner: Describe and compare the pictures of the sea/coast.

2 Skimming

a) *Look through the text quickly. Do not read every word. Concentrate on keywords. Mark the keywords with a coloured pen.*

b) *Now tell your partner in one or two sentences what your text is about.*

3 Scanning

a) *Look at the text again. Do not read every word. Is there any information about these things? Tick the correct boxes.*

changes in the sea	☐	ways of travelling to Britain	☐	battle	☐
sea industries	☐	Britain's coast	☐	day trips	☐

b) *Tell your partner about the things in a). Then find out about the other things from your partner.*

[1]**rough** [rʌf] = rau • [2]**strong tide** [ˈstrɒŋ taɪd] = starke Strömung

Lösung: 3a) sea industries, day trips, changes in the sea

KV 7: Bingo

Work in groups of 4–6 pupils. In your group decide who is the quizmaster. All the other group members cut out one of the grids and write down four words from each list. Don't let the others see your words! Start the game. The quizmaster reads out the words from the lists in a mixed order. When you find one of the words in your grid cross it out. The first one with four words in a row[1] (→ ↓ ↙ ↘) shouts "Bingo!" and wins the game. Change the quizmaster and play again. Have fun!

1. verbs	2. adjectives	3. languages/accents	4. regional aspects
to make fun of	interactive	Welsh	industry
to scan	recently	Punjabi	culture
to be on the move	quite	English	landscape
to be proud of	awful	German	exhibition
to hang out	factual	Asian	waterfront
to get tired of	regional	Indian	coal mine
to skim	definite	Turkish	leisure centre
to sound	rude	Scottish	male voice choir

[1] **row** [rəʊ] = Reihe

KV 8: Wordwise

a) Cut out the cards. Which words have the same sound as 'close', 'down', 'pair' and 'year'? Read them out to your neighbour. Make a grid in your exercise book and stick the words in the right place.

| close | down | pair | year |

close	down	pair	year
broken	cloud	compare	slow
loud	fair	proud	poet
scary	show	cafeteria	dear
sofa	chair	there	clown
share	almost	about	shower
hair	here	alone	ago
care	wear	clear	disappear

b) Use the following suffixes to form as many words as you can remember. Write the word class in brackets (n = noun, adj = adjective).

| -ity | -ful | -ness | -less | -ion | -ment | -or/-er |

Now write down the rule:

The suffixes _____

The suffixes _____

Lösung: a) **close:** broken, slow, poet, sofa, ago, almost, alone; **down:** cloud, proud, loud, about, clown, shower; **pair:** fair, compare, scary, chair, share, hair, there, care, wear; **year:** cafeteria, here, clear, dear, disappear.
b) The suffixes -ity, -ness, -ion, -ment, -or/-er form nouns; the suffixes -ful, -less form adjectives.

GREEN LINE 3

KV 9: Benny's flight to Tunisia

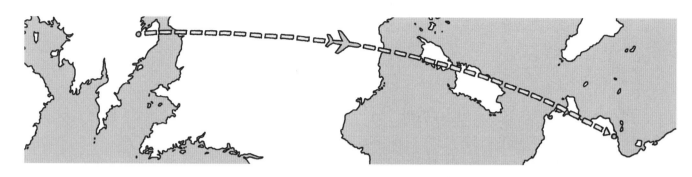

For Benny it was a long way to Tunisia. Look at the pictures and write about his journey. Use your exercise book.

1. (check in)
2. (listen to)
3. (take off)
4. (be)
5. (arrive)
6. (collect)
7. (show)
8. (ask)
9. (not able to read)
10. (find)
11. (tell)
12. (meet)

¹(to) declare [dɪˈkleə] = verzollen

Lösung: 1 Benny checked in at Terminal 1. 2 Then he listened to the announcement. 3 The plane to Sfax took off at 8.30. 4 Benny was on the plane for more than six hours. 5 Finally, the plane arrived in Sfax at 14.45. 6 Next Benny collected his suitcase in the baggage hall. 7 He showed his passport to the policemen. 8 One of the policemen asked him: "Anything to declare?" 9 In Sfax Benny wasn't able to read the signs. 10 But he found a taxi. 11 He told the taxi driver: "To Marhaba village, please." 12 There he met Mr Khayssi.

KV 10: Tunisia

a) Mr Khayssi tells Benny and his family about the worst things that could happen to them in Tunisia. What dangers are these? Answer the questions and find out. Use the text on pages 72–73 in your book for help.

1						A											
2						D											
3						V											
4						E											
5						N											
6						T											
7						U											
8						R											
9						E											

1. When the warning lights don't work here, you don't hear the train coming.
2. People who fight aggressively for what they think is right.
3. Mr Khayssi tells the Shaws to … carefully because of all the traffic.
4.
5.
6. The … of an insect can hurt very badly.
7.
8. When people on the streets start fighting, there are …
9. A small motorbike is a …

b) When Benny meets Omar he gets to know a different Tunisia. Have a look at Omar's photo album. Then write a short paragraph about how he sees his country.

Lösung: 1 *train tracks* 2 *fundamentalists* 3 *drive* 4 *snake* 5 *scorpion* 6 *sting* 7 *mosquito* 8 *riots* 9 *mobylette*

KV 11: Stationenlernen Unit 4 (Language 2)

Station 1: Colourful adjectives

a) *Do you remember how to form adverbs from adjectives? Colour in each box with a different colour.*

1. + -ly ☐   2. -ful → -fully ☐   3. -y → -ily ☐   4. -le → -ly ☐   5. irregular ☐

b) *Read the adjectives and colour them in with the right colour from a).*

c) *Make adverbs from the adjectives.*

d) *Make a grid with the categories in a) and write down the adjectives and the adverbs. Use your exercise book.*

slow	excited	careful	easy	nervous	loud
heavy	horrible	angry	fast	terrible	
grumpy	friendly	different	good	normal	hard
hungry	quick	beautiful	awful	polite	

✂··

Station 2: A letter grid

a) *Think of different adjectives and adverbs. Write them on a piece of paper. Don't show them to your partner.*

b) *Write the adjectives and adverbs in the grid: ↑ ↓ ↗ →   Fill the empty boxes with letters.*

c) *Cut out the grid and give it to your partner.*

d) *Work with your partner's grid and find the adjectives and adverbs.*

e) *Make a grid in your exercise book and write down the words: adjective – adverb.*

f) *Choose three adjectives and three adverbs and write a sentence for each.*

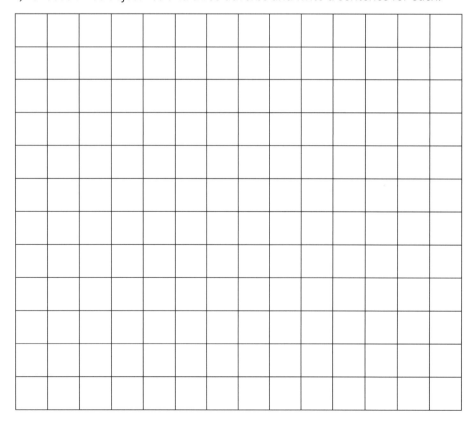

KV 12: Stationenlernen Unit 4 (Language 2)

Station 3: Memory

a) *Cut out the cards and sort them: verb forms – adverbs/adjectives.*

b) *Mix the verb forms and put them face down on the table. Do the same with the adverbs/adjectives. Sort them this way:*

c) *Play memory. When you get a pair, form a sentence. If the sentence is correct, keep the cards.*

become	good	fast	taste
famous	badly	sing	great
cry	feel	hungrily	get
write	slowly	smell	eat
beautiful	calm	walk	unusual
look	bad	terribly	sound
tired	be	strange	stay

GREEN LINE 3

KV 13: Stationenlernen Unit 4 (Language 2)

Station 4: At the bus stop

a) *Look at the picture. What can you see? Choose a verb and an adjective/adverb and form a sentence. Be careful with the verb forms.* Example: The hamburger tastes …

b) *Compare with your partner.*

| sound | dangerous | friendly | talk | great | eat | taste |
| be | look | run | ride | sad | hungry | angry | fast | awful |

Station 5: Move!

a) *Each of you: Think of four activities you can do in class.*

b) *Think of adverbs: How can you do the activities?*

c) *Write them in the grid.* Example: Walk very slowly (to the board and back).

d) *Cut out the sentences, mix them and put them face down on the table.*

e) *Take turns to take a card and do the activity. Let the others guess.*

1	2
3	4

KV 14: Stationenlernen Unit 4 (Language 2)

Station 6: A game

You need a dice and a watch.

a) Decide who starts. Throw the dice, move, read the verb and find as many adverbs for it as you can in one minute. The others check the time and count the adverbs. Write down the number in the grid.
b) The next player on the right goes on.
c) The game is over when the first player gets to FINISH. The winner is the one with the most adverbs.

Name ↓	player	1	2	3	4	5	6	7	8	9	10
	1										
	2										
	3										
	4										

eat	sound	play	START → FINISH	chat	fight	get	smell
work							sing
behave							look
feel							swim
write							become
read							walk
drive							shout
seem	cry	listen	taste	speak	stay	live	be

Verbs inside the face: stay, feel, taste, smell, be, look, sound, seem, get, become

GREEN LINE 3

KV 15: Stationenlernen Unit 4 (Language 2)

Station 7: A poem

How did you feel or look when you were younger? What did you do and how did you do it?
Look at the example and write a poem about yourself. Write it in your exercise book and decorate it. Read it to your class. Have fun!

When I was six

I walked to school slowly

I often sang nicely

I always felt great

And I never was late

But all I want today

Is to dance and shout "Hooray!"

When I was _____

I _____

I _____

I _____

And I _____

But all I want today

Is to _____

Station 8: Mistakes

a) *Read the text. Add the correct punctuation marks " " , : . ? !*
b) *Read the text again. Find and correct five more mistakes (adjectives – adverbs).*
c) *Compare texts with your partner. Then have a look at page 63 in your book and compare again.*

I didn't know you had so many relatives here Rhona said to Shirin quietly She looked around the room at ten of Shirin's aunts uncles and cousins Aunt Zeba put the sixth different kind of food on the table I know you feel hungrily after the long trip she said so don't be shy – eat The Asian food looked unusually to Rhona but most things smelt and tasted well and she ate hungrily When Rhona listened to some of Shirin's older relatives she was surprised They spoke a language she couldn't understand That's Punjabi Shirin's cousin Tariq explained I don't speak it very good I understand it but I usually answer in English Mum gets angrily about that Has Shirin told you anything about Manchester he asked Yes it sounds great replied Rhona

Lösungen zu den Stationen

Station 1

+ -ly	- ful → -fully	-y → -ily	-le → -ly	irregular
slowly	carefully	easily	horribly	fast
excitedly	awfully	heavily	terribly	well
politely	beautifully	angrily		in a friendly way
nervously		grumpily		hard
differently		hungrily		
loudly				
normally				
quickly				

Station 4

1 The hamburger tastes awful. 2 The music sounds great. 3 The old man looks friendly. 4 The woman is sad. 5 The (business)man is talking angrily. 6 The woman is eating hungrily. 7 The man is running fast. 8 The little girl is riding her bike dangerously.

Station 8

a) Siehe Schülerbuch Green Line 3, S. 63.
b) feel hungry; looked unusual; smelt and tasted good; I don't speak it very well; gets angry

⟨Revision for tests⟩ Unit 3–4

Seite 74–75

Ziele
- Den Wortschatz zum Thema *food* wiederholen und festigen
- Einen Hörtext zum Thema „Hausarbeit" verstehen
- Eine E-Mail an Freunde schreiben
- Eine unangenehme Situation sprachlich bewältigen
- Einen Text erschließen und in ein Theaterstück umwandeln

Üben | **1 Mixed bag: British food** | Seite 74

Ziel
- Verschiedene Wortarten erkennen und einsetzen
- Die Zeitenfolge in den *if-clauses type 2 and 3* wiederholen und festigen

Strukturen
- *If-clauses type 2 and 3, simple present, simple past, present perfect, each other*

Methodisches Vorgehen
- L erinnert die S daran, bei Fragen selbstständig im *Dictionary*- bzw. im Grammatikanhang nachzuschlagen. Außerdem sollte L auf die Berücksichtigung des Gesamtzusammenhangs hinweisen.
- Die Aufgabe wird in Einzelarbeit gelöst; anschließend Kontrolle in PA. Problemfälle können im Plenum besprochen werden.

TIP
Nachschlagen im *Dictionary*- bzw. im Grammatikanhang

Erweiterung
- Nachdem in der Aufgabe der Wortschatz zum Thema *food* umgewälzt wurde, bietet sich eine schriftliche Erweiterung an: *Can you have lunch at school? Write a short text (3–4 sentences) about food at your school. If you can't have lunch there, write about the food you eat at home.* Hier können die S auch dazu aufgefordert werden, eine *if-clause*-Struktur einzubauen.

Lösung
1 *angry* 2 *proud* 3 *cook* 4 *have* 5 *at* 6 *awful* 7 *were/was* 8 *would*
9 *the* 10 *cakes* 11 *ate* 12 *would* 13 *taught* 14 *become* 15 *behave*
16 *each* 17 *of* 18 *jeans* 19 *was* 20 *turned* 21 *have*

Tipps für junge Lehrer
Bei solchen Aufgaben können auch *skimming* und *scanning* als Lesetechniken geübt werden, indem die alten Unit-Texte auf der Suche nach Lösungshilfen überflogen werden (siehe *Skills* S. 66). L: *Don't always expect the answers to jump out of the page. Sometimes you have to search for them!*

Material
Workbook S. 51/1

L **Üben** | **2 Listening: Helping the family** | Seite 74

HV-Text

Rachel: Hello, everyone. Many older people say modern teenagers are lazy, selfish people who don't help at home. Today we want to hear from some of those teenagers. Here's our first caller – Justin from Birmingham. Hello, Justin.
Justin: Hello, Rachel.
Rachel: Now, Justin, you don't agree with those older people I was talking about.
Justin: No, I don't. I think teenagers help their parents a lot.
Rachel: Right, Justin, let's take you as an example. Tell us what a typical Saturday looks like in your house.
Justin: OK, well, we get up later, of course, because nobody has to go to work.
Rachel: Do you get the breakfast ready?
Justin: No, my dad does that. Our dog has his breakfast first.
Rachel: Then you walk the dog.
Justin: No, then we have our breakfast. Then my *mum* walks the dog. She says she needs the exercise. And I put all the breakfast things into the dishwasher.
Rachel: Wow! That must be hard work! Do you start on your homework after that?
Justin: No, I usually do that on Friday. No, after breakfast Dad always has to go to

⟨Revision B⟩ R

the DIY shop to buy things. He's not happy at the weekend if he's not building a wall or putting in new windows or something. He usually asks me to come and help him to carry the things. That's OK with me.

Rachel: Is that the last of your Saturday jobs?
Justin: No, then I help in the kitchen. It's my job to get rid of the rubbish and the empty bottles.
Rachel: That doesn't sound too bad. Do you have a garden at your place?
Justin: Oh, don't remind me! Mum and Dad spend hours working there. But it isn't my idea of fun. Our garden isn't even big enough for football.
Rachel: I'm sure your parents would be happy if you helped them.
Justin: Maybe, but I don't have time – I have to tidy up the chaos in my room in the afternoon. My mum says if I leave all that junk around, I'll have mice in there.
Rachel: How sweet! No, seriously – do you really tidy up your room every week?
Justin: Yes, I do. If I didn't, I wouldn't get much pocket money.
Rachel: Ah, I get it! Well, thank you, Justin, –
Justin: Just a minute! I must tell you about the work I really like. If I'm not out with my friends on Saturday evening, I usually cook dinner at home, and I always try out something new. I'm into Indian food at the moment.
Rachel: That's great! What do your parents think of your food?
Justin: They love it. Of course, Dad always says, like, "This looks weird. I think I'll go and get a pizza later." … But he never does!

Ziel
- Das Hörverstehen durch die Anordnung von Bildern überprüfen
- Über die persönliche Einstellung zum Thema „Hausarbeit" sprechen

Methodisches Vorgehen
- Der HV-Text ist relativ schwierig und nach einmaligem Hören werden einige S Probleme haben, die Bilder richtig anzuordnen. Um die Aufgabe vorzuentlasten, können die S das *listening grid* in ihre Hefte übernehmen (siehe TA).
- L betrachtet die Bilder im SB mit den S und stellt die Frage: *What is Justin doing in picture 1?* Erwartungshorizont: *He is carrying things from the DIY store to the car* (siehe TA). Die S tragen die Antwort in das *grid* ein.
- Beim Hören tragen die S die richtige Reihenfolge in die rechte Spalte ein und die Antwort zu b): *What job is missing?* zusätzlich in die unterste Zeile.
- Diese Aufgabe – einschließlich der Erweiterung – bietet sich als Wiederholung zum Thema *family life* an. Anschließend könnte mit Hilfe der *Useful phrases: Finding a compromise* (S. 46) eine Diskussion im Plenum stattfinden.

TIP
Ein *listening grid* erstellen

TA

Picture	Job	Right order
1	carrying things from DIY store	
2	cooking in kitchen	
3	putting things into dishwasher	
4	walking dog	
5	tidying up room	
no picture		

Erweiterung
- Zur Erweiterung der Aufgabe diskutieren die S in PA über das Thema „Hausarbeit": *Interview your partner about the jobs he or she does around the house.*

Lösung
a) 3, 1, 5, 2; picture 4 is wrong: Justin's mum walks the dog.
b) getting rid of the rubbish and the empty bottles

Tipps für junge Lehrer
Pre-listening activities wie das Erstellen eines *listening grid* verhelfen vor allem schwächeren S bei solchen Höraufgaben zu einem Erfolgserlebnis.

Material
L 3/10

R ⟨Revision B⟩

ⓢS ⓢL **Üben**		**Listening: Telephone messages**	Workbook Seite 51
HV-Text Workbook		**a)** Shirin: Hello, this is Shirin. I'm just calling to say that I can't go to the cinema this evening, but I'll be able to go to the film at the Riverside Film Centre at six o'clock tomorrow. Could you call me back, please?	
		b) David: I'm afraid I forgot to write down the title of our Geography project – and I need to search the Internet for some ideas. Please ring me at home after seven. Thanks – David.	
		c) Shirin: Hello Rhona. It's me again, Shirin. Sorry, we can't go to the cinema tomorrow either. I forgot to tell you. There's a rehearsal for the school play at six – and the new drama teacher says we must try on our costumes at five thirty. Bye. I'll speak to you later.	**Material** ⓢS 2/9 ⓢL 3/11 Workbook S. 51/2

Üben	**3**	**An e-mail to friends in London**	Seite 74
Ziel	•	Eine E-Mail an Freunde schreiben	**TIP**
	•	Kenntnisse über britische Städte/Regionen in einer E-Mail kreativ nutzen	Informationen aus früheren Texten kreativ nutzen
Methodisches Vorgehen	•	Die Notizen für Fionas E-Mail sollten von den S mit Ideen aus Unit 4: *The UK on the move* ergänzt werden (siehe Tipps für junge Lehrer).	
	•	Die S bearbeiten die Aufgabe selbstständig – entweder in Einzelarbeit oder als Hausaufgabe.	
Erweiterung	•	Die S formulieren die Antwort zu Fionas E-Mail aus der Sicht eines/einer früheren Klassenkameraden/in.	

Lösung

> *Erwartungshorizont:*
> *Hi, it's me, Fiona. The move up here was awful – nobody knew where anything was in the new house. What a mess! But after a few weeks my room is looking better. It was strange at first – the new neighbours, the class, the town, but everybody is very helpful. They all talk differently. The accent sounds really cool. There's a big open-air rock festival here next week. I'm going with some of the people in my new class. I really miss the skate park and football at Chelsea. But what I miss most is all of you in my old tutor group. We are coming back to London at Christmas to stay with Grandma. See you all then maybe???*
> *Love to all, Fiona*

Tipps für junge Lehrer	Die S tun sich schwer damit zu „lügen", d. h. sie klauen ungern Ideen aus einem Text, um sie in einem anderen kreativen Kontext zu verwenden. Die Texte von *Changing places* (S. 67–69) bieten einige Ideen, die die S für Fionas E-Mail benutzen können. Der Inhalt der E-Mail muss nicht den Tatsachen entsprechen, aber er sollte glaubwürdig sein.	**Material** Workbook S. 51/3

Üben	**4**	**Role play: Hey! What do you think you're doing?**	Seite 74
Ziel	•	Eine unangenehme Situation sprachlich bewältigen	**TIP**
Methodisches Vorgehen	•	Die S lesen die Aufgabe eigenständig durch und überlegen, welche der *Useful phrases* von *Talkwise: Dealing with problems* (S. 62) im Rollenspiel verwendet werden könnten.	Kleine Ermunterung an die S: *Don't learn by heart. Be spontaneous!*
	•	Anschließend spielen die S das Rollenspiel in PA durch; nach dem ersten Durchgang tauschen sie die Rollen.	

⟨Revision B⟩ R

Erweiterung
- Die S denken sich eine weitere unangenehme Situation aus und überlegen sich auch dazu ein Rollenspiel.
- Einige der Rollenspiele können vor der Klasse vorgespielt werden.

Lösung

> *Erwartungshorizont:*
> Nicola: *Hey! What do you think you're doing? I almost hit you and fell off my bike. You silly idiot. You can't sit in the road like that.*
> Boy: *But I fell over and hurt my knee.*
> Nicola: *Oh, I'm terribly sorry. Have you hurt yourself badly?*
> Boy: *I don't think so.*
> Nicola: *Shall I help you to get up?*
> Boy: *Oh, thanks.*
> Nicola: *Just take your time. Are you OK?*
> Boy: *Yes, I think so. You've been a great help. I'll be OK now.*

Tipps für junge Lehrer
Die S können während der Erarbeitungsphase gefragt werden, ob sie ihr Rollenspiel vor der Klasse vorspielen wollen. Wenn einige Freiwillige feststehen, können peinliche Situationen vermieden werden. Nach der Frage: *Who wants to act their role plays in front of the class?* melden sich evtl. weitere S.

Material
Workbook S. 51/4

Üben

5 Good for business   Seite 75

Ziel
- Einen Text eigenständig erschließen
- Die Lesetechniken *skimming* und *scanning* anwenden und festigen
- Ein kurzes Theaterstück schreiben

Methodisches Vorgehen
- L erinnert an den Unterschied zwischen *skimming* und *scanning* (siehe TA).
- Die S erledigen die Teilaufgaben a)–c) eigenständig und kontrollieren ihre Antworten in PA.
- d) sollte als längerfristige Hausaufgabe bearbeitet werden.

TA

> skimming = reading a text quickly to find out what the text is about
> scanning = reading a text to find information on a topic

Erweiterung
- In Gruppen zu je 4–5 S wird zunächst das beste Theaterstück der Gruppe ausgewählt (*relay check*).
- L sammelt anschließend die ausgewählten Stücke ein und kopiert die drei oder vier besten davon, um allen S in der Klasse die Möglichkeit zu geben, in einem Stück mitzuspielen – abhängig von der jeweiligen Anzahl der Charaktere.
- Das Vorspielen der Stücke kann als Abschluss der Unit-Reihe im SB erfolgen.

Lösung

> a) *Erwartungshorizont: Diana tells the reader about her job as a guide at Redstone Castle, the home of old Sir Clarence. One afternoon a tourist falls after she has seen a ghost and her son is missing. The boy comes back with the ghost's scarf and Redstone Castle becomes very popular.*
> b) *Diana's family – no; British history – no; people she works for – yes; the tourist industry – yes*
> c) *lives in Redstone Castle – mean old man – wears an old school scarf – happy about the ghost – thinks tourists come to see the Redstone Ghost*
> d) *Individuelle S-Antworten*

Tipps für junge Lehrer
Wenn die S ein Theaterstück schreiben, sollten sie die Möglichkeit bekommen, es auch vorzuspielen. Ansonsten wäre die Arbeit nicht authentisch.

Material
Workbook S. 52/5

Planung Unit 5

Übersicht

Bearbeitungszeitraum: 22 Unterrichtsstunden

Abschnitt	SB-Seiten	Ziele	Wortschatz/Grammatik & skills	WB-Übungen	CD-Tracks Kopiervorlagen Folien DVD	Gramm. Anhang (SB)
Check-in Media messages	76–77	Über Informationsgehalt und Glaubwürdigkeit verschiedener Medien sprechen Eigene Mediengewohnheiten beschreiben	Wortfeld „Medien" Radiosendungen verstehen	S. 53/ex. 1, 2	Schüler-CD 2/10–12 Lehrer-CD 3/12–14, 15–17 DVD: Recent news, Part A	
Language 1 Casting for a daily soap	78–80	Einen Artikel über die Rollenbesetzung für eine *soap opera* lesen und verstehen Über eigene Lieblingssendungen berichten	*Passive: simple present, simple past, present perfect* R: *If-clauses type 2 and 3*	S. 54/ex. 3–5 S. 55/ex. 6, 7 S. 56/ex. 8, 9	Lehrer-CD 3/18 Folie 12 DVD: Recent news, Part B DVD: Ending	G 19, 20
Talkwise Talk about media in your life	81	Über die Bedeutung von Medien für das eigene Leben berichten Vor- und Nachteile verschiedener Medien diskutieren	Ein Radiointerview verstehen *Useful phrases: Personal media vocabulary*	S. 57/ex. 10–12	Schüler-CD 2/13 Lehrer-CD 3/19, 20	
Language 2 Advertising	82–84	Den Aufbau von Werbeanzeigen verstehen und diskutieren	*Writing texts*: Eine Internetanzeige erstellen *How to*: Die Arbeit eines anderen prüfen *Past perfect passive, personal passive* R: *Simple past vs. present perfect*	S. 58/ex. 13, 14 S. 59/ex. 15, 16	Lehrer-CD 3/21 KV 1, 2 Folie 13	G 21, 22
Skills Writing a newspaper report	85	Die Struktur eines Zeitungsberichts erkennen Einen Zeitungsbericht schreiben	*Writing skills*: Einen Zeitungsbericht schreiben	S. 60/ex. 17	KV 3	
Text No couch potatoes!	86–87	Über die positiven Auswirkungen verschiedener Medien lesen und diskutieren Eine Umfrage zu Mediengewohnheiten in der Klasse durchführen	Ein *media survey* durchführen	S. 61/ex. 18–20	Schüler-CD 2/14–15 Lehrer-CD 3/22–23 KV 4a+b, 5a+b	

Abschnitt	SB-Seiten	Ziele	Wortschatz/Grammatik & skills	WB-Übungen	CD-Tracks Kopiervorlagen Folien DVD	Gramm. Anhang (SB)
Wordwise	88	*Polite answers* anwenden Betonungsvarianten erkennen und differenzieren Einem Lied Informationen entnehmen	Wortschatzarbeit: *polite answers* Sounds: *Strong and weak forms*	S. 62/ex. 21	Lehrer-CD 3/24, 25 KV 6a+b	
Check-out	89	Selbstkontrolle Die Lernziele der Unit 5 überprüfen	Wortschatz- und Grammatikschwerpunkte der Unit: „Medien", Zeitformen des *passive* Einen Zeitungsbericht schreiben Eine Werbeanzeige erstellen	S. 63/ex. 24–26		
⟨Text⟩ *Big mouth and ugly girl*		Einen Auszug aus einem Jugendroman eigenständig erschließen		S. 64	Schüler-CD 2/16 Lehrer-CD 3/27	

Unit 5 Media messages

Hinweise

LANDESKUNDE

In the modern world the **media** have come to play a decisive role in everyday life. People cannot imagine being without various forms of media. They may even be completely unaware of how much they depend on the entertainment and information industry. The visual elements of the media in particular have gained increasing importance, especially for young people. Producers are conscious of the influence they have on the viewers and make great efforts to design their images accordingly. The word 'media' can refer to various aspects: recording/print media, electronic media (multimedia, hypermedia, digital media), published media (mass media, broadcast media, news media), media meshing (combining media), new media (to be used with modern computer processing power), media for advertising.

Shout is a UK magazine for teenage girls. The first issue was published in 1993. It carries articles on fashion, celebrities, true stories, problems and embarrassing moments. It is published fortnightly, and is read by more than 520,000 people. It is a magazine for 10–14 year old girls and aims to help them look and feel great. For more information check: http://www.shoutmag.co.uk

Smash hits was a pop music based magazine, aimed at children and young teenagers and originally published in the UK. It ran from 1978 to 2006 and was issued fortnightly for most of the time. The backbone of the magazine in its early years was the publication of Top 20 song lyrics. In the 1990s the magazine's circulation slumped and it was overtaken by the BBC's magazine *Top Of The Pops*. The magazine was also available in Europe, especially in Germany. In 2006 publication was ceased due to declining sales, but the digital television, digital radio and website services continue.

The Times is a daily national newspaper published in the UK since 1785. With its sister paper, *The Sunday Times*, it is published by Times Newspapers Limited, a subsidiary of News International, itself wholly owned by Rupert Murdoch's News Corporation group. Though traditionally a moderately centre-right newspaper and a supporter of the Conservatives, it supported the Labour Party in the 2001 and 2005 general elections. The newspaper was printed in broadsheet format for 200 years, but switched to compact size in 2004, in an attempt to appeal to younger readers. The circulation figures for 2006 show that *The Times* sold an average of 692,581 copies per day.

The Sun was launched on September 15, 1964. It is a tabloid daily newspaper published in the UK and the Republic of Ireland with the highest circulation of any daily English-language newspaper in the world, standing at 3,126,866 copies daily in October 2007. It is published by the News Group Newspapers of News International, itself a subsidiary of Rupert Murdoch's News Corporation. *The Sun* was launched as a rival to *The Daily Mirror*, which it copied in several ways. It was the same size and colour and its front page had the same general style. It rapidly overtook *The Daily Mirror* in sales to become the fastest growing daily newspaper. From the start, sex was used as an important element in marketing the paper. *The Sun* was a very strong supporter of the Conservative Prime Ministers Margaret Thatcher and John Major but switched to support Labour in March 1997. It relies on stories about the entertainment industry, gossip concerning the British monarchy and sports as well as news and politics, with many items revolving around celebrities.

The Daily Mirror, often referred to simply as *The Mirror*, is a British tabloid daily newspaper founded in 1903. It is the only British national newspaper to have consistently supported the Labour Party since 1945. *The Mirror* was originally launched as a newspaper for women, run by women. It was not a success, and in 1904 it was turned into a pictorial newspaper. Circulation continued to grow and in the 1930s *The Mirror* was selling more than one million copies per day. In the late 1930s it transformed itself from a respectable, conservative, middle-class newspaper into a sensationalist left-wing paper for the working class. By the late 1940s, it was selling 4.5 million copies a day. At the time it was produced in one of the most technically advanced printing works in the world. By the mid-1970s, *The Sun* had overtaken *The Mirror* in circulation. In recent years the paper's circulation has also been overtaken by that of *The Daily Mail*. The circulation figures show that on average *The Mirror* sold 2,353,807 copies per day in 2006.

Arctic Monkeys are an English Indie rock band from High Green, a suburb of Sheffield. It was formed in 2002 and has reached several number one positions in the UK Singles Chart. *Arctic Monkeys* achieved their success through fan-made demo tapes and online file sharing. They were heralded as one of the first acts to come to public attention via the Internet.

Sir Tim(othy John) Berners-Lee (born June 8, 1955) is an English developer who invented the World Wide Web in March 1989. He implemented his invention in 1990 with the first successful communication between a client and a server via the Internet on December 25, 1990.

HTML, an acronym of **Hypertext Mark-up Language**, is the predominant mark-up language for web pages. It provides a means to describe the structure of text-based information in a document.

The World Wide Web (commonly shortened to the Web) is a system of interlinked hypertext documents accessed via the Internet. With a web browser, a user can view web pages with texts, images, videos and other multimedia and navigate between them by using hyperlinks.

Capital 95.8 is a London radio station owned by GCap Media. The station, which was based at Euston Tower until early in 1997, was originally named Capital Radio or Capital FM and was launched by then-chairman Richard Attenborough at 5.00 am on Tuesday, October 16, 1973. Capital went on air as the second legal commercial radio station in the UK. In March 2007 the station was renamed Capital 95.8 and its slogan became 'The Sound Of London'. Today the studios are located in Leicester Square.

50 Cent is the stage name of Curtis James Jackson III (born July 6, 1975), an American rapper, who was born in South Jamaica, Queens, New York. He began drug dealing at the age of twelve. After having started a rap career, he was shot nine times in 2000. 50 Cent was discovered by rapper Eminem, and he adopted his nickname as a metaphor for 'change'. The name was derived from Kelvin Martin, a 1980s Brooklyn robber known as '50 Cent'. Jackson chose the name "because it says everything I want it to say. I'm the same kind of person 50 Cent was. I provide for myself by any means".

A **soap opera** is an ongoing, episodic work of fiction, usually broadcast on television or radio. The name 'soap opera' stems from the original dramatic serials broadcast on radio that had soap manufacturers such as Colgate-Palmolive and Lever Brothers as the shows' sponsors. These early radio serials were broadcast in weekday daytime slots when mostly housewives would be available to listen, thus the shows were aimed at and consumed by a predominantly female audience. The main characteristics that define soap operas are the emphasis on family life, personal relationships, sexual dramas and emotional and moral conflicts set in familiar domestic interiors with only occasional excursions into new locations.

Coronation Street is an award-winning British soap opera. It is the longest-running television soap opera in the UK, first broadcast on Friday, December 9, 1960. The programme is consistently one of the highest-rated programmes on British television. *Coronation Street* (commonly nicknamed as 'Corrie') is set in a fictional street in Weatherfield, a fictional suburb of Manchester. The programme focuses on the experiences and driving forces behind the residents of Coronation Street and examines families and individuals within the community who are of different ages, classes and social structure. Since January 2008, *Coronation Street* has broadcasted two episodes at 7.30 and 8.30 pm on Monday and Friday, and one episode at 7.30 pm on Wednesday, losing its Sunday episode.

Leanne Battersby and **Danny Baldwin** are fictional characters in *Coronation Street*. Leanne and her family were introduced in 1997 as the new 'common family'. Leanne was, at that time, a mischievous troublemaker, who very much resembled a 'second-hand Spice Girl'. She married, got divorced, took drugs and 'disappeared' in 2000. In 2004 she returned to Coronation Street and started a relationship with Jamie Baldwin, and later an affair with his father Danny Baldwin whom she then blackmailed with his father's last will. In 2006 she made her exit to Spain but returned in March 2007 to shock 'the whole street' with the fact that she had worked as an escort before she started a career in the restaurant business.

Neighbours is an Australian soap opera, which began its run in March 1985. The series follows the daily lives of several families who live in six houses at the end of Ramsay Street in the fictional, middle class suburb of Erinsborough. Storylines explore the romances, family and domestic problems and other key events affecting the various residents. *Neighbours* features a large proportion of young actors including Kylie Minogue and Jason Donovan. Throughout its entire run, *Neighbours* has screened as five 22-minute episodes (excluding advertisement breaks) a week, shown each week in an early-evening slot.

Emmerdale (known as *Emmerdale Farm* until November 1989) is an award-winning and critically acclaimed British soap opera, set in the fictional village of the same name (known as Beckindale until 1994) in West Yorkshire, England. Much of the action takes place within the fictional village pub, The Woolpack. *Emmerdale* is the third-highest-rating soap opera on British television, after *Coronation Street* and *EastEnders*. The series was first aired on October 16, 1972. It is shown from Sunday to Friday at 7.00 pm on ITV. Repeat episodes and the omnibus of the show can be seen on ITV2.

EastEnders is a popular and award-winning BBC television soap, first broadcast in the UK on BBC 1 on February 19, 1985. *EastEnders*' storylines examine the domestic and professional lives of the people who live and work in Albert Square, a Victorian square with terraced houses, a pub, a street market and various small businesses in the East End of London. The series was originally screened as two half-hour episodes per week. Today four episodes are broadcast each week on BBC1 and an omnibus edition screens on Saturday afternoons. It is one of the UK's highest-rated programmes. The average audience share for an episode is currently between 35 and 45 %.

RCA, formerly an acronym for the Radio Corporation of America, is now a trademark owned by Thomson SA. RCA was formed in 1919 as a publicly held company. Its intent was to form a holding company that would use various legal means to attempt to monopolize the radio business. In 1949, RCA developed and released the first 45 rpm record to the public, answering CBS/Columbia's 33⅓ rpm 'LP'. In 1953, RCA's all-electronic colour-TV technology was adopted as the standard for American colour TV. RCA was one of the eight major computer companies in the 1960s, but abandoned computers in 1971. At present, the RCA trademark is used by two companies: Sony BMG Music Entertainment (RCA Victor and RCA Records) and Thomson SA (telephones, audio/video, remote controls, antennas, televisions, car stereos, microwaves, mobiles).

The British Broadcasting Corporation, which is usually known simply as the BBC, is the largest broadcasting corporation in the world in terms of audience numbers and revenues. It has 26,000 employees in the UK alone and a budget of more than £ 4 billion. It was founded on October 18, 1922 and made a state-owned corporation in 1927. The corporation produces programmes and information services, broadcasting globally on television, radio and the Internet. The mission of the BBC is "to inform, educate and entertain". Its domestic programmes and broadcasts are primarily funded by television licence fees. UK audiences often refer to the BBC as 'the Beeb'. Another nickname, now less commonly used, is 'Auntie', said to originate from the old-fashioned 'Auntie knows best' attitude in the days when John Reith, the BBC's founder, was in charge. The BBC has five major national radio stations: Radio 1 (new music and entertainment), Radio 2 (popular music) – the UK's most listened to station with 12.9 million weekly listeners, Radio 3 (special interest music e. g. jazz, classical), Radio 4 (current affairs), Radio 5 Live (24 hour news, sports, talk).

Lycos is a search engine and web portal centred upon broadband entertainment content. It began as a search engine research project by Dr. Michael Loren Mauldin of Carnegie Mellon University in 1994. It was incorporated in 1995 and went on to become one of the most visited online destinations in the world with a global presence in more than 40 countries.

STORYLINE

Die Bedeutung verschiedener Medien und ihre Wirkung auf den Konsumenten bilden den inhaltlichen Schwerpunkt dieser Unit. Ausgehend von einer Darstellung der wichtigsten Medien, einem Artikel über die Rollenbesetzung für eine Seifenoper und zwei autobiografische Berichte über eigene Medienvorlieben, sollen die S ihr eigenes Medienverhalten beschreiben und Vor- und Nachteile verschiedener Medien diskutieren. Die Analyse zweier Produktanzeigen, das Schreiben eines Zeitungsberichtes und das Erstellen einer Umfrage zum Thema Mediengewohnheiten runden die inhaltliche Arbeit ab.

| | | Check-in | **5** |

Check-in

Seite 76–77

Ziele
- Britische Zeitschriften, Zeitungen, Radio- und Fernsehprogramme kennen lernen
- Über eigene Mediengewohnheiten sprechen
- Ausschnitte aus Radiosendungen inhaltlich zuordnen

Text/Fotos **Media messages** Seite 76–77

Ziel
- Bildern und Texten Informationen zum Thema „Medienvielfalt in GB" entnehmen

Wortschatz *medium pl. media, celeb(rity), to copy, to change, quality, popular newspaper, newspaper, to create, the public, studio, concert, awesome, main, entertainment (no pl.), soap (opera), realistic, violence (no pl.), housewife pl. housewives, to advertise, soap (no pl.), cleaning product, nickname, copy*

Methodisches Vorgehen
- Zur Einstimmung auf den inhaltlichen Schwerpunkt der Unit präsentiert L eigenes Material zum Thema Medien: Deckblätter von Zeitungen, z. B. lokale Tageszeitung, „Frankfurter Allgemeine", „Süddeutsche Zeitung", „Bild"-Zeitung o. Ä.; Zeitschriften, z. B. „Bravo"/„Mädchen", „Gala"/„Vanity Fair"; Magazine von *soaps* (z. B. „Gute Zeiten, schlechte Zeiten"), eigenes Handy, usw.
- L gibt kurze Erläuterungen zu den mitgebrachten Materialien und verwendet dabei neuen Wortschatz (auch Kurzformen wie *celeb, fave, …*!).
- Die S äußern sich zu der Frage: *What kinds of media do you use? What kinds of media do you not use?*
- Alternative: L beginnt die Einstimmung zur Unit mit einem *brainstorming*: *List up all forms of media you know and use. You have one minute to write them down.* Die Ergebnisse der kurzen Einzelarbeit werden an der Tafel zusammengetragen.
- L leitet zum SB über. Die S beschreiben die Fotos. Anschließend werden die Informationstexte arbeitsteilig gelesen: Die S bereiten in PA einzelne Texte vor, schlagen ggf. unbekanntes Vokabular nach.
- Verschiedene Schülerpaare lesen die einzelnen Texte laut vor und erklären die unbekannten Vokabeln.

TIP
Eigene Materialien mitbringen

TA

Media I know	Media I use	Media I don't use
newspaper		
magazine		
books		
dictionary		
Internet		
television		
mobile		

Erweiterung
- Je nach Leistungsstärke und Interesse der Klasse kann der Bereich *soap opera* weiter thematisiert werden. Es ist durchaus möglich, bereits an dieser Stelle typische Charakteristika einer *soap* zu sammeln und aufzulisten. L kann außerdem ein paar kurze Informationen zur *storyline* der im SB aufgeführten *soaps* geben (siehe Landeskunde).

Material
Zeitungen, Magazine, Poster etc.

Üben **1 Media** Seite 76

Ziel
- Den Informationszuwachs durch einzelne Medien beurteilen

Methodisches Vorgehen
- a) Siehe Einstimmung auf den inhaltlichen Schwerpunkt der Unit
- Alternative: L bereitet ein Arbeitsblatt vor, in das die Ergebnisse von a) und b) eingetragen werden können (siehe Lösung). Die S beschäftigen sich mit den Aufgaben in PA.

TIP
Useful phrases, S. 156, S. 213

253

5 Check-in

- L hat das Arbeitsblatt als Folie vorbereitet. Die S tragen abwechselnd ihre Ergebnisse in die Tabelle ein. Teilaufgabe b) kann auch Begriffe wie *horoscope, crossword etc.* enthalten. L ergänzt Begriffe auf Nachfrage der S hin.

Erweiterung
- c) Leistungsstärkere S können diese Teilaufgabe als schriftliche Hausaufgabe erledigen. Es ist aber auch denkbar, dass die S im Unterricht gemeinsam eine Antwort formulieren. Als Hilfestellung sollte L auf die *Useful phrases*, S. 156 und S. 213, hinweisen.

Auch als HA geeignet

Lösung

a) + b)

Kinds of media	Do you use them?	What can people "get"?
youth magazine		news about celebs, fashion, make-up, music
quality newspaper		news from Germany/international news
popular newspaper		news from Germany, news about celebs, a few international news
mobile		talking to people, texts, Internet
radio		news, music, weather report, sports, traffic news, ads
TV (television)		soaps, films, shows, news, ads, weather report, sports news, talk shows, shopping TV, entertainment

c) *Individuelle S-Antworten*

Tipps für junge Lehrer
Die S neigen zu Kurzantworten, um komplexere Satzstrukturen zu vermeiden. Durch das kontinuierliche Anwenden von *Useful phrases*, die den S bereits seit *Green Line* 1 angeboten werden, sollten die S an das Antworten in vollständigen Sätzen gewöhnt werden. Die Ergebnisse der Teilaufgaben a) und b) bieten sich hierzu an.

Material
Workbook S. 53/1
Ggf. Leerfolie

S L Üben **2 Listening: On the radio** Seite 77

HV-Text

Number 1
Male radio voice: This is John Adams for BBC Kent. This morning at nine thirty there was a road accident on the A26, four miles south of Tunbridge Wells. Three people were injured. A farmer's lorry full of pigs overturned on the A26 and two cars crashed into the lorry with the pigs. When the police arrived at the scene of the accident, pigs were running about everywhere. It took four hours to catch all of them again …

Number 2
Female radio voice: Hi there, listeners everywhere in the South Downs! This is the Fiona Noble Show again. Got your phones ready, girls and ladies? Got your ears ready, boys and very old boys? It's time for: Name the song! Here we go with the first question: Who sang this great hit back in the 1980s? … Yes, hello?
Caller: Uh, hello, this is Wayne … uh … I think … is it Freddy Mercury?
Female radio voice: Oh, sorry, Wayne! Wrong, wrong, wrong! Freddy Mercury didn't sing this cool hit. Well, let's listen again …

| | | Check-in | 5 |

Number 3

Female radio voice: Listen to Entertainment Weekly on Sunday evenings for hot interviews, the best music and a funny look at what's going on in the world of media – music, film and lots more. Entertainment Weekly is our awesome, two-hour weekly special from 7–9 pm with DJs Justin Wilkes, Elsie Mann and Tony Shepherd. They bring you a wild, celebrity-filled entertainment programme. Plus, lots of music and all you ever wanted to know about your fave (and not so favourite) celebs. Wherever the stars go, we're there!

Ziel
- Kurze Ausschnitte aus Radiosendungen inhaltlich und sprachlich analysieren

Wortschatz *programme*

Methodisches Vorgehen

Pre-listening:
- L bereitet die S kurz auf die HV-Texte vor: *You are going to listen to three short radio programmes. The programmes have different topics. Listen carefully: The radio people have different voices and use different phrases.*
- Alternative: Ein/e S liest die Aufgabenstellung vor, L konzipiert ein Lösungsraster an der Tafel/auf Folie. In leistungsschwächeren Klassen empfiehlt es sich, anfangs auf Teilaufgabe c) zu verzichten und sie ggf. im Anschluss gemeinsam zu bearbeiten.

While-listening:
- Die S übernehmen das Lösungsraster in ihre Hefte.
- L präsentiert die drei Hörbeispiele nacheinander von CD und macht jeweils eine kurze Pause, damit die S sich Notizen machen können.
- In einem zweiten Durchgang werden alle drei Mitschnitte unmittelbar hintereinander vorgespielt; die S vervollständigen ihre Notizen.

Post-listening:
- Vergleich und Diskussion der Ergebnisse in PA; anschließend Besprechung im Plenum.

TA

Programme	Topic	Voices/phrases
1. news	about a road accident with a lorry full of pigs	voice: formal phrases: This is … This morning …
2. entertainment	music quiz show	voice: happy phrases: Hi there, listeners … Got your phones/ears ready …? Wrong, wrong, wrong! Well, let's listen again …
3. information	ad for an entertainment programme about music, films, celebs and more	voice: excited phrases: Listen to … … is our awesome … They bring you … … we're there!

Lösung *Siehe TA*

Tipps für junge Lehrer
Die Anzahl der Wiederholungen oder Unterbrechungen bei Hörverstehensaufgaben richtet sich nicht nur nach der Leistungsstärke der Klasse, sondern auch nach den äußeren Bedingungen (Raum, technische Ausstattung, Unterrichtsstunde). Dies sollte bei der Planung und Durchführung dieses Aufgabentyps immer berücksichtigt werden.

Material
◎ S 2/10–12
◎ L 3/12–14, 15–17
Workbook S. 53/2
Ggf. Leerfolie

5 Check-in | Language 1

			Seite 77
Üben	**3 Your turn: You and the media**		
Ziel	• Über persönliche Medienvorlieben sprechen • Zur Bedeutung von Medien im eigenen Alltag Stellung nehmen		
Methodisches Vorgehen	• Zuerst notieren die S in Einzelarbeit, welche Medien ihnen besonders gefallen, und führen Gründe für ihre Auswahl an. • Einzelne S präsentieren ihre Ergebnisse an der Tafel (zusammenfassende Übersicht/Strichliste möglich: *class survey*); dabei werden vor allem die Gründe gesammelt und aufgelistet.		

TA	What?	TV	Youth magazine	...
	Why?	funny films, interesting news, soaps	information about trendy clothes, interesting information about celebs, ...	

Erweiterung	• Wenn die S Freude an der Präsentation der eigenen Meinung zeigen, wäre es bereits zu diesem Zeitpunkt möglich, die Aufgabe ⟨A media survey⟩ (S. 87) durchzuführen.	**Material** Im Anschluss an *ex*. 3: *Action UK!* 3, Recent news, Part A: *Detectives at work* sowie *Action UK!* 3, Begleitheft zu den Filmsequenzen, Unit 5 A
Tipps für junge Lehrer	Gerade bei den Aufgaben im Bereich *Your turn* ist darauf zu achten, dass die Ergebnisse in zusammenhängender Form vorgetragen werden. Auch hier können die zuvor gesammelten *Useful phrases* hilfreich sein.	

Language 1

Seite 78–80

> **Ziele**
> • Einem Text zielgerichtet Informationen entnehmen
> • Die verschiedenen Zeitformen des Passivs erkennen und differenzieren
> • Die Passivformen anwenden

L Text	**Casting for a daily soap**	Seite 78
Ziel	• Das Leseverstehen üben	
Wortschatz	*passive, to discover, to cast, agent, file, script, sides, to reread, Don't get your hopes up too high., assistant, to sign, contract, super*	
Strukturen	• *Passive forms*	
Methodisches Vorgehen	• Bei geöffnetem SB präsentiert L den Text von CD. Die S lesen mit und notieren sich unbekannte Wörter. Alternativ kann jede/r S eine Folie über den Text legen (siehe LB, Unit 4, S. 217) und die unbekannten Wörter mit einem Folienstift markieren. • L semantisiert den neuen Wortschatz. Der Text wird erneut vorgespielt und im Anschluss daran von mehreren S abschnittsweise laut vorgelesen.	**Material** ⊙ L 3/18

Üben	**1 Soap stars**	Seite 78
Ziel	• Einem Text zielgerichtet Informationen entnehmen	

Language 1 | 5

Methodisches Vorgehen	• a) Die S lesen die Aufgabenstellung, L schreibt den Beispielsatz an die Tafel. Die S sollten an dieser Stelle darauf hingewiesen werden, dass die Reihenfolge der Schritte logisch sein muss (Chronologie) und nicht alle Sätze wortwörtlich übernommen werden können. • Die S lesen den Text erneut und unterstreichen die entsprechenden Sätze. Anschließend beantworten sie die Aufgabe schriftlich. • Zwei S schreiben ihre Ergebnisse an die Tafel.
TA	Siehe Lösung
Erweiterung	• b) Die Aufgabenstellung wird im Unterricht besprochen und von den S als Hausaufgabe bearbeitet. Als Hilfestellung kann zuvor ein gemeinsames Argument formuliert werden. Die Anzahl der zu findenden Argumente sollte je nach Leistungsstärke der S variiert werden.

Lösung

a) *Find an agent. Give him/her your photo. Get an invitation to a casting. Read your script carefully. Learn your role well. Follow the directions of the Casting Director. Act your role well. Don't get your hopes up too high. Be better than the other people.*

b) *Erwartungshorizont:*

I would like to be a soap star because …	*I wouldn't like to be a soap star because …*
– *I would love to be famous* – *I would make a lot of money* – *I would meet interesting people* – *I would travel a lot* – *I would meet celebs* – …	– *I would have to work hard* – *I wouldn't have much free time* – *I would have to get up early* – *everybody would know me* – *fans can be difficult* – …

Tipps für junge Lehrer	Es bietet sich an dieser Stelle an, die Modalverben und ihre Ersatzformen zu wiederholen (G 8 und G 9).
Üben	**2 Find the rule** Seite 78
Ziel	• Die Passivformen erkennen und differenzieren • Eine Regel zur Bildung des Passivs formulieren
Strukturen	• *Passive forms*
Methodisches Vorgehen	• L erläutert den Begriff *passive* (Vergleich mit dem Deutschen, Begriff *active/ aktiv* berücksichtigen). • L hat Folie vorbereitet, die dem Muster im SB entspricht (zur besseren Übersicht sollten die *tenses* untereinander angeordnet werden). L trägt das erste Beispiel in die Tabelle ein. • Je nach Leistungsstärke der Klasse wird die Aufgabe in PA oder im Plenum erarbeitet. Dabei werden die einzelnen Formen deutlich im Text markiert. Achtung: Fragebildung als Sonderform erläutern! • Die S übernehmen die Ergebnisse in ihre Hefte und formulieren eine Regel zur Bildung des Passivs. • Alternative: siehe Tipps für junge Lehrer
TA	Siehe Lösung

5 Language 1

Lösung

Present tense		
Subject	to be	Past participle
The agent	is	phoned
Your photo	is	sent
This script	is	called

Past tense		
Subject	to be	Past participle
I	was	informed
The script	was	given
I	was	invited
I	was	chosen

Present perfect			
	Subject	to be	Past participle
Have	you	ever been	invited?
	About 30 people	have been	invited

Rule: You use a form of the verb to be and the past participle to make the passive. You can have passive sentences in different tenses. You must only change the form of to be.

Tipps für junge Lehrer
Bei dieser Aufgabe ist es wichtig, auf den Satzbau (Aussagesatz, Fragesatz) hinzuweisen. Gerade leistungsschwächere Klassen brauchen zum Erkennen der *passive forms* Hilfestellung. Deshalb wäre es eine Alternative, die Formen an die Tafel zu schreiben, im Text unterstreichen und anschließend nach *tenses* ordnen zu lassen.

Material
Ggf. Leerfolie

Üben   **3 How a daily soap is made**   Seite 79

Ziel
- Das *present passive* anwenden

Wortschatz   to discuss, to film

Strukturen
- *Present passive*

Methodisches Vorgehen
- Gemeinsames Lesen der Aufgabenstellung. L weist darauf hin, dass zunächst das Subjekt des Passivsatzes bestimmt werden muss.
- Nachdem ein weiteres Beispiel im Plenum besprochen wurde, bearbeiten die S die Aufgabe in Einzelarbeit; anschließend Partnerkontrolle und Vergleich der Ergebnisse im Plenum/an der Tafel.

TIP
Singular/Plural differenzieren

TA   Siehe Lösung

Erweiterung
- Leistungsstärkere S können noch weitere Aufforderungssätze formulieren, die dann von den anderen S ins *present passive* umgewandelt werden.

Lösung
1 *A story idea is discussed.*   2 *A script is written.*   3 *Actresses and actors are cast.*   4 *The script is discussed with the cast.*   5 *A place for the scenes is found.*   6 *Clothes are bought.*   7 *The scenes are filmed.*   8 *The soap is shown on TV.*

Material
Workbook S. 54/3

Üben   **4 How did Matt get the role?**   Seite 79

Ziel
- Das *past passive* anwenden

Wortschatz   to photograph

Strukturen	• *Past passive*	
Methodisches Vorgehen	• Zunächst gemeinsames Beschreiben der Bilder mit Stichworten an der Tafel (vor allem Verben auflisten). • Die Aufgabe wird von den S in PA bearbeitet; danach Vergleich im Plenum. • Alternative: Sollen *ex.* 3 und *ex.* 4 unmittelbar hintereinander bearbeitet werden, bietet es sich an, die S mit *Workbook* S. 54/4 zunächst auf das *past passive* einzustimmen und erst im Anschluss daran *ex.* 4 bearbeiten zu lassen. Diese Reihenfolge ermöglicht eine größere Selbstständigkeit.	
TA	photograph — Matt give — photo to agent phone — agent send — Matt's photos choose — Matt invite — Matt	
Lösung	1 *Matt was photographed.* 2 *His photo was given to an agent.* 3 *Matt's agent was phoned.* 4 *Matt's photos were sent to the Casting Director.* 5 *He was chosen.* 6 *Matt was invited.*	
Tipps für junge Lehrer	Siehe Alternative	**Material** *Workbook* S. 54/4

Üben	**5 Don't watch this film!**	Seite 79
Ziel	• Die verschiedenen Zeitformen des Passivs anwenden	
Strukturen	• *Simple present passive, simple past passive, present perfect passive*	
Methodisches Vorgehen	• Als Einstimmung auf diese Aufgabe empfiehlt sich *Workbook* S. 54/5. Im Anschluss daran sollte G 19 gemeinsam gelesen werden. Empfehlung: Zusammenstellung von Signalwörtern für die einzelnen *tenses.* Die S übernehmen die Tabelle in ihre Hefte (ggf. auch als Ergänzung für die Tabellen in *ex.* 2 möglich!). • Die Lösungen für die Lücken 1–4 werden gemeinsam erarbeitet. Anschließend arbeiten die S in Einzelarbeit. Um dem unterschiedlichen Arbeitstempo der S gerecht zu werden, hat L die Lösungen auf Blätter kopiert (3–4 pro Klasse), die im Klassenraum ausgelegt werden und mit denen die S ihre Lösungen individuell abgleichen können. • Vergleich der Lösungen im Plenum: Jede Zeitform sollte von den S begründet werden (Signalwörter einbeziehen!).	**TIP** G 19 Tabelle mit Signalwörtern für die einzelnen *tenses* erstellen
TA	Siehe Lösung	
Erweiterung	• Als Hausaufgabe empfiehlt sich das individuelle Lesen/Wiederholen von G 19. • **Folie 12: What is done here?** übt die verschiedenen Zeitformen des Passivs.	
Lösung	1 *has* 2 *been called* 3 *has* 4 *been made* 5 *was written* 6 *was filmed* 7 *was given* 8 *were asked* 9 *are killed* 10 *was given* 11 *is* 12 *discovered*	
Tipps für junge Lehrer	*Workbook* S. 55/6 sollte zu Beginn der nächsten Unterrichtsstunde eingesetzt werden, nachdem die S noch einmal G19 wiederholt haben. Auch hier empfiehlt es sich, die Lösungen vorzubereiten und an die S zu verteilen, damit diese in PA die Sätze ihrer Partner korrigieren können. Anschließend sollte auch bei dieser Aufgabe eine gemeinsame Besprechung erfolgen.	**Material** *Workbook* S. 54/5, 55/6 Folie 12

5 Language 1

Üben	**6 From active to passive**	Seite 80
Ziel	• Aktivsätze in Passivsätze umwandeln	
Wortschatz	*active, by*	
Strukturen	• *Active, passive*	
Methodisches Vorgehen	• Da diese Aufgabe noch einmal das Grundprinzip der Umwandlung von Aktivsätzen in Passivsätze verdeutlicht, sollte sie als Bewusstmachung genutzt werden. Die S schreiben die Sätze ab und unterstreichen die Satzteile im Aktivsatz (Subjekt, Verb, Objekt) und ihre neue Funktion im Passivsatz mit verschiedenen Farben. Anhand des Beispielsatzes wird dieses Vorgehen zunächst an der Tafel verdeutlicht. L weist dabei auf die Beachtung der verschiedenen *tenses* hin. • Die S bearbeiten die Aufgabe in Einzelarbeit oder PA; anschließend Besprechung der Ergebnisse im Plenum.	**TIP** G 20
TA	Teenagers buy TEENBUZZ. TEENBUZZ is bought by teenagers.	
Erweiterung	• Leistungsstärkere S können weitere Beispiele formulieren (inhaltliche Orientierung an S. 76 und S. 77) und diese Sätze dann der Klasse präsentieren, die sie ins Passiv umwandelt.	
Lösung	2 *The first colour TV was made in 1954 by RCA.* 3 *Media messages are believed by too many people.* 4 *Soap and cleaning products were advertised by radio dramas.* 5 *Radio stars were forgotten by most people after the invention of TV in the 1950s.* 6 *The stars' faces were now seen by everyone.* 7 *The BBC is called 'the Beeb' by listeners.* 8 *The script is often written five or ten times by the script authors!*	**Material** Workbook S. 55/7

Üben	**7 Passive or not?**	Seite 80
Ziel	• Die Verwendung von Aktiv und Passiv begründen	
Strukturen	• *Active, passive*	
Methodisches Vorgehen	• Ein/e S liest die *Tip*-Box vor; L erläutert die Aufgabenstellung. • Die S überlegen in PA, warum die Informationen im *active* bzw. *passive* ausgedrückt werden (ggf. erneutes Lesen von G 19 und G 20). • Die S präsentieren ihre Ergebnisse im Plenum. L sollte darauf achten, dass nach Beendigung der Aufgabe die S einen zusammenfassenden Satz auf Englisch formulieren (siehe TA), den sie sich als „Mustersatz" einprägen können.	**TIP** G 19, 20
TA	When it is clear who did the action → active When the action is important or we don't know who did the action → passive	
Erweiterung	• Leistungsstärkere S bearbeiten b) in Einzelarbeit oder als Hausaufgabe. Leistungsschwächere S konzentrieren sich auf einen der drei Beispielsätze.	Auch als HA geeignet

Lösung	a) 1 *The passive form is used in the police report to stress what happened. Here it is important that a red bike was stolen – and not a blue or a green one. We don't know who stole it.*
	   2 *The sentence is in the active form because it tells us who does the action: It's Jim's mum who will pick him up.*
	   3 *In this sentence the passive is used because it's the action that is important and we don't know who did the action.*	

	4 *In this sentence the action is important and not the person who did the action. This is why the passive is used.*
	b) Erwartungshorizont:
	  1 *I would use the active form because the person who did the action is important: "I did more work in the garden than you."*
	  2 *I would use the passive form to stress the action. It is important that my money was stolen, but I don't know who did it: "My money was stolen from my locker."*
	  3 *I would use the active form because the person who did the action is important: "I built the tree house – all by myself."*
		Material
		Workbook S. 56/8

Üben   **8 Your turn: Watching TV**   Seite 80

Ziel
- Über eigene Fernsehgewohnheiten berichten
- Eine Szene aus einer TV-Sendung vorspielen

Methodisches Vorgehen
- Diese Aufgabe kann als langfristige Hausaufgabe eingesetzt werden, um so auch leistungsschwächeren S die Möglichkeit zu geben, sich vorzubereiten und aktiv mündlich zu beteiligen. Als Vorbereitung empfiehlt es sich, dass die S in PA oder GA *Useful phrases* individuell zusammenstellen (ggf. bestehende Wortlisten ergänzen, siehe TA). L wirkt dabei nur beratend und weist im Vorfeld auf einige sinnvolle Seiten im SB hin (z.B. *Useful phrases*, S. 156).
- Die S bereiten ihre individuelle Antwort zu Hause vor und präsentieren sie (nach Absprache mit L) im Unterricht.

TIP
Useful phrases,
S. 156
Als langfristige HA nutzen

TA
I like to watch …
I didn't/don't like that …
I think that …
My favourite show/programme is … because …

Erweiterung
- Da die meisten S sehr konkrete Vorstellungen von ihren Lieblingsfernsehsendungen haben und im Allgemeinen auch über die technischen Mittel verfügen, Sendungen aufzuzeichnen, kann diese Aufgabe erweitert werden. Die S präsentieren nicht nur ihre eigene Meinung zu ihrer Lieblingssendung, sondern geben zusätzlich Informationen über die *storyline* oder die *characters*. Wenn dies im Klassenraum möglich ist, zeigen sie anschließend einen kurzen Filmausschnitt auf Video/DVD (max. 2 Min.) und erläutern diesen kurz. L kann vorab entscheiden, ob er die Aufgabe freiwillig stellt oder gezielte Aufträge an einzelne S vergibt. Statt Video-/DVD-Ausschnitten können auch andere Materialien (Fotos, Magazine, Fanartikel, usw.) zur Veranschaulichung eingesetzt werden.

Lösung   *Individuelle S-Antworten*

Tipps für junge Lehrer
Teilaufgabe b) sollte nur auf freiwilliger Basis bearbeitet werden und kann als Ergänzung/Alternative zu den Tipps in der Erweiterung dienen.
Als weitere Alternative bietet sich ein TV-Quiz an, bei dem die S die Lieblingssendungen anderer S durch Fragen (nur *Yes-/No-questions*) erraten müssen, oder die S ihre Lieblingssendung durch kurze Informationen so umschreiben, dass die anderen S möglichst lange brauchen, um den Titel zu erraten.

Material
Im Anschluss an *ex.* 8: *Action UK!* 3, Recent news, Part B: *The Highland Hound* sowie *Action UK!* 3, Begleitheft zu den Filmsequenzen, Unit 5 B
Action UK! 3, Ending: *A surprise*

Üben   **9 Revision: If-clauses (type 2 and 3)**   Seite 80

Ziel
- Die *if-clauses type 2 and 3* wiederholen und festigen

5 Language 1

Strukturen	• *If-clauses type 2 and 3*
Methodisches Vorgehen	• Je nach Leistungsstärke der Klasse kann diese Aufgabe in Einzelarbeit oder PA bearbeitet werden. Dabei sollten alle Sätze ins Heft geschrieben werden, nachdem sie im Plenum oder mit dem/der Partner/in verglichen wurden. Es empfiehlt sich, im Vorfeld mit G13 die Zeitenfolge zu wiederholen. Eine kurze Zusammenfassung der Regeln an der Tafel ist dabei sinnvoll.
	• In leistungsschwächeren Klassen können die einzelnen Sätze auf Folienstücke geschrieben werden, die mit Hilfe von L auf dem OHP zusammengesetzt werden.

TIP
G13 wiederholen

TA

```
                Conditional sentences
type 1:  if-clause     simple present
         main clause   will future
type 2:  if-clause     simple past
         main clause   conditional (would + infinitive)
type 3:  if-clause     past perfect
         main clause   conditional perfect (would + have + past participle)
```

Erweiterung
• Die S fertigen einen kurzen Text an unter Verwendung von *conditional sentences*, die sinnvoll aufeinander aufbauen. Beispiel: *If I had money, I would buy a big house with a garden. If I had a big house with a garden, I would buy a dog. …*

Lösung
1 *If the driver had been driving more slowly, he would have seen the cow on the road.*   2 *If the driver had seen the cow sooner, the van wouldn't have crashed.*   3 *If the van hadn't crashed, the pigs wouldn't have fallen out.*   4 *If the cow wasn't so silly, it wouldn't go onto the road so often.*   5 *If the driver drove more carefully, he wouldn't have accidents like this.*

Tipps für junge Lehrer
L sollte darauf hinweisen, dass die Reihenfolge der Sätze logisch aufeinander aufbauen sollte („Konsequenzgedanke").

Material
Workbook S. 56/9
Ggf. Leerfolie

!

TIPPS VON MARIO RINVOLUCRI – THE ALTERNATIVE WAY

3rd conditional near-miss stories
Revision: If-clauses (p. 80)

a) In preparation, bring to mind the story of a near-miss you have had and be ready to tell it in class. Give the story a near-miss punch line. Something like, for example:
If the lorry wheel had been six inches nearer the toddler's bootee, he would have been a goner.

b) In class, tell your near-miss story and put your punch line up on the board. Ask if any of the pupils have a near-miss story to tell. Help the first volunteers to tell their story, supplying any words needed, and help them to get their punch line up on the board correctly. Do the same with a second volunteer.

c) Ask the pupils to stand up, mill around and find some one to tell them a near-miss story. (They will tend to cluster round the more extrovert and self-expressive students.)

d) Round off this part of the lesson by asking all the story tellers to put their punch lines on the board which normally leads to some of the stories being re-told.

Variation:	A sadder version of this activity has students working on very good things that nearly happened, but didn't. Near successes!
Pluses:	The activity brings the grammar structure off the page and uses it to carry vivid student experience. It breathes emotional life into the so-called third conditional.
Minuses:	At *Green Line* 3 level the activity is a bit elitist, favouring the students who already have a better command of English.
Acknowledgement:	This idea is from *Grammar in Action Again*, Christine Frank et al., Prentice Hall, 1987.

Talkwise
Seite 81

Ziele
- Das eigene Medienverhalten beschreiben
- Ein Radiointerview zum Thema „Medien" verstehen
- *Useful phrases* zum Thema „Medien" sammeln
- Über Vor- und Nachteile von Medien sprechen
- Einen Cartoon beschreiben und verstehen

Üben **Talk about media in your life** Seite 81

Wortschatz *discussing, pros and cons (pl.)*

Methodisches Vorgehen
- Die Reihenfolge der Aufgaben lässt sich variieren. So wäre ein Beginn mit ex. 3 denkbar, um die S dazu zu animieren, nach jeder weiteren Aufgabe ihre *Useful phrases* zu ergänzen.

TIP
Reihenfolge der Aufgaben variieren

Fotos/Üben **1 Couch potato?** Seite 81

Ziel
- Mit Hilfe von Fotos das eigene Medienverhalten beschreiben

Wortschatz *couch potato, maniac, bookworm*

Methodisches Vorgehen
- a) Die S betrachten die Fotos und entscheiden sich für „ihren" Favoriten.
- b) Die S tauschen sich mit einem/r Partner/in über das von ihnen gewählte Foto aus. Anschließend formulieren sie 2–3 Sätze, in denen sie ihr Foto kurz beschreiben und begründen, weshalb sie dieses Foto favorisieren. Kontrolle der eigenen Schreibleistung in PA.
- L fordert einige S auf, ihre Auswahl zu präsentieren oder zu begründen, warum keines der Fotos ihren Vorstellungen entspricht. Die S können dabei auch neue Begriffe erfinden.
- Alternative: L erfragt die Ergebnisse im Plenum und hält sie in einer Strichliste an der Tafel fest *(class survey)*. Anschließend spricht L gezielt die S an, die sich z. B. als *bookworm, couch potato*, etc. bezeichnen: *Please tell us why you are a bookworm, couch potato …* Auch neue Begriffe können in die Übersicht eingefügt werden.

5 Talkwise

TA

> How many of you are ...?
> magazine junkies
> music maniacs
> bookworms
> super surfers
> couch potatoes
> (mobile fans)
> (soap lovers)

Lösung | *Individuelle S-Antworten*

Tipps für junge Lehrer Es empfiehlt sich, die S einige Sätze schreiben zu lassen, damit sie ihre Gedanken ordnen können. Dies gibt vor allem auch leistungsschwächeren S die Möglichkeit, sich vorzubereiten, bevor sie sich mündlich äußern.

Üben 2 Listening: Interesting people   Seite 81

HV-Text

Jane Wallace: This is Jane Wallace and you're listening to BBC 2. This is *Focus on people*. We've got three interesting media people at the studio tonight to talk about media in their lives. Tonight the question is: Do we really need the media so much? My first guest this evening is Lilian Swane, editor of *Shout* magazine. Lilian, you work for a very popular teen magazine.

Lilian Swane: Thanks, Jane. I think our magazine is very important for teenage girls. We do important teen topics like friends, school problems or fights with parents. We've got a great agony aunt, too. Teen girls are given a lot of information about fashion, celebs and make-up. *Shout* isn't very expensive, so lots of teens can buy it. And they need it!

Jane Wallace: When I was young, I did too! But tell us about yourself: Did you read a lot of magazines when you were growing up?

Lilian Swane: I didn't get enough pocket money to buy magazines, so no, I didn't read them when I was young. In our house TV was very important. It was on all the time.

Jane Wallace: So you were allowed to watch TV?

Lilian Swane: Oh, yeah. The whole family sat together and watched. It was really our only entertainment. TV had a big influence on me. But it's changed. Today TV has too much violence.

Jane Wallace: I agree! But let's talk to our youngest guest, Tony Shepherd. Tony, you're 16 and a pupil at Thomas Tallis School in Greenwich. But on Friday and Saturday night – wow! – you're a disco DJ. We can all guess that you like music, Tony …

Tony Shepherd: … like it? I love it, Jane!

Jane Wallace: I bet! But what other media do you use, Tony? Magazines? TV?

Tony Shepherd: You won't believe this, Jane, but when I was a little boy, uh, about three years ago, I was a real book worm. I read every book that Dickens had written! I was crazy about *Moby Dick*, too! But now I'm a weekend DJ, so I read music magazines and watch MTV – always something to do with music. That's how I spent all my pocket money. Music has kept my mates and me together. My parents always said, "DJ? It's a waste of time and money." But look where I am now – I work with trendy music. My hobby has become my job.

Jane Wallace: So you can't imagine a world without music?

Tony Shepherd: Never! Music is life. Uh, well, it's *my* life.

Jane Wallace:	And what a great life it is, Tony! And now, our next guest today, Matt Stirling. You can see him on the successful BBC soap *East-Enders*. He plays a teen character, Justin. Matt, do you watch a lot of TV, too?
Matt Stirling:	No, I don't. I usually get everything I need from the Internet. And sometimes from books.
Jane Wallace:	Why are you such an Internet fan?
Matt Stirling:	Well, I can communicate, listen to the radio and music, watch films and get information, all on my computer. It's so convenient because with a laptop I can do all those things anywhere!
Jane Wallace:	And what about computer games?
Matt Stirling:	No, don't like them! I can surf for hours on the Internet, though, because there's so much information out there. Sometimes that's the problem. It's not easy to find good information. I surf and surf and surf … and before I know it, it's time for bed. So sometimes I find a great book, and it's the same problem: I read and read and read … and before I know it, it's time for bed!
Jane Wallace:	Now we know all about everyone's media tastes here, so let's get back to tonight's question: Do we really *need* the media so much? What about you, Lilian? Of course it's your job …

Ziel
- Einem HV-Text zielgerichtet Informationen entnehmen

Methodisches Vorgehen

Pre-listening:
- L macht Vorgaben für Notizen zum HV-Text (TA/Folie); die S übernehmen diese Liste in ihre Hefte (auch als Arbeitsblatt möglich).

While-listening:
- a) L präsentiert den HV-Text in Abschnitten (Pause nach jeder Person) und fordert die S auf, sich beim ersten Hören nur auf die genannten Medien zu konzentrieren. Im Anschluss werden die Ergebnisse von verschiedenen S auf einer Folie eingetragen (wieder einsetzbar in nächster Stunde) und von den übrigen S ggf. ergänzt.
- Beim zweiten Hören ergänzen die S auf ihren Arbeitsblättern die Bedeutung der Medien für die interviewten Personen. Die Höraufgabe sollte arbeitsteilig gestellt werden, damit sich die S besser auf einzelne Aussagen konzentrieren können und genügend Zeit für ihre Notizen haben.

Post-listening:
- Vergleich im Plenum; L oder die S ergänzen die Ergebnisse an der Tafel/auf der Folie. Wenn nötig, können einzelne Passagen erneut abgespielt werden.

TIP
Als Arbeitsblatt vorbereiten

TA

Jane Wallace from BBC 2

a) Kinds of media they are talking about
Lilian Wallace:
Tony Shepherd:
Matt Stirling:

b) Important for them because …
Lilian:
Tony:
Matt:

- Einzelne S fassen die Hörergebnisse in vollständigen Sätzen zusammen.
- Je nach Interesse/Bereitschaft der S kann der gesamte Text noch einmal zusammenhängend präsentiert werden.

Erweiterung
- Da die S den HV-Text mehrmals anhören, steht es L frei, ergänzende Inhaltsfragen oder *Right or wrong?-questions* zu stellen, um sich einen Eindruck über die Hörverstehenskompetenz der S zu verschaffen.

5 Talkwise

Lösung

a) *Lilian: magazine (Shout, teen magazine), TV; **Tony**: books, music magazines, TV (MTV); **Matt**: Internet/computer/laptop, books*

b) *Lilian: teen magazines: important information for teenage girls, important teen topics, agony aunt, TV: only entertainment as a child, watched by the whole family; **Tony**: crazy about books (book worm), music magazines and MTV for his job as a DJ; **Matt**: information from the Internet and from books, can listen to the radio/ music, watch films, communicate*

Material
◉L 3/19
Ggf. Leerfolie,
Arbeitsblatt

◉S ◉L **Üben** **Listening: Eric's world** Workbook Seite 57

HV-Text Workbook

Narrator: A monster Robo-Tiger was coming at him from the left. Eric saw the scary yellow eyes and thought he would never see his sixteenth birthday. He ran to the river. The Robo-Tiger followed him slowly. Its wet red tongue hung from a mouth that was full of long, white teeth. The animal was hungry and could eat the boy in one bite. Its orange and black plastic skin shone in the light.

The water moved so fast that it was white, and it was deep, too. Eric did not know how to swim. He had to decide. If he jumped into the water, he might drown. He had heard about people who lived a long time ago that were able to keep their heads out of the water and move through it. But he could not. Anyway, Robo-Tigers could move in water. If he did not go into the water, the Robo-Tiger would get him and eat him in one bite. There was no more fire left in his gun.

Mother: "Eric!"

Narrator: Eric heard a voice and looked to see if it was the Robo-Tiger.

Mother: Eric! Eric!

Narrator: Suddenly, his mother's head was in the picture.

Mother: You have to finish your game. Put the calm-down belt on. We're going to eat in a few minutes.

Narrator: Eric pushed a button. The Robo-Tiger, the river and the whole picture became grey, and then it disappeared.

Eric loved to play games with the Holo-Comm machine. It was fun to enter exciting new worlds. Some of his friends had told him that if a Robo-Tiger, or one of the other monsters in the games, caught you, you would really die. It was like in a dream, where you are falling – people said that if you hit the floor, you would never wake up. He found the idea really scary.

Now it was time for the calm-down belt. It would calm his heart and help him to relax. His hands shook as he put the belt around his body. It was difficult to put it on because he was still so full of scary ideas. He pushed a button. A new picture came to his room. The room was full of pink light. He could not hear, smell, feel or taste a thing – the belt stopped everything else. There was only the colour pink.

Eric knew that the colour pink helped to calm people down – that was why the World was almost all pink. Every room in every family's home was one kind of pink or another. Eric's grandfather remembered a time when there were many different colours. In those days there were five billion people on earth, but now there were only twenty million people left who lived in the World.

The belt told him he had calmed down now. Eric took off the belt and thought about the World and what his grandfather had told him.

© by Charles Ferro, Pink Paradise?; www.easyreader.dk

Material
◉S 2/13
◉L 3/20
Workbook S. 57/10

			Talkwise 5

Üben	**3 Collect phrases**	Seite 81
Ziel	• *Useful phrases* zum Thema „Medien" selbstständig zusammenstellen	
Methodisches Vorgehen	• Da es Ziel dieser Aufgabe ist, die Selbstständigkeit der S zu trainieren, empfiehlt es sich, den S genügend Zeit zu geben, damit sie alle Möglichkeiten des SB nutzen können.	**TIP** Als PA oder GA durchführen
	• L erklärt das Ziel der Aufgabe und weist darauf hin, dass neben den in der Aufgabe genannten Seiten das gesamte SB genutzt werden kann. Neben *phrases* können auch einzelne Wortarten gesammelt werden (kurze Gliederung an der Tafel möglich).	Auch als HA geeignet
	• Die S arbeiten in PA oder GA (beide Sozialformen sind auch parallel möglich) und besprechen ihre Vorgehensweise (Aufgabenverteilung).	
	• Im Anschluss an die Arbeitsphase geben die S ihre Listen ab. L überprüft die Arbeit der einzelnen Paare/Gruppen und stellt eine Gesamtliste zusammen (Folie). In der folgenden Unterrichtsstunde ergänzen die S ggf. ihre eigenen Listen mit Hilfe der Folie.	

TA

> My personal media vocabulary
> kinds of media: …
> verbs: …
> adjectives: …
> phrases: …
> names for media users: …

Lösung	**media:** *magazines, quality/popular newspapers, books, mobiles, TV, Internet, …* **verbs:** *to watch, to listen, to write, to text, …* **adjectives:** *interesting, boring, fast, slow, cheap, expensive, …* **phrases:** *I like/don't like, I use/don't use, I think, For me, …* **media users:** *magazine junkie, music maniac, bookworm, super surfer, couch potato, …*

Tipps für junge Lehrer	Natürlich kann diese Aufgabe auch in Einzelarbeit oder als Hausaufgabe bearbeitet werden. Es bietet sich jedoch an, die S intensiver mit dem SB arbeiten zu lassen und sie gleichzeitig anzuleiten, Aufgaben sinnvoll zu verteilen und so zu gemeinsamen Ergebnissen zu gelangen.	**Material** *Workbook* S. 57/11 Ggf. Leerfolie

Üben	**4 Your turn: Pros and cons of media**	Seite 81
Ziel	• Vor- und Nachteile von Medien diskutieren	
Methodisches Vorgehen	• L schreibt das Thema der GA an die Tafel und erläutert die Vorgehensweise. Anschließend werden Gruppen mit max. 5 S bestimmt (Sitzordnung verändern).	
	• L weist die S auf die inhaltlichen und lexikalischen „Hilfen" der vorausgegangenen Aufgaben hin.	
	• Die S einigen sich auf zwei Medientypen und bearbeiten anschließend Teilaufgabe 2; L leistet individuelle Hilfestellung.	
	• L verteilt Folienstücke, auf denen die Ergebnisse der GA eingetragen werden. L wählt verschiedene Gruppen aus, die ihre Argumente zu jeweils einem Medientyp präsentieren.	
	• Die S vergleichen die präsentierten Argumente mit den Ergebnissen ihrer eigenen Gruppen und ergänzen ggf. ihre Listen.	
	• Anschließend begründen die Gruppen ihre Entscheidung anhand einzelner Beispiele.	

5 Talkwise — Language 2

TA

Pros and cons of media		
	Pros	Cons
Medium 1		
Medium 2		

Erweiterung
- Alternative: Als Vorbereitung für die GA eignet sich *Workbook* S. 57/12. Diese Aufgabe kann auch als Hausaufgabe bearbeitet werden, so dass sich die einzelnen S direkt in die GA einbringen können.

HA
Material
Workbook S. 57/12
Ggf. Leerfolie

Üben 5 ⟨A cartoon⟩ Seite 81

Ziel
- Die Aussage eines Cartoons verstehen und versprachlichen

Methodisches Vorgehen
- Die S schauen sich den Cartoon an und beschreiben ihn kurz. L gibt ggf. Vokabelhilfen, aber da das Thema Computer bereits im *Project: English and Computing* thematisiert wurde, sind kaum lexikalische Nachfragen zu erwarten.
- Die S äußern sich spontan zum Inhalt des Cartoons. Alternativ kann L Fragen stellen: *What is the boy doing? Why are his parents worried? What makes you smile when you look at this cartoon? What is the main message?*

TIP
Cartoon auf Folie kopieren

Lösung

Erwartungshorizont:
There are three people in the cartoon: a man, a woman and a boy. In the centre you can see a desk. On the desk you can see a computer and a joystick. The man and the woman are standing on the left, the boy is sitting on the floor next to the desk. The boy is reading a book. The title of the book is 'Oliver Twist'. The man and the woman are looking at the boy. They seem worried.

Tipps für junge Lehrer
Es empfiehlt sich, den Cartoon auf Folie zu kopieren, um so die Aufmerksamkeit der S direkt auf die Bildaussage zu lenken.

Material
Ggf. Leerfolie

Language 2
Seite 82–84

Ziele
- Produktanzeigen beschreiben und verstehen
- Über die Wirkung von Werbeanzeigen sprechen
- Das *personal passive* kennen lernen
- Die verschiedenen Zeitformen des Passivs anwenden

 Text/Fotos

Advertising Seite 82

Ziel
- Über Werbeanzeigen sprechen

Wortschatz *advertising (no pl.), to be worth, smooth, look, tube, soccer, product*

Methodisches Vorgehen
- Die S betrachten die beiden Werbeanzeigen und äußern spontan ihre Meinung zum beworbenen Produkt.
- L oder ein/e S liest die Werbetexte vor; L erläutert die neuen Vokabeln.
- L präsentiert ggf. vergleichbare (deutsche) Werbeanzeigen und befragt die S nach ihren Eindrücken. Alternative: Die S äußern sich zu ihrer Lieblingswerbung und begründen, warum sie diese Werbung favorisieren. Ggf. bittet L die S, ihre Lieblingswerbung zur nächsten Stunde mitzubringen.
- L leitet direkt zu *ex.* 1 über.

TIP
Eigene Werbeanzeigen mitbringen

Material
L 3/21
Ggf. deutsche Werbeanzeigen

		Language 2	5

Üben	**1 What's in an ad?**	Seite 82

Ziel
- Werbeanzeigen beschreiben und über ihre Wirkung sprechen

Wortschatz *ad(vertisement)*

Methodisches Vorgehen
- a) Die S beschreiben in PA jeweils eine der beiden Werbeanzeigen und benennen das entsprechende Produkt. Sie machen sich Notizen in ihre Hefte, bevor die Ergebnisse im Plenum mündlich zusammengetragen werden (Stichworte an der Tafel/auf Folie möglich). Anschließend werden die Stichworte als zusammenhängender Text formuliert.
- b) Die S äußern sich mündlich, ob sie diese Produkte kaufen würden und begründen ihre Meinung (ggf. lexikalische Hilfen durch L an der Tafel).

TA Siehe Lösung

Erweiterung
- Die S beschreiben kurz die von ihnen mitgebrachten Werbeanzeigen. Anschließend nennen sie Gründe, warum diese Anzeigen besonders wirkungsvoll/ansprechend sind.
- c) Da dieser Aufgabenteil recht schwierig ist, sollte er im Plenum besprochen werden. L oder leistungsstärkere S halten die Ergebnisse an der Tafel/auf Folie fest. Die S übertragen die Ergebnisse anschließend in ihre Hefte.

Lösung
a) *Erwartungshorizont:*
In the picture I can see .../The picture shows a young woman who is smiling. She wears a red jacket and a white T-shirt. She has a black helmet on her head. The ad is about bikes/bicycles/SPIN bikes.
In the picture I can see .../The picture shows a young man with dark/brown/ black hair and dark/brown eyes. He is looking at you. He doesn't wear a shirt. The ad is about hair gel.
b) *Individuelle S-Antworten*
c) *Erwartungshorizont:*
The ad for the bikes uses big letters and different colours. The young woman seems to be happy, she is smiling, she likes her new bike and shows this. The young man has an interesting face. You have the feeling that he is looking at you. He looks sexy.

Material
Werbeanzeigen
Ggf. Leerfolie

Üben	**2 Put in the past perfect passive**	Seite 82

Ziel
- Das *past perfect passive* anwenden

Strukturen
- *Past perfect passive*

Methodisches Vorgehen
- L und die S lesen die *Tip*-Box zur Bildung des *past perfect passive* gemeinsam, L schreibt die Regel an die Tafel.
- Der erste Satz der Aufgabe wird gemeinsam formuliert, L schreibt ihn (zur Regel passend) an die Tafel.
- Die S bearbeiten die weiteren Sätze in Einzelarbeit, L leistet individuelle Hilfestellung.
- Gemeinsames Abgleichen der Ergebnisse an der Tafel. Alternative: L hat die Lösungen auf Blätter geschrieben, die im Klassenraum ausliegen und es den S ermöglichen, ihre Lösungen individuell abzugleichen (je nach Arbeitstempo). Anschließend kurze Besprechung im Plenum.

TIP
G 21

TA
had + been + past participle
They had been asked to act in an ad.

5 Language 2

Lösung
1 *had been asked* 2 *had not been* 3 *had not been sent* 4 *had been changed* 5 *had been forgotten* 6 *had been given*

Tipps für junge Lehrer Da Passivformen im Deutschen seltener gebraucht werden, empfiehlt es sich, einzelne Sätze übersetzen zu lassen, um die Betonung der einzelnen Satzteile zu verdeutlichen.

Material *Workbook* S. 58/13

Üben **3 You're on TV!** Seite 83

Ziel
- Das *personal passive* kennen lernen und anwenden

Strukturen
- *Personal passive*

Methodisches Vorgehen
- L und die S lesen G 22 und die *Grammar*-Box gemeinsam. L verdeutlicht, dass es Sätze mit zwei Objekten gibt (unbedingt die Begriffe Akkusativ- und Dativ-Objekt bzw. direktes und indirektes Objekt verwenden!) und führt den Begriff des *personal passive* ein.
- L schreibt den ersten Satz der Aufgabe an die Tafel. Dieser Satz wird gemeinsam umgeformt und der TA entsprechend ergänzt. Die S markieren die Satzteile im Aktivsatz farbig und unterstreichen ihre neue Position im Passivsatz. L kann den TA zusätzlich durch Pfeile ergänzen.
- Die S bearbeiten die Aufgabe in Einzelarbeit, anschließend Vergleich im Plenum. L bestimmt mehrere S, die jeweils einen Lösungssatz an die Tafel schreiben.

TIP G 22

TA
> Personal passive
> They have offered me the role of the rock star.
> I have been offered the role of the rock star by them.

Erweiterung
- Die *I*-Sätze werden in *he/she*-Sätze umgewandelt (drei Sätze mündlich, drei Sätze schriftlich: *He/She has been offered …; He/She has been sent …*), damit den S die Bildung dieser Form vertraut wird.

Lösung
1 *I have been offered the role of the rock star (by them).* 2 *I have been sent all the information (by the Casting Director).* 3 *I have been given £ 1000 for new clothes (by her).* 4 *I have been promised my own car (by the film people).* 5 *I have been shown the studio (by one of the actors).* 6 *I have been taught how to dance (by some of the actors).* 7 *I have been told crazy stories about the studio (by them).*

Material *Workbook* S. 58/14

Üben **4 Let's go to the studio** Seite 83

Ziel
- Sätze mit *will future passive* formulieren

Strukturen
- *Will future passive*

Methodisches Vorgehen
- L und die S lesen gemeinsam die Aufgabenstellung; L weist auf den veränderten Satzbau bei der Formulierung von Fragen hin (ggf. Regel und Beispielsatz an der Tafel).
- L und die S besprechen die Aufgabe gemeinsam (zunächst mündlich), anschließend schreiben die S die Lösungen in ihre Hefte (Varianten innerhalb der Aufgabe möglich). Gemeinsames Abgleichen der Ergebnisse an der Tafel.

TIP G 21

TA
> Questions in the will future passive
> Will + pronoun + be + past participle   ?
> Will   we   be   taken   to the cafeteria?

Language 2 | **5**

> Answers in the will future passive
> Pronoun + will + be + past participle
> You   will be   taken   to the cafeteria.

Lösung

> Will we be taken to the studio cafeteria? – Yes, you will. You will be shown all around the studio. I've been here before. Our pictures will be taken at the end – maybe even with a celeb. – Right! But this is new: You will even be given a little present. Will we be told stories about the actors? – Yes, you will. And you will be given the chance to look at the actors' costumes in our museum, too. Will we be brought back here? – Yes, you will. (Alternativen möglich)

Material
Workbook S. 59/15

Üben | **5 ⟨Put in the correct passive tense⟩** | Seite 83

Ziel
- Die verschiedenen Zeitformen des Passivs anwenden

Strukturen
- *Passive forms*

Methodisches Vorgehen
- L weist auf G 20 und G 21 und auf die Beachtung der Signalwörter hin. Die S bearbeiten die Aufgabe in Einzelarbeit.
- L hat die Lösungen auf kleine Zettel geschrieben, die ausgeteilt werden, nachdem alle S ihre Arbeit beendet haben. Korrektur in PA.

TIP
G 20, 21

Lösung

> 1 *was born* 2 *was cast* 3 *was flown* 4 *has been seen* 5 *had been given*
> 6 *was asked* 7 *Will she be given* 8 *have been offered*

Tipps für junge Lehrer
Bei dieser zusammenfassenden Aufgabe sollte sich L möglichst zurückhalten und nur vor Beginn der Arbeitsphase einige Hinweise zum Erkennen der *tenses* geben.

Üben | **6 Writing texts: An ad** | Seite 84

Ziel
- Eine eigene Werbeanzeige konzipieren

Wortschatz
headline, to get sb's attention

Methodisches Vorgehen
- L macht zu Beginn deutlich, dass es sich bei dieser Aufgabe um eine individuell zu erledigende Aufgabe handelt, die im Unterricht begonnen, dann aber als Hausaufgabe beendet werden muss (mehr Zeit einplanen). Alternative: L trifft Absprache mit L für Kunst, damit die S ggf. praktische Hilfe bei der Umsetzung ihrer Ideen bekommen.
- L und die S lesen die Aufgabenstellung gemeinsam (zur Orientierung werden die wesentlichen Punkte an die Tafel/auf Folie geschrieben); L fordert die S auf, sich über „ihr" Produkt Gedanken zu machen. Alternative: Kataloge o. Ä. mitbringen oder Kärtchen vorbereiten, auf denen L bereits Produkte aufgeklebt hat. Die S, die sich für kein eigenes Produkt entscheiden können, ziehen ein Kärtchen (es darf einmal getauscht werden, Dopplungen möglich).
- Die S sammeln in einer kurzen Einzelarbeitsphase passende Adjektive für ihre Werbeanzeigen (Wörterbücher dürfen benutzt werden). Anschließend werden diese an der Tafel/auf Folie gesammelt und von den S in ihre Hefte übertragen.
- Die S bereiten ihre Werbung individuell vor; L leistet Hilfestellung. Empfehlung: Termin für die Präsentation bereits in dieser Stunde festlegen.

TIP
Als langfristige HA formulieren

TA

> Writing an ad
> 1. Headline
> 2. Picture/photo/drawing
> 3. Text with information and good adjectives
> 4. Why you need this product

5 Language 2

Erweiterung	• Folie 13: **Advertising** kann als Vorbereitung auf *ex.* 6 eingesetzt werden.	**Material** *Workbook* S. 59/16 Folie 13 Ggf. Leerfolie Wörterbücher Karteikarten, Kataloge/Werbung
Lösung	*Useful adjectives: active, beautiful, brilliant, clear, cool, crazy, exciting, famous, fantastic, free, funny, great, lucky, good-better-best, interesting, surprising, …*	
Tipps für junge Lehrer	Auch wenn bei der Erstellung der Werbeanzeige Phantasie gefragt ist, sollten Grammatik und Orthografie nicht vernachlässigt werden. L bietet deshalb den S an, ihre Texte zu korrigieren, bevor sie sie auf ihr Werbeposter schreiben.	

Üben	**7 How to: Check each other's ad**	Seite 84
Ziel	• Arbeiten anderer kritisch beurteilen und Verbesserungsvorschläge machen	
Methodisches Vorgehen	• a) Um zu verhindern, dass „alte" Paare ihre Arbeiten unkritisch bewerten, sollte L vor Beginn dieser Übung „neue" Paare zusammenstellen (ggf. auch Gruppen mit drei S möglich). Die S tauschen ihre Arbeiten aus. Wichtig: L sollte sicherstellen, dass alle S ihre Werbeanzeigen dabei haben. Deshalb empfiehlt es sich, die Arbeiten in der vorherigen Stunde einzusammeln. • L verteilt **KV 1: How to: Check each other's ad** und legt diese als Folie auf. Kurze Besprechung der einzelnen Untersuchungskriterien. • b) Die S begutachten in Einzelarbeit die Werbeanzeige ihres/r Partners/in und formulieren ihre Verbesserungsvorschläge. L geht herum und leistet individuelle Hilfestellung. • c) Die Arbeiten werden dem/der Partner/in zurückgegeben. Die Verbesserungsvorschläge werden kritisch hinterfragt und ggf. verworfen. • L fordert einige Paare auf, ihre Ergebnisse vorzustellen. Dabei ist darauf zu achten, dass nicht nur die Ergebnisse der Kopiervorlage abgelesen werden, sondern die S eine individuelle (kurze) Stellungnahme formulieren. L kann besonders gute Leistungen (für den Bereich mündliche Mitarbeit) benoten.	**TIP** Neue Schülerpaare zusammenstellen
Erweiterung	• Die S, die ein Feedback zu ihrer Werbeanzeige wünschen, können sie in der folgenden Stunde abgeben, nachdem sie die Verbesserungsvorschläge ihres/r Partners/in eingearbeitet haben oder logisch begründen (schriftlich), warum sie diese nicht berücksichtigt haben.	
Lösung	*Individuelle S-Antworten*	
Tipps für junge Lehrer	Kreative Aufgaben sind gerade für leistungsschwächere S eine gute Möglichkeit, sich in den Unterricht einzubringen. Dies sollte bei der Auswahl der zu präsentierenden Arbeiten und bei der Benotung berücksichtigt werden.	**Material** Kopiervorlage 1 Ggf. Leerfolie

Üben	**8 Revision: Simple past and present perfect**	Seite 84
Ziel	• Die Unterscheidung von *simple past* und *present perfect* wiederholen und vertiefen	
Strukturen	• *Simple past vs. present perfect*	
Methodisches Vorgehen	• L und die S lesen die Aufgabenstellung und besprechen das erste Beispiel. Anschließend werden die Beispielsätze ins Deutsche übersetzt. L weist dabei auf den zeitlichen Bezug zwischen den *tenses* hin und betont besonders den zweiten Satz: *But I haven't seen it yet.* = Aber ich habe sie (die Werbung) **noch** nicht gesehen. L: *That means that it can still happen. So you use the present perfect for this part of the sentence.* • Die S bearbeiten die Sätze in PA; L leistet individuelle Hilfestellung. • Gemeinsames Abgleichen an der Tafel; dabei werden die Sätze übersetzt und die Verwendung der beiden Zeitformen begründet.	

Language 2 | **5**

TA	Siehe Lösung

Erweiterung
- Die S formulieren in PA weitere Sätze (auch auf Deutsch), um ihr Verständnis für den differenzierten Gebrauch der *tenses* zu dokumentieren.
- Als Hausaufgabe kann **KV 2: Simple past or present perfect?** eingesetzt werden.

Lösung

> *Erwartungshorizont:*
> 1 B: *Yes, I saw him on TV yesterday.* 2 B: *Yes, I was in Hollywood with my parents two years ago.* 3 B: *I haven't tried the new crisps yet.* 4 B: *I haven't been on a tour of the studio so far.* 5 B: *Yes, I saw it on TV yesterday evening.*
> 6 B: *Yes, they gave me my own TV for my last birthday.*

Tipps für junge Lehrer
Es ist sehr wahrscheinlich, dass die S die Regeln für die Verwendung von *simple past* und *present perfect* nicht mehr genau kennen. Deshalb sollte L vorbereitet sein und ggf. eine Übersicht (Signalwörter, weitere Beispielsätze) zusammengestellt haben.

Material
Kopiervorlage 2

Üben | **9 Your turn: Celebrities and ads** | Seite 84

Ziel
- Über die Wirksamkeit von Werbung durch Prominente sprechen

Methodisches Vorgehen
- a)+b)+c) L bittet die S, aus Zeitschriften Werbeanzeigen auszuschneiden, auf denen Prominente für Produkte werben. Alternative: TV-Werbespots können aufgenommen und im Unterricht gezeigt werden.
- Die S präsentieren ihre Werbung, beschreiben das Produkt und formulieren ihre persönlichen Eindrücke zu dieser Werbeanzeige.
- Die S überlegen gemeinsam Gründe, warum Werbung mit Prominenten so erfolgreich ist.
- Abschließend schreiben die S in Einzelarbeit einen kurzen Text zu ihrer Werbung. L erstellt ein zusammenfassendes Tafelbild als Orientierungshilfe.

TA

> This is ... He/She is advertising ...
> He/She is a famous ...
>
> I like/don't like the ad because ...
> I think this ad is ... because ...
>
> c) Erwartungshorizont:
> I think famous people help to sell a product. When people see the ad they
> think when a famous and beautiful man/woman uses this ... they will look as
> good as he/she does when they use this product, too.

Erweiterung
- Die S formulieren (mündlich) Ideen, welche/r Prominente zu bestimmten Produkten passen würde.

Lösung | *Siehe TA*

Tipps für junge Lehrer
L sollte ebenfalls Werbeanzeigen sammeln oder aufschreiben, welche Prominente im TV Werbung für welche Produkte machen, um ggf. Material zur Hand zu haben. Da Werbung auch ein Thema des Deutschunterrichts ist, kann hier eine fächerverbindende Arbeit angestrebt werden.

Material
Werbeanzeigen

5 Skills

Skills
Seite 85

 Ziele
- Die Struktur eines Zeitungsberichts kennen lernen
- Einen Zeitungsbericht schreiben
- Passivformen in eigenen Texten verwenden
- Arbeiten anderer kritisch beurteilen und Verbesserungsvorschläge machen

Text **Writing a newspaper report** Seite 85

Ziel
- Das Textverständnis üben
- Die Struktur eines Zeitungsberichts kennen lernen

Wortschatz *LAN (Local Area Network), beginning, basic, to attend, to organise, youth, to raise money, argument, violent, noise, background, police department, to give one's opinion, opinion*

Methodisches Vorgehen
- L liest den Zeitungsbericht laut vor, die S lesen leise mit. Anschließend lesen die S den Text erneut durch; unbekannte Vokabeln werden danach gemeinsam semantisiert. Alternative: L hat die neuen Vokabeln auf Folie geschrieben, so dass die S den Text individuell erschließen können.
- L und die S besprechen die Struktur des Textes (auf die unterschiedliche Funktion der gegebenen Informationen hinweisen!) und stellen an der Tafel/auf Folie eine Liste der Gliederungspunkte zusammen. Der Begriff *conclusion* wurde bereits auf einer Kopiervorlage (LB, Unit 1, **KV 1: Preparing a talk to the class**) verwendet. Sollte er nicht bekannt sein, gibt L eine kurze Erklärung.

TIP
Neues Vokabular auf Folie schreiben

TA

> Writing a newspaper report
> 1. Headline
> 2. Beginning: basic information
> 3. Interesting details
> 4. Background information
> 5. End: useful information/conclusion
>
> Use the passive when you don't know who did the action or when you want to stress the action.
> Don't give your opinion.

Tipps für junge Lehrer Da die S in Zukunft noch häufig die Struktur eines Textes analysieren müssen, empfiehlt es sich, schon früh auf die Bedeutung der Textstruktur hinzuweisen. Eine Zusammenarbeit mit dem Fach Deutsch ist auch hier wünschenswert.

Material Ggf. Leerfolie

Üben **1 Violence in Dorchester** Seite 85

Ziel
- Einen Zeitungsbericht unter Verwendung der *passive forms* schreiben

Wortschatz *to allow*

Strukturen
- *Passive forms*

Methodisches Vorgehen
- L und die S lesen die Aufgabenstellung gemeinsam. L weist auf die Struktur eines Zeitungsberichts hin (siehe TA/Folie oben) und empfiehlt den S, vor dem Schreiben eine Gliederung ihres Berichts zu erstellen.
- Die S lesen die Notizen von der Pressekonferenz; L leistet individuelle Hilfestellung (ggf. einige Vokabeln vorher an die Tafel schreiben).
- Die S bearbeiten die Aufgabe in Einzelarbeit oder als Hausaufgabe.

Auch als HA geeignet

Lösung
Erwartungshorizont:
Violence at Redwood School!/Redwood School – A Place Of Violence!

		Skills **5**

> *"I was shocked that this could happen at my school." –* These were the words of the headmaster of Redwood School last Friday, after a mobile with violent scenes had been found by a teacher at his school. The police was/were called.
> Violent scenes in the school and in the playground had been filmed by a Redwood pupil. His mobile was checked. It showed a scene where a 10-year-old pupil was hit by three other pupils. All attend Redwood School.
> Violent scenes on mobiles are becoming a problem in Britain. The film scenes are sent to friends' mobiles. Many pupils think that it is cool to have more violent scenes than others.
> The headmaster has decided that mobiles are not allowed at Redwood School now. The school does not want any more violence. *"There is enough violence on TV,"* the headmaster said. *"Parents should check their children's mobiles."*

Tipps für junge Lehrer   Da die S bekanntlich sehr ungern schreiben, ist es wichtig, Schreibaufgaben vorher gründlich vorzubereiten. Dies muss individuell auf eine Klasse abgestimmt werden. Deshalb sollte L die Bedürfnisse der S berücksichtigen und ggf. weitere lexikalische Hilfen o. Ä. vorbereitet haben.

Üben   **2 A better report**   Seite 85

Ziel
- Arbeiten anderer kritisch beurteilen und Verbesserungsvorschläge machen

Wortschatz   *to exchange, to rewrite*

Methodisches Vorgehen
- Im Anschluss an die Einzelarbeit/Hausaufgabe tauschen die S ihre Arbeit mit ihrem/r Partner/in aus. L legt als Orientierung die bereits erstellte Folie (S. 84, *ex.* 7) auf.
- Die S formulieren Verbesserungsvorschläge (mündlich/schriftlich) und markieren Stellen (mit Bleistift), die sie verbessern würden.
- L gibt den S Zeit, ihre Berichte zu überarbeiten. Anschließend (auch in der nächsten Stunde möglich) werden die korrigierten Berichte eingesammelt und von L überprüft und kommentiert (nicht bewerten!).
- L liest verschiedene Berichte im Plenum vor und weist auf die Schwachstellen oder besonders gelungene Passagen hin.

TIP
Useful phrases,
S. 176

Üben   **3 News in your town**   Seite 85

Ziel
- Einen Zeitungsbericht verfassen

Methodisches Vorgehen
- Es empfiehlt sich, diese Aufgabe längerfristig zu stellen. Da manche S zu Hause über keine Tageszeitung verfügen, sollte L kurze Zeitungsartikel sammeln und den S zur Verfügung stellen.
- Alternative: **KV 3: Dog News**
- Die S schreiben ihren Artikel als Hausaufgabe. L korrigiert die Texte. Anschließend werden verschiedene Texte vorgelesen. Der beste/lustigste/verrückteste Artikel wird prämiert.

TIP
Zeitungsartikel sammeln

HA

Erweiterung
- Da diese Aufgabe sehr anspruchsvoll ist, kann sie ggf. freiwillig gestellt werden. L kann auch bestimmte S gezielt ansprechen und die Leistung entsprechend honorieren.

Material
Workbook S. 60/17
Kopiervorlage 3

5 Text

Text
Seite 86–87

Ziele
- Über die positiven Auswirkungen des Fernsehens diskutieren
- Einen Text eigenständig erschließen
- Über eigene Erfahrungen mit Büchern/Fernsehen sprechen
- Eine Umfrage zu Mediengewohnheiten in der Klasse durchführen

Üben

1 Before you read
Seite 86

Ziel
- Themenbezogene Argumente formulieren

Methodisches Vorgehen
- L erläutert die Ausgangssituation und gibt den S fünf Minuten Zeit, um in Einzelarbeit Argumente für die weitere Nutzung des TV zu sammeln.
- Die S erstellen eine Argumentationsliste, die sie anschließend mit der Liste des/der Partners/in vergleichen und ggf. ergänzen.
- Die S diktieren ihre Argumente, L hält sie auf Folie fest; die S vergleichen und ergänzen ihre Listen.
- Verschiedene S fassen die Argumente in vollständigen Sätzen zusammen.
- Alternative: L verkörpert die Position der Eltern, die S tragen die vorher gesammelten Argumente vor.

Erweiterung
- Nachdem die Argumente für den Erhalt des TV gesammelt wurden, sucht L verschiedene S aus, die die Gegenposition der Eltern einnehmen sollen.
- Diese S überlegen sich gemeinsam Gegenargumente, die sie in einem Dialog/Gespräch mit den „Kindern" einbringen. Wichtig: Die S sollten sprachlich so gewandt sein, dass sie direkt auf die Argumente der „Kinder" reagieren können und nicht nur ihre Gegenargumente ablesen.

Lösung

> *Erwartungshorizont:*
> *Watching TV is important because …*
> - *you get news/information*
> - *you can relax*
> - *you have entertainment (in the evening) and don't have to go to the cinema*
> - *it belongs to our modern time*
> - *it can help you with your homework*
> - *you get to know other cultures/landscapes/traditions*
> - *…*

Material
Ggf. Leerfolie

 Text **No couch potatoes!**
Seite 86–87

Ziel
- Einen unbekannten Text eigenständig erschließen

Wortschatz
to convince, cereal (no pl.), magic, to get sb to do sth, pile, to fall off, ramp, to disappear, to crack, cold, spinach (no pl.), to admit, to walk past, above, outline, roof, to cut, pipe, gash, blood, patient, to distract, bandage, emergency, to tie, tight, ambulance, to rescue, to grow up

Methodisches Vorgehen
- Gemeinsames Lesen des Einführungsabschnitts *Mariah's media corner*.
- Da die Anzahl der neuen Vokabeln für die beiden Texte recht übersichtlich ist, bietet es sich an, die S die Texte eigenständig erschließen zu lassen. Dazu hat L den neuen Wortschatz der beiden Texte jeweils auf kleine Zettel kopiert und verteilt diese (verdeckt) an die S, die sich dann mit dem entsprechenden Text beschäftigen müssen.
- Die S lesen „ihren" Text in Einzelarbeit und verwenden dabei die Vokabelhilfen. Weiteres Vokabular schlagen sie ggf. im *Dictionary* im Buchanhang nach.
- Anschließend werden die beiden Texte (nacheinander, mit Unterbrechungen) von CD vorgespielt. Die S lesen mit.

TIP
Texte arbeitsteilig erarbeiten lassen

	• Anschließend führen die jeweiligen Gruppen in den neuen Wortschatz der beiden Texte ein. Gleichzeitig äußern sie ihre Ideen zu dem jeweiligen Text. Die S der anderen Gruppen stellen Fragen zum Inhalt und bitten ggf. um die Erläuterung weiterer Vokabeln. • Zum Abschluss werden beide Texte von den S laut vorgelesen.
Erweiterung	• Um sicher zu gehen, dass wirklich alle S die beiden Texte sprachlich und inhaltlich verstanden haben, sollten die S als Hausaufgabe den jeweils anderen Text nochmals lesen. Als weitere Hausaufgabe formulieren die S vier Inhaltsfragen zu „ihrem" Text und schreiben diese auf kleine Zettel.
Tipps für junge Lehrer	Die in der Hausaufgabe geforderten Fragen können den Anfang der nächsten Stunde bilden. Es ist auch möglich, zu Beginn der nächsten Stunde eine kurze mündliche/schriftliche Kontrolle einzuplanen. Dabei zieht L einige der Fragezettel und wählt Fragen aus, die von allen S mündlich/schriftlich beantwortet werden müssen.

Material
◎s 2/14–15
◎L 3/22–23
Vokabelzettel

Üben	**2 What do you think?**	Seite 87
Ziel	• Die eigene Meinung zu einem Text formulieren und begründen	
Methodisches Vorgehen	• a) Zur Einstimmung auf die Aufgabe bieten sich die von den S als Hausaufgabe formulierten Inhaltsfragen an. • Die S formulieren ihre Meinung in 2–3 Sätzen und vergleichen ihre Antwort mit der des/der Partners/in. In leistungsschwächeren Lerngruppen können vorab *Useful phrases* zum Formulieren der eigenen Meinung gesammelt werden (siehe TA).	
TA	I like/don't like this story because ... I think it's good/interesting/brilliant/funny/really exciting ... I think it's sad/terrible/boring ... I think Bill/Janice is an interesting/strange/annoying ... character. This is the reason why ...	
	• Im Anschluss lesen verschiedene S ihre Antworten vor. • b) Diese Teilaufgabe wird nur diejenigen S ansprechen, die sich gerne mündlich einbringen. L sollte die Bearbeitung dieser Aufgabe von der allgemeinen Klassensituation abhängig machen.	
Erweiterung	• Bevor die S ihre Stellungnahme aufschreiben, kann die Liste der *Useful phrases* ergänzt werden. Dabei machen die S Vokabelvorschläge, die L übersetzt. Diese Ergänzung ist sinnvoll, auch wenn die gewünschten Vokabeln im SB noch nicht vorgesehen sind. Zur weiteren inhaltlichen Arbeit eignet sich **KV 4a+b: No couch potatoes!**	
Tipps für junge Lehrer	Auch wenn das schriftliche Formulieren immer zeitaufwendiger ist, sollte es kontinuierlich eingesetzt werden. Bei mündlichen Aufgaben beteiligen sich oft nur wenige S, auf die sich die anderen verlassen. Schriftliche Aufgaben verlangen die Mitarbeit aller S und können mündliche Beiträge vorentlasten.	

Material
Workbook S. 61/18, 19
Kopiervorlage 4a+b
Ggf. Leerfolie

Üben	**3 Your turn: Books and TV**	Seite 87
Ziel	• Über persönliche Lesegewohnheiten berichten • Über den Nutzen der eigenen Lieblingssendung sprechen	
Methodisches Vorgehen	• a) Es empfiehlt sich, den S für die Bearbeitung dieser Aufgabe mehr Zeit zu geben. Sie könnte im Zusammenhang mit einer kurzen Buchvorstellung	

TIP
Als langfristige HA nutzen

	eingesetzt werden. Auch eine Zusammenarbeit mit dem Fach Deutsch könnte hier hilfreich sein.	
Erweiterung	• b) Es ist sehr wahrscheinlich, dass die S Fernsehsendungen nennen werden, die beratenden/informativen Charakter haben. Auch dies entspricht dem Ziel dieser Aufgabe.	**Material** Workbook S. 61/20

Üben	**4 ⟨A media survey⟩**	Seite 87
Ziel	• Eine Umfrage zu Mediengewohnheiten in der Klasse durchführen	
Wortschatz	*survey, habit, adult, to report, result*	
Methodisches Vorgehen	• L und die S lesen die Aufgabenstellung gemeinsam; Klären von Fragen. L stellt die Gruppen zusammen und verteilt **KV 5a: A media survey**. • Die S führen erste Befragungen durch und besprechen die Präsentation ihrer Ergebnisse in der Gruppe. Die Befragung der „Erwachsenen" erfolgt als Hausaufgabe. Dazu **KV 5b: A media survey**.	
Erweiterung	• L kann ggf. Hilfestellung bei der Entscheidung über die Präsentationsform geben. Auch Formulierungen zur Präsentation können auf der Kopiervorlage zusammengestellt/ergänzt werden.	**Material** Kopiervorlage 5a+b

Wordwise

Seite 88

> **Ziele**
> • Höfliche Antworten geben
> • Zwischen *strong* und *weak forms* bei der Betonung einzelner Wörter unterscheiden
> • Einen *Songtext* inhaltlich verstehen und interpretieren

> **TIP**
> Die Ergebnisse der Stationen am Ende zu 2–3 Zeitschriften zusammenfügen

Stationenlernen	• Vor oder nach *Wordwise* kann das Stationenlernen durchgeführt werden (**Kopiervorlagen 7–11**). Der Arbeitsbericht hierzu findet sich als **KV 17** bei Unit 1. • In den einzelnen Stationen erstellen die S unterschiedliche Teile einer Jugendzeitschrift. Es bietet sich an, die Stationen gleichmäßig zu verteilen, so dass am Ende 2–3 Zeitschriften zusammengestellt werden können.	**Material** Kopiervorlagen 7–11 Kopiervorlage 17 (Unit 1)

Üben	**1 Find the polite answer**	Seite 88
Ziel	• Auf Fragen mit der korrekten höflichen Antwort reagieren	
Methodisches Vorgehen	• Bearbeitung der Aufgabe in PA, wobei die Partner alle Frage-Antwort-Kombinationen laut vorlesen und stimmlich variieren. • Präsentation der Ergebnisse im Plenum.	
Erweiterung	• Die S überlegen sich weitere Frage-Antwort-Kombinationen mit Auswahlmöglichkeiten.	
Lösung	*1b) 2c) 3b) 4c)*	

		Wordwise	**5**

Tipps für junge Lehrer	Diese Aufgabe ist besonders geeignet, um den S zu verdeutlichen, dass ein Variieren der Stimme für den Inhalt eines Satzes von großer Bedeutung sein kann. L sollte ggf. die vorgegebenen Sätze etwas überbetont vorlesen.	Material *Workbook* S. 62/21

◉L Üben **2 Sounds: Strong and weak forms** Seite 88

HV-Text   Identisch mit SB-Text

Ziel
- Bei der Betonung einzelner Wörter zwischen *strong* und *weak forms* unterscheiden.

Methodisches Vorgehen
- Die S lesen die Aufgabenstellung; L gibt ggf. kurze Erläuterungen dazu.
- L spielt die Sätze komplett vor; die S lesen leise mit.
- L spielt die CD ein zweites Mal vor und macht nach jedem Satz eine Pause, so dass die S den Satz laut nachsprechen können (im Chor, einzeln, in Gruppen).
- Nachdem alle Sätze präsentiert wurden, lesen verschiedene S die einzelnen Sätze erneut vor. Gemeinsames Erarbeiten der Betonungsunterschiede im Plenum (ggf. auch anhand von deutschen Satzbeispielen).

> **TIP**
> Deutsche Beispiele geben

Material
◉L 3/24

◉L Song **3 ⟨A song: *Sk8er boi* by Avril Lavigne⟩** Seite 88

HV-Text
He was a boy
She was a girl
Can I make it any more obvious?
He was a punk
She did ballet
What more can I say?
He wanted her
She'd never tell secretly she wanted him as well
But all of her friends
Stuck up their nose
They had a problem with his baggy clothes.

Chorus:
He was a skater boy
She said see you later, boy
He wasn't good enough for her
She had a pretty face
But her head was up in space
She needed to come back down to earth.

Five years from now
She sits at home
Feeding the baby
She's all alone
She turns on TV
Guess who she sees?
Skater boy rockin' up MTV.
She calls up her friends
They already know
And they've all got tickets to see his show
She tags along,
Stands in the crowd
Looks up at the man that
She turned down

Chorus:
He was a skater boy
She said see you later boy

279

5 Wordwise

He wasn't good enough for her
Now he's a super star
Slamin' on his guitar
Does your pretty face see what he's worth?
He was a skater boy
She said see you later boy
He wasn't good enough for her
Now he's a super star
Slamin' on his guitar
Does your pretty face see what he's worth?

Sorry girl but you missed out
Well tough luck that boy's mine now
We are more than just good friends
This is how the story ends
Too bad that you couldn't see
See the man that boy could be
There is more than meets the eye
I see the soul that is inside
He's just a boy
And I'm just a girl
Can I make it any more obvious?
We are in love
Haven't you heard
How we rock each other's world

Chorus:
I'm with the skater boy
I said see ya later boy
I'll be back stage after the show
I'll be at a studio
Singing the song we wrote
About a girl you used to know
I'm with the skater boy
I said see ya later boy
I'll be back stage after the show
I'll be at a studio
Singing the song we wrote
About a girl you used to know

Text: Scott David Alspach/Lauren Christy/Graham Edwards/Avril Ramona Lavigne. © 2001 by WARNER-TA-MERLANE PUBLISHING CORP/RAINBOW FISH PUBLISHING/MR. SPOCK MUSIK/FERRYHILL SONGS/WB MUSIC CORP./ALMO MUSIC CORPORATION; SLV NEUE WELT MUSIKVERLAG GMBH&CO.KG/RONDOR MUSIKVERLAG GMBH

Ziel	• Einen Songtext verstehen und interpretieren
Wortschatz	*obvious, ballet, to stick up one's nose, baggy clothes, space, now, all alone, to rock, to tag along, to turn down*
Methodisches Vorgehen	*Pre-listening:* • L schreibt den Titel des Songs an die Tafel; die S ergänzen bzw. korrigieren den Titel *(Skater boy).* • L gibt ein paar kurze Informationen über die Sängerin Avril Lavigne: *Avril Lavigne Whibley, better known by her birth name Avril Lavigne, was born on September 27, 1984 in Belleville, Ontario, Canada. She is a punk pop singer, musician, fashion designer and actress. She has won several awards and was nominated for the Grammy Awards for her single 'Sk8er boi'.* (L kann nach Vorabsprache auch eine/n S bestimmen, die/der diese Einführung übernimmt.) • L schreibt die Höraufgabe an die Tafel.

| | Wordwise | Check-out | 5 |

While-listening:
- Der Song wird das erste Mal präsentiert. Die S lesen mit und notieren sich unbekannte Vokabeln.
- Anschließend kurze Semantisierung. Die S äußern erste Vermutungen zur Höraufgabe.
- Erneutes Abspielen des Songs von CD. Die S lesen mit und machen sich Notizen.
- Die S beantworten die Höraufgabe in vollständigen Sätzen. Dabei achtet L darauf, dass die S möglichst eigene Worte benutzen. Anschließend Besprechung der Ergebnisse im Plenum.

Post-listening:
- L verteilt **KV 6a+b: A song: *Sk8ter boi* by Avril Lavigne** an je eine Hälfte der Klasse. Die S bearbeiten die Aufgaben in PA. Anschließend Vergleich der Ergebnisse im Plenum (auf Tafel oder vorbereiteter Folie).
- Erneutes Abspielen des Songs (falls gewünscht) zum Genießen.
- Ggf. stellt L weiterführende Fragen: *Can you understand the girl's reaction when she was young? Do you know people who have problems with other people's clothes? Are the right clothes important for you?* etc.

TA
Sk8er boi = Skater boy
What mistake did the girl make? (siehe Lösung)

Erweiterung
- Um die *Writing skills* zu schulen, kann im Anschluss der Songtext zu einem durchgängigen Text umgeschrieben werden.

Auch als HA geeignet

Material
L 3/25
Kopiervorlage 6a+b
Ggf. Leerfolie

Lösung
The girl didn't tell the boy that she wanted him. She listened to her friends who didn't like him and his strange clothes. The girl thought the skater boy was not good enough for her.

Check-out

Seite 89

Ziele • Die Lernziele der Unit in Selbstkontrolle überprüfen

Üben **1 Matt Stirling**

Seite 89

Ziel
- Sätze durch Einsetzen verschiedener *passive forms* vervollständigen

Strukturen
- *Passive forms*

Methodisches Vorgehen
- L weist auf G 19 und G 21 hin und erinnert an die Bedeutung von Signalwörtern, um die korrekte Zeitform zu erkennen.
- Die S bearbeiten die Aufgabe in Einzelarbeit; anschließend Kontrolle in PA.

TIP
G 19, 21

Material
Workbook S. 63/24

Lösung Siehe SB S. 215

Üben **2 Put these sentences into the passive**

Seite 89

Ziel
- Aktivsätze in Passivsätze umwandeln

Strukturen
- *Passive forms*

5 Check-out

Methodisches Vorgehen	• L weist auf G 20 und G 22 hin; die S schlagen ggf. im Grammatikanhang nach. • Die S erledigen die Aufgabe in Einzelarbeit schriftlich; anschließend Kontrolle in PA.	**TIP** G 20, 22
Lösung	Siehe SB S. 215	**Material** Workbook S. 63/25

Üben 3 Your turn: A school magazine report — Seite 89

Ziel	• Einen kurzen Bericht für die Schülerzeitung schreiben • Den Bericht eines/einer Mitschülers/in korrigieren	
Methodisches Vorgehen	• L erläutert die Aufgabenstellung und weist auf lexikalische Hilfen hin. • Die S wählen ein Thema aus und schreiben ihren Bericht in Einzelarbeit. Sollten L oder die S andere Themenvorschläge haben, können diese selbstverständlich ebenfalls zur Wahl gestellt werden. • Alternative: Die Aufgabe wird als Hausaufgabe gestellt. • Die S tauschen ihre Berichte aus und machen ggf. Verbesserungsvorschläge; L leistet individuelle Hilfestellung. • Alternative: Einige Berichte werden in der Klasse laut vorgelesen.	**TIP** *Useful phrases* nutzen Auch als HA geeignet **Material** Workbook S. 63/26
Lösung	Siehe SB S. 215	

Üben 4 Write an ad — Seite 89

Ziel	• Eine Werbeanzeige konzipieren	
Methodisches Vorgehen	• L erläutert die Aufgabenstellung; L und die S lesen S. 84, *ex.* 6 nochmals gemeinsam durch. • Die S wählen ein Produkt aus – oder entscheiden sich für ein anderes Produkt (Kataloge o. Ä. mitbringen) – und schreiben eine Werbeanzeige. • Die S präsentieren ihre Ergebnisse in der Klasse und stimmen anschließend über die beste Werbeanzeige ab.	**TIP** Andere Produkte vorschlagen
Erweiterung	• Diese Aufgabe kann auch als längerfristige Hausaufgabe gestellt werden. Die S sollten dann nicht nur eine Werbeanzeige verfassen, sondern ein Plakat/Poster o. Ä. für ihr Produkt gestalten.	Auch als HA geeignet
Lösung	Siehe SB S. 215	

Dictation

How to become a celebrity

For many teenagers it seems that the most important thing in their lives is to become a celebrity. They forget that you need talent, luck and also a good agent. A lot of hard work is necessary and good contacts to famous people can help you, too.
First you talk to an agent and give him or her your photo. If you are lucky, you will be phoned by your agent and be told that a Casting Director has chosen you for a casting. When you get there, make sure you know your role well. Listen carefully to the Casting Director's suggestions when you act your role. If you are chosen, this can be the beginning of a successful future.
But don't forget: Many stars who are famous today will be forgotten tomorrow.

⟨Text⟩

⟨Text⟩

Ziele
- Einen adaptierten Auszug aus einem Jugendroman eigenständig erschließen
- Das *reading between the lines* üben

○s ○L **Text** ⟨Big mouth and ugly girl⟩ Workbook Seite 64

Wortschatz Annotationen S. 64

Methodisches Vorgehen

Pre-reading:
- Die S lesen den kursiv gedruckten Einführungstext. Unbekanntes Vokabular wird durch die Annotationen oder ein Wörterbuch erschlossen.
- L stellt einführende Fragen: *Think about a newspaper article or a radio/TV programme that reported on something you knew a lot about. Was all the information correct? How did you feel when you read or heard the news?*

While-reading:
- L leitet zur Lektüre des Textes über. Präsentation von CD, die S lesen leise mit. Während des Hörens/Lesens machen sich die S Notizen zu folgender Aufgabe: *Now listen to the short text. Try and find out as much as possible about Ursula, the person who tells the story.*
- Die S lesen den Text erneut und erschließen unbekannten Wortschatz durch die Annotationen/ein Wörterbuch.

Post-reading:
- Gemeinsames Sammeln der Ergebnisse an der Tafel.
- L stellt eine weiterführende Frage zum Text: *Why do you think Ursula is so angry about the news programme?*

Erweiterung
- a) Zur weiteren Analyse stellt L eine Frage zur Darstellung der Nachrichtensendung: *How is the news programme presented to us?*
- b) *What do we find out about Ursula's family between the lines?*

Lösung

Erwartungshorizont:
While-reading: goes to Rocky River High School; the 'ugly girl'; knows that what they say about Matt isn't true; is not afraid to speak out; doesn't want to talk to her mother; jealous of her younger sister
Post-reading: Ursula is angry because she knows that what they say about Matt is not true.
Erweiterung: a) The cuts show how silly the whole thing is; no one says anything of real importance.   b) Ursula and her mother don't get on very well with each other, Ursula doesn't talk; jealous of her younger sister; the mother wants to talk to her daughter; the father has not come home and the mother doesn't know where he is; the mother seems to have problems, she drinks alcohol

Material
○s 2/16
○L 3/27

5 ⟨Freiarbeit⟩

⟨Freiarbeit⟩

Ziele
- Eigene Werbespots entwickeln und vergleichen
- Die *Presentation skills* erweitern und vertiefen

Methodisches Vorgehen
- Die S erarbeiten in GA einen Werbespot zu einem bei Jugendlichen beliebten und als wichtig erachteten *Lifestyle*-Produkt (siehe **KV 12a+b: An advertising campaign – A competition**). Zur Gewährleistung einer besseren Vergleichbarkeit der Werbespots sollten alle Gruppen sich auf ein zu bewerbendes Produkt einigen.
- Anschließend werden die Werbespots auf Video aufgenommen oder in der Klasse vorgespielt und im Hinblick auf die auf **KV 12a** genannten Kriterien bewertet. Am Ende steht die Wahl des besten Werbespots, die von den S gut begründet werden sollte.

Erweiterung
- Der Wettbewerbsaspekt kann zugunsten der Vielfalt zu bewerbender Produkte aufgegeben werden. Die Schüler entwerfen dann Werbespots zu einem von ihnen selbst ausgewählten Produkt.

Lösung *Individuelle S-Antworten*

TIP
Zeitrahmen:
2–3 Stunden Planung,
1 Stunde Übung bzw. Aufnahme des Werbespots,
1 Stunde Präsentation und Wahl des besten Werbespots

Material
Kopiervorlage 12a+b
Ggf. Videokamera

KV 1: How to: Check each other's ad

My name: _____   My partner's name: _____

a) *Look at your partner's ad from page 84, exercise 6 in your book. Answer the following questions:*

   1. What can you see in the ad/on the poster? _____
   _____
   _____

   2. What is the ad about? _____
   _____

   3. Would you buy this product? Why or why not? _____
   _____
   _____

   4. Is the ad interesting? Why or why not? _____
   _____
   _____

b) *Make suggestions to improve the ad. Write a short text. You can use the following phrases:*

| It would be better if you … | You should … | I don't understand this sentence. |
| If I were you, I would … | Could you write …? | How about …? |

_____
_____
_____
_____

c) *Now discuss your ideas with your partner.*

KV 2: Simple past or present perfect?

Put the words in the correct order. Use the simple past or the present perfect.

1. Reese Witherspoon • in Louisiana • be born • on March 22, 1976

   _____

   _____

2. She • her first film • make • when • she • a teenager • be

   _____

   _____

3. Reese Witherspoon • in many successful films • already • acted

   _____

   _____

4. She • American actors • one of the most famous • become

   _____

5. *Walk the line* • in the film • have • a leading role[1] • she

   _____

6. many interesting roles • film producers • her • so far • offer

   _____

[1] **leading role** ['liːdɪŋ rəʊl] = Hauptrolle

Lösung: 1 *Reese Witherspoon was born in Louisiana on March 22, 1976.* 2 *She made her first film when she was a teenager.* 3 *She has already acted in many successful films.* 4 *She has become one of the most famous American actors.* 5 *She had a leading role in the film Walk the line.* 6 *So far film producers have offered her many interesting roles.*

KV 3: Dog news

Read the following article, take notes and write a report in English. You don't have to translate every word!

Hund beißt[1] Polizisten und pinkelt[2] ins Auto

Ein Hund hat gestern zwei Polizisten viel Ärger gemacht.
Die Polizisten beobachteten eine betrunkene[3] Frau, die versuchte, ihren immer wieder auf die Straße laufenden Hund einzufangen. Einer der Polizisten bot dem Hund Süßigkeiten an. Als der Hund näher kam, versuchte der Polizist, ihn einzufangen. Der Hund biss ihn daraufhin in beide Hände. Die Polizisten gaben jedoch nicht auf, und kurze Zeit später konnten sie den Hund einfangen.
Sie brachten die Frau mit ihrem Hund zum Polizeirevier. Während der Fahrt roch es plötzlich merkwürdig. Der Hund hatte ins Auto gepinkelt. „Gut, dass wir Tiere mögen", sagte einer der Polizisten. „Aber schön war es nicht." Die Polizisten fuhren zum Arzt, wechselten das Auto und arbeiteten weiter.

© Süddeutsche Zeitung vom 11.12.2007

Notes:

_____
_____
_____
_____
_____

Report:

_____
_____
_____
_____
_____
_____
_____
_____
_____
_____
_____

[1]**beißen** = to bite, bit, bitten [2]**pinkeln** = to pee, peed, peed [3]**betrunken** = drunk

KV 4a: No couch potatoes!

Bill, age 13, Southampton

a) *Read the following sentences. Are they right or wrong? Check with the text on page 86 in your book. Correct the wrong sentences.*

	Right	Wrong
1. Bill's first book was *King Arthur's Legend*.	☐	☐
2. Bill and his mother go to the library twice a week.	☐	☐
3. Bill used a *Harry Potter* book as a ramp when he was skateboarding.	☐	☐
4. Bill's skateboard cracked and he broke his arm.	☐	☐
5. Bill had to stay in hospital for a few weeks.	☐	☐
6. Bill's friends brought him the book from the skateboard ramp.	☐	☐
7. After the fifth chapter, Bill sold the book to the doctor.	☐	☐
8. Bill will read the second *Harry Potter* book soon.	☐	☐

_____

_____

_____

_____

_____

_____

_____

b) *What do you think about books? Explain why you like/don't like reading. Write 3–4 sentences in your exercise book.*

Lösung: 1 Bill's first book was 'Harry Potter'. 2 It's only Bill's mother who goes to the library twice a week. 4 Bill broke his leg. 7 After the fifth chapter, there was spaghetti for lunch. 8 Bill liked the book but we don't know if he'll read the second one.

KV 4b: No couch potatoes!

Janice, age 14, Manchester

a) *Use the text on page 87 in your book and complete the following sentences:*

1. When Janice went home after school last September she _____

2. She was walking past an old factory that _____

3. When she looked up she saw _____

4. She looked for a place _____ to help the boy.

5. The boy looked white in the face and Janice _____

6. Janice used her T-shirt as _____ and told the boy _____

7. While they waited for the ambulance _____

8. After Janice had rescued Ricky, she was _____

9. Janice was sent _____

10. When she grows up, she wants _____

b) *What would you do if you were Janice? Write 3–4 sentences in your exercise book.*

Lösung: 1 suddenly heard that someone or something was crying. 2 had been closed years before. 3 the outline of someone on the roof / a little boy on the roof and he was crying. 4 to climb up to the roof 5 was scared. 6 a bandage – her favourite joke. 7 she held the boy's hand / talked to him calmly like the doctors on the show. 8 invited to tell her story everywhere. 9 12 new ManU T-shirts from all over England. 10 to be a doctor or an actress.

© Ernst Klett Verlag GmbH, Stuttgart 2008. Alle Rechte vorbehalten.
ISBN 978-3-12-547143-6

GREEN LINE 3

KV 5a: A media survey

Write the results of your media survey in the grid.

Name:	Which kind of media do you like?	How much money do you spend on them?	How much time do you spend on them every week?
Your group:			
1.			
2.			
3.			
4.			
5.			
Adults:			
1.			
2.			
3.			
4.			
5.			

KV 5b: A media survey

Now present your media survey to your class. The following phrases can help you with your presentation. You can also use the Useful phrases on page 213 in your book and the word lists in your folder.

1. *How to start your presentation:*

   We asked … people about their media habits.
   Here are their answers./Here are the results of our media survey.
   Many …/Most of …/Only …

2. *How to give examples from your survey:*

   … people said that they like … best./… spend € … on …/… spend … hours on … every week.

3. *How to finish your presentation:*

   I am surprised that …/I think that …/I can't understand why …/For me …

_____

_____

_____

_____

_____

_____

_____

_____

_____

_____

KV 6a: A song: *Sk8er boi* by Avril Lavigne

a) *Read the lyrics of the song on page 88 in your book again. Make notes about the girl's situation in the past and in the future (keywords only!).*

In the past	In the future (five years from now)

b) *Write a short text about the girl's life (5–6 sentences). Use your notes from a).*

_____

_____

_____

_____

_____

_____

_____

_____

_____

_____

Lösungsvorschlag: In the past: ballet girl; wanted him as a friend but didn't tell him; her friends didn't like him; had a pretty face; thought she was better than him;   In the future: sits at home; has a baby; is alone; sees him on TV; calls her friends who already have tickets; stands in the crowd; looks up at him

KV 6b: A song: *Sk8er boi* by Avril Lavigne

a) *What are the differences between the girl and the boy? Fill in the grid (keywords only!).*

Girl	Boy

b) *Write a short text about why the two couldn't/cannot come together (5–6 sentences). Use your notes from a).*

_____

_____

_____

_____

_____

_____

_____

_____

Lösungsvorschlag: girl: ballet girl; pretty face; she didn't tell him she wanted him; had her head up in space; is a young mother; watches TV; is alone at home; looks up at the boy   boy: skater boy/punk; baggy clothes; he wanted her; worked on his career (not directly in the text); is a famous MTV star; is on TV; crowd is waiting for him; has his own show/is loved by his fans

KV 7: Stationenlernen Unit 5 (Wordwise)

Station 1: Horoscopes

a) *Have a look at the pictures and the names of the signs (you can use a dictionary). Which name goes with which picture? Cut out the cards and arrange them on a piece of paper.*
b) *Work with a partner. Find three sentences for each sign: One positive sentence, one sentence about an event/ action that will/won't have happened by the end of the week and one tip for the week. Write them next to the pictures.*

Example: 1. You're lucky! – This week you will meet your new boyfriend/girlfriend.
2. By the end of the week you will have sorted out your problems with someone in your family.
3. Don't be shy – talk about your feelings on Sunday!

Aries	Libra	Taurus	Scorpio	Gemini	Sagittarius
21 Mar – 20 Apr	24 Sept – 23 Oct	21 Apr – 21 May	24 Oct – 22 Nov	22 May – 21 June	23 Nov – 21 Dec
Cancer	Capricorn	Leo	Aquarius	Virgo	Pisces
22 June – 22 July	22 Dec – 20 Jan	23 July – 23 Aug	21 Jan – 19 Feb	24 Aug – 23 Sept	20 Feb – 20 Mar

✂ ....

Station 2: An ad

a) *Think of a product for which you would like to write an ad in a magazine. You can think of a funny product, too.*
b) *Make a mindmap with ideas.*
c) *Write the ad. Use pictures and/or sentences from real magazines that can help you.*

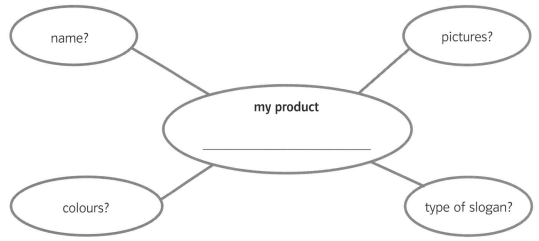

KV 8: Stationenlernen Unit 5 (Wordwise)

Station 3: Film news

a) *Think of three films you like or don't like. For each film make notes about:*
- *What happens in the film (It's a film about …)*
- *The place and time*
- *The actresses/actors*
- *Action*
- *Feelings*
- *Music*

b) *Think about the films again and grade¹ them: from 'not good' ☆ to 'very good' ☆☆☆.*
Explain why you like/don't like the films.

	Place and time	Actresses/Actors	Action	Feelings	Music	Personal opinion
Film 1						
Film 2						
Film 3						

Station 4: Chart news

a) *Write down your personal TOP TEN of English songs. Don't forget the titles and the names of the singers/bands.*
b) *Choose one of the songs. Give a short summary of what the song is about. Use your dictionary.*
c) *Add some information about the singer/band and/or the album.*
d) *Create a Chart news! page for your magazine. Use pictures, if you like.*

My Top Ten	
1	6
2	7
3	8
4	9
5	10

¹**(to) grade sb/sth** [greɪd] = jmdn./etw. benoten/bewerten

KV 9: Stationenlernen Unit 5 (Wordwise)

Station 5: A crossword puzzle

a) *Collect all the media words you know and write them on a piece of paper.*
b) *Arrange as many words as you can in a crossword puzzle.*
c) *Write down the German words in the puzzle and draw* ▶ ▼ *.*
d) *Cut out the puzzle, stick it on a piece of paper and design¹ it for your magazine. Don't forget the title.*

	Seifenoper ▼											
Drehbuch ▶												

¹**(to) design** [dɪˈzaɪn] = entwerfen, gestalten

KV 10: Stationenlernen Unit 5 (Wordwise)

Station 6: Problem corner

a) *Have a look at 'A letter to an agony aunt' on page 49 in your book. Read the letter and the answer.*
b) *Work with a partner. Think of a problem: at school, at home, with your friends … If you can't think of one yourself, choose from the following:*

Your parents seem to like your brother more than you. He always gets everything he wants. When you protest, they get angry.	Your best friend has become a couch potato, but you would like to go out and enjoy 'real life' with him/her.	Your friend had a fight with one of your other friends. You feel bad because you said something about him/her which is not true.

c) *Write your letter and the agony aunt's answer. Design¹ it for your magazine.*

Station 7: A picture story

a) *Create a picture story about a casting. Think of the kind of casting, who the people are and what happens.*
b) *Draw pictures and speech bubbles and write down short sentences to describe the situation.*
c) *Cut out the story and stick it on a piece of paper. Don't forget the title.*

¹(to) design [dɪˈzaɪn] = entwerfen, gestalten

KV 11: Stationenlernen Unit 5 (Wordwise)

Station 8: The interview of the week

a) *Work with a partner. Decide who is the interviewer and who is the star (singer, actor, model …).*
b) *Think of questions and answers. Take notes.*
c) *Write down the interview.*
d) *Cut out the interview and stick it on a piece of paper. Think of a headline and write a short paragraph with information about the star. Draw/Use pictures (from magazines) and design¹ the page.*

⑤ ?	② ?	⑧ ?
⑦ ?	③ ?	⑥ ?
④ ?		① ?

✂ ....

Station 9: The cover page

Design¹ the title/cover page for your magazine. Find a trendy title for it.

¹**(to) design** [dɪˈzaɪn] = entwerfen, gestalten

KV 12a: An advertising campaign[1] – A competition

a) *You and your group work for an advertising agency[2].*
You want to be in the competition for the best TV commercial for ...

TIP
For help look at pages 82, 84 and 123 in your book.

a mobile phone

or

a lemonade

or

an MP3 player

... for young people of your age. This grid can help you to decide on the different parts of your commercial:

Don't forget to find a name.	Create a short slogan that you can remember.
Who should buy your product?	How can you make it interesting for them?

You can ...		
... use something funny or cool:	... show a famous person:	... use something strange or unusual:
... tell a story (who? what? where?):	**PRODUCT**	... play a jingle:
... show everyday life[3]:	... inform about the product:	... ?

b) *Now think about what comes first, second, ... in your commercial. The storyboard in KV 12b can help you to plan the different steps. Collect the things you need and practise your commercial. You can make a video or present it in class. Vote for the best commercial. Have fun!*

[1]**advertising campaign** [ˈædvətaɪzɪŋ kæmˌpeɪn] = Werbekampagne • [2]**advertising agency** [ˈædvətaɪzɪŋ ˌeɪdʒnsi] = Werbeagentur • [3]**everyday life** [ˌevrɪdeɪ ˈlaɪf] = Alltag(sleben)

KV 12b: An advertising campaign – A competition

⟨Project⟩ P

⟨Project⟩ English and Geography

Seite 90–91

Ziele
- Den im Lehrwerk integrierten *skills*-Lehrgang erweitern und vertiefen
- Eine Wettervorhersage erstellen
- *Project skills*: Projektergebnisse präsentieren
- Ein Projekt über das Klima in GB durchführen

STEP 1

Text/Üben	**Find out about the weather**	Seite 90
Ziel	• Die regional unterschiedlichen Niederschlagsmengen in GB kennen lernen • Den Zusammenhang zwischen Niederschlagsmenge und Relief verstehen	
Wortschatz	*Viking, rainstorm, annual average rainfall total, atlas, relief, highland, lowland, area*	
Methodisches Vorgehen	• Die S lesen den Einführungstext und beantworten die Frage: *What is funny about the cartoon?* Anschließend leitet L durch eine weitere Frage zu den Teilaufgaben a) und b) über: *Yes, a lot of people think it always rains cats and dogs in Britain, but is that true?* • Die S bearbeiten die Teilaufgaben in PA; anschließend Besprechung der Ergebnisse im Plenum. L führt hierbei keine weiteren Fachtermini ein. Auch auf den Begriff *rain shadow* im TA kann verzichtet werden. Er bietet sich hier aber an und ist mit einem kleinen Diagramm an der Tafel leicht zu visualisieren. Die S kennen den Stoff bereits aus dem Erdkundeunterricht in Klasse 5 und 6.	
TA	<u>Does it rain cats and dogs everywhere in GB?</u> a) In the highland areas the annual average rainfall totals are higher. In the lowland areas it rains less. b) When the wet air from the west climbs over the highland areas in the west of Britain, there are clouds and it rains. In the lowland areas to the east there is less rain. They are in the rain shadow.	
Erweiterung	• Im Atlas suchen die S zum Vergleich die Niederschlagsmengen für deutsche Städte heraus: z. B. Berlin: 563 mm, Frankfurt: 601 mm, Hamburg: 726 mm, München: 855 mm, Stuttgart 677 mm.	
Lösung	*Siehe TA*	
Tipps für junge Lehrer	Es geht hier nicht darum, sämtliche Fachbegriffe auf Englisch kennen zu lernen, sondern die bisherigen Englischkenntnisse sinnvoll anzuwenden. Die Kenntnis einiger Fachbegriffe erleichtert jedoch das Unterrichtsgespräch: *You've already learnt about weather and climate in your Geography lessons. Try to use your English to explain what you want to say. But remember: Geography words make it easier to talk about the subject.* Die S können die Fachbegriffe in einem „Fachteil" ihrer Wortschatzsammlung bzw. in einer *mindmap* zusammenstellen. Für die Dauer des Projekts sollten den S ausreichend Wörterbücher zur Verfügung stehen.	**Material** Wörterbücher, Atlas

P ⟨Project⟩

STEP 2

Üben	**Collect weather words**	Seite 90

Ziel
- Die Definition des Begriffs „Wetter" kennen lernen
- *Weather words* in einer *mindmap* sammeln
- Das aktuelle Wetter beschreiben

Wortschatz *atmosphere*

Methodisches Vorgehen
- L liest den Einführungstext zu STEP 2 vor und führt die Definition des Begriffs „Wetter" ein: *It's what the atmosphere is like in one place at one time.*
- In PA bzw. in Kleingruppen sammeln die S *weather words* in einer *mindmap*.
- Mit dem gesammelten Wortschatz schreiben sie einen kurzen *weather report* über das aktuelle Wetter am Schulort.

Erweiterung
- Die S können den Bericht etwas interessanter als Radiobericht verfassen und anschließend vortragen. Beispiel: *Well, we hope it's not so cold where you are this morning, but here in Stuttgart it's just 8 °C. Looking out of the studio window, it's raining hard and lots of people are carrying umbrellas …*

Auch als HA geeignet

Lösung *Individuelle S-Antworten*

Tipps für junge Lehrer Es ist eine zusätzliche Motivation für die S, einen etwas trockenen Bericht über das Wetter *(excuse the pun!)* kreativ gestalten zu können.

STEP 3

ⓛ Üben	**Make a weather forecast**	Seite 90–91

HV-Text

Female DJ: *(mild Welsh accent)* … so thanks very much for all your e-mails. Now it's time to have a look at the weather with our sunny weatherman John Mills. Hello, John.

Weatherman: *(mild Welsh accent)* Hello, Susan, and good morning to our listeners. Here is the weather forecast for Wales for today, Monday the 14th of April. It will be cloudy over most of the country, with some sun in the South in the late afternoon. There will be heavy rain in the North this afternoon, and we may even see some thunderstorms in the mountains later this evening. Watch out for some strong winds on the north-west coast this evening, too. Tomorrow, things will be more or less the same, with a greater chance of sun throughout the country. That's all for now and now back to Susan in the studio.

Ziel
- Eine Wettervorhersage verstehen
- Die Regionen auf der Wetterkarte und einfache Wettersymbole kennen lernen
- Eine Wettervorhersage erstellen

Wortschatz *forecast, symbol, Met, light rain*

Methodisches Vorgehen
- *Pre-listening:*
  Die S überlegen sich ein *listening grid*, z. B. mit den Fragen: Where? Weather? When? (siehe TA).
- *While-listening:*
  L spielt die Wettervorhersage von CD ab. Beim zweiten Durchlauf machen sich die S Notizen in ihrem *listening grid*.
- *Post-listening:*
  Die S wiederholen anhand ihrer Notizen die Wettervorhersage in PA.

TIP
Einen deutschen Wetterbericht als Beispiel anführen

⟨Project⟩ P

- b) Im nächsten Schritt betrachten die S mit dem/der Partner/in die Wetterkarte mit den Regionen und Wettersymbolen auf S. 91 und fragen sich gegenseitig, z. B. *What's the weather like in Northern Scotland? There's some heavy rain.* Anschließend bearbeiten die S **KV 1: The different regions on the weather map**, Teilaufgabe a), indem sie die Karte annotieren: *Northern Scotland – heavy rain.*
- c) Die S nutzen die Ergebnisse von **KV 1**, Teilaufgabe a), und schreiben in **KV 1**, Teilaufgabe b), eine Wettervorhersage für das UK. Hierbei können ihnen die *Useful phrases* auf S. 90 helfen.
- d) Die S tragen ihre Wettervorhersage dem/der Partner/in vor. Dies könnte auch als PA-Kontrolle der Hausaufgabe zu Beginn der nächsten Stunde erfolgen.

Auch als HA geeignet

TA

Weather forecast for Wales: Monday 14th April					
Where?	most of Wales	South Wales	North Wales	in the mountains	north-west coast
Weather?	cloudy	some sun	heavy rain	thunderstorms	strong winds
When?	all day	late afternoon	afternoon	later in the evening	evening

Erweiterung
- Die S schreiben die Radio- bzw. TV-Wettervorhersage für ihre Heimatregion mit und versuchen, so viel wie möglich davon auf Englisch wiederzugeben. L weist die S darauf hin, dass es nicht notwendig ist, sich an den genauen Wortlaut zu halten.

Auch als HA geeignet

Material
◎L 3/26
Kopiervorlage 1

Lösung | a) Siehe TA   b)–d) Individuelle S-Antworten |

STEP 4

Üben **Give a presentation**   Seite 91

Ziel
- Projektergebnisse in geeigneter Form präsentieren
- *Useful phrases* für eine Präsentation sammeln

Wortschatz *introduction, (to) summarize*

Methodisches Vorgehen
- Auf den vorherigen *Project*-Doppelseiten haben die S die ersten *Project skills* kennen gelernt. In STEP 4 lernen die S nun als weiteres wichtiges *Project skill*, Ergebnisse in geeigneter Form zu präsentieren.
- Die S bearbeiten **KV 2: Project skills: Giving a presentation**. Dabei sollten sie ermuntert werden, bei Gelegenheit weitere *Useful phrases* zu ergänzen, z. B. *To start with …; First of all, I'd like to …; In conclusion …* etc. Sie können selbstverständlich auch eigene Listen anfertigen, wenn der Platz auf der Kopiervorlage nicht ausreicht.

TIP
Useful phrases: Giving a presentation sammeln

Auch als HA geeignet

Erweiterung
- Die S ergänzen noch in der Stunde **KV 2** durch weitere *Useful phrases.*

Lösung | *Siehe SB S. 91 und KV 2* |

Tipps für junge Lehrer
Die meisten S lernen nicht systematisch genug. Wenn sie *words* und *phrases* zu einem bestimmten Thema zusammenstellen, werden sie ihre Englischkenntnisse längerfristig erfolgreicher anwenden können.

Material
Kopiervorlage 2

STEP 5

| Üben | Do a project: Britain's climate | Seite 91 |

Ziel
- Ein Projekt zum Thema *Britain's climate* durchführen
- Die gelernten *Project skills* anwenden
- Kooperatives und soziales Arbeiten erleben

Wortschatz climate, sunshine

Methodisches Vorgehen
- L fragt nach dem Unterschied zwischen *weather* und *climate*.
- a) Die S bilden fünf Gruppen, die sich mit den fünf Regionen: *Northern* und *Southern England, Wales, Scotland* und *Northern Ireland* befassen.
- b)+c): L erinnert an das bereits erlernte *Project skill: Finding information on the Internet* (siehe S. 23). Innerhalb der Gruppen werden anschließend die Aufgaben verteilt: *annual rainfall, average temperature, hours of sunshine*. Als Hausaufgabe suchen die S auf der Internetseite des Met Office (www.metoffice.gov.uk) Informationen zu ihrer Region in Großbritannien und auf ähnlichen Seiten (z. B. Deutscher Wetterdienst: www.dwd.de) Informationen zum Klima in ihrer Heimatregion.
- In einer der folgenden Stunden tragen die Gruppen ihre Ergebnisse aus der Hausaufgabe zusammen und vergleichen das Klima in Großbritannien mit dem in ihrer Heimatregion. Anschließend besprechen sie den Präsentationsverlauf (*introduction, main ideas, summary*). Die Präsentation kann entweder als Einzel- oder als Gruppenvortrag erfolgen. Aus Gründen der Anschaulichkeit sollten sich die S Visualisierungsmöglichkeiten überlegen, z. B. Bilder, Karten, Balkendiagramme, usw.

> **TIP**
> Hilfreiche Internetseiten: www.metoffice.gov.uk und www.dwd.de (Deutscher Wetterdienst)

Erweiterung
- Eine der Gruppen könnte als „Filmcrew" eine kurze Dokumentation der Projektarbeit drehen. Die anschließende Präsentation in der Klasse oder an einem Elternabend bietet eine zusätzliche Motivation.

Lösung *Individuelle S-Antworten*

Tipps für junge Lehrer Zum Abschluss der drei *Project*-Doppelseiten sollten die S versuchen, bei diesem Projekt alle erlernten *Project skills* sinnvoll einzusetzen.

KV 1: The different regions on the weather map

a) *Look at the weather map and the weather symbols on page 41 in your book. Write down the name of the region and what the weather will be like.*

b) *Write a weather forecast for the United Kingdom.*

KV 2: Project skills: Giving a presentation

a) *What do you have to do to give a good presentation? Use the Project skills on page 91 in your book to help you to find the missing words.*

b) *Look at page 91 again. Write down Useful phrases for each presentation step. Add your own Useful phrases.*

Prepare your presentation	1. Collect _____ .
	2. _____ the information you have chosen.
Give your presentation	3. Start with an _____ .
	–
	–
	–
	4. _____ your information and ideas.
	–
	–
	–
	5. _____ the main points.
	–
	–
	–
	6. _____ questions.
	–
	–
	–

Lösung: 1 (important) information 2 organize 3 introduction 4 present 5 summarize 6 answer

GREEN LINE 3

Planung Unit 6

Übersicht

Bearbeitungszeitraum: 22 Unterrichtsstunden

Abschnitt	SB-Seiten	Ziele	Wortschatz/Grammatik & skills	WB-Übungen	CD-Tracks Kopiervorlagen Folien DVD	Gramm. Anhang (SB)
Check-in *Time to travel*	92–93	Berühmte Weltreisende kennen lernen Ein Gespräch über eine Reise nach Australien verstehen Eigene Wunschreiseziele präsentieren	Wortfeld *travelling*	S. 65/*ex.* 1, 2	Schüler-CD 2/17 Lehrer-CD 4/1, 2 KV 1	
Language 1 *To the ends of the earth*	94–95	Ein Gespräch über ein Computerspiel lesen und verstehen Berichten, was jemand gesagt hat Ein selbst verfasstes Interview als Rollenspiel einüben	Indirekte Rede mit *tense shift* Zeitangaben in der indirekten Rede	S. 66/*ex.* 3, 4 S. 67/*ex.* 5	Lehrer-CD 4/3–4 KV 2, 3 Folie 14	G23–25
Talkwise *Read the book, watch the film, play the game*	96	Einen Ratschlag erteilen Fragen zum Inhalt eines Mediums formulieren Empfehlungen aussprechen	*Useful phrases: Giving advice* Wortfeld *media*	S. 68/*ex.* 7, 8		
Language 2 *Emergency on the motorway*	97–99	Einen Unfallbericht verstehen Berichten, was jemand gefragt oder befohlen hat	Fragen und Aufforderungen in indirekter Rede *How to:* Hilfe in einem Notfall anfordern *R: Questions with prepositions*	S. 69/*ex.* 9–11 S. 70/*ex.* 12–14	Schüler-CD 2/18 Lehrer-CD 4/5, 6–8, 9 KV 4, 5	G 26–28
Skills *Small talk*	100	*Small talk* als wichtiges Element der Kommunikation kennen lernen und anwenden Im Gespräch Interesse zeigen Füllwörter in einem Gespräch heraushören und sammeln	*Speaking skills:* Plaudern Wortfeld *fillers*	S. 71/*ex.* 15, 16	Lehrer-CD 4/10 KV 6	
Text *My big adventure*	101–103	Eine Abenteuergeschichte lesen und verstehen Eine Textpassage in einen Dialog umwandeln	Das Leseverstehen üben *Writing texts:* Eigene narrative Texte interessanter gestalten	S. 72/*ex.* 17–19	Schüler-CD 2/19–22 Lehrer-CD 4/11–14, 15 KV 7, 8 Folie 15	

6

Abschnitt	SB-Seiten	Ziele	Wortschatz/Grammatik & skills	WB-Übungen	CD-Tracks Kopiervorlagen Folien DVD	Gramm. Anhang (SB)
Wordwise	104	Den Wortschatz der Unit umwälzen und vernetzen Unbekannte Wörter erschließen Wörter mit gleicher Aussprache richtig zuordnen	Wortfeld *travelling*	S. 73/*ex.* 21, 22	Lehrer-CD 4/16 KV 9	
Check-out	105	Selbstkontrolle Die Lernziele der Unit 6 überprüfen *Green Line* 3 kritisch reflektieren	Wortschatz- und Grammatikschwerpunkte der Unit: Wortfeld *travelling*, *small talk*, indirekte Rede in Aussage-, Frage- und Aufforderungssätzen	S. 74/*ex.* 23, 24	KV 10	
⟨Text⟩ *Treasure Island*	106–107	Einen Auszug aus einem (klassischen) Abenteuerroman lesen und verstehen	Das Leseverstehen schulen		Schüler-CD 2/23–26 Lehrer-CD 4/17–20 KV 11	

Unit 6 Time to travel

Hinweise

LANDESKUNDE

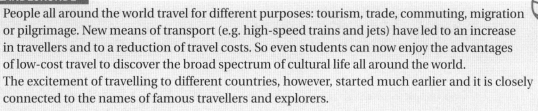

People all around the world travel for different purposes: tourism, trade, commuting, migration or pilgrimage. New means of transport (e.g. high-speed trains and jets) have led to an increase in travellers and to a reduction of travel costs. So even students can now enjoy the advantages of low-cost travel to discover the broad spectrum of cultural life all around the world.
The excitement of travelling to different countries, however, started much earlier and it is closely connected to the names of famous travellers and explorers.

Marco Polo
Marco Polo (1254–1324) is probably the most famous European who travelled on the Silk Road through Asia and who, according to his own account, went further than any of his predecessors. On his 24-year voyage he travelled beyond Mongolia to China where he became a confidant of Emperor Kublai Khan. On special missions in China, Burma and India he saw many places which no European would set foot on for the next centuries.
After returning home to Italy, Marco Polo dictated the story of his travels, known in his time as *The Description of the World* or *The Travels of Marco Polo*. Many of his stories have been considered fairy tales: e.g. the monstrous birds which drop elephants from a height and devour their broken carcasses. However, his account of the wealth of China, the might of the Mongol empire, and the exotic customs of India and Africa became one of the most popular books in medieval Europe. It paved the way for the arrival of thousands of Europeans in the centuries to come.

James Cook
Captain James Cook (1728–1779), the pioneer of modern travelling, was an English explorer, navigator and cartographer. He was the first European who reached the eastern coastline of Australia and the Hawaiian Islands, and the first to circumnavigate New Zealand. Cook charted many areas and recorded several islands and coastlines on European maps for the first time. Thus he contributed much to the European knowledge of the area. He died in Hawaii in a fight with native inhabitants during his third exploratory voyage to the Pacific in 1779.

Charles Darwin
Charles Robert Darwin (1809–1882) was an English naturalist and biologist. He proposed and provided scientific evidence that all species of life have evolved over the ages from common ancestors through a process he called 'natural selection'. Darwin developed his interest in natural history while studying first medicine at Edinburgh University and then theology at Cambridge. His five-year voyage on the 'Beagle' established him as a biologist and the publication of his journal of the voyage made him famous as a popular author.

Gladys Aylward
Gladys Aylward (1902–1970) was born of a working-class family in Edmonton, London. Although forced into domestic service at an early age, she had always wanted to go overseas as a missionary. In 1930, she spent her life savings on a passage to Yuncheng, Shanxi Province, China, where she founded 'The Inn of the Eight Happinesses' in a remote and backward area. The inn was a regular overnight stopping place for muleteers who passed through Yuncheng. Every evening when the muleteers were resting, Gladys Aylward told them stories from the Bible.
In 1938, the region was invaded by Japanese forces, and Aylward led 94 children to safety over the mountains. She remained in China after World War II, but in 1947 she had to move back to England because of serious health problems. When she finally decided to return to China, she was denied re-entry by the Communist Chinese government and settled in Taiwan in 1953.

Neil Armstrong
Neil Alden Armstrong, born August 5, 1930 is a former American test pilot, university professor, and United States Naval Aviator. His second and last spaceflight was as mission commander of the

6 Check-in

Apollo 11 moon landing mission on July 20, 1969. When Armstrong placed his left foot on the surface of the moon, he spoke his famous words: "That's one small step for [a] man, one giant leap for mankind."

Ellen MacArthur
Dame Ellen Patricia MacArthur, born July 8, 1976 is an English yachtswoman from Whatstandwell near Matlock in Derbyshire. She is best known as a solo long-distance yachtswoman. On February 7, 2005 she broke the world record for the fastest solo circumnavigation of the globe, a feat which cemented her international renown. Francis Joyon, the Frenchman who had held the record before MacArthur, recovered it in early 2008.

STORYLINE

In dieser Unit spielt das Reisen um die Welt eine zentrale Rolle. Die S lernen verschiedene Formen des Reisens kennen. Darüber hinaus führt die Unit in Notfallsituationen auf Reisen ein und gibt den S Redemittel für Smalltalk an die Hand. Die S lesen eine Abenteuergeschichte, die an den Roman "In 80 Tagen um die Welt" von Jules Verne angelehnt ist. Auch der zweite Text, ein Auszug aus dem Buch „Die Schatzinsel", ist eine Abenteuergeschichte, die von Segelschiffen und Piraten handelt.

Check-in
Seite 92–93

Ziele
- Berühmte Weltreisende kennen lernen
- Ein Gespräch über eine Reise nach Australien verstehen
- Eigene Wunschreiseziele präsentieren

| Text/Fotos | **Time to travel** | *Seite 92–93* |

Ziel
- Fotos beschreiben und Bezug zum Thema der Unit herstellen
- Informationen über berühmte Weltreisende lesen und verstehen

Wortschatz *traveller, journey, noodle, plant, evolution, missionary, moon, step, giant, leap, mankind, challenge, to take, first language, per cent*

Methodisches Vorgehen
- Als Einstieg in die Unit lässt L mit Hilfe von **KV 1: Time to travel**, *ex.* a), die S eine *mindmap* zum Thema *travelling* erstellen. Da die S auch in *Green Line* 1 und 2 immer wieder Vokabular zu diesem Wortfeld kennen gelernt haben, werden sie zahlreiche Wörter finden, die sie reaktivieren können.
- Alternative: L vergibt bereits 2–3 Wochen vor Beginn der Arbeit an der Unit kleine Referate über die im SB genannten Persönlichkeiten. Die Ergebnisse können im Anschluss an eine kurze Wortschatzarbeit (*mindmap*, siehe **KV 1**, *ex.* a)) oder nach einer Beschreibung der Bilder im SB präsentiert werden.
- Die S beschreiben im Unterrichtsgespräch die Bilder auf der *Check-in*-Doppelseite (*Describe what you can see on page 92–93./What is shown in the pictures?*). Anschließend lesen die S die Texte über berühmte Weltreisende und deren Unternehmungen. Da die S nun schon gewohnt sind, Texte eigenständig zu erschließen, kann auf eine Semantisierung des unbekannten Vokabulars verzichtet werden. Zur Sicherung des Leseverständnisses bietet sich **KV 1**, *ex.* b), an.
- Alternative: L stellt Fragen zum Textverständnis, z. B. *How did Ellen MacArthur travel around the world? How long did Marco Polo travel through Asia? Who was the first person on the moon? What was Gladys Aylward's job?* Eine weitere Möglichkeit wäre es, die Jahreszahlen an die Tafel zu schreiben und die S bei geschlossenem SB die wichtigsten Fakten noch einmal kurz zusammenfassen zu lassen.

	Check-in 6

- L stellt den S die Frage, welche Rolle Englisch in ihrem Alltag spielt. Wichtige Punkte werden an der Tafel gesammelt. Anschließend Lesen der *Did you know?*-Box und Ergänzung des TA.

TA

English: a world language
- computer games
- chatrooms
- music
- used by young people (cool, trendy etc.)
- Internet (more than 85 per cent of all messages)
- first language: more than 330 million people, official language: 400 million people
- more learners than any other language

Tipps für junge Lehrer Wenn am Ende des Schuljahres genügend Zeit bleibt, kann in interessierten Lerngruppen aus der Thematik auch eine Gruppen-/Projektarbeit entstehen, in der verschiedene Weltreisende und deren Unternehmungen dargestellt werden. Wünschenswert ist dabei, dass es sich um Reisen im englischsprachigen Raum handelt *(Commonwealth countries)*. Andere Fächer wie Geschichte oder Erdkunde könnten hier in die Arbeit miteinbezogen werden.

Material
Kopiervorlage 1

Üben 1 Find headings for the photos Seite 92

Ziel
- Passende Überschriften zu den Fotos finden und in der Klasse vergleichen

Methodisches Vorgehen
- Die S bearbeiten die Aufgabe zunächst in Einzelarbeit, um möglichst viele verschiedene Vorschläge für Überschriften zu erhalten. Anschließend Vergleich der Ergebnisse im Plenum.
- Alternative: Die Aufgabe wird im Rahmen der Bildbeschreibung (siehe oben) mündlich durchgeführt. Anschließend leitet L zu den Informationen über die Weltreisenden über.

Lösung *Erwartungshorizont:* A *Holidays* B *Business trip* C *Arrival in a new world* D *A trip to the moon* E *Adventure trip*

Üben 2 Talk about journeys Seite 92

Ziel
- Über Gründe für das Reisen in Vergangenheit und Gegenwart sprechen

Methodisches Vorgehen
- L stellt den Arbeitsauftrag kurz vor, dann bearbeiten die S beide Teilaufgaben in PA. Dabei können die S ihre Ergebnisse in einer Tabelle festhalten (siehe TA). Die Sicherung der Ergebnisse erfolgt an der Tafel oder auf Folie.
- Alternative: Die Aufgaben werden in arbeitsteiliger GA erledigt. Die vier Gruppen bearbeiten jeweils eine Teilfrage (siehe TA): 1. *Reasons for travelling in the past* 2. *Reasons for travelling in the present* 3. *Journeys in the past* 4. *Journeys in the present*. Die Ergebnisse werden auf vier Folienstücken präsentiert, die nebeneinander gelegt werden. Die Überschriften wurden zuvor von L auf der Folie eingetragen.

TA

Reasons for travelling in the past	Reasons for travelling in the present
People were looking for adventures and wanted to discover the world.	People are looking for better jobs.
People wanted to find out more about other people, plants and animals.	People want to learn more about other cultures.
People wanted to help in other countries (missionaries).	People want to relax in their holidays.
	People want to help poor countries.

6 Check-in

> **Journeys in the past**
> Trips took very long.
> Transport was difficult and much slower than today.
> Journeys cost a lot of money, so only rich people could travel a lot.
> Wars made trips very dangerous.
> People were not allowed to go wherever they wanted.
> …

> **Journeys in the present**
> Trips don't take long.
> Journeys are not very expensive.
> Many people can go on holidays because it is not expensive.
> For many countries you only need your passport.
> …

Tipps für junge Lehrer Damit die Gruppen effektiver arbeiten können, bietet es sich an, die Klasse in acht Gruppen einzuteilen und die Aufgaben doppelt zu belegen. Bei der anschließenden Präsentation ergänzen die „Kontrollgruppen" ggf. die Ergebnisse der jeweils anderen Gruppe. Alternativ wäre innerhalb der Großgruppen die Bearbeitung der Aufgaben in PA möglich. Hierbei wird jeweils eines der Schülerpaare aufgefordert, Ergebnisse auf der Folie einzutragen.

Material
Workbook S. 65/1
Ggf. Leerfolie

Üben

3 Listening: A trip to Australia

Seite 92

HV-Text

Ryan: Where, Dad? Australia?!
Father: Yes, I have to go and work there for two weeks. I wasn't expecting it. Someone else from the office was planning to go, but she's ill, so I'm taking her place at the last minute.
Ryan: At the last minute? Does that mean you're going soon?
Father: Yes. The day after your birthday.
Ryan: Oh, next Wednesday. Wow, you're so lucky, Dad! I'd love to go to Australia.
Father: Yes, I'm sure it'll be interesting. I've never been there before. The only thing I'm not so happy about is the flight.
Ryan: Why? What's the problem with the flight?
Father: It's so long. It takes twenty-four hours to fly from the UK to Australia.
Ryan: That's nothing! That's only one day. I mean, it took Captain Cook eight months to get there! We're learning about him in History at the moment.
Father: Good! I'm glad to see you're learning *something* at school!
Ryan: Dad!
Father: Just joking! Anyway, if I had to go to Australia by ship, I wouldn't go at all!
Ryan: And you wouldn't *want* to go in one of those old ships, I can tell you! It was terrible! There was no fresh food, so people became ill and their teeth fell out. Some people died on long voyages, and …
Father: Well, I don't expect to die on my trip! But planes aren't very good for you, you know. I mean it isn't healthy to sit for a long time with not much room for your legs.
Ryan: You can do some of Mum's relaxation exercises, can't you? I wouldn't worry about a long flight, I can tell you! If I had the chance, I'd be on that plane with you. I never get the chance to travel anywhere.
Father: Yes, you do. You're going to France next month!
Ryan: Oh yes. The school trip to France. I'd forgotten about that.
Father: You were really excited about it yesterday.
Ryan: I know. It's just that if I had to choose one country in the world that I could visit, it would be Australia. Don't forget to take a camera, Dad. And hey, how hot will it be at this time of year? I mean, the seasons are different there, aren't they? And do you think you'll have time to …

Ziel • Einem Gespräch über eine Reise zielgerichtet Informationen entnehmen

| | | Check-in | Language 1 | 6 |

Methodisches Vorgehen	*Pre-listening:* • L leitet zum HV-Text über (*You will now hear a dialogue between Ryan and his father. It's about a trip to Australia.*) und gibt den S einige Minuten Zeit zum Lesen der Höraufträge. *While-listening:* • Die S hören den Dialog bei geschlossenem SB und machen sich Notizen zu den einzelnen Höraufträgen. *Post-listening:* • Nach zweimaligem Hören Vergleich der Ergebnisse im Plenum. Die S ergänzen ggf. ihre Notizen. • In leistungsschwächeren Lerngruppen sammelt L die Ergebnisse an der Tafel und spielt anschließend den Dialog noch einmal vor.
Lösung	1 Ryan's father is going to Australia because someone else from the office is ill. 2 He is not so happy about the long flight – 24 hours on the plane. 3 The journey took eight months and many people got ill. 4 Ryan is going on a school trip to France.
Tipps für junge Lehrer	Die S können sich einen solchen Dialog auch anhand der *wh*-Fragen erschließen. Hierzu schreiben die S die *question words* auf ihren Stichwortzettel und ordnen die Informationen entsprechend zu.

Material
◎s 2/17
◎L 4/1, 2
Workbook S. 65/2

Üben	**4 Your turn: See the world** Seite 93
Ziel	• Ein Wunschreiseziel präsentieren und dessen Auswahl begründen
Methodisches Vorgehen	• Die Vorbereitung der Aufgabe eignet sich als Hausaufgabe. Die S zeigen Fotos, die sie z. B. aus dem Internet oder im Reisebüro gesammelt haben. Sinnvoll ist es, eine kleine Collage anfertigen zu lassen, auf der die S auch die Gründe für ihre Wahl des Reiseziels schriftlich fixieren können. Wenn der Klassenraum über Pinnwände o. Ä. verfügt, können die S ihre Fotos für die Dauer der Unterrichtsreihe im Klassenraum aufhängen.
Erweiterung	• Die Aufgabe kann auch als Grundlage für Präsentationen/Referate einzelner S oder Kleingruppen dienen. In diesem Fall zeigen die S nicht nur Fotos, sondern sammeln auch Hintergrundinformationen (z. B. Größe, Bevölkerung, Geographie, Tierwelt, Klima) zu dem von ihnen ausgewählten Reiseziel.
Lösung	*Individuelle S-Antworten*

HA

TIP
Umfang der Präsentationen hängt von der zur Verfügung stehenden Zeit ab

Material
Fotos, Pappe, Kleber

Language 1
Seite 94–95

Ziele
• Ein Gespräch über ein Computerspiel lesen und verstehen
• Die Regeln zu Bildung und Gebrauch der indirekten Rede in Aussagesätzen kennen lernen und anwenden

◎L Text   **To the ends of the earth**   Seite 94

Ziel	• Ein Gespräch über ein Computerspiel lesen und verstehen
Wortschatz	*reporting what someone said, to mention, disappointing, to get bored*

6 Language 1

Strukturen	• *Indirect speech with tense shift in statements*
Methodisches Vorgehen	• Bevor die Texte gelesen werden, führt L kurz in die Situation ein: *Four young people talk about the same computer game: First you're going to hear Ryan and Jade when they meet at the shops. Then you're going to hear two phone calls: Ben talks to Ryan, and Kelly talks to Jade.* In verteilten Rollen können nun zunächst die Sprechblasen und dann der Dialog zwischen Ryan und Jade vorgelesen werden. Anschließend leitet L zu *ex.* 1 über.
	• Alternative: Bei geschlossenem SB präsentiert L den Dialog von CD. Anschließend geben die S zunächst den Inhalt wieder. Grundlage können wieder die fünf *wh*-Fragen sein. Dann leitet L zu *ex.* 1 über.

TIP
Die *tenses* wiederholen

Material
◎ L 4/3–4

Üben 1 What do you think?   Seite 94

Ziel	• Einen Ratschlag erteilen und begründen
Methodisches Vorgehen	• Diese Aufgabe bezieht sich auf die inhaltliche Sicherung des Textes. Die S werden in einem kurzen Unterrichtsgespräch aufgefordert, Ryan einen Ratschlag zu erteilen und diesen zu begründen.

TIP
Als mündliche Aufgabe geeignet

Lösung

> *Erwartungshorizont:*
> – *I wouldn't buy the computer game, because it sounds very boring to me, too. Maybe Ryan can ask Nick to lend it to him. I think he should buy another computer game with his money.*
> – *I think Ryan should buy the computer game. Sometimes girls and boys don't like the same things, so I think that Ryan should try it out.*

Üben 2 Find the rule   Seite 94

Ziel	• Den *tense shift* von direkter zu indirekter Rede erkennen und systematisieren
	• Verben zur Einleitung der indirekten Rede sammeln
Wortschatz	*to report, to introduce, direct speech, indirect speech*
Strukturen	• *Indirect speech with tense shift in statements*
Methodisches Vorgehen	• a) Die S erstellen in Einzelarbeit eine Tabelle nach dem Muster im SB. Anschließend Sammeln der Ergebnisse an der Tafel/auf Folie.
	• b) L fordert die S auf, Regeln zum *tense shift* zu formulieren. Diese werden ebenfalls an der Tafel/auf Folie festgehalten.
	• c) Sammeln von Verben zur Einführung der indirekten Rede an der Tafel/auf Folie.
	• Alternative: Die S sammeln die Veränderungen in a) gemeinsam und formulieren anschließend die Regeln im Plenum.

TIP
G 23, 24

TA Siehe Lösung

Lösung

a) *direct speech* ⟶ *indirect speech*

Ben	*Ryan*
is	*was*
I	*he*
have played	*had played*
borrowed	*had borrowed*
had promised	*had promised*
am going to buy	*was going to buy*
can	*could*
will love	*would love*

Language 1 | 6

Kelly	Jade
lent	had lent
me	her
was disappointing	was disappointing
got bored	had got bored
went back	had gone back
am reading	was reading

b) *Tenses change from*
  simple present → past
  present perfect → past perfect
  simple past → past perfect
  past perfect → past perfect
  can → could
  will → would
  present progressive → past progressive

c) *to say, to tell (sb), to mention, to think, …*

Tipps für junge Lehrer L sollte unbedingt auf die Besonderheit beim Verb *to tell* hinweisen, da dies für die S eine häufige Fehlerquelle ist.

Material
Ggf. Leerfolie

Üben **3 An interview with Ellen MacArthur** Seite 95

Ziel • Die Regel für die Bildung der indirekten Rede anwenden und festigen

Wortschatz *welcome*

Strukturen • *Indirect speech with tense shift in statements*

Methodisches Vorgehen • Die Aufgabe eignet sich als erste Festigung der in *ex.* 2 erarbeiteten Regeln zur indirekten Rede. Dabei wird b) vor allem von leistungsstärkeren S erledigt werden können. Da die Aufgabe sehr umfangreich ist, sollte sie nicht komplett als schriftliche Aufgabe gegeben werden.

Auch als HA geeignet

Lösung
> Ellen told the reporter she was very tired after her trip. She explained that she had sailed through some terrible storms, so she hadn't got the chance to sleep much. She said she felt excited, and couldn't believe that she had broken the world record. She thought she would never forget her welcome home because thousands of people had come to see her. She told the reporter that she had no idea what her next challenge would be, and that she didn't even want to think about it yet. She explained that the first thing she was going to do was sleep.

Erweiterung • **Folie 14: What did he say?** übt die indirekte Rede mit Zeitverschiebung.

Material
Workbook S. 66/3
Folie 14

Üben **4 An e-mail from Ryan's father** Seite 95

Ziel • Die Regeln für die Bildung der indirekten Rede anwenden und festigen
  • Die Veränderung von Zeitangaben in der indirekten Rede kennen lernen

Wortschatz *two days earlier, the day before, to ask about sb/sth*

Strukturen • *Indirect speech with tense shift, expressions of time in indirect speech*

TIP
G 24, 25

Methodisches Vorgehen • Nach einer kurzen Erläuterung zu weiteren Verschiebungen in der indirekten Rede (vgl. G 24 und 25) können die S diese Aufgabe schriftlich in Einzelarbeit oder PA erledigen.

Auch als HA geeignet

Erweiterung • Zur Festigung und Vertiefung bietet sich **KV 2: Computer games** an.

6 Language 1

Lösung

> My dad sent an e-mail from Australia last week. He said that it was warm but not too hot there, because it was June and the winter was starting. He wrote that the day before he had been in the office, but that day he had had time for sightseeing. He told me that that morning he took a boat round Sydney harbour and under the famous bridge. He explained that the next day he was planning to visit Bondi Beach, but he said he wouldn't go swimming because two days earlier someone had seen a shark! He explained that he was glad that he remembered to take a camera – he had got some great photos. He wrote one day I would be able to go to Australia myself!

Material
Workbook S. 66/4, 67/5
Kopiervorlage 2
Ggf. Leerfolie

Tipps für junge Lehrer
Aus zeitökonomischen Gründen kann L eine Folie vorbereiten, auf der nur die Zeitverschiebungen eingetragen werden.

Üben

5 Role play: Around the world

Seite 95

Ziel
- In einem Interview über die Aktivitäten einer berühmten Persönlichkeit sprechen
- Als Reporter über das Interview berichten

Strukturen
- *Indirect speech with tense shift*

Methodisches Vorgehen
- a) Bei dieser Aufgabe sind Fertigkeiten von den S gefordert, die über das bloße Üben der neuen Strukturen hinausgehen. Zunächst macht sich jede/r S in einer kurzen Einzelarbeitsphase Notizen, die als Grundlage für das nachfolgende Gespräch dienen. Anschließend spielen jeweils zwei S den Dialog nach. Dabei macht sich der/die Reporter/in Notizen zu dem, was die berühmte Persönlichkeit gesagt hat. Mit Hilfe der Unterlagen kann der/die Reporter/in danach unter Verwendung der indirekten Rede die Klasse über die Inhalte des Interviews informieren.
- c) Nachdem mehrere Interviews vorgespielt wurden, kann sich eine kurze Reflexionsphase anschließen, in der die S ihre Meinung zu den Interviews äußern. Leistungsschwächeren S sollte dabei die Möglichkeit gegeben werden, sich vorab Notizen zu ihrer persönlichen Stellungnahme zu machen.
- Bei der Bearbeitung der Aufgabe kann leistungsschwächeren S zusätzlich **KV 3: An interview** als Hilfestellung angeboten werden. Die S können entweder im Plenum über den Inhalt des vorgegebenen Interviews berichten oder durch kleine Änderungen ein neues Interview verfassen.

TIP
KV 3 zur Differenzierung geeignet

Lösung

> Individuelle S-Antworten

Tipps für junge Lehrer
Je nach Leistungsbereitschaft können die Telefongespräche in der Klasse nachgespielt werden, d. h. zwei S setzen sich Rücken an Rücken und verwenden ausgeschaltete Handys, um das Telefoninterview möglichst authentisch nachzuspielen. Diese Vorgehensweise ist deutlich anspruchsvoller, als wenn die S nebeneinander sitzen.

Material
Kopiervorlage 3
Ggf. ausgeschaltete Handys

| | | Talkwise | 6 |

Talkwise
Seite 96

Ziele
- Verschiedene Arten von Büchern, Filmen und Computerspielen zuordnen
- *Useful phrases* zur Formulierung von Ratschlägen sammeln
- Ratschläge erteilen
- Empfehlungen aussprechen

| Üben | **Read the book, watch the film, play the game** | Seite 96 |

Hinweis Als Vorbereitung zu dieser Unterrichtsstunde kann L die S auffordern, eigene Bücher, Filme oder Computerspiele mitzubringen.

Wortschatz *giving advice*

| Üben | **1 What kind of books, films and games are these?** | Seite 96 |

Ziel
- Verschiedene Arten von Büchern, Filmen und Computerspielen zuordnen

Wortschatz *biography, comedy*

Methodisches Vorgehen
- Die S schauen sich zunächst in Einzelarbeit die Abbildungen der verschiedenen Bücher, Filme und Computerspiele an und lesen die Begriffe rechts neben den Abbildungen. L erläutert ggf. unbekanntes Vokabular (*comedy: it's nearly the same word in German – a very funny film where people laugh a lot; biography: the German word is also nearly the same – it's about the life of a famous person*). Anschließend ordnen die S den Abbildungen die entsprechenden Begriffe zu. In leistungsstärkeren Lerngruppen kann auf die Einzelarbeit zu Beginn verzichtet werden.

Erweiterung
- Wenn die S selbst eigene Bücher, Filme oder Computerspiele mitgebracht haben, können diese jetzt im Unterrichtsgespräch einer der Kategorien zugeordnet werden.
- Ergänzend können die S aufgefordert werden, den Inhalt eines ausgewählten Mediums kurz zu beschreiben.

Lösung
a) *The Life of Marco Polo – biography; The Heart Speaks – love story; Dark Secret – thriller; Kill or Die – battle game; Road King – car game; Champion! – sports game; Aliens – science fiction film; Fun Farm – comedy; Shy Pirate – action film*
b) *Individuelle S-Antworten*

Tipps für junge Lehrer Es sollte darauf geachtet werden, dass die S nicht zu ausführlich beschreiben, da hierdurch die Zeit für das eigentliche Thema der Stunde (*giving advice*) nicht ausreichen würde. Alternativ veranschlagt L zwei Stunden für die *Talkwise*-Seite.

Material Workbook S. 68/7 Filme/Bücher/ Computerspiele

| Üben | **2 Collect phrases that give advice about things** | Seite 96 |

Ziel
- *Useful phrases* zur Formulierung von Ratschlägen sammeln

Wortschatz *to recommend*

Methodisches Vorgehen
- Die Aufgabe wird im Plenum erarbeitet. Zunächst lesen zwei S die beiden Kommentare, anschließend werden die *Useful phrases* an der Tafel gesammelt. In leistungsschwächeren Lerngruppen sollte L ein Beispiel vorgeben (*You should ...*) und auch das Verb *to recommend* semantisieren (*to tell sb that a book/film is good and he/she should read/watch it*). Gemeinsam können weitere Ausdrücke ergänzt werden (siehe TA).

6 Talkwise

TA

> **Useful phrases: giving advice**
> You should .../shouldn't ...
> I'd recommend ...
> I'm sure you'd love it.
> If I were you, I would/wouldn't ...
> If you want my advice ...
> ...

Erweiterung
- Obwohl der Schwerpunkt der *Talkwise*-Seite auf der mündlichen Arbeit liegt, sollten die S die *Useful phrases* in ihren *folder* übertragen, da diese Formulierungen auch später immer wieder verwendet werden können.
- Zur Festigung formulieren die S Empfehlungen zu den mitgebrachten Büchern/Filmen/Computerspielen. Der TA kann dabei als Hilfestellung dienen.

Lösung Siehe TA

Üben **3 What can you ask?** Seite 96

Ziel
- Fragen zum Inhalt von Büchern, Filmen und Computerspielen formulieren

Wortschatz *Who's in it?*

Methodisches Vorgehen
- Aus zeitökonomischen Gründen können die S in drei Gruppen (oder sechs Gruppen, von denen je zwei die gleiche Aufgabe erhalten) eingeteilt werden; jede Gruppe bearbeitet ein Medium (Bücher, Filme, Computerspiele). Die einzelnen Gruppen erhalten vorbereitete Folienstücke, auf denen sie ihre Fragen fixieren und anschließend im Plenum vorstellen.

TIP
Eigene Materialien mitbringen

TA

Books	Films	Computer games
What's it about?	What kind of film is it?	What do you have to do?
Is it easy to read?	Who's in it?	Is it exciting?
Is it for young people only?	Are the actors good?	Can you play it with a friend or only alone?
What other books has the author written?	How long is the film?	How much is it?
	Was it a success?	

Lösung Siehe TA

Tipps für junge Lehrer Zur Ergebnissicherung kann L die Folien anschließend als Arbeitsblatt für die S kopieren. Das hat den Vorteil, dass keine Zeit für die schriftliche Sicherung eingeplant werden muss, sondern die S sofort mit der nächsten Aufgabe fortfahren können.

Material
Workbook S. 68/8
Ggf. Leerfolie

Üben **4 Your turn: What would you recommend?** Seite 96

Ziel
- Empfehlungen aussprechen und begründen
- Informationen über Bücher, Filme und Computerspiele erfragen

Methodisches Vorgehen
- Die S finden sich in kleinen Gruppen zusammen (Aufteilung aus vorheriger GA, siehe *ex.* 3) und sprechen über Bücher, Filme und Computerspiele, die sie kennen. Der TA bzw. die Folien können dabei als Unterstützung dienen. Idealerweise stehen die beschriebenen Medien in der Stunde zur Verfügung. Dies erhöht die Anschaulichkeit und damit die Motivation der S.
- Alternative: Es ist auch eine Besprechung im Plenum denkbar. Allerdings könnten sich hier nicht so viele S aktiv beteiligen, wie dies in der Gruppe der Fall ist.

Erweiterung	• Neben den oben genannten Medien können die S auch ihre bevorzugten CDs/ Musikvideos vorstellen. Die Aufgabe, Empfehlungen auszusprechen, kann anhand zahlreicher weiterer Themen geübt werden (z. B. Zeitschriften/Magazine, Sportarten).	Auch als HA geeignet
Lösung	*Individuelle S-Antworten*	
Tipps für junge Lehrer	L sollte darauf achten, dass die S wirklich Englisch sprechen und vor allem auch Fragen in der Fremdsprache formuliert werden.	

Language 2

Seite 97–99

Ziele
- Einen Unfallbericht lesen und verstehen
- Berichten, was jemand gefragt oder befohlen hat
- Hilfe in einem Notfall anfordern

ⓞL Text	**Emergency on the motorway**	Seite 97
Ziel	• Einen Unfallbericht lesen und verstehen	
Wortschatz	*coach, police officer, dangerous, chemical, to warn sb, service, paramedic, whether, firefighter, area, to advise (sb to do sth)*	
Methodisches Vorgehen	• Als Einstimmung in die Thematik fordert L die S auf, über Unfälle zu berichten, die sie schon erlebt haben. Anschließend präsentiert L den Unfallbericht von CD, die S lesen mit. In leistungsschwächeren Lerngruppen sollte L die für das Verständnis wichtigen neuen Wörter semantisieren und an der Tafel festhalten *(coach: it's a big bus; dangerous is the opposite of safe; chemical: the word is nearly the same in German* (evtl. auf deutschen Begriff verweisen)*; paramedics help doctors in an ambulance to take care of people; firefighters are people who fight against a fire)*. • Alternative: In leistungsstärkeren Lerngruppen präsentiert L den Unfallbericht bei geschlossenem SB ohne Vorentlastung, zumal so der höchste Grad an Authentizität erreicht wird. Ggf. kann der Bericht ein zweites Mal angehört werden, bevor die S *ex.* 1 bearbeiten.	
Tipps für junge Lehrer	Auch wenn die S nicht auf Anhieb alles verstehen, sollte der Unfallbericht zunächst bei geschlossenem SB vorgespielt werden. Dies ist nicht nur im Hinblick auf die Authentizität, sondern auch auf die Schulung des Hörverstehens die wirkungsvollere Methode.	Material ⓞL 4/5

!

TIPPS VON MARIO RINVOLUCRI – THE ALTERNATIVE WAY

From blank page to reading text
Emergency on the motorway (p. 97)

a) Tell each pupil to take a blank sheet of paper.
Tell the pupils that the page has a transcript of a TV reporter's script, written on it in invisible ink. The story is about a lorry, a coach and a crash on the motorway.

6 Language 2

> Ask them to stare at the page until, here and there, some words become visible.
> Ask them to write down 10–12 of these words wherever they 'appear' on the page.
>
> b) Tell the pupils to swap papers with a partner. They now try and write the whole passage from the words their partner has 'seen' and written down.
>
> c) Ask four or five pupils round the group to read out what they have written to the whole class.
>
> d) The pupils open their books on p. 97 so that they can compare their texts to the book text.
>
> *Pluses:* The pupils shock themselves with how well their imaginations work when confronted with a page of invisible writing! This is a joyous exercise.
>
> *Minuses:* Many teachers find it hard to believe this mechanism will work in *anybody's* class, let alone in theirs. I have to admit that when I first tried the activity I had my heart in my mouth and was ready with something else to do, should the activity go pear-shaped. Instead it went swimmingly. The exercise is unlikely to work well unless the class is decently warmed up.
>
> *Acknowledgement:* This exercise is developed from an idea in *Vocabulary*, John Morgan et al., Oxford University Press, 2004 (2nd edition).

Üben — **1 What can you remember?** — Seite 97

Ziel
- Informationen über den Unfallhergang wiedergeben
- Das momentane Geschehen beschreiben

Methodisches Vorgehen
- Die Aufgabe kann im Plenum erarbeitet werden. L erhält so einen Eindruck, wie viel die S nach dem ersten Hören bzw. Lesen verstanden haben.
- Alternative: L setzt zur Verständnissicherung **KV 4: Emergency on the motorway** ein. Diese dient der Differenzierung nach oben, da die S hier selbst Sätze formulieren müssen, um die Unterschiede zum Text im SB zu beschreiben.

Material
Kopiervorlage 4

Üben — **2 Report the police officer's words** — Seite 97

Ziel
- Berichten, was jemand gesagt hat
- Den Unterschied zwischen indirekter Rede mit und ohne *tense shift* kennen lernen

Strukturen
- *Indirect speech with and without tense shift*

Methodisches Vorgehen
- a) L führt kurz in die Situation ein und bespricht mit den S die *Tip*-Box. Anschließend bearbeiten die S die Aufgabe in Einzelarbeit oder, in leistungsstärkeren Lerngruppen, mündlich im Plenum.
- Durch b) soll der Unterschied zwischen indirekter Rede mit und ohne *tense shift* deutlich gemacht werden. In leistungsstärkeren Gruppen kann dies mündlich erfolgen oder die Teilaufgabe ggf. auch weggelassen werden.

TIP
G 26

Lösung
a) *That police officer says we have to leave again right away. She says there has been an accident. It happened a short time ago, and the emergency services are*

	trying to do their work. She says we can't do anything to help and we are just getting in the way. And she says we'll find out about it all in the newspapers tomorrow. b) *A police officer told us we had to leave again right away. She said that there had been an accident. She explained to us that it had happened a short time ago, and the emergency services were trying to do their work. The police officer also told us that we couldn't do anything to help. She said we were just getting in the way. She told us we would find out about it all in the newspapers the next day.*

Tipps für junge Lehrer	Ob a) und b) mündlich oder schriftlich bearbeitet werden, sollte L vom Leistungsstand und der Motivation der S abhängig machen. Wurde die indirekte Rede zuvor schon intensiv geübt, kann auf Teilaufgabe b) verzichtet werden.	**Material** *Workbook* S. 69/9

Üben	**3 What did the police officer ask?**	Seite 98
Ziel	• Fragen in der indirekten Rede stellen	
Strukturen	• *Indirect questions*	
Methodisches Vorgehen	• Bei geschlossenem SB fordert L die S auf, Fragen zu formulieren, die ein *police officer* am Unfallort stellen könnte. Diese Fragen hält L an der Tafel oder auf Folie fest und setzt dann 2–3 Sätze beispielhaft in die indirekte Rede um (siehe TA). Anschließend versuchen die S selbstständig, Regeln zu Fragen in der indirekten Rede zu formulieren, die auch an der Tafel fixiert werden können (siehe *Tip*-Box S. 98). Anschließend bearbeiten die S *ex*. 3 schriftlich. • Alternative: L weist auf die *Tip*-Box im SB hin, und die S erarbeiten selbstständig die Regeln zu Fragen in der indirekten Rede sowie *ex*. 3. Anschließend Besprechung der Ergebnisse im Plenum.	**TIP** G 27

TA	**Direct questions** — Where do the pupils come from? / How many boys and girls were on the bus? / Has anybody else seen the accident? **Indirect questions** — The police officer asked where the pupils came from. / She wanted to know how many boys and girls had been on the bus. / She asked if anybody else had seen the accident.

Lösung	1 *She asked how the accident had happened.* 2 *She asked how far I had been behind the coach.* 3 *She wanted to know why I hadn't seen the brake lights.* 4 *She asked what I was carrying on the lorry.* 5 *She wanted to know where I had come from.* 6 *She wanted to know when I had started my journey.* 7 *She asked how fast I usually drove.* 8 *She wanted to know when my last break had been.*	**Material** Ggf. Leerfolie

Üben	**4 What did the paramedic want to know?**	Seite 98
Ziel	• Fragen in der indirekten Rede ohne Fragewörter kennen lernen	
Strukturen	• *Indirect questions without question words*	
Methodisches Vorgehen	• Wenn die Fragen in der indirekten Rede mit Hilfe eines ausführlichen TA (siehe oben) eingeführt wurden, können die S diese Aufgabe in Einzelarbeit erledigen. L verweist zuvor auf die *Tip*-Box S. 98. Die Besprechung erfolgt anschließend im Plenum.	

6 Language 2

Erweiterung
- Alternative: In leistungsschwächeren Lerngruppen können zunächst 2–3 Fragen im Plenum besprochen werden.
- Zur Festigung und Vertiefung der neuen Struktur kann **KV 5: A school exchange**, Teilaufgabe b), eingesetzt werden.

Lösung

> She asked if I was OK. She wanted to know whether anything hurt. She asked if I could remember the accident. She wanted to know if I had got a shock. She wanted to know whether I had hit my head. She asked whether I had got a headache. She asked if I felt sick. She asked whether anyone had given me something to drink. She asked if I wanted to sit in the ambulance.

Material
Workbook S. 69/10
Kopiervorlage 5

Üben | **5 Indirect commands** | Seite 98

Ziel
- Indirekte Aufforderungssätze kennen lernen und anwenden

Wortschatz *command, to ask sb to do sth*

Strukturen
- *Indirect commands*

TIP
G 28

Methodisches Vorgehen
- Zunächst werden die S aufgefordert, die in a) angegebenen *commands* aus dem Text S. 97 herauszusuchen. L hält die Aufforderungen an der Tafel fest und weist auf die Besonderheit bei der Satzstellung hin (siehe *Grammar*-Box S. 98). Diese wird leistungsschwächeren S sicherlich Schwierigkeiten bereiten. Farbige Markierungen für Objekt und Infinitivform können hier hilfreich sein.
- b) kann im Plenum bearbeitet werden, indem jeweils ein S die Sätze ins Deutsche übersetzt.
- c) sollte zunächst mündlich besprochen werden (auf die einführenden Verben hinweisen!). In leistungsschwächeren Lerngruppen kann die Aufgabe anschließend noch einmal schriftlich – auch als Hausaufgabe – bearbeitet werden.

Auch als HA geeignet

TA

	Indirect commands		
The lorry driver	warned	everyone	to get off …
The firefighters	have told	people	not to go …
The police officer	told	everyone	to get back …
	verb	object	(not) to + infinitive

Erweiterung
- Zur Festigung und Vertiefung bietet sich **KV 5: A school exchange**, Teilaufgabe a), an.

Lösung
a) *Siehe TA*
b) 1 *Der LKW-Fahrer warnte jeden, den Bus schnell zu verlassen und wegzulaufen.* 2 *Die Feuerwehrmänner haben den Leuten gesagt, nicht in die Nähe des LKWs zu gehen.* 3 *Die Polizisten forderten die Leute auf, in ihre Autos zurückzugehen und wegzufahren.*
c) 1 *His mother told Ben to watch out for traffic on the right. She warned him not to have an accident in France.* 2 *His father warned him not to lose his passport. He advised him to keep it somewhere safe. He told him to look after his money, too.* 3 *Ben's sister told him not to behave like an idiot with Ryan. She asked him to bring her a nice present back.* 4 *His grandma asked him to take some nice photos. She told him to have fun and enjoy his trip.*

Tipps für junge Lehrer
Deutsche S haben mit den Infinitivkonstruktionen (auch bei *want sb to do sth*) immer wieder Schwierigkeiten, da solche Sätze im Deutschen zumeist mit einem „dass"-Satz umgesetzt werden (z. B. Er warnte ihn, dass er auf seinen Pass aufpassen solle.). L sollte hier also ganz besonders auf Fehler achten.

Material
Workbook S. 69/11
Kopiervorlage 5

| | | | Language 2 | 6 |

Üben **6 Listening: Emergency calls** Seite 99

HV-Text

Number 1
Operator: Which service do you need?
Caller: Fire! Quick! Quick!
Voice: Fire service here.
Caller: Help! There's a fire!
Voice: Please tell me where you are and what the emergency is.
Caller: I'm in Green Street. There's a fire here.
Voice: Where exactly is the fire?
Caller: It's at – number 16.
Voice: Is number 16 a house?
Caller: No, a shop.
Voice: So you're saying the fire is in a shop.
Caller: No, no! It's in a flat *over* the shop.
Voice: Is anyone in the flat?
Caller: I don't know. It looks terrible! Smoke is coming out of the windows!
Voice: OK. Please wait there, but don't go near. We'll be there as soon as we can. Could I also have your name and address, please?
Caller: Oh, right. Yes. It's Mrs …

Number 2
Operator: Which service do you need?
Caller: The ambulance service, please.
Voice: This is the ambulance service. Please explain the emergency.
Caller: There has been an accident at the corner of London Road and Devon Street. A car has hit a boy on a bike. The boy is lying next to his bike. He isn't moving.
Voice: Thank you. We'll send an ambulance right away. I also need your details, please.
Caller: Of course. My name is Rachel Thompson and my address is …
(fade out)

Number 3
Operator: Which service do you need?
Caller: Sorry?
Operator: Do you need the fire, police or ambulance service?
Caller: Oh, I see. The police, please.
Voice: Police service here. What's the emergency?
Caller: Well, this is Michael Potts speaking. And – the thing is, I think there might be a burglar in a house in my street. I'm on my way home, you see. I've been to the cinema. That's why I'm walking down the street so late in the evening. I'm outside the house at the moment. And I know that the people are away on holiday this week. So –
Voice: Excuse me. What's the address of the house?
Caller: 39, Brook Way. And I live at number 21.
Voice: Why do you think there's a burglar at number 39? Can you see anybody in the house?
Caller: No, but I can see a light in a room downstairs, and – no, I really don't think it's normal.
Voice: Well, two police officers will come and check. You can go home now and they'll visit you later.

Ziel
• Notrufe verstehen und den richtigen Bildern zuordnen

Methodisches Vorgehen
Pre-listening:
• Die S beschreiben kurz die in den Bildern dargestellten Situationen.

6 Language 2

While-listening:
- a) L präsentiert die Dialoge von CD. Die S machen sich Notizen, um ihre Zuordnung begründen zu können. In leistungsschwächeren Klassen kann ein weiteres Abspielen der Dialoge notwendig sein. Besprechung der Ergebnisse im Plenum.
- b) L spielt die Dialoge noch einmal vor. Die S machen sich Notizen zu den beiden Fragen.

Post-listening:
- Anhand ihrer Notizen beantworten die S die Fragen in Einzelarbeit; Besprechung der Ergebnisse im Plenum.

Lösung
a) *1 B, 2 A, 3 A*
b) *Erwartungshorizont: Dialogue 2 is the best one, because the caller says what has happened, where it has happened and who is hurt. The caller speaks clearly and only talks about important things. The caller in dialogue 3 talks about a lot of unimportant things first and the caller in dialogue 1 is too nervous.*

Material
L 4/6–8

Üben — Listening: An accident in Upton Road — Workbook Seite 70

HV-Text Workbook

Woman 1: Hello, Stockwood Emergency Services.
Man: Oh, hello – er, – we need some help here.
Woman 1: Which service do you need, sir?
Man: A girl has hurt herself –
Woman 1: So it's ambulance you want.
Man: Oh, – er, – yes –
Woman 2: Ambulance Service here. How can we help?
Man: There's a girl – just outside my window.
Woman 2: Can I have name and address, please.
Man: I don't know the girl's name.
Woman 2: Your name, sir. I'd like your name and address.
Man: Yes, of course. My name's Harold Watts, W – A – double T – S, and my address is 10 Upton Road.
Woman 2: Up-ton – Road. Thank you. Now, what has happened and where?
Man: Well, I'm not sure, really. I was having my lunch here. I always sit at the window, then I can see what's going on –
Woman 2: And what did you see?
Man: Well, nothing at first. I was just eating my salad –
Woman 2: Yes, Mr Watts. Go on, please. I need the facts.
Man: I heard a loud shout, so I looked out – and there she was.
Woman 2: The girl?
Man: Yes, that's right. She had fallen out of the big tree, and she was lying on the ground. She's there now, and her head is bleeding. There are –
Woman 2: Right, we'll send an ambulance at once.
Man: Oh, I can hear an ambulance now! Somebody was quicker than me.
Woman 2: That's good! Thanks Mr Watts. Bye!

Material
S 2/18
L 4/9
Workbook S. 70/12

Üben — 7 How to: Get help in an emergency — Seite 99

Ziel
- Notfallrufe mit Hilfe von *Useful phrases* einüben

Wortschatz *burglar, to be trapped*

Methodisches Vorgehen
- Die S erarbeiten in PA Notfallrufe mit Hilfe der *Useful phrases*. Leistungsschwächere S können sich als Hilfe zunächst Notizen machen und die Anrufe

Language 2 | 6

dann nachspielen, leistungsstärkere S simulieren die Situationen direkt. Einige Dialoge können zur Sicherung exemplarisch in der Klasse vorgespielt werden.

Lösung

Erwartungshorizont:
Operator: *Which service do you need?*
Caller: *The ambulance service, please.*
Voice: *This is the ambulance service. Please explain the emergency.*
Caller: *There has been an accident in London Street. A lorry has crashed into a car. The drivers are still in their cars, they can't get out.*
Voice: *Thank you. We'll send an ambulance right away. I also need your details, please.*
Caller: *Of course. My name is Thomas Smith and my address is 5 Park Road, Nottingham. My telephone number is …*

Tipps für junge Lehrer Beim Vorspielen sollten die S ausgeschaltete Handys benutzen und Rücken an Rücken sitzen. Dies entspricht eher der authentischen Situation, als wenn die S nebeneinander am Tisch sitzen.

Material
Workbook S. 70/13
Ggf. ausgeschaltete Handys

Üben | 8 Revision: Questions with prepositions
Seite 99

Ziel
- Die Wortstellung in Fragen mit Präpositionen wiederholen

Strukturen
- *Questions with prepositions*

Methodisches Vorgehen
- Aufgrund des Frage-Antwort-Charakters der Aufgabe sollte sie in PA erledigt werden.

Lösung

2 Who is Ben talking to? – He is talking to his exchange partner. 3 What is Ben spending money on? – He is spending money on a computer magazine. 4 What is Ben looking for? – He is looking for his camera. 5 What is Ben laughing about? – He is laughing about his friend's joke. 6 Who is Ben taking a photo of? – He is taking a photo of his best friend.

Tipps für junge Lehrer Diese Aufgabe kann durchaus auch an anderer Stelle (z. B. im Rahmen der *Check-out*-Seite) erarbeitet werden, falls die S nach der Einführung der *indirect speech* eine kleine „Grammatikpause" benötigen.

Material
Workbook S. 70/14

Üben | 9 Your turn: Good advice for a trip
Seite 99

Ziel
- Über Ratschläge für eine Reise berichten

Methodisches Vorgehen
- Diese Aufgabe kann sowohl mündlich im Plenum als auch schriftlich in Einzelarbeit/als Hausaufgabe bearbeitet werden.

Auch als HA geeignet

Lösung

Erwartungshorizont:
My mother told me not to lose my passport. She told me to put it under my T-shirt. My father warned me not to take too much money with me. And he warned me to be careful with my camera.

The advice my parents gave me was very useful, but sometimes I forgot about it of course …

6 Skills

Skills
Seite 100

Ziele
- *Small talk* als wichtiges Element der Kommunikation kennen lernen und anwenden
- Im Gespräch Interesse zeigen
- Füllwörter in einem Gespräch heraushören und sammeln

Text: Small talk
Seite 100

Ziel
- *Small talk* als wichtiges Element der Kommunikation kennen lernen und anwenden

Wortschatz *second language*

Methodisches Vorgehen
- L setzt sich zwischen die S und beginnt ein Gespräch mit einem/r (leistungsstärkeren) S, z. B. über das Wetter, Sport, das letzte Wochenende, … Auch wenn der/die S eigentlich nicht mehr weiterreden möchte, stellt L wieder eine Frage und bekundet stets – ein wenig übertrieben – sein Interesse. Dann wendet er sich einem/r anderen S zu, beginnt ein Gespräch (gelangweilt und mit gespielt düsterer Miene), das aber genauso schnell wieder abebbt, weil L nicht nachhakt. Anschließend versuchen die S, den Unterschied zwischen den Gesprächen zu beschreiben. L leitet dann zum Thema der *Skills*-Seite über und erläutert, wie wichtig es ist, auch in der Fremdsprache *small talk* betreiben zu können.

Üben: 1 Show that you are listening
Seite 100

Ziel
- Mit Hilfe von *Useful phrases* Interesse an einer Unterhaltung bekunden

Wortschatz *I see., fantastic, Right?, annoying, And you.*

Methodisches Vorgehen
- a) L erklärt die Aufgabenstellung, dann lesen zwei S den Dialog in verteilten Rollen. Im Plenum sammelt die Lerngruppe anschließend *words/phrases*, mit denen man Interesse an der Fortführung einer Unterhaltung bekunden kann. Diese werden an der Tafel/auf Folie festgehalten, so dass die S sie für *ex.* 2 und 4 verwenden können.
- b) Mit Hilfe der *words/phrases* aus a) wird es den S leicht fallen, diesen Aufgabenteil zu bearbeiten.

TA

```
            Show that you are listening
Oh, I see.          Oh no! It's so ..., isn't it?
Really?             Yes, I know.
You say you're ...  Exactly.
```

Erweiterung
- Zur Vertiefung verfassen die S in PA einen Dialog wie in a). Dabei können sie einen ganz neuen Dialog schreiben oder den bestehenden Dialog abändern (leistungsschwächere S).

TIP Zur Differenzierung geeignet

Lösung
a) Siehe TA.
b) 1 *Oh no! It's so annoying, isn't it?* 2 *Really? How fantastic!* 3 *Oh, I see.* 4 *Exactly. It's very expensive.* 5 *Really? That's great.* 6 *Yes, I know.*

Material
Workbook S. 71/15
Ggf. Leerfolie

Üben: 2 Show that you are happy to talk
Seite 100

Ziel
- Über Kommunikation reflektieren
- Die Bedeutung von Kommunikationsstrategien und -signalen beschreiben

Methodisches Vorgehen	• Diese Aufgabe sollte im Plenum besprochen werden. Sie dient in erster Linie der Bewusstmachung verschiedener Redemittel und -signale.
Lösung	*Erwartungshorizont:* *A and B don't just say 'yes' to answer the questions, but they give some more details. They both ask questions and use question tags (right?/isn't it?/don't you?).*
Tipps für junge Lehrer	Möglicherweise fällt es leistungsschwächeren S hier schwer, die Strategien in der Fremdsprache zu benennen. Sie sollten die Möglichkeit erhalten, sich vor Besprechung der Aufgabe Notizen zu machen.

ⓛ Üben 3 Listening: Fillers   Seite 100

HV-Text	A: What an interesting trip! So – um – what's your favourite country so far? B: That's hard to say. The thing is – I've had a good time everywhere. A: Yes, but – you know – if you could go back to just one country, where would it be? B: Let's see. Germany was great – and – well, I enjoyed France, too. But Italy was like, just so brilliant. I mean the weather and the food and everything. A: So Italy's your favourite. B: Hm. Yes, I think so far it is. But you never know. I'm going to Greece next, and that might be even more – er – even *more* brilliant!
Ziel	• Füllwörter in einem Gespräch heraushören und sammeln
Wortschatz	*filler, extra*
Methodisches Vorgehen	*Pre-listening:* • L führt den Begriff *filler* ein: *'Well' is a filler – it's a word with no real meaning in the sentence.* *While-listening:* • Der Dialog wird zweimal vorgespielt. Die S sammeln die gehörten Füllwörter in einer Liste. *Post-listening:* • Vergleich der Ergebnisse im Plenum. Die S ergänzen ggf. ihre Listen. • b) wird anschließend im Plenum besprochen.
TA	
Lösung	a) *Siehe TA* b) *Erwartungshorizont:* *People use these phrases to have more time to think about what they want to say. When you can't find the right words, fillers like 'er' or 'um' can help you. Some people think it's cool to use these words. Everybody uses them.*
Material	ⓛ 4/10

Üben 4 A game: Small talk champion   Seite 100

Ziel	• Einen *Small-talk*-Wettbewerb durchführen
Methodisches Vorgehen	• L stellt die Regeln des Wettbewerbs vor: Es wird nur Englisch gesprochen und das Paar, dessen Unterhaltung am längsten dauert, gewinnt. Um sicher zu stel-

6 Skills Text

len, dass die Regeln eingehalten werden, können einige S als „Schiedsrichter" bestimmt werden. L sollte zur Motivation eine kleine Belohnung bereithalten (z. B. Gutschein für 1x hausaufgabenfrei).
- L verweist auf TA/Folie aus *ex.* 1 und *ex.* 3 und fordert die S auf, ganz bewusst die zuvor gesammelten *words/phrases* zur Intensivierung des Dialogs einzusetzen.

Erweiterung
- Damit die S auch im Nachhinein überprüfen können, ob sie Füllwörter verwendet haben und ihr Interesse am Gespräch positiv hervorheben konnten, empfiehlt es sich, die Dialoge aufzunehmen (idealerweise auf Video) und anschließend zu besprechen.
- Zur weiteren Festigung der gelernten *Speaking skills* eignet sich auch **KV 6: Travel situations**.

Lösung | *Individuelle S-Antworten*

Material
Workbook S. 71/16
Kopiervorlage 6
Ggf. Videokamera

Tipps für junge Lehrer | Um sehr leistungsschwache S nicht zu frustrieren, können diese die Rolle des Schiedsrichters übernehmen.

Text
Seite 101–103

Ziele
- Eine Abenteuergeschichte lesen und verstehen
- Eine Textpassage in einen Dialog umwandeln
- Eigene narrative Texte interessanter gestalten

S L Text | **My big adventure** | Seite 101–103

Hinweis | Die Geschichte lehnt sich inhaltlich an den Abenteuerroman *Around the world in 80 days* von Jules Verne an, in dem der Protagonist Phileas Fogg, ein reicher Londoner, nach einer Wette in 80 Tagen um die Welt reisen muss. Diese Reise birgt zahlreiche Abenteuer und Erlebnisse, von denen einige wenige hier im Text aufgegriffen werden.

Wortschatz | *to complete, seat, princess, to save, railway, track, prairie, to slow down, bellow, to jump out of one's skin, skin, buffalo pl. buffalo, delay, bet, to continue, on foot, to take the chance, whistle, to make it, side, scream, to scream, Sioux pl. Sioux, frightening, gun, to shoot, danger, on time*

Material
S 2/19–22
L 4/11–14

Text/Üben | **1 Before you read** | Seite 101

Ziel
- Eine Abenteuergeschichte lesen und verstehen

Methodisches Vorgehen
- *Pre-reading:* Bevor die S den Text lesen, sollten sie in Einzelarbeit oder als vorbereitende Hausaufgabe Ideen sammeln, was in einer Abenteuergeschichte vorkommen sollte. Verschiedene Beiträge können dann als Einstimmung auf den Text im Plenum vorgestellt werden. Alternative: L schreibt zu Beginn der Unterrichtsstunde das Stichwort *adventure story* an die Tafel und die S äußern ihre Ideen dazu.
- Anschließend wird den S die Abenteuergeschichte als Ganzes von CD präsentiert, in leistungsstärkeren Lerngruppen bei geschlossenem SB. Nach dem ersten Hören sammelt L, was die S von der Geschichte verstanden haben und klärt ggf. Wortschatzfragen. Allerdings sollte auf eine Semantisierung aller neu-

Auch als HA geeignet

	en Vokabeln verzichtet werden, da dies eher demotivierend auf die S wirken könnte. • Zur Sicherung des Verständnisses kann **KV 7: My big adventure** eingesetzt werden. Anschließend werden die Aufgaben im SB bearbeitet.	
Erweiterung	• Vor dem Lesen kann **Folie 15: My big adventure** eingesetzt werden Die S machen sich anhand der Bilder Gedanken darüber, was in der Geschichte passieren könnte.	
Tipps für junge Lehrer	Der „Lesegenuss" sollte nicht durch eine abschnittsweise Präsentation und Zwischenfragen zum Detailverständnis unterbrochen werden. Nur in sehr leistungsschwachen Lerngruppen macht eine abschnittsweise Präsentation Sinn, um die S nicht zu demotivieren.	**Material** Kopiervorlage 7 Folie 15

Üben	**2 Talk about the end of the story**	Seite 103
Ziel	• Das Ende der Geschichte reflektieren	
Methodisches Vorgehen	• Diese Aufgabe wird mündlich bearbeitet. Hierzu können kleine Gruppen von 4–5 S gebildet werden, die auch für die Arbeit an den nachfolgenden Aufgaben zusammenbleiben. Alternativ kann das Ende der Geschichte im Plenum besprochen werden.	
Lösung	a) *Erwartungshorizont:* – *At the end Jade is hurt or even dies, so we don't learn anything about how Mr Fogg's story ends. I like that because an open end is very exciting.* – *I don't like the end of the story. It's not a happy ending because I think Jade is hurt and we don't know what will happen next.*	
Tipps für junge Lehrer	Teilaufgabe b) ist optional. Möglicherweise gibt es S, die die Geschichte kennen und das Ende nacherzählen können. Allerdings wird dann die Spannung genommen, so dass L abwägen muss, ob diese Teilaufgabe tatsächlich bearbeitet werden soll.	**Material** *Workbook* S. 72/17

Üben	**3 ⟨Compare then with now⟩**	Seite 103
Ziel	• Die Reisebedingungen in der Geschichte mit den heutigen Bedingungen vergleichen	
Wortschatz	*then, now*	
Methodisches Vorgehen	• Die Aufgabe kann wahlweise im Plenum oder in den Kleingruppen (siehe *ex.* 2) mündlich bearbeitet werden. • Wenn das Hören bzw. Lesen und die erste Besprechung des Inhalts eine ganze Unterrichtsstunde in Anspruch genommen hat, kann diese Aufgabe auch als Hausaufgabe schriftlich bearbeitet werden.	Auch als HA geeignet
Lösung	*Erwartungshorizont:* a) *problems in the story: dangerous people attack the train, animals are on the track, bridge was not safe; the same problems can happen today, too* b) *problems today: sometimes there are trees on the track; nice things missing: you cannot see much of the country because the trains are so fast*	

Üben	**4 Write and act a dialogue**	Seite 103
Ziel	• Eine Textpassage in einen Dialog umwandeln	

6 Text

Methodisches Vorgehen
- In PA oder in den Kleingruppen (siehe *ex.* 2 und 3) schreiben die S mit Hilfe der Fragen im SB einen Dialog. L hat hier nur unterstützende Funktion (z. B. Vokabelhilfen). Anschließend werden mehrere Dialoge vor der Klasse vorgespielt.

Lösung

Erwartungshorizont:
Man on foot: *I've come from Medicine Bow. You can't go there! The bridge over the river is not safe for such a heavy train!*
Passepartout: *Oh, no! This is terrible for Mr Fogg! What can we do?*
Passenger: *I don't want to stop here! I must go to New York! How can we go on if we can't cross the bridge?*
Train Driver: *I don't want to give up so easily. I think we must go very fast. Then it'll be okay! What do you think?*
Mr Fogg: *Yes, let's try! It's our only chance!*
Man on foot: *You're really crazy! You're all risking your lives! Stop!*
Passengers: *No, no, we're going on. That's our only chance! Let's go!*

Tipps für junge Lehrer
Nicht alle S dieses Alters spielen gerne vor der Klasse vor, deshalb sollte die Art und Weise der Ergebnissicherung von der Bereitschaft der Lerngruppe abhängen. Alternativ kann zur Sicherung eine der Gruppen gebeten werden, ihren Dialog auf Folie zu schreiben. Dieser kann dann exemplarisch im Plenum besprochen werden.

Material
Workbook S. 72/18
Ggf. Leerfolie

Üben | **5 Writing texts: Make a story more interesting** | Seite 103

Ziel
- Eigene narrative Texte interessanter gestalten

Methodisches Vorgehen
- a) L erläutert kurz die Aufgabenstellung, dann suchen die S in Einzelarbeit weitere *phrases* aus dem Text. Aus zeitökonomischen Gründen kann der Text auch in mehrere Abschnitte aufgeteilt werden, die die S in den Gruppen bearbeiten (siehe *ex.* 2–4).
- b) Auch diese Teilaufgabe kann in den Gruppen bearbeitet werden. Anschließend Besprechung der Ergebnisse im Plenum.
- c) Dieser Arbeitsauftrag eignet sich gut als Hausaufgabe. Zur Ergebnissicherung werden in der nächsten Stunde einige Beispiele im Plenum besprochen.
- Die S heften die in der Aufgabe gesammelten *words/phrases* in ihrem *folder* ab.

TIP
Sammeln von *words/phrases* für den *folder*

Auch als HA geeignet

Lösung

a) *weitere Beispiele: long whistle (l. 77), began to shake (l. 78), then – crash! (l. 84); loud bangs and screams (ll. 89–90), frightening faces (l. 97), a giant leap (l. 110); felt the shock (l. 120)*
b) *Try to make the reader interested. – I had spoken too soon.*
Show that the characters are nervous. – I almost jumped out of my skin!
Give the reader a shock. – But the Sioux wasn't dead!
Describe the action in short sentences. – We began to move. Fast, then faster.
Use words that describe sounds. – Crash!
c) *Individuelle S-Antworten*

Tipps für junge Lehrer
Teilaufgabe c) ist sehr anspruchsvoll und dürfte je nach Leistungsstand der S sehr unterschiedlich ausfallen. Wichtig ist aber auf jeden Fall, dass die S die Hilfen aus a) und b) berücksichtigen. Als weitere Übung bietet sich für leistungsstärkere S **KV 8: A scary castle** an.

Material
Workbook S. 72/19
Kopiervorlage 8

| Text | 6 |

⊚L Song **6 ⟨A song: Hit me with your rhythm stick⟩** Seite 103

In the deserts of Sudan
And the gardens of Japan,
From Milan to Yucatan
Every woman, every man

Chorus:
Hit me with your rhythm stick.
Hit me! Hit me!
Je t'adore, ich liebe dich.
Hit me, hit me, hit me!
Hit me with your rhythm stick.
Hit me slowly, hit me quick.
Hit me! Hit me! Hit me!

In the wilds of Borneo
And the vineyards of Bordeaux
Eskimo, Arapaho
Move their body to and fro.

Chorus:
Hit me with your rhythm stick.
Hit me! Hit me!
Das ist gut! C'est fantastique!
Hit me, hit me, hit me!
Hit me with your rhythm stick.
It's nice to be a lunatic.
Hit me! Hit me! Hit me!

In the dock of Tiger Bay
On the road to Mandalay
From Bombay to Santa Fe
Over hills and far away

Chorus:
Hit me with your rhythm stick.
Hit me! Hit me!
C'est si bon, mm? Ist es nicht?
Hit me, hit me, hit me!
Hit me with your rhythm stick.
Two fat persons, click, click, click.
Hit me! Hit me! Hit me!

Text: Ian Dury/Charles Jeremy Jankel.
© by TEMPLEMILL MUSIC LD/WARNER/CHAPPELL MUSIC; SLV: NEUE WELT MUSIKVERLAG GMBH & CO.KG/RONDOR MUSIKVERLAG GMBH

Ziel
- Ein Lied hören und verstehen

Wortschatz *rhythm, desert, the wilds, vineyard, Arapaho, to and fro*

Methodisches Vorgehen

Pre-listening:
- Das Lied kann nach der Arbeit mit dem Text als Auflockerung eingesetzt werden.
- L teilt den S das Lied als Kopie aus, wobei die Strophen untereinander vermischt sind. Zum besseren Verständnis werden die im Text vorkommenden Namen und geografischen Bezeichnungen kurz angesprochen. Ggf. Einführung unbekannter Vokabeln.

While-listening:
- Das Lied wird von CD vorgespielt. Die S nummerieren die richtige Reihenfolge der Strophen.
- Kontrolle der Ergebnisse durch nochmaliges Vorspielen. Die S machen sich Notizen zum Rhythmus des Liedes.

Post-listening:
- Besprechung der Ergebnisse im Plenum. Das Gespräch über den Rhythmus des Liedes sollte aber nicht unnötig in die Länge gezogen werden.

Material
⊚L 4/15

6 Wordwise

Wordwise
Seite 104

Ziele
- Unbekannte Wörter erschließen
- Das Hörverstehen schulen
- Festigung des Vokabulars zum Thema *travelling*

Üben ### 1 Guess new words
Seite 104

Ziel
- Unbekannte Wörter erschließen

Methodisches Vorgehen
- a) Obwohl die S die Strategien zum Erschließen von unbekannten Wörtern durchaus schon häufig – bewusst oder unbewusst – angewendet haben, sollte L noch einmal auf die *Tip*-Box hinweisen.
- Die Aufgabe kann sowohl mündlich im Plenum als auch schriftlich in Einzelarbeit oder PA bearbeitet werden. Vorteil bei der schriftlichen Bearbeitung ist es, dass alle S aktiv sind, während im Unterrichtsgespräch die leistungsstärkeren S schnell eine Lösung präsentieren und damit die leistungsschwächeren S frustrieren können.
- b): Die Dialoge werden zunächst in PA vorbereitet. L sollte die S auf die auf der *Skills*-Seite (S. 100) erlernten *words/phrases* und Strategien hinweisen. Zur Sicherung werden möglichst viele Dialoge vorgespielt.

Lösung
a) *Individuelle S-Antworten*
b) *Erwartungshorizont:*
A: *Hello, what can I do for you?*
B: *We would like two adults and one child to Bristol, please.*
A: *Would you like single or return tickets?*
B: *Are the return tickets cheaper?*
A: *Yes, they are. A single ticket for adults is £21, a return ticket is £38.*
B: *Oh, I see! It's clever to take the return tickets then. And what about the children's ticket?*
A: *Well, how old is your daughter?*
B: *She is four years old.*
A: *You don't have to pay for her ticket then.*
B: *Great! That's two return tickets to Bristol then.*
A: *Here you are! Have a nice journey.*
B: *Thanks a lot! Bye!*

⊚L Üben ### 2 Listening: Sounds and spelling
Seite 104

HV-Text
1. Last year we rode our bikes from England to Spain and back.
2. The fare for the ferry is cheaper in winter than in summer.
3. Ask whether we can get a meal on the train.
4. If you don't want an accident, you should check that brake!
5. All the departures are shown on the information board.
6. I don't agree – women are *not* too weak for the challenge!

Ziel
- Wörter mit gleicher Aussprache aber unterschiedlicher Bedeutung richtig zuordnen

Methodisches Vorgehen
- a) L erklärt die Aufgabenstellung und präsentiert die Sätze von CD. Nach dem zweiten Vorspielen werden die Ergebnisse im Plenum verglichen.
- b) Diese Teilaufgabe kann wahlweise mündlich im Plenum oder zunächst schriftlich in Einzelarbeit bearbeitet werden. In beiden Fällen sollte allerdings eine Sicherung an der Tafel erfolgen, damit die S die unterschiedlich geschriebenen Wörter auch wirklich „vor Augen haben".

	Wordwise **Check-out**	**6**

Erweiterung
- **KV 9: Sounds and spelling**, Teilaufgabe a), bietet weitere Beispiele zu Teilaufgabe b). Sie kann zusätzlich als Hausaufgabe oder als schriftliche Aufgabe im Unterricht eingesetzt werden.

Auch als HA geeignet

Material
◎L 4/16
Workbook S. 73/21
Kopiervorlage 9

Lösung
> a) 1 *rode* 2 *fare* 3 *whether* 4 *brake* 5 *board* 6 *weak*
> b) *see/sea; their/there; know/no; meet/meat; would/wood*

Üben **3 Mixed bag: Complete the missing words** Seite 104

Ziel
- Das Leseverstehen schulen
- Die Vokabeln zum Thema *travelling* festigen

Methodisches Vorgehen
- Die Aufgabe eignet sich in erster Linie zur schriftlichen Bearbeitung, so dass auch langsamere und leistungsschwächere S die Chance haben, die Wörter selbstständig einzusetzen.
- Alternative: In leistungsschwächeren Lerngruppen kann zunächst **KV 9: Sounds and spelling**, Teilaufgabe b), eingesetzt werden. Hier sind alle fehlenden Begriffe aus *ex. 3* versteckt. So haben die S das notwendige Vokabular präsent und müssen nur noch die passenden Begriffe in die Lücken einsetzen.

TIP
KV 1

Erweiterung
- Haben die S zu Beginn der Arbeit an Unit 6 eine *mindmap* zum Thema *travelling* erstellt (siehe **KV 1**), können sie diese mit den hier einzusetzenden Vokabeln ergänzen.

Material
Workbook S. 73/22
Kopiervorlage 9
Ggf. Leerfolie

Lösung
> *airport, drive, park, railway, journey, take, driver, warn, track, accident, slow, delay, time, arrive, late, desk, flight, late, passengers, plane, annoying*

Check-out

Seite 105

Ziele • Die Lernziele der Unit in Selbstkontrolle überprüfen

Üben **1 Report a call from France** Seite 105

Ziel
- Einen Telefonanruf in indirekter Rede wiedergeben

Strukturen
- *Indirect speech in statements and questions*

Methodisches Vorgehen
- Die Aufgabe dient der Festigung der Regeln zur indirekten Rede. Sie kann sowohl mündlich als auch schriftlich bearbeitet werden. L sollte vorab noch einmal auf die Regeln zum *tense shift* in der indirekten Rede hinweisen. Die Sicherung der Ergebnisse erfolgt in Selbstkontrolle oder in PA.

Auch als HA geeignet

Material
Workbook S. 74/23

Lösung
> *Siehe SB S. 215–216*

Üben **2 Complete the dialogues at the airport** Seite 105

Ziel
- Indirekte Aufforderungen formulieren

Strukturen
- *Indirect commands*

6 Check-out ⟨Text⟩

Methodisches Vorgehen	• Die Aufgabe wird in PA bearbeitet; dabei wechseln sich die S ab (1. und 2. Sprecher), so dass sie abwechselnd die *indirect commands* formulieren müssen.	
Lösung	*Siehe SB S. 216*	

Üben	**3 Improve the conversation**	Seite 105
Ziel	• Gelernte Strategien der Gesprächsführung anwenden	
Methodisches Vorgehen	• Die Aufgabe dient zur Vertiefung der erlernten Strategien. Sie sollte zunächst schriftlich bearbeitet werden. Zur Ergebnissicherung können die S in verteilten Rollen vorlesen.	Auch als HA geeignet
Lösung	*Siehe SB S. 216*	

Üben	**4 Your turn: What do you think of Green Line 3?**	Seite 105
Ziel	• Die eigene Meinung zum Lehrbuch in einer Diskussion vertreten	
Methodisches Vorgehen	• Die S schreiben zunächst in Einzelarbeit ihre Meinung zu Band 3 in Stichworten auf, so dass sie über eine Grundlage für die anschließende Diskussion verfügen. Anschließend präsentieren sie ihre Argumente in Kleingruppen. L hält sich im Hintergrund und versucht Eindrücke zu sammeln, um abschließend im Plenum die wichtigsten Positionen zusammenzufassen.	
Erweiterung	• Als Vorbereitung für die Aufgabe bearbeiten die S **KV 10: Do you remember?**, in der sie spielerisch ihr Wissen aus *Green Line* 3 unter Beweis stellen können. • Alternative: Die S bereiten in zwei Großgruppen ein eigenes Quiz vor. Anschließend beantworten sie bei geschlossenem SB die Fragen der jeweils anderen Gruppe.	**Material** *Workbook* S. 74/24 Kopiervorlage 10
Lösung	*Siehe SB S. 216*	

⟨Text⟩

Seite 106–107

 Ziele • Einen Auszug aus einem Abenteuerroman lesen und verstehen

ⓢ ⓛ Text	**⟨Treasure Island⟩**	Seite 106–107
Hinweis	Der vorliegende Text ist ein Auszug aus dem Roman *Treasure Island* von Robert Louis Stevenson, erschienen im Klett Verlag als *Easy Reader*-Ausgabe (ISBN 3-12-536241-3).	
Ziel	• Einen Auszug aus einem Abenteuerroman lesen und verstehen	
Wortschatz	Annotationen S. 106/107	
Methodisches Vorgehen	• *Pre-reading:* Als Einstimmung schreibt L den Titel des Romans an die Tafel und die S spekulieren über den Inhalt. Alternative: L legt **KV 11: Treasure Island**, Teilaufgabe a), als Folie auf. Hier sind zahlreiche Bilder zum Romanauszug ab-	

gebildet. Die S spekulieren, um welche Art von Geschichte es sich handeln könnte und begründen ihre Aussage.
- L präsentiert den Text von CD, die S hören wahlweise bei geöffnetem/geschlossenem SB zu (abhängig vom Leistungsstand der Lerngruppe). Eine Unterbrechung der Präsentation sollte vermieden werden, das ganzheitliche Erschließen eines Textes steht hier im Vordergrund.
- Nach dem Hören/Lesen überprüft L das Textverständnis durch **KV 11: Treasure Island**, Teilaufgabe b), oder anhand der *wh*-Fragen. Sammeln von Stichpunkten an der Tafel/auf Folie.

TA

```
                    Treasure Island
Who?    Jim, his mother, the captain, the blind beggar, the neighbours
When?   18th century, one evening/night
Where?  In the 'Admiral Benbow' inn in Bristol
What?   The captain dies after he got a piece of paper from a blind beggar.
        Jim and his mother want money from the captain.
        They go to their neighbours.
        They take money from the sea chest and run away.
Why?    The captain didn't pay for his bed in the inn.
        The neighbours are too scared to help.
        Jim and his mum run away after they have taken the money because
        they are afraid, too.
```

Erweiterung
- In Anlehnung an *ex.* 4 zum Haupttext der Unit *(My big adventure)* schreiben die S eine Textpassage aus dem Romanauszug in einen Dialog um. Anbieten würde sich hier z. B. das Gespräch mit den Nachbarn (Z. 19–26).

Material
s 2/23–26
L 4/17–20
Kopiervorlage 11
Ggf. Leerfolie

Dictation

Last week I listened to the news on TV. It was very interesting. Someone talked about the first trip to the moon. That was a fantastic journey but also a dangerous one! Later a reporter talked about an accident in Spain. A coach full of German tourists crashed into a lorry. A fire broke out and the firefighters had to come. There were many police officers and paramedics around who helped the tourists out of the coach. Many people screamed but in the end everybody was safe. Some tourists had to go to hospital but many were able to continue their trip by train …

6 ⟨Freiarbeit⟩

⟨Freiarbeit⟩

Ziele
- Informationen aus einem Text visualisieren
- Logisches Denken fördern
- Das Wortfeld *geography* wiederholen und vertiefen

Üben — **A treasure map**

Methodisches Vorgehen
- Die S vervollständigen die Flaschenpost (**KV 12a: A treasure map**). Anschließend beschriften sie die Karte der Insel, indem sie mit Hilfe der Hinweise auf der Schatzkarte auf die Lage der beschriebenen Orte schließen (**KV 12b+c: A treasure map**). Dies kann sowohl in Einzelarbeit, PA oder auch in Kleingruppen erfolgen.
- Die Freiarbeit zu Unit 6 bietet sich als Ergänzung zum bilingualen Sachfachunterricht in Klasse 7 an (i. d. R. Erdkunde), da sie sowohl fachspezifische Methoden (Kartenarbeit) aufgreift als auch geographisches Vokabular vertieft.

Erweiterung
- Die S können die Schatzkarte bunt gestalten und im Klassenraum aufhängen.
- Alternativ können sie eigene Schatzkarten entwerfen und die Mitschüler/innen mit Hilfe von **KV 12c** „ihren" Schatz finden lassen.

> **TIP**
> Der Zeitrahmen für die Freiarbeit umfasst 1–2 Unterrichtsstunden inkl. HA

Lösung

KV 12a: year – world/sea/ocean – ship – strong wind/storm – scared – wave – beach – sun – dead – wood – dangers – island – fish – animals – people – alone – gold/silver/diamonds – letter/message – save/rescue – promise

KV 12c:

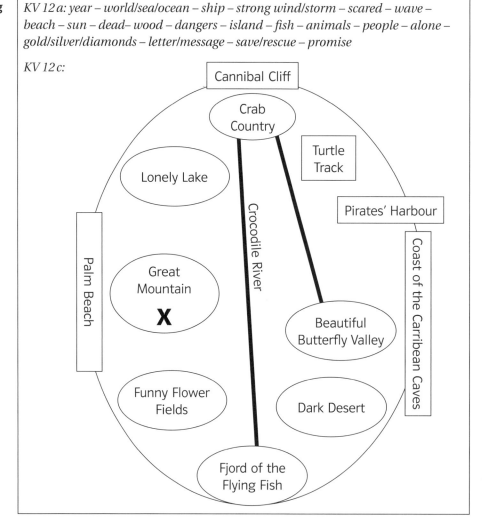

Material
Kopiervorlage 12a–c
Wörterbücher
Buntstifte

KV 1: Time to travel

a) *Draw a mindmap. Here are some key words that can help you to start:*

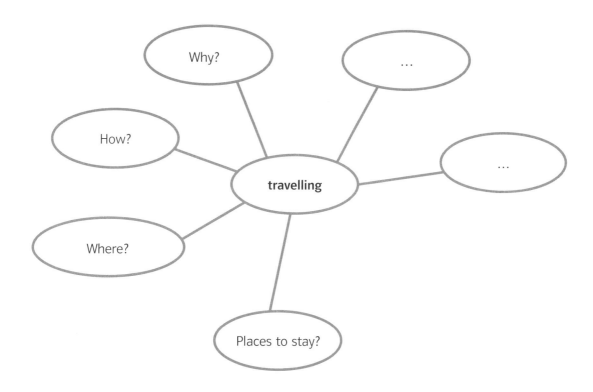

b) *Do this quiz about famous travellers and their journeys and English as a world language. Tick (✔) the right answers.*

1. Marco Polo travelled through …
   - [ ] Asia
   - [ ] America
   - [ ] Africa

2. Marco Polo brought back from his journey:
   - [ ] potatoes
   - [ ] noodles
   - [ ] apples

3. The *Beagle* was the ship of …
   - [ ] Marco Polo
   - [ ] Charles Darwin
   - [ ] Ellen MacArthur

4. Neil Armstrong landed on the moon in …
   - [ ] 1963
   - [ ] 1965
   - [ ] 1969

5. Ellen MacArthur …
   - [ ] sailed around the world
   - [ ] travelled to the moon
   - [ ] travelled to China to work as a missionary

6. English is the first language of more than …
   - [ ] 300 million people
   - [ ] 330 million people
   - [ ] 400 million people

7. English is used for more than 85 per cent of all …
   - [ ] phone calls around the world
   - [ ] Internet messages
   - [ ] official letters

Lösung: 1 *Asia* 2 *noodles* 3 *Charles Darwin* 4 *1969* 5 *sailed around the world* 6 *330 million people* 7 *Internet messages*

KV 2: Computer games

Report what the boys and girls said about computer games in an interview for the school magazine.

¹**software engineer** [ˈsɒftweər ˌendʒɪnɪə] = Programmierer

Lösung: 1 Kelly said it wasn't easy to find good computer games which weren't too expensive. 2 Ben explained that he wanted to become a software engineer. Then he could make his own games. 3 Rhona said she didn't like computer games. 4 Michael mentioned that last week his grandma had given him money for a new game. He said that had been really great. 5 Wayne explained that 'Kings and Knights' was fantastic. 6 Tariq said he had played a new game the day before but it had been boring after some time.

KV 3: An interview

This is an interview between a famous pop star, Joe X, and a reporter, Rick, from a music magazine.
You are Rick. Report to your readers what Joe X said in the interview.

Reporter: Hi Joe! It's great to have you here! How are you?
Joe X: Hi Rick! I'm fine, thanks.
Reporter: Well, Joe, how is life as a pop star?
Joe X: Oh, it's cool and very exciting. Last week, for example, I made a video for my new single in Berlin and yesterday I went to the studio in New York to record the new album.
Reporter: Oh, that's fantastic. What's the name of your new album?
Joe X: Sorry, I can't tell you. It's still a secret.
Reporter: I see. – So you're going on tour soon, are you?
Joe X: Yeah, that's right. I'm starting the tour in Los Angeles next week.
Reporter: Great. And what are your plans for after the tour?
Joe X: I'll need a break! I'm planning a holiday in Bali.
Reporter: That sounds awesome. OK, Joe, thanks a lot for the interview.
Joe X: No problem, Rick. Goodbye!

_____
_____
_____
_____
_____
_____
_____
_____
_____

Lösungsvorschlag: I did an interview with Joe X. He told me that he was fine. He said that life as a pop star was cool and very exciting. The week before, for example, he had made a video for his new single in Berlin and the day before he had gone to the studio in New York to record the new album. He couldn't tell me the name of the new album. He explained that it was still a secret. He said that he was going on tour soon and that he was starting the tour in Los Angeles the following week. At the end of the interview, he told me that after the tour he would need a break and that he was planning a holiday in Bali.

KV 4: Emergency on the motorway

What is different from the report on page 97 in your book? Look at the picture and find the mistakes. Write complete sentences.

Lösung: *The accident happened on the M20. / The accident was between a lorry and a coach. / The coach was bringing pupils back from France. / Two ambulances were there. / Two girls came out of the field. / There were many people who wanted to watch or help. / The police officer was very busy and had a lot to do.*

KV 5: A school exchange

a) *Before the pupils leave the bus to meet their German families, the teacher, Mr Morgan, tells Robin and the other pupils what to do/not to do. Later Robin tells Michael, his German friend, what the teacher said.*

Start: Mr Morgan told us …

| Speak as much German as possible. | Never forget your mobile! | Phone me if there is a problem. |

| Try every meal the family offers you. | Don't be too quiet. | Don't go out alone! |

b) *The first evening Robin phones his mother and tells her what his German family asked him. Write down what Robin said.*

Start: They wanted to know …

- Have your friends also come to Germany?
- Would you like to go to school with Michael tomorrow?
- Was the journey very long and boring?
- Why can you speak German so well?
- Have you ever been to Germany before?
- Do you like pizza?

Lösung: a) Mr Morgan told us to speak as much German as possible. He warned us not to be too quiet. And he advised us to try every meal our family offered us. Then he asked us not to go out alone and he told us never to forget our mobile. He advised us to phone him if there was a problem. b) They wanted to know if my friends had also come to Germany. Then they asked me if I would like to go to school with Michael the next day. Michael asked me if I liked pizza and his mother wanted to know if the journey had been very long and boring. Then Michael's father asked me if I had ever been to Germany before. Michael's sister wanted to know why I could speak German so well.

6 Kopiervorlagen

KV 6: Travel situations

a) *At the travel agency: the conversation is not in the correct order. Make a dialogue from the sentences. Then finish the conversation.*

- Good morning!
- Oh, that's a great idea.
- Well, I would like to go on a beach holiday.
- I can offer you a wonderful hotel in Barcelona!
- Good morning. What can I do for you?
- I see. That's no problem. Let's have a look.
- I want to go on holiday to Spain.

A: Good morning! _____

B: _____

b) *At the airport: rewrite the conversation. Use phrases and fillers to show that the people are happy to talk to each other. Finish the dialogue and act it with a partner. Use your exercise book.*

A: Hello.
B: Hello.
A: Can you help me?
B: What do you want?
A: I've lost my ticket. My flight number is LH 109 to Paris.
B: I can't help you. You must phone the ticket hotline.
A: Have you got the number?
B: …

Lösung: a) *Lösungsvorschlag:* A: Good morning! B: Good morning. What can I do for you? A: I want to go on holiday to Spain. B: Oh, that's a great idea. I can offer you a wonderful hotel in Barcelona! A: Well, I would like to go on a beach holiday. B: I see. That's no problem. Let's have a look. A: Yes, I will. B: Okay, here you are. I've got a hotel on the Costa Brava and I think it's really cheap. A: How much is it? B: It's £ 100 for one week in a single room! A: Oh, that's great. I'll take that.
b) *Lösungsvorschlag:* A: Hello. B: Hello! A: Can I help you? B: Well, I hope you can. A: Yes, what's the problem? B: You see, I've lost my ticket. My flight number is LH 109 to Paris. A: Oh, that's terrible! But I'm sorry, I can't really help you. You must phone the ticket hotline. B: Mmm, have you got the number for me? A: Yes, wait a moment, please. I'll get it for you.

342 © Ernst Klett Verlag GmbH, Stuttgart 2008. Alle Rechte vorbehalten. GREEN LINE 3
ISBN 978-3-12-547143-6

KV 7: My big adventure

What happened to Mr Fogg, Passepartout, Aouda and the other passengers on their way from San Francisco to New York? Find the correct order.

	A. There were many buffalo on the track and the train had to wait until all the animals had left the track.
	B. The train was going as fast as possible but the Sioux were on the train.
	C. The journey started in San Francisco. All the passengers wanted to go to New York.
	D. A man told them the bridge was not safe for a heavy train.
	E. A mile from the next station the train stopped again.
	F. The passengers tried to shoot the Sioux.
	G. Suddenly the passengers heard loud bangs and screams.
	H. The train driver didn't give up and the train went over the bridge at a very high speed.
	I. Hundreds of Sioux were attacking the train.
	J. The next morning the train came to Nevada.
	K. Suddenly the train stopped and the passengers could hear a loud bellow.
	L. Then they came through Utah and went up the Rocky Mountains.

Lösung: 1-C; 2-J; 3-K; 4-A; 5-L; 6-E; 7-D; 8-H; 9-G; 10-I; 11-F; 12-B

KV 8: A scary castle

Linda, 13, had to write about her holiday for her English test. Read what she wrote and then make Linda's story more interesting! Look at the tips on page 103 in your book.

On the last day of my holiday I went on a trip with my parents and my brother. We wanted to visit a castle. We had to walk up a mountain for some miles and the weather got worse in the afternoon. It started to rain and it was very stormy. When we arrived at the castle we bought our tickets. Then we went through dark, empty rooms. I thought about how the people had lived in the past.
What was that? I heard a noise.
I looked for my parents but I couldn't see them. Where were they?
I heard the noise again. Then I saw a shadow on the wall and I heard steps and the noise again. I wanted to run away but I couldn't because I was so scared. Suddenly the man from the ticket office was there and he said: Hello, I just wanted to see if all the windows are closed. It's raining and the storm is getting stronger. We must be careful ...

KV 9: Sounds and spelling

a) *Find two different spellings for these sounds!*

1. [hɪə] 2. [ðeə] 3. [sʌn] 4. [wiːk]

_____ _____ _____ _____

_____ _____ _____ _____

5. [weə] 6. [fɔː]

_____ _____

_____ _____

b) *Find 21 words in this word search puzzle. Most of the words have to do with TRAVELLING. The more words you find, the easier exercise 3 on page 104 will be!*

B	A	N	N	O	Y	I	N	G	R	W	S	T	D	R	I	V	E	R	T
A	F	A	A	S	D	W	E	G	F	D	S	L	K	L	O	I	N	M	R
C	G	H	I	J	F	L	I	G	H	T	U	Z	O	T	R	E	E	W	A
C	R	E	W	Q	A	S	D	C	V	B	N	M	V	W	X	Y	A	S	C
I	A	S	Y	D	P	L	O	P	A	S	S	E	N	G	E	R	I	Z	K
D	E	R	T	U	I	O	P	U	Z	H	K	T	L	H	G	F	D	S	A
E	R	T	E	F	D	C	R	A	S	L	R	K	I	M	N	A	B	H	U
N	J	W	A	R	N	L	O	T	H	A	G	T	R	R	E	R	W	S	D
T	W	E	R	T	Z	U	I	O	C	P	K	L	L	J	H	R	F	R	S
A	W	S	E	D	R	F	T	K	G	Z	H	U	A	J	I	I	I	L	J
F	R	G	T	H	Z	H	U	J	I	K	O	L	T	U	H	V	B	V	O
T	X	C	T	I	M	E	D	F	G	H	J	K	E	T	E	E	A	S	U
A	R	F	Z	H	R	A	I	L	W	A	Y	A	S	W	E	D	R	F	R
K	G	H	J	K	I	U	I	O	P	L	Z	P	J	K	Z	H	T	G	N
E	G	T	H	D	E	L	A	Y	U	I	T	Z	A	R	E	W	A	A	E
G	H	J	K	I	L	O	M	N	B	Z	T	R	E	R	W	E	C	S	Y
Y	P	L	A	N	E	D	F	G	D	E	S	K	T	H	K	U	J	K	I

Lösungen a) 1. *to hear/here* 2. *their/there* 3. *sun/son* 4. *week/weak* 5. *where/wear* 6. *for/four* b) → *annoying; driver; flight; passenger; warn; time; railway; delay; plane; desk* ↓ *accident; take; late; arrive; track; journey* ↘ *airport; track; slow; drive; park*

KV 10: Do you remember?

Only one of the answers is correct. Do you know which?

1. What is 'the Globe'?
   a) a theatre
   b) a wax museum
   c) a Shakespeare play
   d) a club

2. What band is Liverpool famous for?
   a) The Rolling Stones
   b) The Beatles
   c) The Tom-Toms
   d) U2

3. Shirin's relatives speak
   a) Punjabi.
   b) Turkish.
   c) Spanish.
   d) French.

4. The 'Superbowl' is a
   a) leisure centre.
   b) soap opera.
   c) rock band.
   d) football match.

5. The Pattersons are worried about Grandpa because he
   a) is very ill.
   b) wants to leave the old people's home.
   c) had an accident.
   d) can't look after himself any more.

6. What is the trendiest magazine for teenage girls today in the UK?
   a) Smash hits
   b) Couch potato
   c) Shout
   d) Popcorn

7. Neil Armstrong was
   a) an American president.
   b) an athlete.
   c) the first person on the moon.
   d) a singer.

8. What does Chloe find in her mother's wardrobe?
   a) jewellery
   b) a diary
   c) her pullover
   d) a lot of money

9. Who is Phileas Fogg's servant?
   a) Aouda
   b) Ben Brown
   c) Medicine Bow
   d) Passepartout

10. Mr Patterson's father finally
    a) moves in with his family.
    b) moves in with a friend.
    c) stays in his own flat.
    d) goes into an old people's home.

11. 'Abertawe' is the Welsh name for
    a) Great Britain.
    b) Mount Snowdon.
    c) Swansea.
    d) the Irish Sea.

12. Who was Sir Francis Drake?
    a) a royal servant
    b) a Roman soldier
    c) a pirate
    d) a Spanish king

13. Which of these soap operas is not British?
    a) Coronation Street
    b) Grey's Anatomy
    c) Emmerdale
    d) EastEnders

14. Mr Fogg and the other passengers are attacked by
    a) Sioux.
    b) buffalo.
    c) pirates.
    d) aliens.

15. Who is not a member of the Patterson family?
    a) Amy
    b) Mel
    c) Jake
    d) Miriam

16. Which city is called the 'pop cult capital' of the UK?
    a) London
    b) Manchester
    c) Glasgow
    d) Belfast

17. What is Ryan going to buy with his birthday money?
    a) a DVD
    b) a book
    c) a computer game
    d) an MP3 player

18. Janice can help a little boy because she
    a) watches 'Emergency Room' regularly.
    b) is a doctor.
    c) had some training at school.
    d) is a nurse.

19. What is special about Timothy?
    a) He is an excellent pupil.
    b) He can see things.
    c) He knows a lot of stories.
    d) He speaks five languages.

20. Who is Eddie Edwards?
    a) the winner of a gold medal
    b) a tennis player
    c) an actor
    d) a ski jumper

21. Shirin's family moved to
    a) London.
    b) Edinburgh.
    c) Manchester.
    d) Swansea.

22. When the Pattersons' children are home alone, they
    a) have a party.
    b) tidy up their rooms.
    c) watch TV.
    d) get bored.

23. Windsor is famous for
    a) its castle.
    b) cheese.
    c) music festivals.
    d) its beaches.

24. The Industrial Revolution started in the
    a) 17th century.
    b) 18th century.
    c) 19th century.
    d) 20th century.

25. What can you find in Anfield Road?
    a) the Williamson Tunnels
    b) Swansea Leisure Centre Skatepark
    c) the National Waterfront Museum
    d) Liverpool Football Club

26. Stephen Hoskins worked as a
    a) casting director.
    b) shop assistant.
    c) factory worker.
    d) reporter.

27. Which river runs through Reading?
    a) the Thames
    b) the Mersey
    c) the Tyne
    d) the Severn

28. Amy Patterson is
    a) a football fan.
    b) Jake's twin sister.
    c) a good cook.
    d) a vegetarian.

29. Which of these names is not a British newspaper?
    a) The Times
    b) The Sun
    c) The BBC
    d) The Daily Mirror

30. When Bill is in hospital, he reads
    a) nothing at all.
    b) Harry Potter.
    c) Lord of the Rings.
    d) magazines.

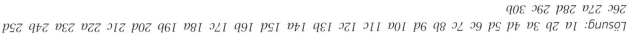

Lösung: 1a 2b 3a 4d 5d 6c 7c 8b 9d 10a 11c 12c 13b 14a 15d 16b 17c 18a 19b 20d 21c 22a 23a 24b 25d 26c 27a 28d 29c 30b

© Ernst Klett Verlag GmbH, Stuttgart 2008. Alle Rechte vorbehalten.
ISBN 978-3-12-547143-6

KV 11: Treasure Island

a) *Say what these objects have to do with the story.*

b) *Tell the story of Jim and his mother with the help of these pictures.*

KV 12 a: A treasure map

You have found a message in a bottle on your favourite beach. The letter inside is wet, and so some words have disappeared. Read the letter. Guess what the missing words are. Exchange letters with a partner and check his/her work.

Lonely Island in the _____ 1798

Dear reader,

I am a man on a lonely island somewhere in the _____. It all happened when I was on my journey to America on a _____ called Mary. One day, I was walking the planks when a _____ came up suddenly, and the ship sank. I was very _____ and couldn't do anything. A large _____ pushed me into the water!

When I woke up again, I wasn't on the ship any more. I was on a sandy _____, and the _____ was shining. I was happy that I wasn't _____. I got up, frightened and hungry, and collected some _____ to make a fire, but I had to be careful. Who knows what _____ were waiting for me here!?

Then I looked around the _____. It has got a green forest, a large mountain, many colourful _____ in a long river, and beautiful trees on the long beach where I had woken up. But one part of the island is hot, dry and full of scorpions and other dangerous _____.

I looked for _____, but I found no one. I am _____ on the island. But you will not believe what I found. I won't say where, because pirates could find it, too, but there is a treasure chest with a lot of _____ hidden somewhere on the island. The treasure map on the back of this _____ will help you to find me and the treasure.

Please come and _____ me. You will get part of the treasure, I _____!

The lonely man

KV 12 b: A treasure map

butterflies

turtle

crab

Palm Beach is not next to Crab Country in the north.
Beautiful Butterfly Valley[1] is in the east,
on the Coast of the Caribbean Caves, south of Pirates' Harbour.
Turtle Track goes from Crab Country to Beautiful Butterfly Valley.
Crocodile River goes from the north to the south of the island
and into the Fjord of the Flying Fish.
Funny Flower Fields are west of Crocodile River, east of Palm Beach,
and south of the Lonely Lake
but they are not next to Beautiful Butterfly Valley.
The Dark Desert is not in the north, west or
east of the island, but it is east of Crocodile River.
Cannibal Cliff is on the coast of Crab Country.
The place where the treasure is hidden
is on the top of the Great Mountain, not in
Crab Country, or in Beautiful Butterfly Valley or in a very hot place.
It is not on the coast but it is on the western side
of Crocodile River.
Are you clever enough to look for these places,
fight the dangers and find the treasure?

field of flowers

cliff

treasure chest

palm tree

crocodile

[1] **valley** ['væli] = Tal

KV 12 c: A treasure map

Work with a partner. Draw the parts of the island which are described in the treasure map (KV 12 b) and find the treasure.

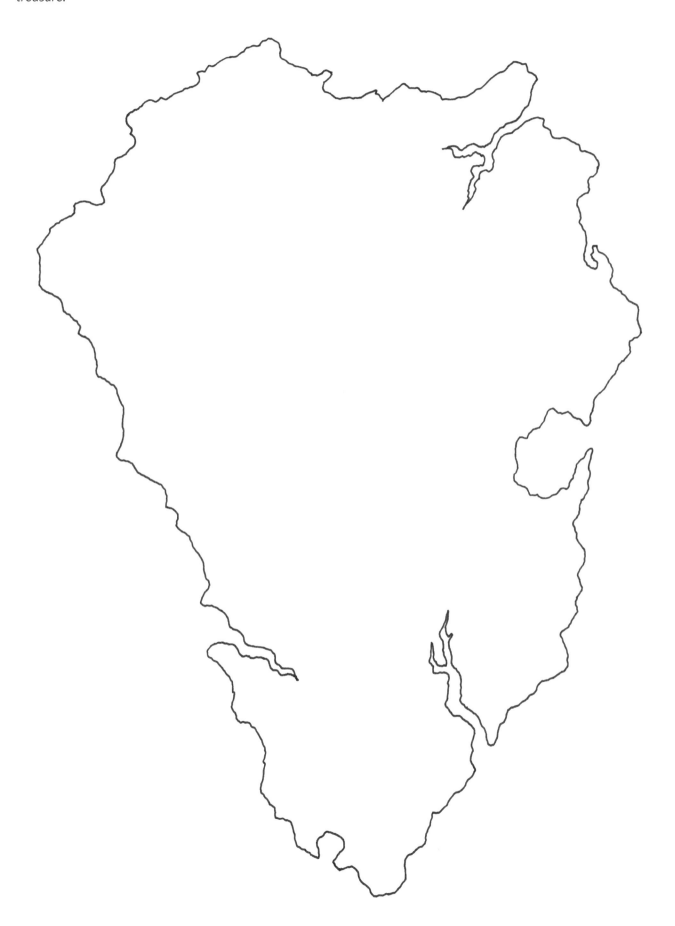

⟨Revision for tests⟩ Unit 5–6

Seite 108–109

> **Ziele**
> - Vorbereitung auf Standardprüfungen
> - Die neuen Grammatikpensen festigen: *passive* und *indirect speech*
> - Einen kurzen biografischen Text schreiben
> - Bei einem Unfall als Sprachmittler auftreten
> - Einem Radiomitschnitt Informationen entnehmen
> - Einen Text über Kinderarbeit verstehen und mit der eigenen Situation vergleichen
> - Einen Artikel für die Schülerzeitung schreiben

Üben   **1 Mixed bag: From Station Road to Hollywood**   Seite 108

Ziel
- Wörter aus dem Textzusammenhang erschließen
- Die neuen Grammatikpensen festigen

Strukturen
- *Passive, indirect questions, indirect commands*

Methodisches Vorgehen
- L weist auf die Notwendigkeit hin, die neu erlernte Grammatik (G 19–22, G 23–28) sowie den Gesamtzusammenhang zu berücksichtigen. Auch die Vokabelanhänge der Units können den gesuchten Wortschatz liefern.
- Die Aufgabe wird in Einzelarbeit gelöst; anschließend Kontrolle in PA. Schwierige Stellen können im Plenum besprochen werden.
- Wenn die Aufgabe für die Lerngruppe zu schwierig erscheint, kann L ein Lösungsblatt mit *scrambled answers* ausgeben (Differenzierung nach unten).

TIP Differenzierung nach unten durch *scrambled answers*

Erweiterung
- Nachdem der Wortschatz zum Thema *media* in der Aufgabe umgewälzt wurde, bietet sich eine schriftliche Erweiterung an: *Would you like to be in a daily soap? Write a short text (3 sentences) and say why or why not.*

Auch als HA geeignet

Lösung

> 1 *celeb*   2 *was*   3 *soap*   4 *had*   5 *commercials/ads*   6 *be*   7 *was*   8 *but*
> 9 *to*   10 *if*   11 *was*   12 *given*   13 *sent*   14 *contract*   15 *been*   16 *already*
> 17 *will*

Tipps für junge Lehrer
Eine Alternative zu den *scrambled answers* sind *letter sandwiches*: Statt *celeb* gibt man nur *c…b* an. *Letter sandwiches* kann L in der richtigen oder in vertauschter Reihenfolge vorgeben.

Material *Workbook* S. 75/1

Üben   **2 Eric Liddell – athlete and missionary**   Seite 108

Ziel
- *Connecting words* sammeln und anwenden
- Einen kurzen biografischen Text schreiben
- Die *Useful phrases: Check each other's …* anwenden
- Das *scanning* anhand von authentischen Texten einüben

Methodisches Vorgehen
- L fragt nach *connecting words* und schreibt einige Beispiele an die Tafel (*so, because, but, when, …*). Dabei betont er die Notwendigkeit, Texte möglichst interessant zu gestalten.
- Die S schreiben anhand der Bilder einen Text in Einzelarbeit oder als Hausaufgabe. Anschließend Partnerkontrolle, ggf. zu Beginn der nächsten Stunde. Dabei sollten die S die *Useful phrases: Check each other's …* (S. 84) benutzen.
- L präsentiert einen Beispieltext auf Folie (siehe Lösung) und fragt nach *connecting words* und anderen sprachlichen Mitteln, die den Text interessant klingen lassen. Gleichzeitig können die S mit Hilfe der *Useful phrases* Verbesserungsvorschläge machen.

TIP *Useful phrases: Check each other's …* (S. 84)

Auch als HA geeignet

⟨Revision C⟩ R

| Erweiterung | • Die S ergänzen den Text mit zusätzlichen Informationen aus dem Internet. Bei Google finden sich mehrere Treffer zu Eric Liddell. Die S sollten die schwierigen Texte aus dem Internet jedoch nur überfliegen (*scanning*) und wichtige Punkte aufgreifen (*making notes*), die sie für ihre Texte nutzen können. L kann auch eine Internetseite vorgeben, z. B. http://www.bbc.co.uk/scotland/sportscotland/asportingnation/article/0019/ |

Lösung

> *Erwartungshorizont:*
> In 1916 Eric Liddell ran in a race at his school in Edinburgh. His teachers got very excited when they saw him win. One of his teachers shouted that Eric was the fastest again. In 1924 the Olympic Games were held in Paris. A friend told Eric that he had to run in the 100 m, but Eric said that he wouldn't run on a Sunday because he was a religious man. So he didn't run in the 100 m on Sunday, but he ran in the 400 m on another day – and won gold for Britain! He couldn't believe it – he felt great. Everybody in the British team was cheering and clapping. Eric was a brilliant athlete and a year later he was told he could be a brilliant scientist, too, but Eric said he was going to be a missionary, like his parents. So Eric became a missionary in China. In 1941 he was asked if he was going back to the UK because China and Japan were at war, but Eric explained that he was staying in China with his pupils.

Tipps für junge Lehrer — Notizen zu authentischen Texten sind eine hervorragende Möglichkeit, *scanning* als Lesetechnik einzuüben.

Material Workbook S. 75/2

Üben 3 Mediation: There's been an accident Seite 108

Ziel
- Bei einem Unfall als Sprachmittler auftreten
- Ein Rollenspiel auswendig vorführen

Methodisches Vorgehen
- Die S bearbeiten die Aufgabe in PA. Alternative: L fordert die S auf, in Kleingruppen ein Rollenspiel vorzubereiten. Dies wirkt an dieser Stelle authentischer als eine bloße schriftliche Bearbeitung der Aufgabe.
- Nachdem die drei Rollen verteilt wurden, machen sich die S zunächst Gedanken über die mögliche Situation. Beispiel: Der verletzte deutsche Tourist sitzt auf dem Boden. Wie verhalten sich der Polizist und der andere Tourist *(you)*? Anschließend entwerfen die S ein Rollenspiel und lernen ihre Rolle als Hausaufgabe auswendig.

HA

Erweiterung — Das Rollenspiel kann auch direkt im Anschluss an die Erarbeitung in den Kleingruppen eingeübt werden. Ziel ist es, mehrere Rollenspiele auswendig vor dem Plenum vorzuspielen.

TIP
Auswendiglernen steigert die Konzentration

Lösung
> Sind Sie verletzt? – He isn't hurt. He only got a shock – Haben Sie gesehen, was passiert ist? – He didn't really, but it looked terrible. – Ist das Auto sehr schnell gefahren? – He says he's sorry, but he can't tell. He wants to know if anybody was hurt. – Ja, der Fahrer wurde verletzt. Er ist mit dem Krankenwagen ins Krankenhaus gebracht worden. – He feels sick. – Er wird einen Sanitäter bitten, sich um Sie zu kümmern. – Thanks a lot.

Tipps für junge Lehrer — Wenn die S ein solches Rollenspiel mehrmals durchspielen, steigert das Auswendiglernen die Konzentration.

Material Workbook S. 76/3

Üben 4 Listening: Which film is right for Julie? Seite 109

HV-Text DJ: And now for all our cinema fans, here's a roundup of some of the films now showing in town.

353

⟨Revision C⟩

Film number one is *Hello, Doc!* at the ABC cinema. It's a hospital drama starring Gary Manning as the nice young doctor who finds answers to all the patients' problems – and to his own, too. Will he fall in love with Farah, the pretty paramedic, or Leila, the girl with the broken leg? People cry a lot in this film, and some nearly die. But there isn't a *lot* of blood, and not much violence, either. There are more love stories than emergencies.

Film number two is *Flight 927* showing at The Odeon, an exciting science-fiction thriller about a group of scientists who are attacked by aliens on their way to the moon. They are beamed to another planet. Maybe you won't find the aliens awfully frightening, but the computer tricks are very clever. Everything looks realistic, and there's always another surprise waiting for you. The music from the soundtrack is a big hit at the moment.

You can see this week's film number three, *Open Country*, at the Plaza. It's all about a journey, too, but this story happened about 200 years ago in Australia. Two Englishmen are sent to make maps of the coast for the British government. The travellers have problems with the weather, the people – and with each other. It was filmed in Australia, and the landscape is fantastic. The film seems very long and slow in some parts, so don't expect non-stop action. It's good entertainment, though.

Ziel
- Einen Radiomitschnitt verstehen
- Eine Entscheidung anhand von Notizen begründen

Methodisches Vorgehen

Pre-listening:
- Die S überlegen sich ein *listening grid*, um die drei Filme nach Julies Interessen beurteilen zu können: *Let's make a listening grid to help us say which film is right for Julie. How can you do it?* Es ist im Sinne einer selbstständigen Vorbereitung auf Standardprüfungen sinnvoll, dass die S solche Hörverstehensstrategien entwickeln lernen. Anschließend werden die Vorschläge kurz im Plenum besprochen und ein gemeinsames *listening grid* an der Tafel erstellt.

While-listening:
- Die S hören den Radiomitschnitt an und machen Kreuze in die entsprechenden Kästchen des *listening grid*.
- Beim zweiten Anhören machen sich die S in einer weiteren Spalte Notizen zu den einzelnen Filmen, um ihre Entscheidung anschließend begründen zu können.

Post-listening:
- Vergleich der Ergebnisse in PA; anschließend Besprechung im Plenum.

> **TIP**
> Hörverstehensstrategien entwickeln

TA

Julie's interests	Notes on films	Films		
		1 Hello, Doc!	2 Flight 927	3 Open Country
taking photos	fantastic landscape			x
travelling to other countries	journey to Australia			x
+ real adventure stories	two Englishmen sent to make maps of coast problems with weather, people and each other			x
+ history	about 200 years ago			x
+ own website				
– silly love stories	young doc + pretty paramedic or + girl with broken leg?	x		

	a lot of crying, more love stories than emergencies	x		
– brother's computer games	clever computer tricks		x	

Lösung

Erwartungshorizont: I think 'Open Country' is the right film for Julie. It has everything she likes – travelling, adventure, history – and pictures of Australia's fantastic landscape. It's a real adventure story about two Englishmen who are sent to Australia by the British government about 200 years ago to map the coast. There they have problems with the weather, the people and with each other.

Tipps für junge Lehrer

Wenn L das *listening grid* vorgeben möchte, sollte auf eine vorherige Sammlung der S-Vorschläge verzichtet werden. Die S könnten sich ansonsten nicht ernst genommen fühlen.

Material
 L 4/21

Üben

5 Who makes our footballs?

Seite 109

Ziel
- Einen Text eigenständig erschließen
- *Skimming* und *scanning* als Lesetechniken einüben
- Einen Zeitungsbericht schreiben

Methodisches Vorgehen
- Die S lesen Teilaufgabe a) und machen sich Notizen. Für die Bearbeitung der Fragen notwendige Vokabeln werden von L auf S-Nachfrage hin an der Tafel gesammelt (evtl. in einer *mindmap*).
- Die S beantworten die Eingangsfragen in Einzelarbeit; Vergleich der Ergebnisse in PA.
- Anschließend lesen die S den Text leise für sich *(skimming)*.
- Teilaufgabe b) sollte als Hausaufgabe bearbeitet werden, möglichst nicht von einem Tag auf den anderen. Hierbei sollen die S das *scanning* als Lesetechnik einüben. L spricht ggf. die einzelnen Arbeitsschritte mit den S durch (siehe TA).
- Die schriftliche Hausaufgabe kann in Kleingruppen kontrolliert werden. Hier bietet sich ein *relay check* an. Die S lesen die Zeitungsartikel der anderen Gruppenmitglieder und besprechen sie nach jedem Lesevorgang, bevor sie weitergegeben werden. Sie sollten dabei die *Useful phrases*: Check each other's … (S. 84) anwenden.
- *Who has written the most interesting text in the group?* Die besten Texte können auf Poster geschrieben und an der Wand des Klassenraums präsentiert werden.

TIP
Think first – then write!

HA

TA

Get ready to write:
1. Scan texts for useful information
2. Make notes
3. Plan your answer – paragraphs!
4. Write
5. Check – spelling, grammar, writing skills (p. 85)

Erweiterung
- Die S können als freiwillige Zusatzaufgabe ein *local radio feature* zum Thema *Jobs children do* schreiben und evtl. aufnehmen.

Lösung

Individuelle S-Antworten

Tipps für junge Lehrer

Die meisten S schreiben, ohne vorher nachzudenken. Es ist daher wichtig, den S die Notwendigkeit einiger Vorüberlegungen zu vermitteln (siehe TA). Kreativität braucht Konzentration und Zeit nach dem Motto: *Think first – then write!*

Material
Workbook S. 76/4
Ggf. Poster

Skills

Workbook Seite 79

Üben — **Listening: Listen for keywords** — Workbook Seite 79

HV-Text Workbook

Woman: Welcome to the information and booking service for the Picturehouse Cinema. Please listen to this list of options and choose the number you require. To book tickets, please press 1. For details about films and performance times, please press 2. For information about film certificates, please press 3. To find out about facilities for the disabled, please press 4. For membership of the Picturehouse Film Club, please press 5. To hear about special events and educational activities, please press 6. For opening times of the Picturehouse café, please press 7. To hear all these options again, please press 8.

Material
S 2/27
L 4/27
Workbook S. 79/1

Üben — **Listening: Take notes while you listen** — Workbook Seite 79

HV-Text Workbook

A: Well, Jessica, let's tell everybody out there what exciting things there are to do in our town this weekend.
B: Sure, Kaleb. Can I start?
A: That's fine with me.
B: Great. Because I've got a top tip for our younger listeners. A fantastic all-day drama workshop! Anyone between the ages of eleven and sixteen can take part. And you don't only learn to act. You also get the chance to work stage lights and try out costumes and put on make-up and design a set and – oh, too many things to mention!
A: Sounds amazing! So when and where is this workshop?
B: It's on Saturday at the Royal Theatre. It starts at nine in the morning and goes on till six o'clock in the evening. And – I think you'll have to agree this is pretty cheap for a whole day – it only costs ten pounds.
A: Well, ten pounds isn't bad, I admit. But my first tip is something that can actually save you money!
B: Save you money? Really?
A: Yes. It's a special promotion by the Italian Kitchen.
B: Italian Kitchen. That's the pizza place in Victoria Street, right?
A: Right. And what they're doing this weekend is giving you two pizzas for the price of one! You have to go with a friend. I mean, you can't go and eat two pizzas yourself! But anyway, two people only pay for one pizza. So that's good news.
B: And is the offer for the whole weekend?
A: It's for Saturday and Sunday, yes. But – and this is important – only until three o'clock in the afternoon.
B: So you need to be hungry early in the day! Well, that's OK for you, Kaleb. You're always hungry!
A: Thank you, Jessica! Now, moving quickly on - what are you going to tell us about next?
B: I'm going to tell you about the Technology Museum. It's just reopened this week.
A: Oh, yes, it was closed for a long time, wasn't it?
B: Well, they wanted to change it all. And I can tell you, they have changed it! It's a really cool place now. I've already been there myself, and it's, like, so hands on, with loads of fun machines you can try out. And there are things there for people of all ages.
A: So it's a good tip for families.
B: Yes, it's perfect for families. And, unlike most museums these days, it's free. It doesn't cost anything at all.

A: Fantastic! Oh, and what about opening hours?
B: It's open every day from ten o'clock to five o'clock, except for Sunday. On Sundays it's only open in the afternoon, from two to half past five.
A: Thanks, Jessica. Now, there's just time for one last idea about what you can do this weekend. Well, it's for Sunday evening, actually. And that's a ghost tour!
B: Ooh! That sounds exciting! I didn't know there were any ghosts around here!
A: There you are, you see. Now is your chance to meet them! The tour starts outside the tourist information centre at half past six, and you walk with the guide around the old part of the town and - well, I'm not going to tell you any more, or it won't be a surprise!
B: How much does it cost?
A: £ 6.50.
B: How much per ghost is that?
A: If you want to know that, you'll have to go on the tour and count the ghosts!
B: I might just do that! Thanks, Kaleb. And thanks to all our listeners. Have a great weekend! Bye now.

Material
◎s 2/28
◎L 4/28
Workbook S. 79/2

Listening: Listen carefully to the sounds of words

Workbook Seite 79

HV-Text Workbook

a)
Julie: Hello. Julie here.
Tom: Hi, Julie. This is Tom. Can I speak to Ed, please?
Julie: Oh hi, Tom. Sorry, but Ed isn't at home just now.
Tom: Oh, well, can you give him a message, do you think?
Julie: Sure, no problem.
Tom: Tell him I've got three tickets for the football match on Saturday.
Julie: Oh, he'll be happy about that!
Tom: And I need to know before tomorrow if he wants one of them. So he should give me a call this evening.
Julie: This evening, you say? Right, I'll tell him.
Tom: Thanks. Bye.

b)
Vicky: Hello.
Kelly: Is that you, Lisa?
Vicky: No, it's Lisa's sister Vicky.
Kelly: Oh, your voice is just like hers!
Vicky: Everybody says that. Anyway, Lisa is out at the moment. So do you want to leave a message?
Kelly: Yeah, that'd be great. Tell her Kelly phoned. That's me. And my boyfriend is having a party tomorrow.
Vicky: Just a moment while I write that down. Kelly – boyfriend – party – OK, got that. Anything else?
Kelly: Er – I'm not sure if she knows his address, so could you give her that, too, please? It's 40, Field Way.
Vicky: Field Way.
Kelly: And the party starts at 7.30.
Vicky: 7.30. Fine. I'll give her the note as soon as she gets home.
Kelly: Thanks very much. Bye.

c)
1. A van hit an actor in the street.
2. It's a very good prize, isn't it?
3. The woman had a problem with her back.
4. I think small glasses are better.
5. He'll be fifty on his next birthday.
6. The two boys never fought about girls.

Material
◎s 2/29
◎L 4/29
Workbook S. 79/3

M | Mediation

Mediation
Seite 110–115

Ziele
- Die Bedeutung von Sprachmittlung verstehen
- Informationen strukturieren und reorganisieren
- Anderen bei Gesprächen als Mittler dienen
- Eine E-Mail und einen Brief verfassen
- Einem HV-Text Informationen entnehmen und diese in der Muttersprache zusammenfassen

Mediation
Seite 110

Methodisches Vorgehen
- Zur Einführung werden die *Mediation skills* S. 110 gemeinsam gelesen und besprochen. Anschließend nennen die S Situationen, in denen sie sich der Bedeutung von Fremdsprachenkenntnissen bewusst geworden sind.
- L betont noch einmal, dass es bei der Sprachmittlung nicht darauf ankommt, wortwörtlich zu übersetzen, sondern die wesentlichen Informationen zu bündeln.

Unit 1 — American Football
Seite 110–111

Ziel
- Die Kernaussagen eines Textes erfassen und in die Muttersprache übertragen.

Methodisches Vorgehen
- L erläutert die Ausgangssituation und die Aufgabenstellung (auf Deutsch), die S hören bei geschlossenem SB zu. Anschließend liest L die einleitenden Sätze zum *American Football* laut vor, die S merken sich ein paar Fakten über Justin Walden und fassen sie anschließend mündlich (auf Deutsch) zusammen.
- L weist erneut auf die Zielsetzung der Aufgabe hin, die S öffnen das SB und orientieren sich am Aufbau des Textes.
- L erstellt eine Tabelle (Tafel/Folie) für den ersten Teil der Aufgabenstellung *(A few basics)*; die S übernehmen die Tabelle in ihre Hefte. Anschließend werden die ersten beiden Informationen zum *American Football* gemeinsam gelesen und in die Tabelle eingetragen.
- Die S beenden den ersten Abschnitt in PA; anschließend Vergleich im Plenum.
- L und die S erstellen eine weitere Tabelle für den zweiten Abschnitt des Textes *(A few rules)*, in die die geforderten Informationen von den S in Einzelarbeit eingetragen werden. Dieser Aufgabenteil ist auch als Hausaufgabe möglich.
- Anschließend präsentieren verschiedene S ihre Ergebnisse, die gemeinsam verglichen und ergänzt bzw. gekürzt werden.
- Alternative: Da der Text sehr anspruchsvoll ist und viele S Schwierigkeiten haben, Wichtiges von Unwichtigem zu trennen, kann der Text auch erst im Plenum (mündlich und/oder schriftlich) erarbeitet werden, bevor die S ihn unter der angegebenen Schwerpunktsetzung zusammenfassen. Dies ist zeitlich aufwändiger, schult aber das Mediationsverständnis der S, die oft Probleme haben, Sachverhalte kompakt in der Muttersprache zu formulieren.

TIP Tabellen anlegen

Auch als HA geeignet

TA Siehe Lösung

Erweiterung
- Die S bereiten eine kurze mündliche Präsentation vor, in der sie die Rolle des kleinen Bruders Jan übernehmen. Hierzu lesen sie erneut den Text und orientieren sich an den zuvor gesammelten Informationen. Während der Präsentation dürfen ausschließlich die beiden Tabellen als Hilfe verwendet werden. Die anderen S übernehmen die Rolle der Freunde, denen Jan die Grundregeln des *American Football* erklären möchte.

Auch als HA geeignet

Lösung

American Football	
Grundlagen	
Wichtig: Amerikaner bezeichnen nur diese Sportart als 'football', den europäischen Fußball nennen sie 'soccer'!	
Anzahl der Spieler	11 Spieler in jedem Team
Spielfeld	91,44 m, zwei Hälften (etwas größer als ein Fußballfeld)
Spielzeit	60 Minuten (vier Viertel mit jeweils 15 Minuten, Halbzeit dauert 12 Minuten)
Ball	ovale Form
Hauptregeln	
Ziel des Spiels	Spieler einer Mannschaft muss mit dem Ball (in den Händen, unter dem Arm) den Bereich hinter dem Tor des Gegners ('end zone') erreichen, gegnerische Spieler verhindern das mit allen Mitteln
Punktesystem/Bewertung	6 Punkte für einen 'touchdown': Ein Spieler erreicht mit dem Ball die gegnerische 'end zone'. 1 Extrapunkt, wenn Ball sofort danach vom 'kicker' über die Torpfosten geschossen wird. 3 Punkte, wenn der Ball vom Spielfeld aus über die Torpfosten geschossen wird

Spielerpositionen	'quarterback'	Angriffsspieler, wirft seinen Mitspielern weite Bälle zu
	'wide-receiver'	fängt die weiten Bälle des 'quarterback' und punktet
Wichtig: 'cheerleaders'	feuern ihr Team an, jubeln, tanzen	

Tipps für junge Lehrer

Die Erweiterung kann dahingehend ausgebaut werden, dass sich mehrere S auf die Rolle des Jan vorbereiten (max. 3–4). Während ein S vor der Klasse spricht, warten die anderen S außerhalb des Klassenraumes. Da die Präsentation nicht mehr als 2–3 Minuten pro S in Anspruch nimmt, ist ein kurzzeitiges Verlassen des Klassenraumes (für S der Klasse 7) durchaus zu rechtfertigen. Im Anschluss entscheiden die „Freunde", welcher „Jan" ihnen die aussagekräftigsten Informationen gegeben hat. Diese Vorgehensweise schult neben der Präsentationstechnik auch die Merkfähigkeit und die komplexe Verwendung der Muttersprache.

Material
Ggf. Leerfolie

Unit 2 — **Einen Besuch im Tower of London planen** — Seite 112

Ziel
- Eine E-Mail mit Hilfe von vorgegebenen Inhalten verfassen

Methodisches Vorgehen
- Die S lesen die Situationsbeschreibung gemeinsam durch; anschließend werden die Aufgabenstellung und die vorgegebenen Fragen gemeinsam besprochen.
- Die S nennen mögliche Grußformeln, L trägt diese auf einer Folie zusammen.
- Gemeinsames Formulieren des Einleitungssatzes; Lösung wird auf Folie fixiert.
- Die S bearbeiten die Aufgabe in Einzelarbeit oder PA; L verteilt Folienstücke, auf denen verschiedene S ihre Lösungsvorschläge zu den einzelnen Fragen eintragen.
- L geht herum und leistet individuelle Hilfestellung.

TIP
Useful phrases,
S. 28

	• Folienstücke werden aufgelegt und gemeinsam korrigiert. L überträgt die korrigierten Sätze auf die „Musterfolie"; die S übernehmen diese in ihre Hefte. • Alternative: L und die S erstellen eine Liste der zu formulierenden Fragen/Inhalte (siehe TA). Anschließend wird die erste Frage gemeinsam formuliert und die E-Mail in Einzelarbeit oder PA oder auch als Hausaufgabe beendet.

Auch als HA geeignet

TA

> 1. pay for tickets — When and how?
> 2. get tickets — Where?
> 3. day of visit, time, London Eye at 14.00, Tower – last admission at 17.00, what happens if late?
> 4. 'Blue Badge Guide' — Who/what is it?

Lösung

> *Erwartungshorizont:*
> *Dear Madam or Sir,*
> *In six weeks my class (25 pupils) and two teachers will go on a class trip to London. I'm responsible for booking the tickets for the Tower. I have looked for information about the Tower in a brochure and on the Internet but I still have some questions. Could you please tell me if we have to pay for our tickets before our trip/right now. If we must/have to pay for them now, how can we do this/so? Where can we get our tickets when we are at the Tower?*
> *We will visit the Tower on Tuesday, April 4, at 17.00/5 p.m. I know that the last admission on Tuesdays in April is 17.00. We have booked the London Eye for 14.00 and we are sure that we can be at the Tower on time. But can we still go in if we are a bit late?*
> *In the brochure I read about a 'Blue Badge Guide'. Could you please tell me who/what that is? Thank you very much for your help.*
> *Yours sincerely,*

Tipps für junge Lehrer Diese Aufgabe zur Mediation ist sehr anspruchsvoll und verlangt ein hohes Abstraktionsvermögen. Da es vielen S schwer fällt, Briefe/E-Mails in ihrer Muttersprache zu formulieren, sind ähnliche Schwierigkeiten auch in der Fremdsprache zu erwarten. L sollte daher unbedingt Hilfestellung leisten und die Aufgabe ggf. in eine gemeinsame „Klassenaktion" umwandeln.

Material
Ggf. Leerfolie

Unit 2 Eine Unterhaltung im V & A   Seite 112–113

Ziel
• Eine Unterhaltung in der Zielsprache führen und gleichzeitig als Sprachmittler auftreten

Wortschatz Annotationen S. 113

Methodisches Vorgehen
• L und die S lesen den Einführungstext und die ersten Sätze der Unterhaltung gemeinsam.
• Ein/e S liest den ersten Satz von Ruby vor *("Oh, thanks a lot … .")*, der gemeinsam ins Deutsche übertragen wird. L hält die Lösung an der Tafel/auf Folie fest.
• Nachdem auch Janines erste Frage („Was ist die Geschichte dieses Kleids?") gemeinsam bearbeitet wurde, übertragen die S Rubys Antwort *("This dress here? … .")* in Einzelarbeit. Anschließend Besprechung im Plenum (mündlich/an der Tafel/auf Folie).
• Die S bearbeiten die restlichen Sätze der Aufgabe in Einzelarbeit. Partnerkontrolle, anschließend Besprechung der Ergebnisse im Plenum.

TA Siehe Lösung

Lösung	*Erwartungshorizont:* *[Ruby]* You: Sie ist/studiert im ersten Jahr an der Modeschule in London. Sie liebt es, historische Kostüme zu zeichnen und dieses hier ist eines ihrer Lieblingskostüme. Sie liebt auch die Geschichte der Kostüme. *[Janine]* You: What is the history of this dress? There is a lot of information in English but it is still too difficult for my friend. *[Ruby]* You: Meinst du dieses Kleid? Eine Sache, die man über historische Kleidung wissen muss ist, dass es nach drei oder vier Jahrhunderten sehr schwierig sein kann, herauszufinden, wem dieses Kleid oder Kostüm gehört hat. Aber bei diesem wundervollen Stück/Kleid hier ist bekannt/weiß man, dass es Elizabeth I. war, die es einmal getragen hat. *[Janine]* You: Was it really a dress of Queen Elizabeth? *[Ruby]* You: Ja, war es. Und man weiß genau, wann sie es getragen hat. Es war ein Geschenk der Königin von Frankreich, die gehofft hat für ihren Sohn, den Herzog von Alencon, eine Heirat mit Elizabeth zu arrangieren. Der Herzog brachte bei einem Staatsbesuch das Kleid nach England mit und Elizabeth liebte es. So hat sie es/das Kleid behalten – den Herzog aber nicht. *[Janine]* You: Elizabeth was very intelligent. My friend likes the story. *[Ruby]* You: Elizabeth liebte die Aufmerksamkeit all der europäischen Prinzen/von all den europäischen Prinzen. Sie alle wollten sie heiraten – und den Thron von England bekommen. Aber Elizabeth hat nie geheiratet. Sie spürte, dass sie „mit England verheiratet" war. Vielleicht war es so besser für sie – und besser für England. *[Janine]* You: This was much more interesting than everything that is written about this museum in her guidebook. Thank you (very much)! It was nice to talk to you.

Material
Ggf. Leerfolie

Unit 3	**Ein Brief an eine Jugendzeitschrift**	Seite 113
Ziel	• Einen Brief an eine Jugendzeitschrift verfassen	
Methodisches Vorgehen	• Es empfiehlt sich, diese Aufgabe mit Unit 3, *Language* 3 (S. 49) oder mit der *Free Section* S. 118–119 zu kombinieren. Die dort präsentierten Leserbriefe können als Muster dienen und ermöglichen es so auch leistungsschwächeren S, einen eigenen Brief zu verfassen. Den S sollte außerdem gestattet werden, das Thema ihres Briefes weiter zu fassen (auch „lustige" Probleme sind erlaubt). • Gemeinsames Lesen der Zielvorgaben; anschließend bearbeiten die S die Aufgabe in Einzelarbeit oder als Hausaufgabe. Je nach Bereitschaft der S werden die Briefe im Unterricht vorgelesen, wenn möglich anonym (die S tippen die Briefe ab; L mischt die Briefe, teilt sie in der Klasse aus; die S lesen die Briefe erst ihrem/r Partner/in vor – ggf. Korrektur mit Hilfe von L – und anschließend der Klasse). Alternative: L sammelt die Briefe ein, korrigiert sie und liest gute Beispiele in der Klasse vor. • Um den S im Vorfeld ein größeres Angebot an Themen zu geben, sollte L ein paar Kärtchen vorbereitet haben, auf denen weitere Ideen stehen (Alternative: Ideen auf Folie), die an die S ausgegeben werden. Auch eigene S-Ideen können umgesetzt werden.	**TIP** Mit Unit 3, *Language* 3 (S. 49) oder *Free Section* S. 118–119 kombinieren Auch als HA geeignet

Erweiterung	• Ideen für weitere Briefe (auf Kärtchen/Folie):
	  – Eltern mögen (neue) Freunde nicht
	  – Deine Freunde mögen deine/n neue/n Freund/in nicht
	  – Du möchtest reiten/Tennis spielen, Eltern wollen nicht für Unterricht zahlen
	  – Du möchtest mit dem Klavierunterricht aufhören/einen Job annehmen/die Schule wechseln, Eltern sind dagegen
	  – Familie muss umziehen wegen neuem Arbeitsplatz des Vaters/der Mutter
	  – Alle Freunde dürfen in die Disko gehen, du nicht
	  – Deinen Eltern gefällt deine Kleidung/Haarschnitt nicht
	  – Du möchtest ein Piercing/Tattoo, deine Eltern sind dagegen
		Auch als HA geeignet

		Material Ggf. Karteikarten, Leerfolie
Lösung	*Individuelle S-Antworten*	

Unit 4 — Neu in der Nachbarschaft

Seite 114

Ziel
- Eine Unterhaltung in der Zielsprache führen und gleichzeitig als Sprachmittler auftreten

Methodisches Vorgehen
- Die S lesen den Einführungstext und die Aufgabenstellung gemeinsam durch.
- L und die S besprechen die ersten beiden Sätze gemeinsam (evtl. Notizen an der Tafel/auf Folie).
- Die S bearbeiten die Aufgabe in Einzelarbeit oder als Hausaufgabe und vergleichen ihre Ergebnisse in PA. Alternative: L hat Lösungsvorschlag kopiert und verteilt diesen an die S. Die S vergleichen in PA ihre Sätze mit dem Lösungsvorschlag und markieren Unterschiede. L geht herum und bespricht die Abweichungen mit den Schülerpaaren individuell.
- Besprechung der Ergebnisse im Plenum.

Auch als HA geeignet

Lösung

Erwartungshorizont:
[Mum]
You: My mother is sorry. She doesn't speak so much English.
[Mark]
You: Mark geht es gut. Du sollst dir keine Gedanken über dein Englisch machen. Sein Deutsch ist viel schlechter.
[Mum]
You: How do you feel after one week?
[Mark]
You: Alle sind nett. Aber er vermisst den 'chippie' – das ist der Fish-and-Chips-Laden an der Ecke seiner Straße in Liverpool.
[Mum]
You: If the question is allowed: Why did you leave England?
[Mark]
You: Sein Vater ist Ingenieur. Vor drei Monaten hat er seinen Job verloren und konnte nirgendwo in Großbritannien einen neuen Job finden. Schließlich hat er hier in Deutschland eine Firma gefunden, die jemanden wie ihn gesucht hat. Deshalb sind sie hier.
[Mum]
You: This must be interesting. A new town, a new language, new friends.
[Mark]
You: Ja und nein. Die Nachbarschaft hier ist sehr nett und sie sind froh/glücklich über den neuen Job seines Vaters. – Ich frage Mark, wo dann das Problem liegt.
[Mark]

> You: Es ist das dritte Mal in sechs Jahren, dass sie umgezogen sind. Ihm reicht es jetzt/Er hat genug davon, aber sie müssen dorthin gehen, wo sein Vater Arbeit findet. Das Problem ist, dass immer wenn er in eine neue Schule geht und neue Freunde findet, sie wieder wegziehen müssen, weil die Verträge seines Vaters normalerweise nur für zwei Jahre sind/nur zwei Jahre laufen. Und dann geht die ganze Sache wieder von vorne los/fängt alles wieder von vorne an.
> [Mum]
> You: My mum understands you. Do you miss your friends?
> [Mark]
> You: Ja. Er vermisst seine Fußballkumpels/-kameraden. Aber ganz besonders vermisst er seine Freundin Sophie.
> [Mum]
> You: It's time for her to go into the house. We two can stay and go on talking about football matches and girlfriends.

Tipps für junge Lehrer

Da die S lernen sollen, sich auf unterschiedliche Partner/innen einzustellen, empfiehlt es sich, die Schülerpaare häufiger auszuwechseln (abzählen, Nummern aus dem Klassenbuch nennen, Junge – Mädchen). Ein Partnertausch ist zwar immer mit einiger Unruhe beim Platzwechsel verbunden, fördert aber die Sozialkompetenz und sollte deshalb so oft wie möglich praktiziert werden.

Material
Ggf. Leerfolie

Unit 5 Ein Filmabend

Seite 114–115

Ziel
- Den Inhalt von Filmen in der Zielsprache zusammenfassen

Methodisches Vorgehen
- L und die S lesen den Einführungstext und die *Mediation skills* gemeinsam. L betont noch einmal, dass unbekanntes Vokabular kein Hinderungsgrund für eine Sprachmittlung sein muss.
- Die S lesen den ersten Text („Der rosarote Panther") und machen sich Notizen zum Inhalt des Films; anschließend Sammeln der wichtigsten Ergebnisse an der Tafel/auf Folie.
- Die S bearbeiten die Aufgabe in Einzelarbeit und verwenden dabei auch das *Dictionary* im Buchanhang, ggf. individuelle Hilfestellung durch L.
- Verschiedene S präsentieren ihre Zusammenfassung in der Klasse; die Inhalte werden mit den Notizen an der Tafel/auf Folie verglichen. In leistungsschwächeren Klassen können die Notizen anschließend auf Englisch übersetzt werden, um den S eine weitere Hilfestellung zu geben.
- Text 2 („Girls Club") wird als Hausaufgabe bearbeitet und die Ergebnisse in der folgenden Stunde von L eingesammelt. Alternative: In leistungsstärkeren Klassen lesen die S beide Texte durch und bearbeiten einen davon im Unterricht, den anderen als Hausaufgabe. (Nachteil: Das gemeinsame Zusammentragen der Notizen als Hilfestellung und somit das Fokussieren auf die wesentlichen Informationen entfällt.)

TIP
Mit *Free Section* S. 123 kombinieren

TA

> Der rosarote Panther
> - Fußballmanager wird ermordet
> - Ring (The Pink Panther) wird gestohlen
> - Inspektor und Detektiv ermitteln
> - treffen Freundin des Toten, Arbeit beginnt Spaß zu machen

Erweiterung
- Erweiterung zu b): Die S bringen weitere Filmzusammenfassungen mit (Kinoprogramm, Fernsehzeitung), die ebenfalls in die Zielsprache übertragen werden. Dies ist auch als längerfristige Hausaufgabe möglich.

Auch als HA geeignet

M | Mediation

Lösung

Erwartungshorizont:
a) *'The Pink Panther'*: In the comedy 'The Pink Panther' a football manager is killed and a famous ring, 'The Pink Panther', is stolen. Steve Martin is Inspector Clouseau and Jean Reno is Detective Ponton. They must find out about the murder. When they meet Xania, the pretty girlfriend of the dead football manager, they have fun with their job. The role of the girlfriend is played by Beyoncé Knowles.

'Girls Club': In the comedy 'Girls Club' Lindsay Lohan plays Cady, a girl who lived in Africa and was taught only by private teachers. At her first public school in the USA she makes friends with the outsiders Jan and Damien who hate the girls of the élite clique 'The Plastics'. The friends push Cady to find out more about this girls' club and to report about its mean activities.

b) *Individuelle S-Antworten*

Tipps für junge Lehrer

Da diese *Mediation* im Rahmen der Bearbeitung von Unit 5 eingesetzt werden kann, sollte L die S auffordern, zwei oder drei Passivformen in ihre Zusammenfassungen einzubauen.

Material
Ggf. Leerfolie

L Unit 6 — Durchsagen am Flughafen — Seite 115

HV-Text

One
Airport announcement: Good morning, ladies and gentlemen. Boarding for British Airways flight 0980 will begin at 8.40. That's flight BA0980 to Munich, from Gate 16. Boarding will begin at 8.40.

Two
Airport announcement: This is a reminder to all passengers: Please do not leave your baggage unattended. Keep your baggage with you at all times. Airport Security will collect all unattended items of baggage, so please save yourself the trouble and watch your things. Thank you.

Three
Airport announcement: We have an announcement for all passengers who are waiting to board British Airways flight 0982 to Berlin. We're very sorry to say that we must delay boarding time until 9.35. The plane was late on arrival from Berlin and our cleaning crew are still busy on board. I repeat, boarding for flight 0982 will not begin until 9.35. Thank you.

Four
Airport announcement: This is an announcement for a passenger on Lufthansa flight LH 4728. Will Mr William Blacksmith please report to the Information Desk at Gate 11. Mr William Blacksmith, please report to the Information Desk at Gate 11. And this is also a last call for Mrs Diane Rooney to board Air France flight 8969 to Paris. Diane Rooney, please go to gate 28 immediately, this is a last call to board Air France flight 8969 to Paris.

Five
Airport announcement: Ladies and gentlemen, we are now ready to board British Airways flight 0982 to Berlin. Please note that the flight will not leave from Gate 40. Your new gate is Gate 14. I repeat, we are now ready to board British Airways flight 0982 to Berlin, but from Gate 14.

		Mediation — **M**

Ziel	• Aus einem HV-Text Informationen entnehmen und in die Muttersprache übertragen
Methodisches Vorgehen	*Pre-listening:* • L und die S lesen die *Mediation skills* gemeinsam; anschließend lesen die S den Einführungstext und die Informationen zur Höraufgabe. • Gemeinsames Formulieren der Zielvorgabe (ggf. Stichworte an der Tafel) mit Hinweisen zum Hörverhalten: *Listen carefully. Which of the five announcements gives us information about the gate number for the flight to Berlin? Concentrate on the name of the airline, the number of the flight and the time. Don't forget: You must find out the number of the gate only.* *While-listening:* • L präsentiert die Durchsagen von CD. Um die Authentizität zu wahren, werden alle Durchsagen ohne Pause präsentiert. • Die S notieren sich die Antwort zur Höraufgabe, die im Anschluss an die Präsentation verglichen und an der Tafel/auf Folie festgehalten wird. Die S übertragen den Antwortsatz ins Deutsche.

TIP
Höraufgaben auf Arbeitsblatt

TA

```
situation:  London Heathrow; British Airways BA0982 to Berlin; 9.15 a.m.
you need:   gate number
solution:   announcement no. 5 – The flight to Berlin will leave from Gate 14.
```

• Zweites Abspielen der CD; die S machen sich Notizen zu den Inhalten der einzelnen Durchsagen.
• Alternative: Die Höraufgabe kann auch arbeitsteilig gestellt werden. Jede/r S konzentriert sich zunächst auf 2–3 Durchsagen und macht sich Notizen. Beim dritten Hördurchgang werden die noch fehlenden Informationen ergänzt und anschließend in PA oder in Kleingruppen verglichen. In leistungsstärkeren Klassen können die o. g. Arbeitsschritte verkürzt/variiert werden.

Post-listening:
• Die S übertragen die Inhalte derjenigen Durchsagen ins Deutsche, die den Flug nach Berlin betreffen. Anschließend Besprechung der Ergebnisse im Plenum.

Erweiterung	• Mögliches Arbeitsblatt: *Announcement 1: Fill in the missing information.* flight to: boarding at: gate number: *Announcement 2: Finish the sentence.* Keep _____ at all times. _____ your things. *Announcement 3: Fill in the information.* announcement for: delay because: boarding later because: boarding will not begin until: *Announcement 4: Finish the sentences.* Mr William Blacksmith must _____ Mrs Diane Rooney must _____
Lösung	*Announcement 2: You:* Wir sollen unser Gepäck nicht unbeaufsichtigt lassen. Der Flughafen-Sicherheitsdienst sammelt alle unbeaufsichtigten Gepäckstücke ein. *Announcement 3: You:* Das Boarding verschiebt sich auf 9.35 Uhr. Der Flieger kam zu spät aus Berlin und jetzt ist das Reinigungsteam noch an Bord.

M | Mediation

> Announcement 5: You: Das Boarding beginnt jetzt. Unser Flug startet nicht von Gate 40, sondern von Gate 14.
>
> Lösungen zum Arbeitsblatt:
>
> Announcement 1: flight to Munich; boarding at 8.40; Gate 16
> Announcement 2: Keep your baggage with you at all times. Watch your things.
> Announcement 3: announcement for passengers who are waiting to board British Airways flight 0982 to Berlin; boarding later because the cleaning crew are still busy on board; boarding will not begin until 9.35
> Announcement 4: Mr William Blacksmith must report to the Information Desk at Gate 11. Mrs Diane Rooney must board Air France flight 8969 to Paris.

Tipps für junge Lehrer Viele S benötigen gerade bei Hörverstehensaufgaben gezielte Hilfestellung im Vorfeld. Deshalb sollten diese Aufgaben systematisch vorbereitet bzw. begleitet werden. Dabei bietet es sich an, die zu überprüfenden Informationen auf einem Arbeitsblatt/auf Folie aufzulisten, um die Aufmerksamkeit der S gezielt auf das Wesentliche zu lenken. Bei der muttersprachlichen Präsentation der Ergebnisse ist darauf zu achten, dass diese in vollständigen Sätzen erfolgt.

Material
◎L 4/22–26
Ggf. Leerfolie, Arbeitsblatt

⟨Free Section⟩

⟨The Spaniards are coming⟩ (after Unit 2)

Seite 116–117

LANDESKUNDE

The Armada was the Spanish fleet which sailed against England in 1588. The fleet set out with 22 warships and 108 converted merchant vessels with the intention of sailing through the English Channel to anchor off the coast of Flanders. There the Duke of Parma's army would stand ready for an invasion of the south-east of England. While awaiting communications from Parma's army, the Armada was driven from its anchorage by an English fireship attack. It managed to regroup and withdraw north, with the English fleet following it up the east coast of England. The fleet sailed into the Atlantic where severe storms disrupted its course, and more than 24 vessels were wrecked on the northern and western coast of Ireland. The survivors had to seek refuge in Scotland. About 50 vessels failed to make it back to Spain.

Sir Francis Drake (1540–1595) was an English privateer, navigator, slave trader, and politician of the Elizabethan era. Drake was knighted in 1581. He was second commander of the English fleet against the Spanish Armada. His exploits were semi-legendary, making him a hero to the English but a simple pirate to the Spaniards. He was known as 'El Draque' ('the Dragon'), and it is said that King Philip II offered a reward of 20,000 ducats (about £6.5 million) for his life.
In 1585 hostilities broke out between England and Spain. Drake sailed to the New World where he sacked the ports of Santo Domingo and Cartagena. Later he captured the Spanish fort of San Augustin in Spanish Florida. This encouraged Philip II of Spain to plan an invasion of England. Drake became vice admiral in command of the English fleet under Lord Howard of Effingham when it overcame the Spanish Armada in 1588.
The most famous anecdote about Drake relates that before the battle he was playing a game of bowls on Plymouth Hoe. On being warned of the approach of the Spanish fleet, Drake is said to have remarked that there was plenty of time to finish the game and still beat the Spaniards. There is no eyewitness account of this incident and the earliest retelling of it was printed 37 years later. Adverse winds and currents caused some delay in the launching of the English fleet as the Spanish drew nearer. So it is easy to see how the popular myth of Drake's cavalier attitude to the Spanish threat may have originated. Sir Francis Drake died after unsuccessfully attacking San Juan, Puerto Rico, in 1595.

Charles Howard of Effingham (1536–1624) was an English statesman and admiral. He was the cousin of Elizabeth I and held several prominent posts during her reign. Effingham was knighted in 1572. In 1585 he became Lord High Admiral and in 1587 commander-in-chief of the English fleet against the Spanish Armada. Effingham ordered a strategy of harassing the Spanish fleet rather than attacking them directly. The strategy succeeded. In 1596 Effingham became Earl of Nottingham. He was at Elizabeth's deathbed in 1603 and later enjoyed the confidence of her successor, James I. He served on the commission of union between England and Scotland and as commissioner at the Gunpowder Plot trial in 1605.

Ziele
- Einen Augenzeugenbericht lesen und verstehen
- Die Erzählperspektive des *first-person narrator* kennen lernen
- Die *Writing skills* fördern

Text/Üben	**The Spaniards are coming!**	Seite 116–117
Hinweis	Der Text bietet einerseits die Möglichkeit, das historisch-landeskundliche Wissen zu Unit 2 zu vertiefen, andererseits können auch die *Reading* und *Writing skills* gefestigt und das selbstständige Lernen der Schüler gefördert werden. L sollte daher vor dem Einsatz des Textes überlegen, welche Schwerpunktsetzung für die individuelle Lerngruppe geeigneter erscheint.	

F ⟨Free Section⟩

Wortschatz Annotationen S. 116–117

Methodisches Vorgehen
- Je nach geplanter Unterrichtszeit und Leistungsfähigkeit der Klasse kann der Text als Hausaufgabe oder im Unterricht lexikalisch vorentlastet werden. Ziel der späteren Arbeit sollte es sein, die S zum eigenständigen Erschließen des Textes anzuregen und die Hilfestellung durch L auf Hinweise zu den Arbeitstechniken (*reading for gist*, Erschließen unbekannter Wörter) zu beschränken.

Variante 1 (inhaltlicher Schwerpunkt):
- L setzt den Text nach SB S. 27, *ex.* 4, ein, so dass die S die Person Sir Francis Drake einordnen können. Alternativ wären Kurzvorträge zu Francis Drake und Elizabeth I. denkbar, die von ausgewählten S vorbereitet werden.
- L klärt abschnittsweise lexikalische Fragen und lässt ggf. einzelne *words/ phrases* von den S erklären.
- Anschließend erhalten die S **KV 1a: The Spaniards are coming!** und lesen die Aufgabenstellung gemeinsam durch, L klärt ggf. Verständnisfragen. Die S bearbeiten die Aufgaben in Einzelarbeit oder PA. Je nach Leistungsstärke der Klasse/ einzelner S kann L festlegen, ob und in welchem Maße das SB bei der Bearbeitung der Aufgaben genutzt werden darf.
- a) + b) L hat die Lösungen für alle S kopiert. Alternativ werden mehrere Lösungsblätter im Klassenraum ausgelegt, so dass die S ihre Ergebnisse individuell abgleichen können.
- c) Um deutlich zu machen, dass gleiche Inhalte durch unterschiedliche Formulierungen ausgedrückt werden können, sollten möglichst viele S ihre Ergebnisse vortragen.

Variante 2 (Förderung von *Reading* und *Writing skills*)
- L klärt abschnittsweise lexikalische Fragen und lässt ggf. einzelne *words/ phrases* von den S erklären.
- Die S erhalten **KV 1b: The Spaniards are coming!** und lesen die Teilaufgaben a) und b) gemeinsam durch. L weist darauf hin, dass zur Beantwortung der Fragen das SB eingesetzt werden darf und die S ihre Antworten durch Zeilenangaben belegen sollen.
- Die S bearbeiten die Aufgaben schriftlich in Einzelarbeit. Ideal wäre es, wenn L die Aufgaben einsammelt und (ohne Benotung) korrigiert. Als Alternative empfiehlt es sich, möglichst viele S-Beiträge anzuhören. Dabei werden die Ergebnisse stichwortartig an der Tafel/auf Folie festgehalten.
- c) + d) können anschließend gemeinsam, schriftlich oder mündlich, bearbeitet werden. Die Ergebnisse werden ebenfalls stichwortartig an der Tafel/ auf Folie festgehalten.

TA

> The way of the Spanish Armada:
> Spain – the Netherlands – the Channel – the French coast – Calais – the North Sea – the north of Scotland – the coast of Ireland – back to Spain

Erweiterung
- Zur weiteren Festigung des Textverständnisses sammeln L und die S die im Text genannten geographischen Punkte zur Route der Armada (siehe TA). Anschließend vollziehen die S die Route im Atlas/auf einer Wandkarte nach.
- Als Auflockerung kann L die S die Gesamtlänge der von der Armada zurückgelegten Strecke bestimmen lassen.

Lösung *Siehe Kopiervorlagen*

Tipps für junge Lehrer Je nach Schwerpunktsetzung und Leistungsfähigkeit der Klasse kann die Reihenfolge der Aufgaben auf den Kopiervorlagen beliebig variiert werden.

Material
Kopiervorlage 1a + b
Ggf. Leerfolie
Atlas/Wandkarte

⟨Authentic Britain⟩ (after Unit 3)

Seite 118–119

Ziele
- Die authentische Problemseite einer Jugendzeitschrift lesen und verstehen
- Ein Wortfeld zum Thema *feelings* zusammenstellen
- *Idiomatic phrases* sammeln
- Eine eigene Problemseite gestalten

Text/Üben	**A problem shared**	Seite 118–119

Wortschatz: *to approve, to make over, to reckon, to replace*

Methodisches Vorgehen

Schwerpunkt 1 (lexikalischer Schwerpunkt):

- Um die S systematisch an die Arbeit mit authentischen Texten heranzuführen, sollten die hier präsentierten Texte nicht detailliert semantisiert werden. Sie sollten vielmehr dazu genutzt werden, Wortbilder und idiomatische Wendungen zusammenzustellen, die dann für andere Aufgaben genutzt werden können.
- L schreibt die o. g. Vokabeln an die Tafel und erläutert sie kurz. Anschließend wird mit Hilfe von Beispielen der Begriff *idiom/idiomatic* eingeführt. L schreibt eine Definition an die Tafel, die die S in ihre Hefte übernehmen.
- Die S arbeiten in GA (max. fünf S, bei größeren Klassen Themen doppeln). L formuliert die Aufgabenstellung: *Read your texts. Make sure that everybody in your group understands them. Find all the words/phrases in your text that have to do with 'feelings'. Then look for idiomatic phrases. Be careful: You can't find idiomatic phrases in every text! Make two lists in your exercise books.* In leistungsschwächeren Klassen sollte innerhalb der GA ggf. auf das Heraussuchen idiomatischer Ausdrücke verzichtet werden.
- Die Gruppen erhalten zusätzlich einige Minuten Zeit, um das Vorlesen der von ihnen bearbeiteten Texte zu üben. Anschließend lesen jeweils zwei S einer Gruppe Brief und Antwort laut vor. Die anderen S können Fragen zum Inhalt/ zu den Vokabeln stellen. Alternative: Die einzelnen Gruppen fassen ihre Texte mit eigenen Worten kurz zusammen.
- Nach dem Vorlesen ihrer Texte präsentieren die einzelnen Gruppen die von ihnen gesammelten *words/phrases*. Die übrigen S ergänzen ihre Listen. Ggf. können anschließend weitere (nicht in den Texten vorkommende) *words/phrases* hinzugefügt werden.

Schwerpunkt 2 (inhaltlicher Schwerpunkt):

- Die S lesen die Texte nochmals durch (auch als Hausaufgabe möglich) und äußern sich zustimmend oder ablehnend zu den Antworten der *agony aunt*. Dabei können die *Useful phrases* auf S. 156 hilfreich sein.
- Die S verfassen in PA/GA Briefe an die *agony aunt* sowie deren Antworten und gestalten ihre eigene Problemseite. Dabei können sie auf die zuvor erarbeiteten Listen mit *words/phrases* sowie auf Unit 3, *Language* 3 (S. 49) und auf die *Mediation* S. 113 zurückgreifen; L leistet individuelle Hilfestellung (LB *Green Line* 3, S. 362, bietet weitere Ideen für Briefe an die *agony aunt*, die hier angeboten werden können).
- Diese Schreibaufgabe ist auch als längerfristige Hausaufgabe möglich. L sammelt die Texte ein und korrigiert sie, bevor sie in der Klasse präsentiert werden. Die Aufgabe kann auch als eine Art Wettbewerb gestaltet werden, wobei eine Jury/die Klasse die besten Arbeiten auswählt, die dann als Wandzeitung/an der Pinnwand präsentiert werden.
- Alternative: Sollte die *Mediation* zu Unit 3 (S. 113) noch nicht bearbeitet worden sein, bietet sie sich an dieser Stelle als kreative Schreibaufgabe an.

> **TIP**
> Mit Unit 3, *Language* 3 (S. 49) und *Mediation* S. 113 kombinieren.

Auch als HA geeignet

TA

> Idiom (adj.: idiomatic):
> An idiom is a group of words which have a different meaning when they are used together.

Erweiterung
- Die S bringen Jugend-/Mädchenzeitschriften mit, die ebenfalls eine Problemseite anbieten und nutzen die dort abgedruckten Beiträge, um sie in der Fremdsprache zusammenzufassen (Mediation) und zu kommentieren oder als Grundlage für eigene Antworttexte zu nutzen.

Auch als HA geeignet

Lösung

Feelings:	*Idiomatic phrases:*
to be stressed, to hate sth, to be nasty, to be unhappy, to be moody and sad, to feel down, to feel lost, to drive sb crazy, to be shy, to be friendly and understanding, to miss sb/sth, to be upset, to be unwanted, to be unloved, etc.	to take it out on sb, to come clean, things are out in the open, a tough time, to go through sth, etc.

Tipps für junge Lehrer
Die hier präsentierte Doppelseite ist ideal, um das Lesen authentischer Texte und die *Writing skills* weiter zu schulen. L sollte sich deshalb auf individuelle Hilfestellung beschränken und die S zur Selbstständigkeit anregen. In leistungsschwächeren Klassen können die gesammelten Vokabeln auch dazu genutzt werden, einfache Texte über sich/andere zu schreiben, bevor es konkret um die oben aufgeführte Umsetzung der Zielvorgaben geht.

Material
Ggf. Leerfolie

⟨Poems⟩ (after Unit 3 or Unit 4)

Seite 120–122

> **Ziele**
> - Gedichte lesen, diskutieren und präsentieren
> - Strukturelle Elemente von Gedichten erkennen und differenzieren
> - Ein eigenes Gedicht schreiben

Text **Poems**

Seite 120–122

Ziel
- Strukturelle Elemente eines Gedichtes kennen lernen

Wortschatz *symbol, to rhyme, brink, metre, leaf pl. leaves*

Methodisches Vorgehen
- Die S lesen den Einführungstext gemeinsam. Anschließend erstellen L und die S ein zusammenfassendes Tafelbild, das die S in ihre Hefte übernehmen und das ihnen als Hilfestellung für die weitere Arbeit mit Gedichten dient. Diese Zusammenfassung kann nach *ex.* 1 ergänzt werden.

TIP
Auch muttersprachliche Beispiele einbringen

TA

```
                    Poems

Symbols              Rhymes                  Metre
→ pictures or objects  → the last word in a line  → the rhythm of the
which stand for something  rhymes with another last  sounds in a poem
else                 word
In modern poems the writer can do everything!
```

Erweiterung
- L und die S sammeln Beispiele, um die o.g. Begriffe zu dokumentieren, z. B. *symbols: heart, rose,* etc.

Tipps für junge Lehrer
L sollte den S unbedingt deutlich machen, dass Gedichte nichts anderes sind als Texte, die in einer anderen Form aufgeschrieben wurden und dass wir täglich mit Gedichten konfrontiert werden, sei es in Liedern oder in der Werbung (hier ist der Einsatz von Beispielen aus dem Alltagsleben sinnvoll).

⟨Free Section⟩ **F**

Üben	**1 Images**		Seite 120

Ziel
- *Images* als Bestandteil von Gedichten kennen lernen

Wortschatz *image, to drift along*

Methodisches Vorgehen
- L und die S lesen Einleitung und Aufgabenstellung gemeinsam; Ergänzung des TA aus *ex.* 1. Anschließend bearbeiten die S die Aufgabe in Einzelarbeit oder PA.
- Verschiedene S tragen ihre Ideen der Klasse vor. Alternative: Die S schreiben ihre Ideen auf kleine Zettel, die L einsammelt und (anonym) vorliest. Die S entscheiden dann, welche Überlegungen am aussagekräftigsten sind.

TA
> Images
> → pictures

Lösung
> *Individuelle S-Antworten*

Tipps für junge Lehrer Viele S dieser Altersgruppe scheuen sich, anderen ihre Ideen, Gedanken und Gefühle mitzuteilen. Deshalb sollte L die S zur mündlichen Beteiligung auffordern, aber auch Möglichkeiten zur schriftlichen Meinungsäußerung anbieten.

Üben	**2 Read poems A to D**		Seite 120–121

Ziel
- Gedichte lesen und verstehen

Wortschatz *choice, fuss, glare, What the heck …?, wreck, stupid, lead, stroke, That's that!, there's no harm, to have a fit, to get into a state, to choke, glee, to swerve, curve, alive*

Auch als HA geeignet

TIP
Die Arbeit an den *poems* ggf. mit *ex.* 4 beginnen

Methodisches Vorgehen
- Die S lesen die Gedichte in Einzelarbeit (auch als vorbereitende Hausaufgabe möglich). L leistet ggf. Hilfestellung bei lexikalischen Problemen.
- Die S fassen den Inhalt der Gedichte in 1–2 Sätzen zusammen; anschließend Partnerkontrolle und Vergleich der Ergebnisse im Plenum.

Üben	**3 Match these images**		Seite 121

Ziel
- Den bekannten Gedichten die passenden *images* zuordnen

Methodisches Vorgehen
- Die S betrachten die Bilder und nennen spontan *words/phrases*, die sie damit verbinden (ggf. an der Tafel sammeln) und auf die sie sich beim erneuten Lesen der Gedichte konzentrieren.
- Die S lesen die Gedichte und ordnen den Bildern die passenden *phrases* aus den Gedichten zu; anschließend Besprechung der Ergebnisse im Plenum.

TA
> Siehe Lösung

Lösung
> 1 *to choke with glee – poem C*   2 *to be all waves in the sea – poem C*
> 3 *to drink to the brink – poem D*   4 *to shake like leaves on a tree – poem C*
> 5 *to feel as heavy as lead – poem A*   6 *to have a fit – poem B*

Üben	**4 The title helps**		Seite 121

Ziel
- Den bekannten Gedichten inhaltlich passende Titel zuordnen

Methodisches Vorgehen
- a) Die S ordnen in Einzelarbeit die Titel den Gedichten zu; Vergleich der Ergebnisse im Plenum.

F ⟨Free Section⟩

- Anschließend bearbeiten die S Teilaufgabe b) in PA und präsentieren ihre Ideen in mündlicher Form.
- Alternative: Die Aufgabe wird zu Beginn der Arbeit mit Gedichten eingesetzt. L schreibt die vier Titel der Gedichte an die Tafel. Die S haben vier Minuten Zeit, um jeweils einen Satz zum möglichen Inhalt der Gedichte aufzuschreiben. Gute Ideen werden an der Tafel gesammelt.
- Anschließend lesen die S die Gedichte in Einzelarbeit und ordnen die Titel zu. Teilaufgabe b) kann als Hausaufgabe bearbeitet werden.

Auch als HA geeignet

Lösung

a) *Poem A – Monday morning, 6 am; Poem B – Such a tiny little thing; Poem C – Help!; Poem D – Why?* b) *Erwartungshorizont: Poem A – Good morning! Poem B – It's not fair! Poem C – HE Poem D – Unanswered Questions*

Tipps für junge Lehrer

Titel von Gedichten und Texten im allgemeinen schaffen sehr gute Sprechanlässe, da die S zum Spekulieren angeregt werden. Diese Vorgehensweise bietet sich allerdings nur bei Texten an, die vorher nicht bekannt sind.

Üben

5 How to: Talk about poems

Seite 121

Ziel
- Über Gedichte diskutieren
- Eine eigene Stellungnahme formulieren

Methodisches Vorgehen
- L teilt die S in Gruppen ein. Diese wählen jeweils ein Gedicht aus, das sie unter Zuhilfenahme der *Useful phrases* diskutieren. Für die spätere Präsentation werden die Ergebnisse in Stichpunkten festgehalten.
- Anschließend werden die Gruppenergebnisse präsentiert. Die anderen Gruppen achten dabei darauf, ob aussagekräftige *phrases* verwendet wurden.

TIP
Useful phrases S. 121 und S. 213

Erweiterung
- Sollten die S weitere Gedichte kennen, können auch diese für die GA verwendet werden.

Tipps für junge Lehrer

Um auch leistungsschwächeren S die Möglichkeit der aktiven mündlichen Beteiligung zu geben, können Teile dieser Aufgabe als Hausaufgabe vorbereitet werden.

Auch als HA geeignet

Üben

6 Present the poem

Seite 122

Ziel
- Ein Gedicht präsentieren

Methodisches Vorgehen
- Präsentation der Gruppenergebnisse aus *ex.* 5. Die übrigen Gruppen achten darauf, ob aussagekräftige *Useful phrases* verwendet werden und kommentieren anschließend die präsentierten Ergebnisse.
- Die positiven und negativen Stellungnahmen zu den Gedichten werden in Form von Stichpunkten an der Tafel gesammelt.
- Abschließend wird ein Klassenranking zu den vier Gedichten erstellt.

TA

	Poem A	Poem B	Poem C	Poem D
+				
–				
Ranking				

Üben

7 Writing texts: Write a poem yourself

Seite 122

Ziel
- Ein eigenes Gedicht schreiben und präsentieren

Wortschatz	*topic, rose*	
Methodisches Vorgehen	• L und die S lesen die Aufgabenstellung gemeinsam. L weist auf die zu berücksichtigenden Elemente hin, betont aber gleichzeitig, dass gerade bei modernen Gedichten die Formvorgaben nicht bindend sind, und dass die S ihr Gedicht frei gestalten können. • Die S verfassen ihr Gedicht in Einzelarbeit oder als Hausaufgabe. Über die Form der Präsentation (Wettbewerb, Ausstellung etc.) entscheidet L je nach Interesse und Fähigkeiten der S.	Auch als HA geeignet
Lösung	*Erwartungshorizont: SPRING/I really love the season of spring,/When flowers grow and birds want to sing./The trees become green – /And have you ever seen/ What joy some sunshine can bring?*	

⟨Working with films⟩ (after Unit 5) — Seite 123

Ziele
- Filmszenen inhaltlich analysieren
- Eine Filmszene schreiben und vorspielen
- Eine Filmszene drehen

Üben 1 Important film questions — Seite 123

Ziel
- Filmszenen anhand von Leitfragen inhaltlich analysieren

Methodisches Vorgehen
- Die im SB abgebildete Szene aus dem Film „Titanic" bietet eine erste Grundlage für die Arbeit mit Filmen, bevor dann in der Anschlussstunde von den S ausgewählte Filmszenen zum Einsatz kommen können.
- Bei geschlossenem SB: L schreibt die Leitfragen und die Fachbegriffe aus der *Tip*-Box an die Tafel/auf Folie. Die S übernehmen diese in ihre Hefte.
- Die S erstellen eine Tabelle, in der sie die Fachbegriffe um den Begriff *feelings* erweitern. L präsentiert eine Szene aus einem Film. Die S ergänzen ihre Tabelle (PA möglich). Sammeln der Ergebnisse an der Tafel/auf Folie.
- Anschließend äußern sich die S zum Film, spekulieren über das Ende oder stellen gezielt Fragen zum Inhalt.
- L präsentiert eine weitere Szene aus dem Film, die die S nach den bekannten Kriterien beschreiben; Vergleich der Ergebnisse im Plenum. Zur Analyse weiterer Filmsequenzen kann die Tabelle beliebig erweitert werden.

TA

Working with films

characters = the people in a film
setting = the place where the characters are
action = sth that happens in a film
plot = the story that the film tells

Title of the film	Scene 1	Scene 2
Characters:		
Setting:		
Action:		
Feelings:		
Plot:		

F ⟨Free Section⟩

Tipps für junge Lehrer	Die Konzentration der S kann gesteigert werden, wenn L Szenen aus einem Film aussucht, der den S nicht bekannt ist. Anschließend können die S weitere Filme vorschlagen, die szenenweise bearbeitet werden.	**Material** Filmausschnitte, DVD-/Videogerät Ggf. Leerfolie
Üben	**2 Let's work with films**	Seite 123
Hinweis	Für die nachfolgende Aufgabe eignen sich Filmszenen aller Art. Je nach Schwerpunktsetzung sollten neben Filmszenen auch Werbespots und Musikclips zum Einsatz kommen. Lustige Werbespots bieten ein hohes Potential an Spekulationsmöglichkeiten und können für Teilaufgabe c) eingesetzt werden, während sich Spielfilmszenen besonders für b) anbieten.	
Ziel	• Über Filmszenen/Werbespots/Musikclips spekulieren	
Wortschatz	*sound*	**TIP** Auch Werbespots oder Musikclips einsetzen
Methodisches Vorgehen	• Die S bearbeiten die Teilaufgaben zunächst in Einzelarbeit; anschließend Diskussion der Ergebnisse im Plenum. L entscheidet über die zeitlichen Vorgaben, die Häufigkeit der Wiederholungen und die weiteren Arbeitsanweisungen für die S.	
Erweiterung	• Wie bei *ex.* 1 ist es auch hier möglich, die S mit der Präsentation von Filmsequenzen zu beauftragen. Beim Einsatz von Werbespots und Musikclips bietet sich darüber hinaus ein Quiz an.	**Material** Filmausschnitte DVD-/Videogerät
Üben	**3 Writing texts: A film scene**	Seite 123
Ziel	• Eine Filmszene schreiben und vorspielen/drehen	
Methodisches Vorgehen	• L präsentiert die *settings* an der Tafel/auf Folie und fordert die S auf, Ideen für Filmszenen zu nennen. Antworten werden an der Tafel/auf Folie gesammelt. Die Liste der *settings* kann auf Wunsch erweitert werden. • Die S finden sich in Gruppen zusammen und diskutieren die weitere Vorgehensweise. L weist darauf hin, dass sich die Szenen auf die Charaktere des SB beziehen können (Alex und Chloe aus Unit 2, die Pattersons aus Unit 3, Rhona, Shirin und Tariq aus Unit 4). Sollten die S andere Ideen für Charaktere haben, sollten auch diese akzeptiert werden. • L weist auf die Struktur eines Skripts hin, welches für die Umsetzung einer Szene konzipiert werden muss (Orientierung an Unit 3, *How to: Put on a play*, möglich) und verweist auf die *Talkwise*-Seiten, die *Useful phrases* und S. 54 (*Describing people*). • Die S schreiben eine kurze Szene, die sie entweder präsentieren (mit verteilten Rollen vorlesen und dabei Informationen über eine mögliche filmische Umsetzung – Kostüme, Musik etc. – geben) oder als Filmszene drehen und abspielen.	
TA	Settings: Ideas: On the bus witness at accident, … In the shop money stolen At home trouble with parents, … At a birthday party ex-boyfriend/girlfriend has new love	**Material** Ggf. Leerfolie

Kopiervorlagen F

KV 1a: The Spaniards are coming!

a) *Read the text and fill in the missing words.*

In July 1588 the English _____ lay at anchor in _____ harbour. The English knew that the _____ wanted to _____ England with the greatest fleet in the world, the _____. The Spaniards had more than _____ ships. They wanted to sail to _____ because they had a large _____ there and wanted to bring it to _____.

Lord Howard, the commander of the English fleet, and _____ were playing _____ when a young officer brought them the _____ that some men had seen the Armada in the English _____. Sir Francis Drake was not _____ and _____ the game.

b) *Choose the correct answer.*

1. The Spanish ships were
   a. faster and heavier than the English ships.
   b. turning away from the English ships.
   c. heavier and slower than the English ships.

2. In the night
   a. the English set fire to the Spanish ships in the Channel.
   b. the English set fire to their own ships and let them drift towards Calais.
   c. the Spanish ships sailed off.

3. The English ships
   a. surrounded some Spanish ships and sank them.
   b. followed the Spanish ships to Ireland.
   c. sailed off to the Netherlands.

c) *Complete the following sentences*

1. The ships of the Armada had to sail to the north because _____.

2. _____ because the Spaniards had lost most of their ships on the coast of Scotland and Ireland.

3. When the English sailors returned home _____.

4. The defeat of the Spanish Armada was _____.

Lösung: a) *fleet; Plymouth; Spaniards; attack; Armada; one hundred; the Netherlands; army; England; Sir Francis Drake; bowls; news; Channel; worried; finished* b) 1 - c; 2 - b; 3 - a c) 1. *a great storm came up.* 2. *Only 54 out of 130 ships returned to Spain* 3. *there was great joy in the country/all the people were dancing/church bells were ringing.* 4. *the greatest victory in English history.*

© Ernst Klett Verlag GmbH, Stuttgart 2008. Alle Rechte vorbehalten.
ISBN 978-3-12-547143-6   GREEN LINE 3   375

KV 1b: The Spaniards are coming!

Read the text on pages 116–117 in your book again and answer the following questions.

a) Describe Sir Francis Drake's two strategies¹ to fight the Armada. Remember to give the line(s)!

b) Give reasons why the Armada lost the battle.

c) What do you think of Sir Francis Drake? Write a short text.   Start: I think Sir Francis Drake was …

d) A first-person narrator² tells the story. Where can you see that in the story? What influence³ does a first-person narrator have on you, the reader?

---

¹**strategy** ['strætədʒi] = Strategie • ²**first-person narrator** ['fɜːst ˌpɜːsn nəˈreɪtə] = Ich-Erzähler • ³**influence** ['ɪnfluəns] = Einfluss

---

Lösung: a) 1. *attack the Armada from behind* (ll. 59–60) – *fire off cannon balls* (ll. 60–61) – *turn away before the Spaniards fire* (ll. 61–62) 2. *fill old ships with pitch and tar* (ll. 68–69) – *set fire to the ships and let them drift towards the Spanish fleet* (ll. 70–71) – *surround some ships and sink them* (ll. 77–78) – *follow the rest of the Spanish ships* (ll. 79–80) – *fire off cannons balls* (ll. 80–81) – *turn back*   b) *heavy ships* (l. 52) – *English ships could sail faster and turn away* (ll. 59, 51–62) – *great storm* (l. 83) – *ships had to sail farther north* (ll. 84–85) – *lost most of their ships on the coast of Scotland and Ireland* (ll. 89–90)   d) *The narrator is a character in the story. He uses the pronouns 'I' and 'we' when he tells us the story about the Armada. You have the feeling that you are in the story together with the narrator. You can understand his feelings. The narrator talks to you and so the story seems to be true.*